Eugene O'Neill
and the American Critic

Eugene O'Neill
and the American Critic

A Bibliographical Checklist

SECOND EDITION, REVISED

JORDAN Y. MILLER

ARCHON BOOKS
1973

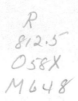

Library of Congress Cataloging in Publication Data

Miller, Jordan Yale, 1919—
   Eugene O'Neill and the American critic.

   1. O'Neill, Eugene Gladstone, 1888-1953—Bibliography
   2. O'Neill, Eugene Gladstone, 1888-1953. I. Title.
Z8644.5.M5   1973   016.812'5'2   72-122403
ISBN 0-208-00939-6

Contents

Contents

Preface

The first edition of *Eugene O'Neill and the American Critic*, published in 1962, was an adaptation and considerable expansion of a doctoral dissertation conceived as far back as 1954, when the name of Eugene O'Neill had all but disappeared as a meaningful reference in the American theatre. At that time an even dozen daring graduate students had ventured to include O'Neill in their doctoral research, among them Doris Alexander, Edwin Engel, and Doris Falk, all now established as leading O'Neill scholars, who had gone so far as to make his plays their sole subject. Others within a year or two, including critic and editor Robert Corrigan, would include O'Neill as an artist, or one or two of his plays, in dissertations involving the drama as a whole, particularly the Electra theme. But where it counted most, in the theatre, and before the playgoing public, Eugene O'Neill was a long-gone has-been. His death in 1953 had evoked virtually no reaction in print except a few choice words from those who cared, such as Brooks Atkinson and Joseph Wood Krutch.

Thus, when this study of the apparently shrunken giant in American dramatic art was undertaken, it had very few companions. Genevra Herndon had treated the subject of O'Neill criticism in her unpublished 1948 Wisconsin dissertation, but there was little else. It seemed, then, a propitious moment for another doctoral aspirant to undertake a comprehensive study of how this artist, now so ignominiously ignored, had been regarded by his critics both during and beyond his active life in the theatre. The end result, it was hoped, would lead to the establishment of some cohesive pattern of the public's reaction, which could point toward some reasonable determination of the

vii

causes behind the decline and fall of this hewer of new ways and cleaver of tomorrow's skylines, who had at one time received the greatest of awards for literary accomplishment, the Nobel Prize.

Once the decision was made, there began a three-year effort culminating in the dissertation itself in 1957. At the time of its acceptance it had become a monster of a typescript consisting of some 1,200 pages of bond paper covered with a mass of factual data and over 2,000 bibliographic references touching every phase of the life, works, and international reputation of Eugene O'Neill that could be gleaned from a variety of major public and university libraries and museums. Introduced by a 120-page summary discussion of the meaning of things as revealed in the annotated listings, this "Critical Bibliography of Eugene O'Neill," as it became known and so remains within *Dissertation Abstracts* and the records of University Microfilms, formed the basis for what eventually emerged as the first edition of *Eugene O'Neill and the American Critic*.

When it came time to consider the possibility of a second edition, it was clear that expansion and correction of the bibliography and its appended reference sections was of primary concern. Within the decade which had been the life span of the first edition, the name of O'Neill had become permanently reinstated as a major force in world theatre. Books, articles, essays of all types, as well as rapidly multiplying doctoral treatises, paid increasingly serious attention to the once nearly eclipsed tragedian. A useful edition of the ten year old bibliography, reflecting this greatly expanded body of domestic critical and biographical literature, had to be compiled. Once done, the corollary question of what to do about the badly outdated introductory summary demanded consideration. It was not very hard to decide what to do.

In its day, first as one of the few academic exercises in O'Neill criticism, and second as the only published discussion of O'Neill and his art derived in this particular fashion, the introductory essay had a certain significance. Once interest in O'Neill's plays, old and new, began to grow into a genuine revival of major proportions, the essay had a further value as an introduction to the contents and the meaning of the bibliography itself. The essay's importance has now greatly diminished, its contribution limited. Short of total revision, best it were omitted entirely.

And so it was. No longer is there need for questions once raised as to the possibility of O'Neill's surviving beyond the revival of the 1950's to be answered. Survival is not an issue. The years have shown that the best of O'Neill's plays need have little fear of eclipse as *THE ICEMAN COMETH* and *LONG DAY'S JOURNEY INTO NIGHT*, for instance, remain unquestioned masterpieces.

Further, the "Unknown Man" has become less and less a matter of importance. During the time that the original dissertation and the first edition were being compiled, Croswell Bowen, writing for O'Neill's younger son, Shane; Agnes Boulton, O'Neill's second wife; and the husband-wife team of Arthur and Barbara Gelb were opening a lot of previously locked doors for which *LONG DAY'S JOURNEY* itself had begun to provide keys. The enigmatic artist, the darkly pondering tragic thinker who seemed to have been to hell and back, who refused to lay aside the mask over his "real" identity, began to appear more and more understandable, more and more "human." With the appearance of Louis Sheaffer's first volume of biography the mask was almost totally removed, and now that the papers so long withheld from public scrutiny by Carlotta O'Neill, the jealous guardian of the trust, are slowly becoming available, the obscurities and the enigmas have all but evaporated.

Finally, the whole concept of whether or not O'Neill surrendered to, or actually triumphed over, some sort of debilitating "romanticism" must be studied and restudied in view of the posthumous plays and whatever revelation lies ready to be discovered within the collected papers. In fact, the final decision to let the Gelbs, Sheaffers, Falks, Raleighs, Carpenters and others carry forward the task of "O'Neill Criticism," limiting the present volume to its basic function as a reference tool, was comparatively easy to make.

Thus, with all the energy of revision devoted toward increasing the value of this volume as bibliographic, rather than critical, importance, what changes of significance may be worthy of note?

First of all, the Chronology of the Life of Eugene O'Neill has been completely recast, with extremely valuable assistance from Louis Sheaffer, whose meticulous search into O'Neill's past has provided more accurate dates and more precise facts.

Second, the Chronology of Composition, Copyright, and Domestic Publication has been updated and amended to provide a complete listing of "first appearances" of all plays and editions of plays through 1972. The Chronology is not intended to be a fully collated index of every manuscript or every volume in the manner attempted initially by Ralph Sanborn and Barrett Clark in their 1937 *Bibliography*, nor does it attempt to trace the many, often confusing, facts surrounding earlier obscure works in the manner attempted with considerable success by Egil Törnqvist in his 1969 *Drama of Souls*. The attempt here, as in the first edition, is to provide an accurate listing of the plays with regard to first copyrights and first appearances in print or, in a few limited cases, dates of composition. Early drafts and truncated or otherwise incomplete versions are not included.

The catalogue of Major Productions has been carefully rechecked and previous errors and omissions corrected, again with the helping hand of Louis Sheaffer and, of course, the amazing Theatre Collection of the New York Public Library and its cordial staff. All pertinent facts are included through the 1972 productions of *MOURNING BECOMES ELECTRA* and *THE GREAT GOD BROWN*.

The format of the Non-Dramatic O'Neill is most significantly altered. Not too many years from now this entire section may well be rendered meaningless, anyway, as the papers in the O'Neill collection at Yale are further opened and the enormous accumulation of letters from all sources is edited and published. For the time being, however, this section serves its limited purpose of including items other than plays which are readily accessible at this time.

The main Bibliography remains essentially as before. The numerical listing has been abandoned, having proved to be an unnecessary editorial restriction serving no practical purpose. The index, accordingly, now contains only page numbers, avoiding the confusion of the first edition in which page and item numbers soon became so hopelessly confused as to baffle the editor who had thought the system up in the first place. Annotations remain as before, mostly factual, occasionally editorial. Entries lacking an annotation are rare, an omission necessitated in most cases by inability to locate the reference by publication deadlines.

The somewhat unorthodox arrangement of the Bibliography has been retained in order to keep the convenient grouping of opening night and subsequent comments in basically chronological rather than alphabetical order. As before, separate introdutions to the various sections provide detailed explanations of the arrangement.

The final section, Graduate Research, will show how far the name of Eugene O'Neill has come as a subject for serious academic consideration since the first edition was published. The original seventeen entries, some of them admittedly a bit shaky, have now been expanded to some seventy, all doctoral dissertations, and all giving more than passing recognition to O'Neill.

The list of Sources Consulted has been omitted. As a part of a doctoral dissertation, it was a necessary guide to the primary and secondary sources from which the material had been compiled, but for present purposes, such a list seems hardly necessary.

What follows, then, represents an effort to provide a reasonably complete reference volume which can yield, however it is used, a detailed and comprehensive picture of domestic critical reactions to Eugene O'Neill through 1972. It is hoped that the gaps are few, and the glaring omissions minimal. An artist in O'Neill's position, apparently firmly established as a subject for continuing theatrical revival as well as scholarly research, will continue to be the source of books, essays, monographs, and dissertations into the indefinite future. This volume, by its very nature, is out of date the day it appears, but it has its important uses. Hopefully, it can retain a modicum of value until such time as this editor or, more likely, another of greater youth and at least equal enthusiasm shall deem it advisable to consider further changes through revision or periodic supplement. May he find the pleasure in so doing as great as that which accompanied the creation of the book now in your hands.

Jordan Y. Miller

Kingston, R. I.
May, 1972

*Eugene O'Neill
and the American Critic*

A Chronology of the Life
of Eugene O'Neill

While the basis of this chronology is a composite from many sources, I am most grateful to Mr. Louis Sheaffer, author of *O'Neill: Son and Playwright* and its forthcoming sequel, for his many detailed suggestions that have helped to make this revised chronology a more accurate and meaningful account of the life of Eugene O'Neill. Until recent years, during which biographers such as Arthur and Barbara Gelb and Louis Sheaffer have so painstakingly sought out the facts, sources for details of this nature were notoriously unreliable. O'Neill himself strongly preferred to keep such information as hazy and vague as possible so that he could have protection, "like a mask" as he once said, for the personal matters which he steadfastly and generally successfully maintained were his own business.

The volumes by the Gelbs and by Sheaffer are now, of course, the best available sources for biographical information, but it is interesting to read others, particularly some of the earlier accounts, for comparison and contrast. Suggested are: "The Tragic Sense," by Hamilton Basso in *The New Yorker*; Barrett H. Clark's *Man and His Plays* series; Croswell Bowen's *The Curse of the Misbegotten*; and the very personal account by O'Neill's second wife, Agnes Boulton, in *Part of a Long Story*.

16 Oct. 1888. Born on third floor of Barrett House, Times Square, New York, corner of 43rd and Broadway. Father: Irish-born James O'Neill, born 1846, Thomastown, Kilkenny County, famous throughout America in title role of *Count of Monte Cristo*. Mother, Ellen (or Ella) Quinlan O'Neill, quiet, beautiful, artistic, born in New Haven, Connecticut, 1857, convent-bred in South Bend, Indiana.

3

1888-1895. Traveled with parents on road tours to important cities all over the United States. Until age seven, under care of Cornish nurse who regaled him with tales of murder and terror.

1895-1900. Attended St. Aloysius Academy for Boys, Riverdale, New York, operated by Catholic Sisters of Charity as part of the Academy of Mount St. Vincent, a girls' school.

1900-1902. Attended De La Salle Institute, New York City, run by the Christian Brothers. Day student the first year, boarder the second.

1902-1906. Attended and graduated from Betts Academy, Stamford, Connecticut (no longer in existence), considered one of the better preparatory schools. Summers spent with family in Pequot Avenue home, New London, Connecticut.

1906-1907. Entered Princeton University in Sept. 1906 as freshman, class of 1910. While perhaps accomplishing somewhat more than the "all play and no work" which he himself spoke of, O'Neill never completed his freshman year. After an episode of throwing rocks at power line insulators along the tracks from Princeton Junction to Princeton ended in breaking a window of the local stationmaster's house, O'Neill was suspended for two weeks effective April 25, 1907, but he never returned and was permanently dropped from the university for "poor scholastic standing."

1907-1908. Lived on West 58th Street, New York, with Frank Best. Held virtually meaningless position of "secretary to the president" of New York-Chicago Supply Co., a third-rate mail order house dealing in cheap jewelry, in which James O'Neill had financial interest. Meanwhile "did the town" with brother James, ten years his senior and eager tutor in ways of the worldly. During this period O'Neill became friendly with his father's press agent, James Findlater Byth, the original of "Jimmy Tomorrow" of *ICEMAN* and the subject of "Tomorrow," O'Neill's only published short story, as well as the early one-act play *EXORCISM*.

1909. In the spring introduced by Frank Best to beautiful Kathleen Jenkins, non-Catholic, daughter of once wealthy New York family. Mrs. Jenkins, separated from her husband, shared with O'Neill's parents strong opposition to any marriage. Hoping to separate them, James O'Neill arranged to send Eugene gold prospecting to Honduras, but marriage took place in secret on October 2 in

Hoboken, New Jersey. By October 16, his twenty-first birthday, bridegroom was sailing off the coast of Mexico.

Spring 1910. After four and one-half months in fruitless search for gold and bad case of malaria, returned to New York. Did not live with Kathleen, even though marriage no longer a secret. In mid-March joined father's road company of *The White Sister* as "assistant stage manager" in St. Louis, remaining until tour folded, Portland, Maine, in April.

5 May 1910. Birth of Eugene Gladstone, Jr. Father and son did not become acquainted until after the child's eleventh birthday, but O'Neill did see the infant upon one known occasion at Kathleen's home.

6 June 1910. Shipped from Boston on Norwegian square-rigged barque, *Charles Racine*, among last of active sailing vessels. At sea 57 days, then jumped ship in Buenos Aires. This outward-bound voyage always considered one of major high points of his life, reflected particularly in lyric remembrance in *LONG DAY'S JOURNEY*.

Fall-Winter 1910-1911. Took jobs in Buenos Aires with Westinghouse (posing as draftsman), Swift and Company (sorting hides), and Singer Sewing Machine Co. (salesman). Was fired from (or quit) each job in matter of weeks. Shipped as seaman on cattle boat to Durban, South Africa, returning to South America and living nearly destitute along waterfront. At one time, as later admitted, almost turned to robbery for money to live on.

Spring 1911. Returned on Easter Sunday to New York aboard British tramp freighter, *Ikala*, real-life model for S.S. *Glencairn*. Began living at Jimmy the Priest's waterfront dive, New York, virtually in destitution. Survived on whisky, free lunch, and allowances from father to pay room rent of three dollars a month. Life here reflected in *ANNA CHRISTIE* and *ICEMAN*.

Summer 1911. Sailed on luxury liner *New York* as ordinary seaman on July 22, returned on sister ship *Philadelphia* in August. Life in stokehole and crew's quarters later reflected in *HAIRY APE* and *GLENCAIRN* plays. Wages: $27.50 a month.

January 1912. Continued to live at Jimmy the Priest's after return from 1911 voyages, though actual date is uncertain, attempted suicide by overdose of veronal. Quick action by friends, particularly James Byth (Jimmy Tomorrow), and possibly insufficient dosage saved his life. Joined father's touring *Monte Cristo* vaudeville troup in New Orleans soon thereafter, with acting debut in Ogden, Utah, end of the month. Acting ability condemned by father and himself. Tour ended in St. Paul in February.

Spring-Summer 1912. In March all the O'Neill family—James, Eugene, and both parents—returned to New London for first time together for any length of time in many years. In mid-August began working as cub reporter on New London *Telegraph* under Judge Frederick P. Latimer, who first felt O'Neill had talent. Ran column of poetry, often maintained by his own contributions, some two dozen of which were signed by various cryptic pseudonyms. Contributed limited number of verses to left wing New York *Call, The Masses,* and Franklin P. Adams' "Conning Tower." Main interest was swimming and boating, rather than journalism. Apparently courted several "nice" girls in town, including Maibelle Scott of New London, model for Muriel in *AH, WILDERNESS!*

10 July 1912. Interlocutory divorce decree from Kathleen Jenkins awarded. (Final decree, on grounds of adultery, awarded October 11.)

December 1912. Having worked through fall and into November on the *Telegraph*, ill-health forced resignation. From December 9 to 11 was patient at Fairfield County State Tuberculosis Sanitorium, Shelton, Connecticut (the charity farm discussed so bitterly in *JOURNEY*). Refusing to remain, had himself discharged. Entered Gaylord Farm Sanitorium, Wallingford, Connecticut, Dec. 24. While a patient began serious interest in reading plays, especially Strindberg. *THE STRAW* based directly on experiences here.

3 June 1913. Discharged from Gaylord Farm as arrested case. Spent remainder of summer with family in New London.

Fall-Winter 1913-1914. Boarded from October to May with family of James Rippin, New London, overlooking Long Island Sound. Always an expert swimmer, continued almost daily dips as health mended. Began serious playwriting, mailing off scripts regularly to New York producers, who never produced them. Twelve short plays and two long ones produced during this time, with *THE WEB* apparently the first, although *A WIFE FOR A LIFE* had been copyrighted in 1913.

Spring 1914. Wrote *BOUND EAST FOR CARDIFF*, to become his first produced play.

16 July 1914. Encouraged by Clayton Hamilton, critic, author, and family friend, applied for admittance to George Pierce Baker's English 47, Dramatic Composition, at Harvard, stating in his letter that he intended to become "an artist or nothing."

August 1914. Publication of *THIRST and Other One Act Plays* by Gorham Press, Boston. James O'Neill, told by Hamilton that his son seemed to have talent, backed publication with $450. Now a valued collector's item, the book had no success whatever, and was reviewed only by Hamilton in *Bookman* of April the following year. O'Neill disowned the volume, prevented its reissue during his lifetime.

Sept. 1914-May 1915. Attended Baker's English 47 class. Generally unimpressed by the works of the leading American playwrights of the day, was remembered by classmates, all younger and less experienced in worldly matters, as nervous, shy, reserved, restless.

Summer 1915. Again spent in New London, with one trip to New York in effort to interest producers in his one-act plays. Romance with "Muriel" (Maibelle Scott) had ended, and second more or less serious interest, this with Beatrice Ashe, also terminated with fall departure for New York.

Fall-Winter 1915-1916. Lived in Greenwich Village, and began to be a "regular" at John Wallace's Golden Swan bar, popularly known as "The Hell Hole" and immortalized in *ICEMAN*. Income consisted of a ten dollar weekly allowance from father. Became friend of political radicals, I.W.W.s, and gang of underworld characters known as Hudson Dusters, many of whom he could drink under the table. Never became a member of any one group, but was always welcomed as drinking companion, entertaining all comers with memorized renditions of Francis Thompson's "The Hound of Heaven." While having little actual contact with typical struggling artists and writers of the Village, did become close crony of Terry Carlin, model for Larry Slade of *ICEMAN*. Although alcoholic sprees were wild and could last for days, a number of them based on discouragement over inability to sell his plays, most evidence proves what Agnes Boulton was to write in her account of life with O'Neill: all drinking stopped completely whenever work was undertaken. Did not write anything while intoxicated, and never took drugs of any kind. During this period learned of death by suicide of Driscoll, stoker friend from *Philadelphia* days, model of same in *GLENCAIRN* plays and model of Yank of *HAIRY APE*. Also became acquainted with original Chris Christopherson of *ANNA CHRISTIE* at the Hell Hole.

28 July 1916. *BOUND EAST FOR CARDIFF*, first play by Eugene O'Neill to be produced anywhere, staged during second season of newly formed Provincetown Players, headed by George Cram Cook and wife, Susan Glaspell, in Mary Heaton Vorse's 50 x 100 foot Wharf Playhouse in Provincetown. An immediate and sensational success. O'Neill had resided during summer in Provincetown, still a haven for artists and not yet a tourist attraction, continuing to write short plays. Introduction into the Players at last opened the doors to active production which O'Neill had so long striven toward.

Fall 1916. Remained in Provincetown until late summer, then took residence at 38 Washington Square South, Greenwich Village, in order to be close to Louise Bryant, with whom he had fallen in love. One of chief models for Nina of *STRANGE INTERLUDE*, she was mistress and wife of John Reed (*Ten Days That Shook the World*). Complex Reed-Bryant-O'Neill triangle endured virtually up to day of wedding with Agnes Boulton in 1918.

3 Nov. 1916. First bill presented by Provincetown Players in Playwrights' Theatre, a converted brownstone at 139 Macdougal Street, Greenwich Village. *BOUND EAST FOR CARDIFF* second work on first bill, with subsequent plays including *BEFORE BREAKFAST, FOG, THE SNIPER*.

13 Nov. 1916. First professional critical notice of O'Neill and the Provincetown Players themselves in item by Stephen Rathbun, New York *Evening Sun*, who praised O'Neill and *CARDIFF* as best of the lot. Though New York drama editors were early aware of existence of the Players, it was some time before regular reviews of the individual plays were undertaken.

28 March 1917. Arrested in Provincetown with friend Harold DePolo, on suspicions of vagrancy. Released without charge, although for some time thereafter, because of habit of roaming Provincetown sands, was carefully observed by authorities on suspicion of wartime "spying."

Summer 1917. Turned down by Navy, and claiming Army exemption as arrested tubercular case, returned to Provincetown and continued to write. Short story forming nucleus of *HAIRY APE* apparently lost or destroyed. First and only short story to be published,

"Tomorrow," appeared in June issue of *The Seven Arts*. Providing first important royalties, $50, it contained elements later to appear in *ICEMAN*.

October 1917. *THE LONG VOYAGE HOME*, first play to be published outside THIRST volume, appeared in *The Smart Set*. Royalties: $75. Met Agnes Boulton, handsome 24-year-old widow, author of short stories and pulp fiction.

Winter 1917-1918. *THE LONG VOYAGE HOME* and *ILE* produced by Provincetown Players in second theatre, converted stable, 133 Macdougal St. Washington Square Players, rival off-Broadway group of the day, staged its first O'Neill play, *IN THE ZONE*, reviewed by major newspaper critics. Although an active contributor to Provincetown productions, still preferred Hell Hole gang. Returned to Provincetown; lived with Agnes Boulton in rented studio on income still provided by father's allowance.

12 April 1918. Married Agnes Boulton in Provincetown.

Spring-Summer 1918. *IN THE ZONE* sold for $75 weekly royalties to Orpheum vaudeville circuit, money split evenly with Washington Square Players. Producer John D. Williams took six-month option on first full-length play, *BEYOND THE HORIZON*. Living in flat over a Provincetown store, wrote further one-acts and first drafts of *CHRIS*, to become *ANNA CHRISTIE*. Brother James a permanent house guest.

Winter 1918-1919. Upon return to New York in November introduced Agnes to elder O'Neills for first time. Resided at Agnes' former home, Old House, West Point Pleasant, New Jersey, within easy commuting distance of New York. Wrote *CHRIS* and the *THE STRAW*.

May 1919. Boni and Liveright published first important collection, *THE MOON OF THE CARIBBEES and Six Other Plays of the Sea*. First meeting with *Smart Set* editor, George Jean Nathan, who had published *LONG VOYAGE HOME*. Start of permanent close friendship.

Summer 1919. Moved into remodeled former Coast Guard station on Peaked Hill Bars, Provincetown, purchased by James O'Neill and given to his son and family as a gift. House so remote from town could be reached only on foot or horseback over dunes.

30 Oct. 1919. Birth of son, Shane, in Provincetown.

3 Feb. 1920. *BEYOND THE HORIZON* produced by John D. Williams at special matinees, Morosco Theatre. Eventual permanent run of 111 performances. Only one of his son's long plays that James O'Neill ever saw. While disapproving of serious and somber realism ("What are you trying to do, send the audience home to commit suicide?") father obviously pleased at son's success.

June 1920. Pulitzer Prize awarded to *BEYOND THE HORIZON*.

10 August 1920. Death of James O'Neill.

Summer-Fall 1920. Residing at Peaked Hill Bars until weather forced return to rented Provincetown house, wrote *GOLD*, turned *CHRIS* (after failure of road tryouts in Atlantic City and Philadelphia in March) into *ANNA CHRISTIE*, completed *EMPEROR JONES* and *DIFF'RENT*. Despite success of *HORIZON*, remained in close financial straits.

3 Nov. 1920. *THE EMPEROR JONES* opened to much acclaim in production staged by Provincetown Players.

Fall-Winter 1921-1922. Lived in New York during rehearsals of *ANNA CHRISTIE*, opening November 2. Wrote *HAIRY APE* in Provincetown. In early 1922 met Eugene, Jr. nearly 12, only recently informed of true parentage. O'Neill immediately took over cost of his private school education.

28 Feb. 1922. Death of Ellen Quinlan O'Neill in Los Angeles. Her death and brother James' drunken return to New London with the body form basis of *MOON FOR THE MISBEGOTTEN*.

May 1922. Pulitzer Prize awarded to *ANNA CHRISTIE*. Weekly royalties permanently removed all financial difficulties.

Fall 1922. Purchased Brook Farm, Ridgefield, Connecticut, as winter home. Peaked Hill Bars still used in summers.

February 1923. Elected to National Institute of Arts and Letters. Awarded gold medal for drama.

8 Nov. 1923. Death of brother James at age 45.

January 1924. O'Neill, Robert Edmond Jones, Kenneth Macgowan operate reorganized Provincetown Players, original group having folded in January 1922, with plans to reopen fall of 1923 never materializing.

Fall 1924. With Jones and Macgowan continued operating Provincetown Playhouse and added new group, Greenwich Village Theatre.

December 1924. Winter months in Campsea, Paget West, Bermuda, working on *GREAT GOD BROWN*.

13 May 1925. Birth of daughter, Oona, at Campsea.

Winter 1925-1926. Rented Bellevue, large Bermuda mansion, while negotiating for purchase of 19th-century estate, Spithead. Worked on *INTERLUDE* and *LAZARUS LAUGHED*.

Spring 1926. O'Neill, Jones, Macgowan end operations connected with Provincetown Playhouse, though others continued.

Summer 1926. Received honorary Litt. D. from Yale, June 23. Resided with family at Belgrade Lakes, Maine. Began acquaintance with Carlotta Monterey, who had appeared in a production of *HAIRY APE*.

Fall-Winter 1926-1927. After Belgrade Lakes a few weeks in New York, then returned to Bermuda, late November, where *STRANGE INTERLUDE* was completed.

Spring-Fall 1927. Lived in Bermuda, with visits to New York in spring and more extended period late August to mid-October, to confer with Theatre Guild on impending productions of *INTERLUDE* and *MARCO MILLIONS*, first of his plays to be undertaken by the Guild.

November 1927. Left Bermuda for rehearsals of *MARCO* and *INTERLUDE*. Although assumption is that return to Bermuda was intended, never visited there again.

February 1928. After January 30 opening of *STRANGE INTERLUDE* left for Europe on three-year exile from United States.

May 1928. Pulitzer Prize awarded to *STRANGE INTERLUDE*.

Oct.-Dec. 1928. Embarked on what has been termed "round the world trip," although voyage was realization of specific life-long dream to visit the Orient. Unable to return to the United States until Agnes consented to divorce, extended Far Eastern trip offered temporary escape. At this time romance with Carlotta Monterey had developed to point of decision to marry her when free. Details of journey gleaned from newspapers of the day remain garbled, involving illness in Shanghai.

January 1929. Took up residence at Villa Mimosa, Cap d'Ail, France.

May 1929. In somewhat grotesque case, sued by Georges Lewys (Gladys Adelina Lewis) for plagiarism of her novel *The Temple of*

Pallas Athene in *STRANGE INTERLUDE.* Case eventually thrown out of court.

2 July 1929. Agnes Boulton granted Reno divorce on grounds of desertion.

22 July 1929. Married Carlotta Monterey.

27 July 1929. Took up residence at Chateau de Plessis, Sainte Antoine du Roches, France, under three-year lease.

6 Jan. 1931. Peaked Hill Bars home destroyed in Cape Cod storm.

17 May 1931. Left France permanently; returned to New York.

Summer 1931. Resided at Northport, Long Island.

14 Nov. 1931. In special ceremonies at Yale, bust executed by Edmond Quinn presented to Department of Drama.

Winter 1931-1932. Resided in Park Avenue apartment.

Summer 1932. Moved to Sea Island Georgia into elaborate home built to specifications. Casa Genotta (the house—though the cognate "castle" seems highly appropriate—of Gene and Carlotta) was noted for its almost museum-like quality of Spanish architecture and its study, built to resemble the captain's quarters in the stern of a sailing vessel. Two plays completed and produced while here were *DAYS WITHOUT END* and *AH, WILDERNESS!*

Sept. 1932. Announced as editor, together with Theodore Dreiser, George Jean Nathan, and James Branch Cabell, of *The American Spectator,* for which three articles contributed before publication folded (see Non-Dramatic O'Neill). On Sept. 19 made associate member of Irish Academy of Letters.

9 Nov. 1933. Elected member of American Academy of Arts and Letters.

1934. Last play to appear in New York before Oct. 1946, production of *ICEMAN, DAYS WITHOUT END,* opened January 8, a total failure. During most of year a near-breakdown forced O'Neill to cease writing altogether, and not until October or November was activity resumed.

1936. Moved to rented house on Puget Sound, Seattle, on November 3. (Casa Genotta sold in January 1937.) Nobel Prize for Literature awarded in November, and, ostensibly to avoid unwanted public contact concerning the prize, fled to San Francisco in

December. On December 26 underwent appendicitis operation in Oakland, and received Nobel Prize from representative of Swedish government while recovering in hospital.

Dec. 1937-Dec. 1943. Lived in Tao House, Chinese-style mansion built to specifications, on 158-acre estate in Contra Costa County, California. Here the last plays were completed—*ICEMAN, LONG DAY'S JOURNEY, MOON FOR THE MISBEGOTTEN, TOUCH OF THE POET*, and various parts of the giant cycle, *A TALE OF POSSESSORS SELF-DISPOSSESSED* were undertaken.

16 July 1943. Marriage of daughter Oona to famed film comedian Charlie Chaplin as his fourth wife. Her age, 18; his, same as O'Neill, 54. While mother, Agnes Boulton, was reported as pleased, O'Neill never forgave her and eventually disinherited her, along with her brother, Shane, and all their issue.

1944. Tao House sold in January; moved to Nob Hill apartment, San Francisco. The hand tremor, similar in effect to that of Parkinson's disease, but actually a different nervous affliction, that had troubled him off and on all his life, now so great as to force total cessation of writing.

1945. Moved to New York in October, living in various hotels and apartments.

1946. Took up residence in the spring in New York apartment, East 84th Street, former home of playwright Edward Sheldon. In June held extremely rare press conference in offices of Theatre Guild. *ICEMAN* opened Oct. 9, last play in New York during his lifetime.

1947. *A MOON FOR THE MISBEGOTTEN*, last play to open anywhere during his lifetime, produced in Columbus, Ohio, February 20. Tryout tour abandoned; play did not enter New York. Continued residence in New York, unable to write because of hand tremor.

1948. Moved in summer to Marblehead, Mass., purchasing shore home. Joined Euthanasia Society of America. Though general health good, could not write, and lived in virtual seclusion.

25 Sept. 1950. Suicide of Eugene, Jr. in Woodstock, New Jersey, after many marital difficulties and many problems with life as classics teacher at Yale and Princeton and as television panelist. A brilliant scholar, he had won wide recognition particularly in classics, but continued emotional disturbances ended in Woodstock death, a profound

shock to O'Neill who had maintained comparatively close relationship with his eldest child, as sharply contrasted to the ultimate complete break with Oona and Shane.

1951. In February charged by Carlotta with "cruel and abusive treatment." Admitted to Salem, Massachusetts, hospital with broken right knee, suffered in fall. Carlotta admitted to McLean Hospital, Belmont, Massachusetts, after breakdown. In March O'Neill signed petition stating Carlotta unable to take care of herself, but eventual reconciliation came in April. O'Neill admitted to Doctors' Hospital, New York, March 31, for further treatment of knee. In May left for residence in Boston and disposed of Marblehead home. While living at Hotel Shelton in Boston most of remaining plays or portions of plays, including large sections of proposed *DISPOSSESSED* cycle, were destroyed.

27 Nov. 1953. Died in Boston. Official cause: bronchial pneumonia. Age: just past 65.

2 Dec. 1953. Interred in Forest Hills Cemetery, Boston.

Chronology of Composition, Copyright and Domestic Publication

This is a chronological listing of significant available facts relating to the composition, copyright, or publication of various versions and editions of all of O'Neill's plays except those included in general anthologies. Acting versions, such as those of Dramatists Play Service or Samuel French, are not included.

Few people realize the great number of apprentice works which O'Neill poured into the U.S. Copyright Office and never published, or which he wrote but never copyrighted. The unauthorized publication of *Lost Plays* by New Fathoms Press in 1950 called attention to a few of these early plays, most of which O'Neill himself thought he had destroyed. If we are to judge the quality of those destroyed by those which New Fathoms resurrected, we can say that the loss was of minor consequence to American drama.

Sources for this chronology are varied. The primary text is Sanborn and Clark's *Bibliography of the Works of Eugene O'Neill*, originally published in 1931 and reissued in offset in 1965. It is the only detailed collation of O'Neill's plays. Clark's *Eugene O'Neill, the Man and His Plays* series has provided further information. Other sources are the U.S. Copyright List of the Government Printing Office, the Greenwich Theatre Playbill No. 3, Season 1925-1926 for THE FOUNTAIN, containing a list of all the destroyed plays, and, of course, the research efforts of biographers such as Louis Sheaffer, to whom I am much indebted. For information relating to the two projected cycles, the epic *TALE OF POSSESSORS SELF-DISPOSSESSED* and the one-act series *BY WAY OF OBIT*, I am further indebted to Mr. Donald Gallup, curator of the O'Neill papers

15

in the American Literature Collection at the Beinecke Library, Yale University.

It is extremely difficult to pinpoint actual dates of composition for many of O'Neill's plays, particularly the very early one-acters. O'Neill himself was often rather obscure concerning the facts, and conflicting opinions among his biographers and historians are not uncommon. In the following listing, therefore, I have limited myself to copyright and publication dates except for those plays known to have been written but destroyed or otherwise withheld from public notice. If one is interested in the most accurate information currently available concerning the order in which O'Neill wrote his plays and their several drafts, he should consult Egil Törnqvist's extremely valuable listing in his study of O'Neill, *A Drama of Souls* (Yale, 1969). Every known fact, including mention of several projected titles which never emerged beyond the idea of scenario stage, is included in Törnqvist's meticulous chronological table.

Plays are grouped under respective years. Titles are in *ITALIC CAPITAL LETTERS*. Plays included in Sanborn and Clark's bibliography are listed with their entry numbers.

1913

(A) WIFE FOR A LIFE
One act. Typewritten; copyrighted 15 Aug.
The earliest recorded play, although *THE WEB* (see below under *THIRST*), based on O'Neill's own written comments, could be considered the first. For explanation of the confusion, see Törnqvist, p. 258. Contents remained unknown until publication of *Lost Plays* in 1950.

1914

BREAD AND BUTTER
Four acts. Typewritten; copyrighted 2 May. First published 1972 in *Children of the Sea*.

CHILDREN OF THE SEA
One act; 13 pages. Typewritten; copyrighted 14 May.
With slight revisions, this became *BOUND EAST FOR*

CARDIFF, which appeared in 1916 in Frank Shay's *Provincetown Plays,* First Series. Original version was never published until 1972 in *Children of the Sea.*

ABORTION
One act. Typewritten; copyrighted 19 May.
Apparently O'Neill worked on this play in Baker's 47 Workshop at Harvard, because it is mentioned in some of the published reminiscences of his classmates. First published 1950 in *Lost Plays.*

THE MOVIE MAN
One act comedy; 11 pages. Typewritten; copyrighted 1 July. First published 1950 in *Lost Plays.*

THIRST AND OTHER ONE ACT PLAYS
Boston, Gorham Press, August 1914. Published as part of "American Dramatists Series."
O'Neill's first published book, an issue of 1,000 copies financed by his father, fell virtually stillborn from the press. Today it commands a high price as a collector's item, available only in large libraries. Its only review was by Clayton Hamilton in *Bookman* of April 1915.
Contents: *FOG, RECKLESSNESS, THIRST, THE WEB, WARNINGS.* None of these plays has been found under any other copyright date. Their date of composition is uncertain (see Törnqvist, p. 258). *THE WEB* is often considered the first play O'Neill ever wrote, probably very close in time to *WIFE FOR A LIFE.*
Sanborn and Clark, No. 4.

SERVITUDE
Three acts. Typewritten; copyrighted 23 Sept. First published 1950 in *Lost Plays.*

1915

THE DEAR DOCTOR
One act, never copyrighted. Date uncertain. (See Törnqvist, p. 259.)

THE SNIPER
One act. Typewritten; copyrighted 13 May. First published 1950 in *Lost Plays*.

BELSHAZZAR
Six scenes. Biblical. Never copyrighted; destroyed. According to Clark, it was written with a classmate, Colin Ford.

A KNOCK AT THE DOOR
One act, comedy. Never copyrighted; destroyed.

THE PERSONAL EQUATION
Four acts. Never copyrighted.

Begun in Prof. Baker's Harvard 47 Workshop as *THE SECOND ENGINEER*. Deutsch and Hanau in *The Princetown* refer to a reading of the first act which O'Neill gave before the Provincetown group, but it was never considered for production. Typescript copy exists at Houghton Library, Harvard.

1916

BOUND EAST FOR CARDIFF
In *The Provincetown Plays*, First Series, edited by Frank Shay. N.Y., November 1916.

The first published version of a major O'Neill play. 1,200 copies were printed, mainly for friends and patrons of the Playwrights' Theatre. Some were sold at the door during intermissions. The book is not as rare as *THIRST, etc.* and can be found in many library collections.

Sanborn and Clark, No. 6.

BEFORE BREAKFAST
In *The Provincetown Plays*, Third Series, edited by Frank Shay. N.Y., December 1916.

The first printing was 500 copies and others were made later without Shay's editing.

Sanborn and Clark, No. 7.

BEFORE BREAKFAST
New York, Frank Shay, December 1916.

Prepared from the original text and type of the Provincetown Third Series above. A rare volume; available in Special Collections,. Butler Library, Columbia, and in American Literature Collection, Beinecke Library, Yale.

Sanborn and Clark, No. 8.

ATROCITY
One act; pantomime. Never copyrighted; destroyed.

THE G.A.N. (Also reported as THE G.A.M.)
One act; farce-comedy. Never copyrighted; destroyed.

Greenwich Village Playbill dates in 1916. Kenneth Macgowan in *Vanity Fair*, April 1922, dates it 1917.

1917

NOW I ASK YOU
Three acts, prologue and epilogue, 98 pages. Typewritten; copyrighted 23 May. First published 1972 in *Children of the Sea*.

THE LONG VOYAGE HOME
In *The Smart Set*, 53 (October 1917) 83-94.

Editors H. L. Mencken and George Jean Nathan were among the very first to recognize O'Neill's importance. O'Neill was extremely grateful to them for their assistance and criticism, and in a letter to Nathan expressed his surprise and pleasure at this publication of his play, since he had submitted it only for comment.

Sanborn and Clark, No. 11.

ILE
In *The Smart Set*, 55 (May 1918) 89-100.

Also issued in printed wrappers extracted from *Smart Set* as part of Flying Stag plays for the little theatre.

Sanborn and Clark, No. 12.

BEYOND THE HORIZON
   Three acts; 128 pages. Typewritten; copyrighted 7 June.
   Three acts; 121 pages. Typewritten; copyrighted 5 Aug.

1918

THE MOON OF THE CARIBBEES
   In *The Smart Set*, 55 (Aug. 1918) 73-86.
   Sanborn and Clark, No. 13.

TILL WE MEET
   One act. Never copyrighted; destroyed.

SHELL SHOCK
   One act. Törnqvist notes it as copyrighted, though Clark, noted
as his source, seems to list it with *TILL WE MEET* simply as
unproduced. First published 1972 in *Children of the Sea.*

1919

CHRIS CHRISTOPHERSON
   Three acts, six scenes; 111 pages. Typewritten; copyrighted 5
June.
   This play appeared on the stage in 1920 as *CHRIS* in an unsuc-
cessful tryout run in Atlantic City and Philadelphia. After its with-
drawal and considerable rewriting, it emerged first as *THE OLE
DAVIL*, then as *ANNA CHRISTIE*. It never appeared in print in either
of its "Chris" forms, and is not included in the Sanborn and Clark
bibliography. A typescript of the produced *CHRIS* is listed in Union
List of Microfilms, and is available at the University of California.
(See note under *THE OLE DAVIL*, below.)

MOON OF THE CARIBBEES and Six Other Plays of the Sea
   New York, Boni and Liveright, June 1919.
   Sanborn and Clark notes differences in various printings. The
dialogue is "rougher" than that in *The Smart Set*. Except for the

unsuccessful and unlamented *THIRST* volume, this is the first publication of O'Neill's plays by an established commercial publisher. The edition consisted of 1,200 copies.

Contents: *THE MOON OF THE CARIBBEES; BOUND EAST FOR CARDIFF; THE LONG VOYAGE HOME; IN THE ZONE; ILE; WHERE THE CROSS IS MADE; THE ROPE.*

Three plays, *ZONE, CROSS* and *ROPE*, received their first publication (and of course first copyright) in this volume.

Sanborn and Clark, No. 14.

THE STRAW
   Three acts, five scenes; 121 pages. Typewritten; copyrighted 19 Nov.

EXORCISM
   One act. Apparently never copyrighted. It was never published, but was given one production by the Provincetown Players in 1920. It is not noted by Sanborn and Clark.

HONOR AMONG THE BRADLEYS
   One act. Never copyrighted; destroyed.

THE TRUMPET
   One act; comedy. Never copyrighted; destroyed.

1920

THE DREAMY KID
   In *Theatre Arts Magazine,* 4 (Jan. 1920) 41-56.
   Sanborn and Clark, No. 16.

BEYOND THE HORIZON
   New York, Boni and Liveright, March 1920.
   First publication of a long play. Second printing in 1923 had minor differences, but was not a separate edition.
   Sanborn and Clark, No. 18.

GOLD
> Four acts; 101 pages. Typewritten; copyrighted 27 July.

THE OLE DAVIL
> Four acts; 119 pages. Typewritten; copyrighted 29 Nov.
> Never published, and not noted separately in Sanborn and Clark. Typescript, like that of *CHRIS*, listed in Union List of Microfilms and available at University of California.
>
> *Note:* Claude R. Flory in "Notes on the Antecedents of *ANNA CHRISTIE*," PMLA, 86 (Jan. 1971) 77-83, gives a detailed analysis of this play and *CHRIS*, pointing out that the original *CHRIS* is about one-third longer than the sharply revised *OLE DAVIL* itself representing about 95% of the final version, *ANNA CHRISTIE*. The only notation of *THE OLE DAVIL* in Sanborn and Clark is passing reference as "in preparation" in entry No. 23, *THE EMPEROR JONES, etc.*, below.

1921

THE EMPEROR JONES
> In *Theatre Arts Magazine*, 5 (Jan. 1921) 29-59.
> The text, with many incidental editorial changes, was used later in Stewart Kidd edition below. Boni and Liveright used text prepared by O'Neill.
> Sanborn and Clark, No. 22.

THE EMPEROR JONES, DIFF'RENT, THE STRAW
> New York, Boni and Liveright, April 1921.
> This is the first of a series of volumes issued by Boni and Liveright using two or more plays on title page. They frequently appeared before the plays were produced and were often given newspaper reviews. 2,200 copies were printed.
> Sanborn and Clark, No. 23.

THE EMPEROR JONES
> Cincinnati, Stewart Kidd Co., Sept. 1921. Edited by Frank Shay.

Adapted from *Theatre Arts* version above. Printed under general title of "Stewart Kidd Modern Plays" and later reprinted as one of "Appleton Modern Plays."
Sanborn and Clark, No. 25.

GOLD
New York, Boni and Liveright, Sept. 1921.
Uniform with *MOON OF THE CARIBBEES*, *etc.*
Sanborn and Clark, No. 28.

THE FOUNTAIN
Nine scenes; prologue; 115 pages. Typewritten; copyrighted 13 Oct.

THE OLDEST MAN
Four acts; 119 pages. Typewritten; copyrighted 13 Oct.
The original title of *THE FIRST MAN*.

1922

THE HAIRY APE, ANNA CHRISTIE, THE FIRST MAN
New York, Boni and Liveright, July 1922.
Uniform with other Boni and Liveright editions.
Sanborn and Clark, No. 29.

THE DREAMY KID
In *Contemporary One-act Plays of 1921 (American)*. Cincinnati, Stewart Kidd, Oct. 1922. Selected and edited by Frank Shay.
Text editorially changed from *Theatre Arts* version above.
Sanborn and Clark, No. 17.

1923

WELDED
Three acts; 73 pages. Typewritten; copyrighted 2 May.

THE MOON OF THE CARIBBEES and Six Other Plays of the Sea

New York, Boni and Liveright, 1923. Introduction by George Jean Nathan.

"The Modern Library of the World's Best Books"—the first of a long series of Modern Library reprints of O'Neill's plays. Merely a re-issue of 1919 edition plus introduction. Not noted in Sanborn and Clark.

THE ANCIENT MARINER

One act, 7 parts. Never copyrighted.

Not actually a play, but an adaptation of Coleridge's poem to a kind of stage pantomime. No definite composition date has been established. Not noted in Sanborn and Clark. (See below, 1960, for publication information.)

1924

ALL GOD'S CHILLUN GOT WINGS

In *The American Mercury,* 1 (Feb. 1924) 129-148.

After the demise of *The Smart Set* Mencken and Nathan founded the *Mercury,* continuing their interest in the fast developing O'Neill. This controversial play was published nearly three months before its production.

Sanborn and Clark, No. 37.

ALL GOD'S CHILLUN GOT WINGS and WELDED

New York, Boni and Liveright, April 1924.

A few minor variations from *Mercury* version. Uniform with previous editions in this series. By now O'Neill was selling well enough to call for a first printing of 3,200 copies.

Sanborn and Clark, No. 38.

DESIRE UNDER THE ELMS

Three parts; 156 pages. Typewritten; copyrighted 29 Aug.

THE REVELATION OF ST. JOHN THE DIVINE

Draft of an adaptation of the last book of the bible. Noted in Donald Gallup's article introducing the published version of *THE ANCIENT MARINER* in *Yale University Library Gazette,* 1960.

1925

MARCO'S [*sic*] *MILLIONS*

    Eight acts, epilogue; 217 pages. Typewritten; copyrighted 28 Jan. The title appears thus in the copyright list. O'Neill held that the play's actual title *MARCO MILLIONS* was meant to convey a surname for the protagonist, rather than to indicate his actual wealth.

The Complete Works of Eugene O'Neill

    New York, Boni and Liveright, Jan. 1925. Actually copyrighted 1924.

    Limited to 1,200 sets. Contain the first printing of *DESIRE.*

    Contents: Vol. I—*ANNA CHRISTIE; BEYOND THE HORIZON; THE FIRST MAN; DIFF'RENT; GOLD; THE MOON OF THE CARIBBEES; BOUND EAST FOR CARDIFF; THE LONG VOYAGE HOME; IN THE ZONE; ILE.*

    Vol. II—*THE EMPEROR JONES; THE HAIRY APE; ALL GOD'S CHILLUN GOT WINGS; DESIRE UNDER THE ELMS; WELDED; THE STRAW; THE ROPE; THE DREAMY KID; WHERE THE CROSS IS MADE; BEFORE BREAKFAST.*

    Sanborn and Clark, Nos. 42 and 43.

DESIRE UNDER THE ELMS

    New York, Boni and Liveright, April 1925.

    "The Provincetown-Greenwich Plays." A separate edition, apparently reprinted from the *Complete Works,* above.

    Sanborn and Clark, No. 44.

THE GREAT GOD BROWN

    Five acts. Copyrighted 2 July 1925. (Törnqvist indicates copyright date as 2 January 1925.)

The Works of Eugene O'Neill

    New York, Boni and Liveright, July 1925.

    In four volumes. Differs from *Complete Works* in omission of sea plays. This is the "trade" edition, with several minor changes.

Contents: Vol. I—*ANNA CHRISTIE; ALL GOD'S CHILLUN; DIFF'RENT.*

Vol. II—*BEHOND THE HORIZON; THE STRAW; BEFORE BREAKFAST.*

Vol. III—*DESIRE UNDER THE ELMS; THE HAIRY APE; WELDED.*

Vol. IV—*THE EMPEROR JONES; GOLD; THE FIRST MAN; THE DREAMY KID.*

Sanborn and Clark, Nos. 45, 46, 47, 48.

1926

THE GREAT GOD BROWN, THE FOUNTAIN, THE MOON OF THE CARIBBEES and other plays

New York, Boni and Liveright, March 1926.

Uniform with 1925 four volume *Works*. 5,000 copies were printed.

Contents, in addition to those in title: *BOUND EAST FOR CARDIFF; THE LONG VOYAGE HOME; ILE; WHERE THE CROSS IS MADE; THE ROPE.*

Sanborn and Clark, No. 53.

THE EMPEROR JONES

"Reading version" in *Everybody's Magazine*, 54 (April 1926) 134-148.

THE EMPEROR JONES

In *Golden Book*, 3 (April 1926) 517-530.

LAZARUS LAUGHED

Eight scenes. Copyrighted 23 June.

1927

MARCO MILLIONS

New York, Boni and Liveright, April 1927.

Uniform with 1925 and 1926 *Works*. Even though the play had not yet been produced, it was considered worth 7,000 copies.
Sanborn and Clark, No. 58.

MARCO MILLIONS

New York, Boni and Liveright, May 1927.
Limited edition, 450 copies signed by the author, of which 440 were for sale. Same as the trade edition, same errors, pagination, etc.
Sanborn and Clark, No. 60.

STRANGE INTERLUDE

Nine acts. Copyrighted 1 July.

LAZARUS LAUGHED

First act only, in *The American Caravan*, edited by Van Wyck Brooks, Lewis Mumford, Alfred Kreymborg, and Paul Rosenfeld. New York, The Macaulay Co., September 1927.
This version of a single act is much different from the later complete edition. It was, according to Sanborn and Clark, submitted at the personal request of the editors.
Sanborn and Clark, No. 62.

LAZARUS LAUGHED, a Play for an Imaginative Theatre

New York, Boni and Liveright, 12 Nov. 1927.
The first publication of the entire play with major changes from *Caravan* version above.
Sanborn and Clark, No. 63.

LAZARUS LAUGHED, etc.

New York, Boni and Liveright, 26 Nov. 1927.
A separate edition of 775 copies, 750 offered for sale, following the precedent established by the limited edition of *MARCO*.
Sanborn and Clark, No. 64.

1928

THE EMPEROR JONES and THE STRAW

New York, The Modern Library, 1928. With an introduction by Dudley Nichols.

Not noted in Sanborn and Clark, but listed in *Publishers Trades List Annual*. Apparently an unsuccessful Modern Library edition. No copy found in any major library consulted.

A PLAY, *STRANGE INTERLUDE*

New York, Boni and Liveright, Feb. 1928.
Uniform with others of this series of *Works* starting in 1925. O'Neill was now popular enough to risk an initial printing of 20,000 copies.
Sanborn and Clark, No. 65.

STRANGE INTERLUDE

New York, Boni and Liveright, March 1928.
Limited edition, 775 copies, 750 for sale. Identical text with February printing, using blue and black inks to distinguish between dialogue and inner thoughts.
Sanborn and Clark, No. 66.

THE EMPEROR JONES

New York, Boni and Liveright, July 1928. With eight illustrations by Alexander King.
Special limited edition of 775 copies, 750 for sale.
Sanborn and Clark, No. 27.

DYNAMO

Three parts. Copyrighted 4 Oct.

1929

ILE

In *Golden Book*, 9 (February 1929) 87-93.

THE HAIRY APE

New York, Horace Liveright, April 1929. With nine illustrations by Alexander King.
Another limited edition of 775 copies, 750 for sale. Uniform with *JONES* 1928.

The Strange Interlude

During the height of the controversy during which Boston banned the play this appeared in pamphlet form, containing excerpts from the dialogue to prove the play "obscene." The long list of passages taken out of context rendered the attack generally meaningless, although those supporting censorship apparently made considerable use of it. The publisher is unidentified. The New York Public Library Theatre Collection has a copy.

Sanborn and Clark, No. 68.

DYNAMO

New York, Horace Liveright, October 1929.

Uniform with the four-volume trade edition of 1925 and subsequent volumes of *Works* series. Sanborn and Clark states that this is the third version. The first was the form presented by the Guild, the second went to the English publisher, and this is yet another. There seem to be substantial differences among all three.

Sanborn and Clark, No. 71.

DYNAMO

New York, Horace Liveright, December 1929.

Limited edition, 775 copies, 750 for sale.

Sanborn and Clark, No. 73. The last play listed in this bibliography.

1930

ANNA CHRISTIE

New York, Horace Liveright, November 1930. With illustrations by Alexander King.

Limited edition, 775 copies, 750 for sale. Uniform with *JONES* and *APE* in this illustrated series.

Sanborn and Clark, No. 33.

1931

MOURNING BECOMES ELECTRA

A trilogy. Copyrighted 12 May.

MOURNING BECOMES ELECTRA
New York, Horace Liveright, November 1931.
The regular trade edition.

MOURNING BECOMES ELECTRA
New York, Horace Liveright, December 1931.
Special edition of 500 copies signed by the author.

Inscription to MOURNING BECOMES ELECTRA
A broadside 28 x 43 cm. was issued reproducing in facsimile
O'Neill's inscription to the final longhand manuscript of the play. 50
copies were printed.

1932

BEFORE BREAKFAST
In *Golden Book*, 15 (February 1932) 151-156.

Nine Plays, selected by the author
New York, Horace Liveright, December 1932. With an introduc-
tion by Joseph Wood Krutch.
Contents: *THE EMPEROR JONES; THE HAIRY APE; ALL
GOD'S CHILLUN; DESIRE UNDER THE ELMS; MARCO
MILLIONS; THE GREAT GOD BROWN; LAZARUS LAUGHED;
STRANGE INTERLUDE; MOURNING BECOMES ELECTRA.*
This edition later became the Modern Library Giant, still in print
and an active seller as of 1973.

Representative Plays by Eugene O'Neill
New York, Liveright, Inc. 1932.
Contents: *MARCO MILLIONS; EMPEROR JONES; ANNA
CHRISTIE; WHERE THE CROSS IS MADE; MOON OF THE
CARIBBEES.*

STRANGE INTERLUDE
New York, Horace Liveright, 1932.
''The Black and Gold Library'' edition.

1933

DAYS WITHOUT END
   Four acts. Copyrighted 20 July.

AH, WILDERNESS!
   Four acts. Copyrighted 8 Aug.

AH, WILDERNESS!
   New York, Random House, October 1933.

AH, WILDERNESS!
   New York, Random House, November 1933.
   Limited edition of 325 copies, autographed, bound in leather.
Published simultaneously by Macmillan in Toronto.

1934

DAYS WITHOUT END: A Drama of Religious Faith
   New York, Random House, January 1934.
   The Yale Library catalogues an "uncorrected page proof" of this
play, with some errors corrected by an unidentified hand. One of 25
copies bound in paper wrappers. The College Library, Columbia
University, also catalogues a copy.

DAYS WITHOUT END: A Play
   New York, Random House, February 1934.
   Limited edition of 325 copies, autographed, bound in leather.
Uniform with *AH, WILDERNESS!* of 1933.

THE EMPEROR JONES
   New York, Appleton-Century, 1934. With a study guide for
screen version by W. Levin and M. J. Herzberg.
   Published in "Appleton Modern Plays."

1934-1935

The Plays of Eugene O'Neill
   New York, Charles Scribner's Sons.

The Wilderness Edition. 12-volume set, with illustrative plates and portrait, limited to 770 copies, signed by the author, with 750 for sale. Copyrighted as follows: Vols. 1 & 2, Nov. 1934; Vols. 3 & 4, Dec. 1934; Vols. 5, 6, & 7, Jan. 1935; Vols. 8 & 9, Mar. 1935; Vols. 10 & 11, May 1935; Vol. 12, June 1935.
Contents, Vol. 1—*STRANGE INTERLUDE*.
Vol. 2—*MOURNING BECOMES ELECTRA*.
Vol. 3—*THE EMPEROR JONES; AH WILDERNESS!*
Vol. 4—*ALL GOD'S CHILLUN; LAZARUS LAUGHED*
Vol. 5—*MARCO MILLIONS; THE HAIRY APE*.
Vol. 6—*BEYOND THE HORIZON; WELDED*
Vol. 7—*DYNAMO; DIFF'RENT*.
Vol. 8—*THE STRAW; THE FIRST MAN*.
Vol. 9—*DAYS WITHOUT END; GOLD*.
Vol. 10—*THE GREAT GOD BROWN; ANNA CHRISTIE*.
Vol. 11—*DESIRE UNDER THE ELMS; THE FOUNTAIN*.
Vol. 12—The *Glencairn* plays; *WHERE THE CROSS IS MADE; THE ROPE; THE DREAMY KID; BEFORE BREAKFAST; ILE*.

1936

ILE
   In *Scholastic Magazine*, 38 (15 Feb. 1936) 4-6.

Nine Plays by Eugene O'Neill
   New York, Random House, 1936. Introduction by Joseph Wood Krutch.
   Same as 1932 edition by Liveright, but issued as "Nobel Prize Edition."

A TOUCH OF THE POET
   Known to have been written during 1936 as part of the projected cycle, *A TALE OF POSSESSORS SELF-DISPOSSESSED*. Apparently not copyrighted until publication in 1957.

1937

THE EMPEROR JONES, ANNA CHRISTIE, THE HAIRY APE
New York, The Modern Library, March 1937. Introduction by Lionel Trilling.
Published simultaneously by Macmillan, Toronto.

1940

THE ICEMAN COMETH
Four acts. Copyrighted 12 Feb.

Sun Dial Press Editions
During 1940 The Sun Dial Press, New York, issued a series of volumes containing over twenty O'Neill plays. They are listed here in alphabetical order.
AH, WILDERNESS!
ANNA CHRISTIE; ALL GOD'S CHILLUN; DIFF'RENT
DAYS WITHOUT END
DESIRE UNDER THE ELMS; THE HAIRY APE; WELDED
DYNAMO
THE EMPEROR JONES; THE FIRST MAN; THE DREAMY KID
THE GREAT GOD BROWN; THE FOUNTAIN; MOON OF THE
CARIBBEES and Other Plays
LAZARUS LAUGHED
MARCO MILLIONS
MOURNING BECOMES ELECTRA
STRANGE INTERLUDE

THE LONG VOYAGE HOME; Seven Plays of the Sea
New York, The Modern Library (Random House), 1940.
A re-issue of the familiar *MOON OF THE CARIBBEES etc.,* with title change in order to capitalize on the successful motion picture, *The Long Voyage Home.*

Nine Plays by Eugene O'Neill
New York, Garden City Publishing Company, 1940. Introduction by Joseph Wood Krutch.

A "deluxe edition" of the same volume issued in 1934 and 1936.

LONG DAY'S JOURNEY INTO NIGHT
Manuscript completed in 1940 and presented to wife, Carlotta, the following year, July 22, 1941, on twelfth wedding anniversary. ". . . a sadly inappropriate gift," wrote O'Neill in his inscription to his wife, "written in tears and blood."

1941

Nine Plays by Eugene O'Neill
New York, The Modern Library (Random House), 1941. Introduction by Joseph Wood Krutch.

The first edition under Modern Library Giant series, where it has remained ever since.

Plays of Eugene O'Neill
New York, Random House, 1941.

A three-volume boxed edition. This is not in the Modern Library series, but is an entirely separate edition. It is not "complete" because of omission of certain early one-acts.

Contents: Vol. 1—*STRANGE INTERLUDE; DESIRE UNDER THE ELMS; LAZARUS LAUGHED; THE FOUNTAIN;* The *Glencairn* plays; *ILE; WHERE THE CROSS IS MADE; THE ROPE; THE DREAMY KID; BEFORE BREAKFAST.*

Vol. 2—*MOURNING BECOMES ELECTRA; AH, WILDERNESS!; ALL GOD'S CHILLUN; MARCO MILLIONS; WELDED; DIFF'RENT; THE FIRST MAN; GOLD.*

Vol. 3—*ANNA CHRISTIE; BEYOND THE HORIZON; THE EMPEROR JONES; THE HAIRY APE; THE GREAT GOD BROWN; THE STRAW; DYNAMO; DAYS WITHOUT END.*

HUGHIE
Only known completed play of projected eight-play cycle of one-act "monologues" known as *BY WAY OF OBIT.* Not published, and apparently not copyrighted, until 1959.

MORE STATELY MANSIONS
    Completed in 1941 in this "final draft" version, second and apparently last surviving play from the *POSSESSORS* cycle. First notes for the play known to have been made in 1935, and even in this version it was recognized by O'Neill as essentially incomplete, for he directed that it be destroyed in case of death. Not copyrighted until 1964.

1942

A MOON FOR THE MISBEGOTTEN
    Completed during 1942, but not produced until 1947 nor published until 1952. Törnqvist indicates original copyright date as 1945.

1946

A TOUCH OF THE POET
    Four acts. Copyrighted 4 Jan.

THE ICEMAN COMETH
    New York, Random House, October 1946.
    Hardback edition. Subsequently published in paperback but retaining 1946 copyright date by Vintage Books.

1949

THE EMPEROR JONES, ANNA CHRISTIE, THE HAIRY APE
    New York, The Modern Library (Random House), 1949. Introduction by Lionel Trilling.
    A new edition, but same contents as 1947 volume.

1950

Lost Plays of Eugene O'Neill
    New York, New Fathoms Press, 1950.
    An unauthorized edition of five very early plays "found" (with the copyright expired) in the Library of Congress. O'Neill at first pre-

pared to fight the publication, but feeling the struggle pointless he dropped his action. Critical reception was mostly unenthusiastic. Many reviewers were disturbed at the publisher's attempt to capitalize on obviously inferior works at the expense of their creator. The book is available in this edition in most libraries and has been reprinted, but as far as is known, it gained New Fathoms Press little if any profit and no prestige whatever.

Contents: *ABORTION; THE MOVIE MAN; THE SNIPER; SERVITUDE; WIFE FOR A LIFE.*

1951

Plays of Eugene O'Neill
    New York, Random House, 1951.
    "Random House Lifetime Library." Same as 1941 edition, but includes *ICEMAN* in Vol. 3.

1952

A MOON FOR THE MISBEGOTTEN
    New York, Random House, 1952.
    Unable to secure a New York production, and the play a catastrophe on the road in its tryouts in Columbus, Pittsburgh, and Detroit, O'Neill submitted the manuscript to the publishers exactly as he had written it, prefaced by his own brief remarks. It was the last publication during his lifetime and the last new O'Neill play to be published by Random House.

1955

LONG DAY'S JOURNEY INTO NIGHT
    Copyrighted as an unpublished work by Carlotta Monterey O'Neill.

1956

LONG DAY'S JOURNEY INTO NIGHT
    New Haven, Yale University Press, February 1956.

O'Neill originally directed that this play not be published or produced until twenty-five years after his death because of its intense personal nature. Before he died, however, he expressed willingness to allow the Royal Dramatic Theatre in Stockholm to produce it. Mrs. O'Neill requested Random House, in whose safekeeping O'Neill had deposited a sealed script, to publish the play. Although legally entitled to do so at Mrs. O'Neill's request as estate executrix, Random House declined. Mrs. O'Neill gave the publication rights to the Yale Library and the Library contracted with the Yale University Press for publication. Royalties are returned to Yale to establish and increase the Eugene O'Neill Memorial Fund to help preserve the O'Neill collection and maintain the O'Neill scholarships at the Yale School of Drama.

THE ICEMAN COMETH
New York, Random House, 1956.

A reprinting of the 1946 edition but including pictures from the successful production at the Circle-in-the-Square. A Vintage Book paperback edition was subsequently issued, minus the pictures, but containing only the original 1946 copyright date.

1957

A TOUCH OF THE POET
New Haven, Yale University Press, September 1957. Cloth and paperback.

Originally written in 1936 and revised in 1939 and 1942, this is one of the two known survivors from the projected *POSSESSORS* cycle. Published in America during the Stockholm production and before the 1958 staging in the United States. As in the case of *LONG DAY'S JOURNEY*, publication rights were given to the Yale Library by Mrs. O'Neill.

1958

Lost Plays of Eugene O'Neill
New York, The Citadel Press, 1958.

A reprinting of the 1950 New Fathoms Press edition.

1959

HUGHIE
New Haven, Yale University Press, February 1959.
The only survivor from the projected one-act "monologue" cycle
BY WAY OF OBIT. Publication rights given to the Yale Library by
Mrs. O'Neill.

1960

THE ANCIENT MARINER
In *Yale University Library Gazette,* 35 (October 1960) 61-68.
Printed from manuscript, with appropriate introductory comments
by Donald Gallup, Curator of the Yale Collection of American Literature, with the permission of Carlotta Monterey O'Neill.

1961 (?)

Three Plays of Eugene O'Neill
New York, Vintage Books, 1961 (?)
This paperback edition in the Knopf-Random House Vintage line
contains *DESIRE, INTERLUDE,* and *ELECTRA.* It has no copyright
date and Union Catalogue indicates uncertainty.

1962

LONG DAY'S JOURNEY INTO NIGHT
New Haven, Yale University Press, 1962.
Paperback edition of the 1956 clothbound volume.

1963

Lost Plays of Eugene O'Neill
New York, The Citadel Press, 1963.
Paperback edition of Citadel's 1958 reprint.

1964

MORE STATELY MANSIONS
  Copyrighted by Carlotta Monterey O'Neill.
  New Haven, Yale University Press, 1964. Prefatory note by
Donald Gallup. Cloth and paperback.
  Title page specifies: "Shortened from the author's partly revised
script by Karl Ragnar Gierow and edited by Donald Gallup." Publication rights given to the Yale Library by Mrs. O'Neill.
  The path of this edition is interesting indeed in view of its "dis-
covery" in the Yale manuscript collection, not generally available to
the public; its subsequent translation and sharp editing for the Stockholm production of 9 November 1962; and its further adaptation from
the Swedish version, with certain additions, by Prof. Gallup. This particular edition also incorporates certain adaptations by José Quintero
for the American production of November 1967. Contains a facsimile
page from the original typescript, showing many of O'Neill's emenda-
tions, plus several of his own sketches and plans for the setting.

Ten "Lost" Plays of Eugene O'Neill
  New York, Random House, 1964.
  Foreword by Bennett Cerf. Contents: *THIRST; THE WEB;
WARNINGS; FOG; RECKLESSNESS; ABORTION; THE MOVIE
MAN; THE SNIPER; A WIFE FOR A LIFE; SERVITUDE.*

1965

Six Short Plays of Eugene O'Neill
  New York, Vintage Books, 1965.
  Paperback edition of *DREAMY KID; BEFORE BREAKFAST;
GOLD; DIFF'RENT; THE STRAW; WELDED.*

1967

The Later Plays of Eugene O'Neill
  New York, The Modern Library, 1967.

Edited by Travis Bogard. Modern Library College Edition (paperback) of *AH, WILDERNESS!; A TOUCH OF THE POET; HUGHIE; A MOON FOR THE MISBEGOTTEN.*

1969

Selected Plays of Eugene O'Neill
New York, Random House, 1969.
More or less similar to the well-established "Nine Plays" editions, this contains *JONES, ANNA CHRISTIE, HAIRY APE, DESIRE, BROWN, INTERLUDE, ELECTRA,* and *ICEMAN.*

1972

CHILDREN OF THE SEA
Washington, Microcard Editions, 1972.
This volume, put out in a regular and a "Collectors" edition, publishes for the first time the original version of *BOUND EAST FOR CARDIFF,* written in 1914 as *CHILDREN OF THE SEA.* Also included: *BREAD AND BUTTER, NOW I ASK YOU, SHELL SHOCK.*

Date Uncertain

THE EMPEROR JONES
New York, Appleton-Century-Crofts. Edited by M. J. Herzberg.

The Two Projected Cycles

O'Neill worked for many years on two multi-play cycles, most of which were destroyed before his death. Details about them during his lifetime were often conflicting, but Mr. Donald Gallup, Curator of the Yale Collection of American Literature, in which the O'Neill papers are preserved, has supplied some very helpful information concerning the over-all plan of the cycles and their plays.

The Long Play Cycle
A TALE OF POSSESSORS SELF-DISPOSSESSED

As early as February 1932 the New York *Times* reported that

O'Neill planned three plays in a series to cover American life from 1776 to the present day. At the time of the Pittsburgh tryout of *AH, WILDERNESS!* newspaper accounts mentioned four plays "based on the Gold Rush," calling them a "monumental" work which would take years to complete and several nights to produce. In 1935 the total had reached seven, to begin with 1829 in New England and encompass five generations. By October 1935 the Theatre Guild seemed to have known of "eight separate dramas" completed, covering 125 years, with one or more soon to be forthcoming.

During 1936 reports about the status of this "octology" appeared frequently. Early in 1937 the Guild was to do two of the eight plays per season, and the following December the total had increased to nine. Throughout the next few years predictions of all kinds appeared concerning possible production. The total number finally reached eleven, the figure confirmed by O'Neill himself in his own Work Diary of 21 May 1941.

Barrett H. Clark's final edition of *Eugene O'Neill: The Man and His Plays* reported in 1947 that O'Neill intended to go back to his old vein of ironic tragedy. From Mr. Gallup's information we learn that the whole series was to begin in 1776 and carry down to at least 1932, tracing the history of an Irish family in America. As far as can be determined, these are the intended plays:

Cycle title: A TALE OF POSSESSORS SELF-DISPOSSESSED
(Originally planned title: *A TOUCH OF THE POET*)
   PLAY I. *(THE) GREED OF THE MEEK.* 1776-1793.
   PLAY II. *AND GIVE ME (US) DEATH.* 1806-1807.
   According to Mr. Gallup the titles of these first two plays at one time were reversed. O'Neill discovered that they were too long for single plays, and faced with the necessity of dividing them, finally destroyed both by burning at Tao House on 21 February 1943. Had they been divided the cycle would have reached the anticipated eleven plays. No additional proposed titles are known, but rough manuscript notes for the four plays do exist.
   PLAY III. *A TOUCH OF THE POET.* 1828 (Originally *(THE) HAIR OF THE DOG.)*
   This is the only play to survive in condition to produce. Drafted in 1936, finished in 1942, it was the first of the cycle to be completed.

PLAY IV. *MORE STATELY MANSIONS*. 1837-1842 (or later). This play survives in a very long third draft form completed by O'Neill in January 1939. It was edited for production by Karl Ragnar Gierow of the Royal Dramatic Theatre, Stockholm, where it appeared in 1962. The 1967 production in the United States is based on the 1964 edition by the Yale University Press, with the addition of a first scene and other adaptations by José Quintero (including substantial cuts toward the end of the play).

PLAY V. *THE CALMS OF CAPRICORN*. 1857.

PLAY VI. *THE EARTH'S THE LIMIT*. 1858-1860.

PLAY VII. *NOTHING IS LOST SAVE HONOR*. 1862-1870.

PLAY VIII. *(THE) MAN ON IRON HORSEBACK*. 1876-1893.

PLAY IX. *(THE) HAIR OF THE DOG*. 1900-1932.

Mr. Gallup reports that O'Neill seemed uncertain about a title for the last play. *TWILIGHT OF THE POSSESSORS* was originally considered before *HAIR OF THE DOG*, which was at first the title of the third play. In 1934 O'Neill was reported at work on *THE LIFE OF BESSIE BOWEN (BROWN, BOLEN)* which Mr. Gallup states finally became the basis of the ninth play. Karl Ragnar Gierow reported in *World Theatre*, Spring 1958, that *BESSIE* was to be about the motor car industry. He also mentioned another play, *THE LAST CONQUEST* or *THE THIRTEENTH APOSTLE* which was to include Christ and Satan as characters, but these were never part of the *POSSESSORS* cycle. Mr. Gallup states that *BESSIE* was finally destroyed in 1947. Mrs. O'Neill affirmed that all others in the cycle were destroyed page by page by O'Neill and herself.

The One-Act Cycle
BY WAY OF OBIT

In 1939 O'Neill was reported at work on a play entitled *BY WAY OF OBIT* but details were lacking. Mr. Gallup reports that this was to be another cycle, to consist of some eight one-act plays or, more accurately, monologues. One play survives, *HUGHIE*, written probably in 1941-1942, and produced in this country in January 1965. The following bits and pieces of information have been supplied by Mr. Gallup:

First draft of *HUGHIE* completed 30 April 1941; second draft May 1941; final "going over" in June 1942.

Brief outlines of five plays were written in November 1940, which seem to have been worked on as follows:

"Miser one" December 1940

"Chambermaid one" and "Blemie [?] one" December 1940

"R.R. man play" and the "Pig H[ell ?] H[ole ?] play" February 1941

"Rudie (the chambermaid play)" was worked on again October 1941

Subsequent references:

"Jimmy the Priest idea of guy who recited Homer" February 1942

"Thompson—rat idea" February 1942

"Minstrel man idea" February 1942

Major Productions of Eugene O'Neill's Plays

This is a chronological list of all important *domestic* productions of O'Neill's plays, limited, with few exceptions, to New York premiers or revivals. O'Neill preferred to open "cold" in New York without the traditional out of town tryouts. A few important productions which did appear first on the road are listed, but no attempt has been made to include the touring productions which went out after the New York openings.

Sources are varied. The greater part of the information comes from the Burns Mantle yearbooks. Early Provincetown data are taken from Deutsch and Hanau's *The Provincetown*. Other material is from newspapers and magazines, playbills of various sorts, and miscellaneous sources in library collections. The ever helpful Louis Sheaffer has also provided factual corrections here and there.

1916

BOUND EAST FOR CARDIFF
Presented 28 July, second bill, Wharf Theatre, Provincetown.

Cast

Yank	George Cram Cook
Captain	David Carb
First Mate	Eugene O'Neill

The first production anywhere of a play by Eugene O'Neill. Mary Heaton Vorse owned the tiny wharf where the newly formed group produced its plays. This second season displayed the talents of the young man who had recently joined them, "dressed like Edgar Allan Poe who had just jumped ship." Only about 60 spectators could crowd into the theatre, but all reports speak of the play as a tremendous experience. This is one of the few appearances of O'Neill as an actor. His stage fright was considerable.

THIRST
Presented Summer, fourth bill, Wharf Theatre, Provincetown.

The three-man cast included O'Neill in the part of the mulatto sailor. There is no record of a second production at any time, nor any record of the play having been reviewed.

BOUND EAST FOR CARDIFF
Presented 3 November, first bill, Playwrights' Theatre, 139 MacDougal Street, New York.

Cast

Yank	George Cram Cook
Driscoll	William Stewart
Cocky	Edw. J. Ballantine
Davis	Harry Kemp
Scotty	Frank Shay
Olson	Bion Nordfelt
Smitty	Lew Parrish
Ivan	Francis Buzzell
Captain	Henry Marion Hall
First Mate	Eugene O'Neill

The first New York production at the newly established theatre in Greenwich Village. The cast probably represents many from the original Wharf production. The performance attracted little attention, and regular New York newspaper reviewers generally ignored it with the important exception of Heywood Broun of the *Tribune*.

BEFORE BREAKFAST
Presented 1 December, third bill, Playwrights' Theatre.

Cast

Mrs. Rowland	Mary Pyne
Alfred, her husband (unseen)	Eugene O'Neill

O'Neill's performance consisted of the insertion of his hand onto the set to take a pan of hot water, and an offstage groan at the climax of the play. It was his last appearance of any kind on any stage.

1917

FOG
Presented January, fifth bill, Playwrights' Theatre.
This is apparently the only production the play ever received. The details of the production are unavailable.

THE SNIPER
Presented 16 February, seventh bill, Playwrights' Theatre.

Cast

Rougon	George Cram Cook
Priest	Donald Corley
German Captain	Theron M. Bamberger
Private of Regiment	Morton Stafford
Another Private	Robert Montcarr
Jean	Ida Rauh

Another of the very early works tried by the Provincetown group. It has never received any other production. It was also ignored by the press.

IN THE ZONE
Presented 31 October, first bill, Washington Square Players, Comedy Theater, New York.

The first O'Neill play produced by Washington Square and the first to be included in Burns Mantle's *Best Plays* (1909-1919). Neither Mantle nor the New York *Times* lists the cast, but actors known to have appeared are Arthur Hohl, Robert Strange, Frederick Roland, and Harry Ehlers. The play became a favorite vaudeville skit, and it brought O'Neill some of his earliest steady royalties.

THE LONG VOYAGE HOME
Presented 2 November, first bill, Playwrights' Theatre.

Cast

Bartender	George Cram Cook
Olson	Ira Remson
Driscoll	Hutchinson Collins
Cocky	O. K. Liveright
First girl	Ida Rauh
Second girl	Alice MacDougal

ILE
Presented 30 November, second bill, Playwrights' Theatre. Directed by Nina Moise.

Cast

Ben	Everett Glass
Steward	Robert Edwards
Capt. Keeney	Hutchinson Collins
Mr. Slocum	Ira Remson
Mrs. Keeney	Clara Savage
Joe	Louis B. Ell

1918

ILE
Presented 18 April, Greenwich Village Players, Greenwich Village Theatre, New York.

Cast

Ben	Everett Glass
Steward	Francis McDonald
Capt. Keeney	Joseph Macaulay
Mr. Slocum	Harold Meltzer
Mrs. Keeney	Margaret Fareleigh
Joe	John Ahearn

THE ROPE
Presented 26 April, seventh bill, Playwrights' Theatre. Directed by Nina Moise.

Cast

Abraham Bentley	O. K. Liveright
Annie	Dorothy Upjohn
Pat Sweeney	H. B. Tisdale
Mary	Edna Smith
Luke Bentley	Charles Ellis

THE ROPE
Presented 13 May, Washington Square Players, Comedy Theatre.

Cast

Abraham Bentley	Whitford Kane
Annie	Josephine A. Meyer
Pat Sweeney	Robert Strange
Mary	Kate Morgan
Luke Bentley	Effington Pinto

WHERE THE CROSS IS MADE
Presented 22 November, first bill, Playwrights' Theatre. Directed by Ida Rauh.

Cast

Nat Bartlett	James Light
Dr. Higgins	O. K. Liveright
Sue Bartlett	Ida Rauh
Capt. Bartlett	Hutchinson Collins

THE MOON OF THE CARIBBEES

Presented 20 December, second bill, Playwrights' Theatre.
Directed by Thomas Mitchell.

Cast

Yank	Harry Winston
Driscoll	Hutchinson Collins
Olson	Wm. Forster Batterham
Davis	W. Clay Hill
Cocky	O. K. Liveright
Smitty	Charles Ellis
Paul	Percy Winner
Lamps	Phil Lyons
Chips	Fred Booth
Old Tom	William Stuart
First Mate	Louis B. Ell
Bella	Jean Hobb
Susie	Bernice Abbott
Pearl	Ruth Collins Allen

1919

THE DREAMY KID

Presented 31 October, first bill, Playwrights' Theatre.
Directed by Ida Rauh.
Settings by Glenn Coleman.

Cast

Mammy Saunders	Ruth Anderson
Coely Ann	Leathe Colvert
Irene	Margaret Rhodes
The Dreamy Kid	Harold Simmelkjaer

1920

BEYOND THE HORIZON
Presented 2 February, Morosco Theatre.
Produced by John D. Williams.
Moved to Criterion Theatre, 23 February; Little Theatre, 9 March.

Cast

Robert Mayo	Richard Bennett
Andrew Mayo	Robert Kelly
Ruth Atkins	Elsie Rizer
Capt. Dick Scott	Sidney Macy
Mrs. Kate Mayo	Mary Jeffery
Mrs. Atkins	Louise Closser Hale
James Mayo	Erville Alderson
Mary	Elfin Finn
Ben	George Hadden
Dr. Fawcett	George Riddell

The first "uptown" production of an O'Neill play, undertaken on an experimental basis by John Williams. It was produced at special matinees, using cast members already committed to regular evening performances elsewhere. The critics welcomed the play and its popularity increased until it finally received, after two subsequent moves, a regularly scheduled run. It brought O'Neill his first Pulitzer Prize.
Total performances: 111

CHRIS
>Presented 8 March by George C. Tyler in Atlantic City, N.J.

Cast

Chris Christopherson	Emmett Corrigan
Anna	Lynn Fontanne
The Mate	Arthur Ashley

This was the abortive road tryout of the first version of *ANNA CHRISTIE*. The newspaper reception was only lukewarm, and after a week in Atlantic City the play moved to Philadelphia where it died an unmourned death. After this failure O'Neill waited four years before permitting another out of town tryout. He never permitted publication of the play, although a typescript exists at the University of California. The original version was considerably changed, apparently became first *THE OLE DAVIL* and then, with further minor modifications, *ANNA CHRISTIE* as we know it.

EXORCISM
>Presented 26 March, fifth bill, Playwrights' Theatre.

Cast

Ned Malloy	Jasper Deeter
Jimmy	M. A. McAteer
Maj. Andrews	William Dunbar
Mr. Malloy	Remo Bufano
Nordstrom	Lawrence Vail

Listed as "a play of anti-climax" and never again produced. The director was Edward Goodman.

THE EMPEROR JONES
>Presented 1 November, Playwrights' Theatre, 139 MacDougal Street.

Moved to Selwyn Theatre 27 December; Princess Theatre 29 January 1921.

Cast

Brutus Jones	Charles Gilpin
Harry Smithers	Jasper Deeter
Native woman	Christine Ell
Lem	Charles Ellis

The sensational success which brought the public crowding up to the tiny Provincetown box office demanding to become members in order to witness this phenomenal play. Thereafter the small theatre in Greenwich Village was never the same, This also marks the first major role for a Negro in the American theatre. Gilpin's tremendous interpretation extended through the season and carried him throughout the nation on an extended tour.
Total performances: 204

DIFF'RENT

Presented 27 December, Provincetown Players.
First performances listed at Playwrights' Theatre, then a transfer uptown on matinee schedule to Selwyn Theatre, 21 January. Later transfers, giving it regular run, to Times Square, 4 February, and Princess, 7 February.

Cast

Capt. Caleb Williams	James Light
Emma Crosby	Mary Blair
Jack Crosby	Eugene Lincoln
Capt. John Crosby	Alan MacAteer
Mrs. Crosby	Alice Rostetter
Harriet Williams	Elizabeth Brown
Alfred Rogers	Iden Thompson
Benny Rogers	Charles Ellis

This was probably a case of pushing good luck too far. The play was given a moderate welcome by the few critics who first saw it. Mary Blair was generally felt to be a more than competent Emma. Because of the apparent success downtown, the transfer was made to capitalize on the fortunes of the *HORIZON* matinees and the *JONES* regular performances. The move was a bad one, and the public would not come. Perhaps a longer run at the smaller theatre would have been more successful, but the play generally is not deemed worthy of much attention anyway.

Total performances: 100

1921

GOLD
Presented 1 June, Frazee Theatre, New York.
Produced by John D. Williams.
Staged by Homer Saint-Taudens.

Cast

Abel	Ashley Buck
Butler	George Marion
Capt. Isaiah Bartlett	Willard Mack
Silas Horne	J. Fred Holloway
Ben Cates	Charles D. Brown
Jimmy Kanaka	T. Tamanoto
Mrs. Bartlett	Katherine Grey
Sue Bartlett	Geraldine O'Brien
Danny Drew	Charles Francis
Nat Bartlett	E. J. Ballantine
Dr. Berry	Scott Cooper

This is often regarded as the "expanded" version of the one-act *WHERE THE CROSS IS MADE*, but O'Neill actually wrote the longer play first, with the fourth act providing most of the material for the more popular shorter piece. *GOLD* was not a success and quickly closed, although Willard Mack received some good notices for his portrayal of the mad captain.

Total performances: 13

ANNA CHRISTIE
Presented 2 November, Vanderbilt Theatre, New York.
Produced by Arthur Hopkins.
Settings by Robert Edmond Jones.

Cast

Johnny-the-Priest	James C. Mack
Chris Christopherson	George Marion
Marthy Owen	Eugenie Blair
Anna	Pauline Lord
Mat Burke	Frank Shannon

The first production of one of O'Neill's busiest seasons, in which four of his full length plays were produced both uptown and down. This rewrite of *CHRIS* won wide critical acclaim both for the writer and the star. It won another Pulitzer Prize and has become one of the most familiar of O'Neill's plays. Many felt the "happy ending" was poor, although O'Neill denied that it was happy. He never liked the play, and did not include it in his own choice of his best plays.
Total performances: 177

THE STRAW
Presented 10 November, Greenwich Village Theatre.
Produced by George C. Tyler.

Cast

Bill Carmody	Harry Harwood
Nora	Viola Ormonde
Tom	Richard Ross
Billy	Norris Millington
Dr. Gaynor	George Woodward
Fred Nicholls	Robert Strange
Eileen Carmody	Margalo Gilmore
Stephen Murray	Otto Kruger
Dr. Stanton	George Farren

Most critics thought this second production of the season was a touching, well-written play, in spite of the distasteful subject of tuberculosis, but that its tragic qualities were debatable. Margalo Gilmore, to star later in *MARCO MILLIONS*, was approved as a warm and charming heroine, but Otto Kruger met unenthusiastic response. The direction of the play was not particularly good and the whole production, which had far more to offer than other of O'Neill's failures, was ineffectively handled and terminated after a disappointing run. For many O'Neill students, however, it has remained one of the better of his less known plays.

Total performances: 20

1922

THE FIRST MAN
Presented 4 March, Neighborhood Playhouse, New York.
Produced by Augustin Duncan.

Cast

Curtis Jayson	Augustin Duncan
Martha	Margaret Mower
John Jayson	Harry Andrews
John, Jr.	Gordon Burby
Richard	Alan Bunce
Esther	Margherita Sargent
Lily	Marjorie Vonnegut
Mrs. Davidson	Marie L. Day
Mark Sheffield	Eugene Powers
Emily	Eva Carder
Richard Bigelow	Frederic Burt

Originally "The Oldest Man." The birth scene and its screams offended most critics, although many caught the humor of the satire of a close-knit family.

Total performances: 27

THE HAIRY APE
Presented 9 March, Playwrights' Theatre.
Produced by the Provincetown Players.
Settings by Cleon Throckmorton and Robert Edmond Jones.

Cast

Yank	Louis Wolheim
Paddy	Henry O'Neill
Long	Harold West
Mildred Douglas	Mary Blair
Her Aunt	Eleanor Hutchinson
Second Engineer	Jack Gude

The sensation of this play's style and subject matter, and the acting of Louis Wolheim, rivalled the furor over *JONES* and the performance of Charles Gilpin. Theatre crowds once more came downtown in such large numbers that the play was forced to move to the Plymouth on 17 April. There were strong reactions from the District Attorney's Office, which threatened to close it as obscene for its shocking, jolting language, but it continued on through the season unmolested.

Total performances: 127

1924

WELDED
Presented 17 March, Thirty-ninth Street Theatre, New York.
Produced by Eugene O'Neill, Kenneth Macgowan, and Robert Edmond Jones in association with the Selwyns.
Directed by Stark Young.
Settings by Robert Edmond Jones.

Cast

Eleanor Owen	Doris Keane
Michael Cape	Jacob Ben-Ami

John Darnton	Curtis Cooksey
A Woman	Catherine Collins

The first of the productions by the newly formed company of O'Neill, Macgowan, and Jones, which broke away from the now disintegrating original Provincetown group. The play, which had tried out in Baltimore to unenthusiastic notices, was a distinct failure. Few critics could find any pleasure or point of view in the sordid, heavily Strindbergian battle of the sexes. Some praise for individual performances could not save it.

Total performances: 24

THE ANCIENT MARINER

Presented 6 April, Provincetown Playhouse (no longer Playwrights').

Directed by Robert Edmond Jones and James Light.

Settings by Robert Edmond Jones.

Masks by James Light.

Cast

Ancient Mariner	E. J. Ballantine
First Wedding Guest	James Shute
Second Wedding Guest	H. L. Rothschild
Third Wedding Guest	Charles Ellis
Helmsman	James Meighan
Bride	Rosalind Fuller
Bridegroom	Gerald Stopp

An attempt at a pantomimic dramatization of the Coleridge poem. Using both original directions and those contained in the poem, and with a combined system of actions and readings of the verse, O'Neill attempted to interpret the story. It was not a success, and most critics felt O'Neill was far away from his element.

Total performances: 29

ALL GOD'S CHILLUN GOT WINGS
Presented 15 May, Provincetown Playhouse.
Directed by James Light.
Settings by Cleon Throckmorton.

Cast

Jim Harris, child	William Davis
Ella Downey, child	Virginia Wilson
Shorty, child	George Finley
Jim Harris, adult	Paul Robeson
Ella Downey, adult	Mary Blair
Mrs. Harris	Lillian Greene
Hattie Harris	Flora Cole
Shorty, adult	Charles Ellis
Joe	Frank Wilson
Mickey	James Martin

Because of muddled censorship attempts from City Hall, offended by the theme of miscegenation, the play was denied the use of children in the opening scene, ostensibly because they were too young. This did not halt production, because James Light, the director, read the passage to the audience, after which the play proceeded without incident. O'Neill always felt the work was badly misunderstood and would some day come into its own among his important plays.
Total performances: 100

S. S. GLENCAIRN
Presented originally 14 August by Barnstormer's Barn, in Provincetown, Massachusetts. Then in New York as follows:
3 November at the Provincetown Playhouse, directed by James Light.
16 December at the Punch and Judy.
12 January 1925 at the Princess.

Cast

Yank	Sidney Machet
Driscoll	Lawrence Cecil
Olson	Walter Abel

Davis	Howard McGee
Cocky	Walter Kingsford
Smitty	E. J. Ballantine
Ivan	James Meighan
Swanson	Samuel Selden
Scotty	Archie Sinclair
Paul	Abraham Krainis
Lamps	Clement O'Loghlen
Old Tom	Stanley Howlett
Big Frank	William Stahl
Paddy	H. L. Remsten
Captain	Edgar Stehli
First Mate	Lewis Barrington
Bella	Mary Johns
Joe	Stanley Jowlett
Nick	Edgar Stehli
Freda	Helen Freeman

The first attempt to bring the four *Glencairn* plays together. It met with considerable critical success and has since been revived many times.

Total performances: 99

DESIRE UNDER THE ELMS

Presented 11 November, Greenwich Village Theatre.
Produced by the Provincetown Players.
Moved to Earl Carroll, 12 January; George M. Cohan, 1 June; Daly's 63rd Street, 28 September.
Settings by Robert Edmond Jones.

Cast

Simeon Cabot	Allen Nagle
Peter Cabot	Perry Ivins
Eben Cabot	Charles Ellis
Ephraim Cabot	Walter Huston
Abbie Putnam	Mary Morris

A success while in the village, this play moved uptown, where it prospered on its notoriety. A campaign was at the time in full swing to "clean up" New York plays by eliminating so much "sex." The long run can in part be attributed to thrill-seekers (most of them keenly disappointed at the lack of "filth" they came to see), but the play did have its merits that were widely recognized by others. It was regarded as the nearest O'Neill had yet come to establishing the feeling of Greek tragedy.

Total performances: 208

1925

THE FOUNTAIN

Presented 10 December, Greenwich Village Theatre.
Produced by Kenneth Macgowan, Robert Edmond Jones and Eugene O'Neill.
Designed by Robert Edmond Jones.
Musical setting by Macklin Morrow.

Cast

Ibnu Aswad	Stanley Berry
Juan Ponce de Leon	Walter Huston
Pedro	William Stahl
Maria de Cordova	Pauline Moore
Luis de Alvaredo	Egon Brecher
Christopher Columbus	Henry O'Neill
Beatriz de Cordova	Rosalind Fuller
Diego Menendez	Crane Wilbur
Nano	Curtis Cooksey

This brief list of major characters gives little indication of the extensive cast which performed against the overwhelming scenery designed by Jones. While critics admired the settings in themselves,

they suffocated what action there was, and O'Neill's attempt at the
romantic and poetic interpretation of history did not succeed.
Total performances: 24

1926

THE GREAT GOD BROWN
Presented 23 January, Greenwich Village Theatre.
Produced by Kenneth Macgowan, Robert Edmond Jones, Eugene
O'Neill.
Staged by Robert Edmond Jones.
Moved to Garrick Theater, 1 March; Klaw Theatre, 10 May.

Cast

William A. Brown	William Harrigan
His Father	Milano Tilden
His Mother	Clifford Sellers
Dion Anthony	Robert Keith
His Father	Hugh Kidder
His Mother	Eleanor Wesselhoeft
Margaret	Leona Hogarth
Cybel	Anne Shoemaker

Despite the complete mystification of the average audience, many
critics and a good part of the public found this play thoughtful and
somewhat profound. The use of masks was confusing, but did not
hinder the viewer's pleasure. The play marked O'Neill's turning point
away from the realism of the past and showed the beginnings of the
mysticism that was to dominate future plays. It was also one of the
few times when O'Neill felt obliged to explain his play's meaning,
which he did by a widely reprinted article for the press.
Total performances: 283

THE EMPEROR JONES
Revived at the Provincetown Theatre, 16 February.
Staged by James Light.

Cast

Brutus Jones	Charles Gilpin
Harry Smithers	Harold McGee
Old native woman	Barbara Benedict
Lem	William Stahl

Revived 10 November, Mayfair Theatre.
Produced by Mayfair Productions.

Cast

Brutus Jones	Charles Gilpin
Harry Smithers	Moss Hart
Old native woman	Hazel Mason
Lem	Arthur Ames

Total performances, second revival: 61
The 10 November Mayfair production is described by Moss Hart
in *Act One*.

BEYOND THE HORIZON
Revived 30 November, Mansfield Theatre.
Produced by The Actors Theatre.

Cast

James Mayo	Malcolm Williams
Kate Mayo	Judith Lowry
Capt. Scott	Albert Tavernier
Andrew Mayo	Thomas Chalmers
Robert Mayo	Robert Keith
Ruth Atkins	Aline MacMahon
Mrs. Atkins	Eleanor Wesselhoeft
Mary	Elaine Koch
Ben	Victor Kilian
Dr. Fawcett	Joseph McInerney

The revival was widely praised by the critics. The performance of Aline MacMahon as Ruth was outstanding.
Total performances: 79

1928

MARCO MILLIONS
Presented 9 January, Guild Theatre, by the Theatre Guild.
Staged by Rouben Mamoulian.
Settings by Lee Simonson.

Cast

Marco Polo	Alfred Lunt
Donata	Natalie Browning
Tedaldo	Morris Carnovsky
Nicolo	Henry Travers
Maffeo	Ernest Cossart
Kublai, the Great Kaan	Baliol Holloway
Chu-Yin	Dudley Digges
Kukachin	Margalo Gillmore

The Guild's first O'Neill, staged lavishly, and moderately successfully. Many felt the Babbitt in oriental dress from Renaissance Italy was not very amusing at this late date, but others saw its merits. It ran concurrently with the sensational *STRANGE INTERLUDE*.
Total performances: 92

STRANGE INTERLUDE
Presented 30 January, John Golden Theatre.
Produced by the Theatre Guild.
Staged by Philip Moeller.
Settings by Jo Mielziner.

Cast

Charles Marsden	Tom Powers
Prof. Leeds	Philip Leigh
Nina Leeds	Lynn Fontanne

Sam Evans	Earl Larimore
Edmund Darrell	Glenn Anders
Mrs. Evans	Helen Westley
Gordon, a boy	Charles Walters
Madeline Arnold	Ethel Westley
Gordon, a man	John J. Burns

The first of O'Neill's over-length plays and, from all angles, the most successful of his works up to this time. It brought his third Pulitzer Prize and was heralded as the beginning of new and wonderful things in the modern drama. Its wide popular support and long run, the longest of any O'Neill play before the 1956 revival of *ICEMAN*, never failed to amaze even O'Neill's most ardent enthusiasts.

Total performances: 426

LAZARUS LAUGHED

Presented 9 April, by the Pasadena, California, Community Playhouse.

This "play for an imaginative theatre" was rumored in production by the Provincetown group, but the Pasadena performance is the only large-scale staging it ever received. The production was lavish, complete with all costumes and masks as directed, and was enthusiastically received. The cast was entirely local, and all work was voluntary.

Total performances: 28

1929

S. S. GLENCAIRN

Revived at the Provincetown Theatre, 9 January.

Cast

Yank	Lionel J. Stander
Driscoll	Byron Russell
Olson	Walter Abel
Davis	Harold McGee
Cocky	George Tawde

Smitty	E. J. Ballantine
Ivan	George Tobias
Scotty	Archie Sinclair
Paul	Richard Gaines
Paddy	H. L. Remsten
Captain	Robert Lucius Cook
First Mate	Max Essin
Bella	Mary Johns
Joe	Robert Lucius Cook
Nick	A. Montague Ash
Freda	Dorothee Nolan

Total performances: 90

DYNAMO
Presented 11 February, Martin Beck Theatre.
Staged by Philip Moeller.
Produced by the Theatre Guild.
Designed by Lee Simonson.

Cast

Rev. Light	George Gaul
Mrs. Light	Helen Westley
Reuben Light	Glenn Anders
Ramsay Fife	Dudley Digges
May Fife	Catherine Doucet
Ada Fife	Claudette Colbert

The first of the proposed trilogy exploring "the sickness of today." O'Neill was unhappy that he had announced a coming trilogy, for many critics reserved judgment until the other two had been produced. The original plan was never carried through. O'Neill also objected to the leggy display of the heroine, who continually detracted from the play's effectiveness. He always felt the play was terribly misunderstood, along with *ALL GOD'S CHILLUN*.
Total performances: 50

BEFORE BREAKFAST
Revived at the Provincetown Theatre, 5 March.

Cast

Mrs. Rowland   Mary Blair

Presented along with Vergil Geddes' *The Earth Between*. An interesting event for two reasons. First, Geddes, in his 1934 pamphlet, *The Melodramadness of Eugene O'Neill*, was to be one of O'Neill's strongest critics. Second, the star of Geddes' piece was hailed as one of great promise. Her name was Bette Davis. Neither play in this bill was very well received.
Total performances: 27

1930

MARCO MILLIONS
Revived by the Theatre Guild, Liberty Theatre, 3 March.

Cast

Marco Polo	Earl Larimore
Donata	Helen Tilden
Nicolo	Frederick Roland
Maffeo	Harry Mestayer
Kublai	Sydney Greenstreet
Chu-Yin	Henry Travers
Kukachin	Sylvia Field

Total performances: 8

1931

MOURNING BECOMES ELECTRA
Presented 26 October, by the Theatre Guild, Guild Theatre.
Staged by Philip Moeller.
Settings and costumes by Robert Edmond Jones.

Cast

Seth Beckwith	Arthur Hughes
Christine	Alla Nazimova
Lavinia	Alice Brady
Peter Niles	Philip Foster
Hazel Niles	Mary Arbenz
Ezra Mannon	Lee Baker
Adam Brant	Thomas Chalmers
Orin	Earl Larimore

This trilogy which ran for many hours and many acts was commonly regarded as O'Neill's masterpiece and the climax of his career. It did have its violent detractors, but probably no more than many other of his plays. O'Neill's published notes report over three years of careful thought and planning, during which time he included and then rejected many of his previous stage effects such as spoken thoughts and masks.
Total performances: 150

1932

MOURNING BECOMES ELECTRA
Revived by the Theatre Guild, 9 May.

Cast

Lavinia	Judith Anderson
Orin	Walter Abel
Christine	Florence Reed
Adam Brant	Crane Wilbur

The road company returned for a brief engagement. Most critics found the play still effective, although the loss of Brady and Nazimova was acutely felt.
Total performances: 16

1933

AH, WILDERNESS!

First performed at Nixon Theatre, Pittsburgh, 25 Sept. Presented 2 October, by the Theatre Guild, Guild Theatre.
Staged by Philip Moeller.
Settings by Robert Edmond Jones.

Cast

Nat Miller	George M. Cohan
Essie	Marjorie Marquis
Arthur	William Post, Jr.
Richard	Elisha Cook, Jr.
Mildred	Adelaide Bean
Tommy	Walter Vonnegut, Jr.
Sid	Gene Lockhart
Lily	Eda Heinemann
David McComber	Richard Sterling
Muriel	Ruth Gilbert
Belle	Ruth Holden

The "new" O'Neill emerged in this play, amazing his friends and critics alike with a nostalgic comedy of "recollection." It was the first time an actor received top billing in a Guild play. The name of George M. Cohan appeared in lights along with that of O'Neill. One of O'Neill's most popular plays, it is a constant favorite of little theatres and college groups.

Total performances: 289

1934

DAYS WITHOUT END

First performed at Plymouth Theatre, Boston, 27 Dec. Presented 8 January, by the Theatre Guild, Henry Miller Theatre.
Staged by Philip Moeller.
Settings by Lee Simonson.

Cast

John	Earl Larimore
Loving	Stanley Ridges
William Elliot	Richard Barbee
Father Baird	Robert Loraine
Elsa	Selena Royle
Lucy	Ilka Chase

The "return to the Cross" signified, for many critics, the "arrival" of Eugene O'Neill. For others it meant the worst play he had ever written. The reviewers in various religious publications, both Catholic and Protestant, overwhelmingly praised it; other critics almost universally condemned it.

Total performances: 57

1937

S. S. GLENCAIRN
Revived by the WPA Federal Theatre Project at the Lafayette Theatre, 29 October.
Staged by William Challee.
Settings by Perry Watkins.

This revival was presented by an all-Negro cast, none of whom achieved fame except Canada Lee, who played Yank. The critics praised O'Neill for having made all his plays available to the Federal Theatre Project, but in the case of the *Glencairn* cycle, it was difficult to adjust to the black cast in such a variety of national roles.

Total performances: 68

1938

DIFF'RENT
Revived by Charles Hopkins for the WPA New York State Federal Theatre Project at the Maxine Elliott Theatre, 25 January.
Settings and costumes by Ben Edwards.
Lighting by Feder.

Cast

Capt. Caleb Williams	Erford Gage
Emma Crosby	Lennore Sorsby
Capt. John Crosby	Gene Webber
Mrs. Crosby	Rose Morison
Jack Crosby	Douglas Campbell
Harriet Williams	Irene Taylor
Alfred Rogers	Jay Velie
Benny Rogers	Frank Daly

1941

AH, WILDERNESS!
Revived by the Theatre Guild, at the Guild Theatre, 2 October.
Staged by Eva Le Gallienne.
Produced by Theresa Helburn, Lawrence Langner, Eva Le Gallienne.
Settings by Watson Barratt.

Cast

Nat Miller	Harry Carey
Essie	Ann Shoemaker
Arthur	Victor Chapin
Richard	William Prince
Mildred	Virginia Kaye
Tommy	Tommy Lewis
Sid	Tom Tully
Lily	Enid Markey
David McComber	Hale Norcross
Muriel	Dorothy Littlejohn
Belle	Dennie Moore

The critics found Harry Carey a pleasing replacement for Cohan but the play was now less of a starring piece.

Total performances: 29

1946

THE ICEMAN COMETH
  Presented 9 October, Martin Beck Theatre.
  Produced by Theatre Guild in association with Armina Marshall.
  Staged by Eddie Dowling.
  Supervised by Theresa Helburn and Lawrence Langner.
  Settings and lighting by Robert Edmond Jones.

Cast

Harry Hope	Dudley Digges
Ed Mosher	Morton L. Stevens
Pat McGloin	Al McGranary
William Oban	E. G. Marshall
Joe Mott	John Marriott
Piet Wetjoen	Frank Tweddell
Cecil Lewis	Nicholas Joy
James Cameron	Russell Collins
Hugo Kalmar	Leo Chalzel
Larry Slade	Carl Benton Reid
Rocky Pioggi	Tom Pedi
Dan Parritt	Paul Crabtree
Pearl	Ruth Gilbert
Margie	Jeanne Cagney
Cora	Marcella Markham
Chuck Morello	Joe Marr
Theodore Hickman	James Barton
Moran	Michael Wyler
Lieb	Charles Hart

The twelve-year drought was broken by this third long play
demanding a dinner hour break. Press conferences, advance publicity,
and O'Neill's return to New York made headlines throughout the
country. It was to be his greatest effort, said George Jean Nathan.
Reception, however, was mixed. It clearly did not herald the long

awaited New Age of O'Neill on the Broadway stage. It was also the last new play presented in New York during O'Neill's lifetime. Total performances: 136

1947

A MOON FOR THE MISBEGOTTEN
Presented 20 February by the Theatre Guild at the Hartman Theatre, Columbus, Ohio.

Cast

Phil Hogan	J. M. Kerrigan
Josie Hogan	Mary Welch
Mike Hogan	J. Joseph Donnelly
James Tyrone, Jr.	James Dunn
T. Stedman Harder	Lex Lindsay

This was the official tryout opening of the last new O'Neill play to see production before his death. It ran its original week in Columbus and journeyed to Pittsburgh and Detroit, where it ran into considerable difficulty with censors. "Casting trouble" finally caused its withdrawal. Of conventional length, it was published with O'Neill's own brief preface, the last to be printed during his lifetime.

1948

S. S. GLENCAIRN
Revived by the New York City Theatre Company, at the New York City Center, 20 May.
Produced by José Ferrer.

Cast: (principals only)

Yank	Richard Coogan
Driscoll	George Mathews
Olson	Ralph Roberts
Cocky	Kenneth Treseder

Smitty	Robert Carrol
Ivan	Harold J. Stone
Bella	Juanita Hall
Captain	Ralph Sumpter
Fat Joe	José Ferrer
Nick	Victor Beecroft
Freda	Nan McFarland

Total performances: 14

LAZARUS LAUGHED
Presented by Fordham University, 8 April.
Staged by Albert McCleery.
Scenery by William Riva.
Costume and masks by Florence Lamont.
Music by Chris Kiernan.
Choreography by Jean Sullivan.
Choral direction by Edgar L. Kloten.

Cast

Lazarus	John Dugan
Miriam	Jean Sullivan
Caligula	Eugene Deserio
Pompeia	Katherine Heekin
Tiberius	Will Walsh

Twenty years after the first performance of this play in Pasadena the Fordham University theatre department presented the second full-length production which, apparently, remains the last to date. The critical reception was lukewarm at best, and the use of a bell to signify the laughter rather than the actor's attempting the real thing was generally regarded with disfavor. There was no extended run, the performance being part of the university's theatre season.

1951

ANNA CHRISTIE

Revived by the New York City Theatre Company, at the City Center of Music and Drama, 9 January.
Staged by Michael Gordon.
Sets and costumes by Emeline Roche.
Production Manager, Billy Matthews.

Cast

Johnny-the-Priest	Frank Rowan
Chris Christopherson	Art Smith
Marthy Owen	Grace Valentine
Anna	Celeste Holm
Mat Burke	Kevin McCarthy

A generally welcomed revival, with main criticism against Miss Holm's interpretation. The play was moved to the Lyceum Theatre for an extended run, but interest suddenly fell and it closed quickly. Total performances: 29

1952

DESIRE UNDER THE ELMS

Revived by the American National Theatre and Academy at the ANTA Playhouse, 16 January.
Staged by Harold Clurman.
Set by Mordecai Gorelik.
Costumes by Ben Edwards.

Cast

Eben Cabot	Douglas Watson
Simeon Cabot	Lou Polan
Peter Cabot	George Mitchell
Ephraim Cabot	Karl Malden
Abbie Putnam	Carol Stone

Another highly praised revival which had more success than the *ANNA CHRISTIE* of City Center, yet was unable to maintain a sustained run. Malden's Cabot was considered to be very powerful.

Total performances: 46

THE LONG VOYAGE HOME

Revived by the American Lyric Theatre—Provincetown Playhouse, August.

Directed by Arch Johnson.

Information found in the New York Public Library Theatre Collection states that the play starred William Whiting as Olson and contained Pernell Roberts, Hal Forrest, Mary Doyle and others in the cast. Reference to the production cannot be found in files of New York *Times*, and no reviews appear in the routine collections of the Theatre Collection itself.

1956

THE ICEMAN COMETH

Presented 8 May at Circle-in-the-Square, New York.

Staged by José Quintero.

Scenery and lighting by David Hays.

Costumes by Diedre Cartier.

Revival supervised by Leigh Connell, Theodore Mann, and José Quintero.

Cast

Harry Hope	Farrell Pelly
Ed Mosher	Phil Pheffer
Pat McGloin	Albert Lewis
Willie Oban	Addison Powell
Joe Mott	William Edmonson
Piet Wetjoen	Richard Abbott
Cecil Lewis	Richard Bowler
James Cameron	James Greene
Hugo Kalmar	Paul Andor
Larry Slade	Conrad Bain

Rocky Pioggi	Peter Falk
Don Parritt	Larry Robinson
Pearl	Patricia Brooks
Margie	Gloria Scott Backe
Cora	Dolly Jonah
Chuck Morello	Joe Marr
Hickey	Jason Robards, Jr.
Moran	Mal Throne
Lieb	Charles Hamilton

This tiny Greenwich Village theatre, in its way closely parallel to the theatres which had done so much to start O'Neill's career nearly forty years earlier, made theatrical history by undertaking this revival. The large cast, extreme length, and previously unsuccessful stage history discouraged conventional staging. Quintero chose to mount it in arena style in this made-over nightclub, and with the audience in close contact with the actors, bringing a greater intimacy and unity to the performance, he found immediate success. Critics on the whole found this production superior to the original in nearly every way. Mrs. O'Neill was so pleased with it that she asked Quintero to produce *LONG DAY'S JOURNEY*.

Total performances: 565

LONG DAY'S JOURNEY INTO NIGHT

Produced 7 November at the Helen Hayes Theatre, New York.
Staged by José Quintero.
Setting by David Hays.
Lighting by Tharon Musser.
Costumes by Motley.
Production supervised by Leigh Connell, Theodore Mann, and José Quintero.

Cast

James Tyrone	Frederic March
Mary Tyrone	Florence Eldridge
James Tyrone, Jr.	Jason Robards, Jr.

Edmund Tyrone	Bradford Tillman
Cathleen	Katherine Ross

The immediate success in February of the Stockholm production and the highly favorable critical reception which greeted the published version brought out by Yale during the same month prompted a demand for a New York production. O'Neill had intended that the play not be released until 25 years after his death, but Mrs. O'Neill admitted that her husband had anticipated release much earlier. He had always admired the work of the Royal Dramatic Theatre in Stockholm and had wanted them to undertake the play, which Mrs. O'Neill permitted them to do much sooner than would have been expected. Then, witnessing the substantial success of Quintero's *ICEMAN* revival, she requested that the same director produce *JOURNEY* on Broadway. Highly praised by the New York critics, this play "written in tears and blood" began the long O'Neill revival.

Total performances: 390

1957

A MOON FOR THE MISBEGOTTEN
Produced 2 May at the Bijou Theatre, New York.
Staged by Carmen Capalbo.
Settings by William Pitkin.
Lighting by Lee Watson.
Costumes by Ruth Morley.
Production supervised by Carmen Capalbo and Stanley Chase.

Cast

Josie Hogan	Wendy Hiller
Mike Hogan	Glenn Cannon
Phil Hogan	Cyril Cusack
James Tyrone, Jr.	Franchot Tone
T. Stedman Harder	William Woodson

Ten years after the Guild failed to bring the first company into New York following its tryout failures, Carmen Capalbo independently staged O'Neill's last play to somewhat reserved critical reception which generally found Wendy Hiller's interpretation of Josie the best aspect of the production.

Total performances: 68

1958

A TOUCH OF THE POET
Produced 2 October at the Helen Hayes Theatre.
Directed by Harold Clurman.
Designed by Ben Edwards.
Produced by Robert Whitehead.

Cast

Mickey Maloy	Tom Clancy
Jamie Cregan	Curt Conway
Sara Melody	Kim Stanley
Nora Melody	Helen Hayes
Cornelius Melody	Eric Portman
Dan Roche	John Call
Patty O'Dowd	Art Smith
Patch Riley	Farrell Pelly
Deborah	Betty Field
Nicholas Gadsby	Luis Van Rooten

Once again Stockholm witnessed an O'Neill premiere, this time in March, before the play was staged in New York. While *MORE STATELY MANSIONS* survives from the many-play cycle, *A TALE OF POSSESSORS SELF-DISPOSSESSED*, in draft form, and had to be sharply edited for production, *POET*, so far as we know, is the only cycle survivor in apparently completed form. Despite its obvious fragmentary nature as part of the much larger cycle concept, the production was enthusiastically received.

Total performances: 284

1959

THE GREAT GOD BROWN
Revived by the Phoenix Theatre at the Coronet Theatre, 6 October.
Directed by Stuart Vaughan.
Settings and costumes by Will Steven Armstrong.
Lighting by Tharon Musser.

Cast

Mrs. Brown	Sasha Von Scherler
Mr. Brown	Patrick Hines
Billy Brown	Robert Lansing
Mrs. Anthony	Patricia Ripley
Mr. Anthony	J. D. Cannon
Dion	Fritz Weaver
Margaret	Nan Martin
Cybel	Gerry Jedd

Total performances: 32

1961

DIFF'RENT
Revived by the Torquay Company and Ruth Kramer at the Mermaid Theatre, 17 October.
Directed by Paul Shyre.

Cast

Mrs. Crosby	Dorothy Patten
Capt. John Crosby	Art Smith
Alfred Rogers	David Ryan
Emma Crosby	Marian Seldes
Capt. Caleb Williams	Michael Higgins
Benny Rogers	Robert Drivas

Jack Crosby	Edwin Sherin
Harriet Williams	Jen Jones

Total performances: 88

THE LONG VOYAGE HOME
Revived by the Torquay Company and Ruth Kramer at the Mermaid Theatre, 4 December.
Directed by Paul Shyre.
Scenery by Richard Kirk.

Cast

Mag	Marian Seldes
Olson	Michael Higgins
Driscoll	Robert Gerringer
Fat Joe	Alfred Hinckley
Freda	Jen Jones
Kate	Dorothy Patten
Nick	Wayne Maxwell
Ivan	John Benson
Cocky	David Ryan

Total performances: 32

1962

LONG DAY'S JOURNEY INTO NIGHT
Presented by the Royal Dramatic Theatre of Stockholm at the Cort Theatre for two performances only, 15 May and 17 May.
Produced by the Seattle World's Fair Performing Arts Division in association with Roger L. Stevens.
Staged by Bengt Ekerot.
Settings by Georg Magnusson.
Costumes by Gunnar Gelbort.

Cast

James Tyrone	Georg Rydeberg
Mary Tyrone	Inga Tidblad
James Tyrone, Jr.	Ulf Palme
Edmund Tyrone	Jarl Kulle
Cathleen	Catrin Westerlund

For this very limited time only New York was permitted to see a presentation by the Royal Dramatic Theatre which had undertaken both this play and *TOUCH OF THE POET* before they had been produced in New York. Though given in Swedish, the performances were well received and generally highly praised.

1963

DESIRE UNDER THE ELMS
Revived at the Circle-in-the-Square by Theodore Mann and José Quintero, 8 January.
Directed by José Quintero.
Scenery and Lighting by David Hays.
Costumes by Noel Taylor.

Cast

Eben	Rip Torn
Simeon	Clifford A. Pellow
Peter	Lou Frizzell
Ephraim	George C. Scott
Abbie	Colleen Dewhurst

Once again Quintero and his Circle-in-the-Square were able to succeed where others had failed. The ANTA revival of 1952 had been a disappointment, and no other major revival of this first of O'Neill's great tragedies had been attempted. Using an imaginative setting of various levels in the arena production, Quintero ended up with a respectable success not far in total performances from the original, even though the great New York newspaper strike prevented the usual coverage by the regular critics.

Total performances: 164

STRANGE INTERLUDE

Revived by the Actors Studio, Inc. by arrangement with the Circle-in-the-Square at the Hudson Theatre, 11 March.
Directed by José Quintero.
Scenery and Lighting by David Hays.
Costumes by Theoni Aldredge for Miss Page and Noel Taylor.

Cast

Charles Marsden	William Prince
Henry Leeds	Franchot Tone
Nine Leeds	Geraldine Page
Edmund Darrell	Ben Gazzara
Sam Evans	Pat Hingle
Mrs. Evans	Betty Field
Gordon, as a child	Richard Thomas
Madeline	Jane Fonda
Gordon, as a man	Geoffrey Horne

After 35 years, O'Neill's first "marathon" play was given its only major revival to date. The reception was mixed, but on the whole recognition was given to an all-star cast that had undertaken the gigantic task. The performance was recorded and is available in a long playing album of five disks.

Total performances: 72

1964

MARCO MILLIONS

Revived by the Repertory Theatre of Lincoln Center at Washington Square, 20 February.
Directed by José Quintero.

Scenery and Lighting by David Hays.
Costumes by Beni Montresor.
Music by Doris Schwerin.

Cast

Marco Polo	Hal Holbrook
Marco's Father	Lou Frizzell
Donata	Crystal Field
Marco's Uncle	Michael Strong
Khan of Persia	Harold Scott
Princess Kukachin	Zohra Lampert
Kublai Khan	David Wayne

The newly formed Lincoln Center company, occupying its Washington Square house before the completion of the Vivian Beaumont Theatre uptown, did not fare particularly well with its initial productions, among them this revival. The critical reception was not strong, and the play did not last for even half of the performances of the limited success of the original.

Total performances: 38

HUGHIE
Produced by Theodore Mann and Joseph E. Levine in association with Katzka-Berne at the Royale Theatre, 22 December.
Directed by José Quintero.
Scenery and Lighting by David Hays.
Costumes by Noel Taylor.

Cast

Night Clerk	Jack Dodson
Erie Smith	Jason Robards

The only one of the proposed one-act cycle to be entitled *By*

Way of Obit to be published and produced. Originally staged in Stockholm in 1958 and published in this country in 1959.
Total performances: 51

1967

A TOUCH OF THE POET
Revived by the National Repertory Theatre, ANTA, 2 May.
Produced by ANTA and Michael Dewell and Frances Ann Dougherty
Directed by Jack Sydow.
Scenery by Will Steven Armstrong.
Lighting by Tharon Musser.
Costumes by Alvin Colt.

Cast

Paddy O'Dowd	Les Barkdull
Cornelius Melody	Denholm Elliott
Nicholas	Herbert Foster
Mickey	Geoff Garland
Sara	Jeanne Hepple
Nora	Priscilla Morrill
Deborah	Sloane Shelton
Patch	Geddeth Smith
Dan	John Straub
Jamie	G. Wood

Total performances: 5

MORE STATELY MANSIONS
Produced by Elliot Martin at the Broadhurst Theatre, 31 October
Directed by José Quintero.
Scenery by Ben Edwards.
Lighting by John Harvey.
Costumes by Jane Greenwood.

Cast

Jamie Cregan	Barry Macollum
Mickey Maloy	Vincent Dowling
Nora Melody	Helen Craig
Sara	Colleen Dewhurst
Simon Harford	Arthur Hill
Cato	John Marriott
Deborah	Ingrid Bergman
Nicholas Gadsby	Fred Stewart
Joel Harford	Lawrence Linville
Benjamin Tenard	Kermit Murdock

Long presumed to have been destroyed, a bulky draft manuscript of this play was discovered in the Yale collection of O'Neill's papers, and Karl Ragnar Gierow of the Royal Dramatic Theatre in Stockholm received permission to copy, adapt, and produce it so long as he did not change O'Neill's words. After five years an actable version appeared and the play was produced in Stockholm on November 9, 1962. Further editing by Donald Gallup of the Yale Library resulted in the American published version brought out by Yale in 1964, upon which the New York production was based. The play was regarded by the critics as in need of further work, and there was broad realization that it represented a fragment rather than a completed effort. Ingrid Bergman received widespread praise for her performance.

Total performances: 142

1971

LONG DAY'S JOURNEY INTO NIGHT
Revived by Edgar Lansbury, Jay J. Fuchs, Stuart Duncan, and Joseph Beruh at the Promenade Theatre, 21 April.
Directed by Arvin Brown.
Setting by Elmon Webb and Virginia Dancy.
Costumes by Whitney Blansen.

Cast

James Tyrone	Robert Ryan
Mary Tyrone	Geraldine Fitzgerald
Edmund Tyrone	James Naughton
James Tyrone, Jr.	Stacy Keach
Cathleen	Paddy Croft

This revival received almost unanimous rave reviews and ran successfully into the summer. Miss Fitzgerald's performance was held in many respects to have been better than Florence Eldridge's original, and the entire production was regarded as a fine rendition of a masterpiece.

MOURNING BECOMES ELECTRA

Presented by the American Shakespeare Festival Theatre, Stratford, Conn., as part of the 1971 summer repertory.
Directed by Michael Kahn.
Settings by William Ritman.
Lighting by John Gleason.
Costumes by Jane Greenwood.

Cast

Ezra Mannon	Lee Richardson
Christine	Sada Thompson
Lavinia	Jane Alexander
Orin	Peter Thompson
Capt. Brant	Roy Cooper
Peter Niles	Robert Staffel
Hazel Niles	Maureen Anderman
Seth Beckwith	Maury Cooper

The first important revival by a professional company of the 1931 tragedy. About one hour was cut from the original running time, but the production received but modest praise.

1972

MOURNING BECOMES ELECTRA
Presented by the Circle-in-the-Square at the Circle-in-the-Square
Joseph E. Levine Theatre, 15 November.
Directed by Theodore Mann.
Settings by Marsha L. Eck.
Lighting by Jules Fisher.
Costumes by Noel Taylor.

Cast

Christine	Colleen Dewhurst
Lavinia	Pamela Payton-Wright
Hazel	Lisa Richards
Adam Brant	Alan Mixon
Ezra	Donald Davis
Orin	Stephen McHattie
Seth Beckwith	William Hickey

This production opened the newly completed uptown theatre of
the Circle-in-the-Square, named for a long-time supporter of the company since its first uncertain days in Greenwich Village. Most critics
found the play appropriate and fitting for this significant new
playhouse, particularly since the Circle had been a strong supporter
of O'Neill revivals since its sensational success with *THE ICEMAN
COMETH* in 1956. Furthermore, it was seen as a major play for a
major breakthrough in the future of New York theatre, since this house
was one of three, together with the American Place and the Uris, to
be erected under relaxed building codes designed to encourage theatre
construction, since 1927. The play itself received mixed reviews, and
was still running into early 1973.

THE GREAT GOD BROWN
Presented by the New Phoenix Repertory Company at the
Lyceum Theatre, 10 December.

Directed by Harold Prince.
Settings by Boris Aronson.
Costumes and masks by Carolyn Parker.
Lighting by Tharon Musser.

Cast

William Brown	John Glover
Mrs. Brown	Bonnie Gallup
Mr. Brown	Paul Hecht
Dion Anthony	John McMartin
Mrs. Anthony	Charlotte Moore
Mr. Anthony	James Greene
Margaret	Katherine Helmond
Cybel	Marilyn Sokol

Presented as part of a two-play repertoire (the other being Molier's *Don Juan*), this production was the first in New York since the original Phoenix attempted it in 1959. Scheduled for a limited run, the play opened to very mixed reviews, but was still playing during the first week of January 1973 when this volume went to press.

The Non-Dramatic O'Neill

O'Neill wrote nothing of permanent significance other than his plays. In 1912, while working on the New London, Conn., *Telegraph,* he edited a poetry column which was often kept going by his own contributions. The left wing New York *Call* and F.P.A.'s "Conning Tower" in the New York *Tribune* printed some of his poems as late as 1917, and Sanborn and Clark, over O'Neill's friendly protest, reprinted several as noted below.

No attempt has been made to track down O'Neill's poems as they appear in their original sources, most of which are accessible only in the New York Public Library or in a very few large academic libraries. Moreover, no recognition has been made of the many manuscript letters available in the various collections at Yale, Princeton, Dartmouth, or elsewhere. The purpose of this section, then, is to list miscellaneous letters and other items which O'Neill wrote and which have appeared, one place or another, in print.

LETTERS

Cargill, Oscar, and N. Bryllion Fagin and William J. Fisher. *O'Neill and his plays*. NY, NYU Press, 1961.
    Subtitled "Four decades of criticism" this large volume includes the following letters or excerpts of letters:
    "I want to be an artist or nothing." 16 July 1914 to George

Pierce Baker, applying for admission to Baker's Harvard English 47, p. 19.

"A yowl at fate." 9 May 1919 to Baker, sending him a copy of the just-published *Moon of the Caribbees and six other plays of the sea* as a token of "all I owe to my year under your guidance," p. 38.

"Inscrutable forces." Excerpt, 1919 (only date given) to Barrett H. Clark, expressing disagreement with Clark's praise of *IN THE ZONE*, p. 99. Originally printed in Clark's *Eugene O'Neill: The man and his plays*, NY, Dover, revised ed. 1947, p. 56.

"Playwright and critic." 20 June 1920 to George Jean Nathan, in response to praise for O'Neill in a *Smart Set* article on American playwrights, p. 101. One of a collection of fourteen letters printed in Goldberg's *The theatre of George Jean Nathan* (see below), from the Boston *Transcript*, 31 Oct. 1925 (*q.v.*).

"O'Neill's ideal of a theatre." 2 June 1930 to manager of Kamerny Theatre of Russia, expressing great pleasure at productions of *DESIRE* and *CHILLUN* in Paris, p. 123. Originally published in New York *Herald-Tribune*, 19 June 1932.

"Neglected poet." Excerpt, 1925 (only date given) to Arthur Hobson Quinn, expressing discouragement at inability of some critics to see precisely what he is driving at, especially in *DESIRE*, p. 125. Originally published in Quinn, *A History of the American drama* (see below).

"Language in a faithless age." Excerpt, 10 Feb. 1932 to Arthur Hobson Quinn, apologizing for lack of great language that is needed for *ELECTRA*, p. 463. Originally in Quinn's *History* (see below).

Clark, Barrett H. *Eugene O'Neill: The man and his plays*. NY, Dover, revised version, 1947.

Beginning with the 1926 version, the thin volume entitled *Eugene O'Neill*, this series relied on use of letters exchanged between Clark and O'Neill for a good amount of biographical and critical data. It is impossible to list each letter of which Clark makes use, but the last version before Clark's death contains a

large, valuable number of letters and excerpts scattered throughout the text. [See Cole, below, regarding reprints.]

COLE, Toby. *Playwrights on playwriting.* NY, Hill & Wang, 1960.
Reprints O'Neill's comments written to Clark and included in
Eugene O'Neill (see above) on Sea Plays, pp. 232-234; *HORIZON*,
p. 234; and *JONES* pp. 234-235. Also includes O'Neill's comments
on *APE* as printed in Mullet's "Extraordinary Story" in *Am. Mag.*,
Nov. 1922, plus O'Neill's explanation of *BROWN*.

Goldberg, Isaac. *The theatre of George Jean Nathan.* NY, Simon &
Schuster, 1926.
Contains fourteen letters to Nathan concerning attitudes
toward work, producers, critics, pp. 143-165. Letters originally
appeared as a group under title "Playwright and critic: The record
of a stimulating correspondence," in the *Boston Transcript,* 31
Oct. 1925. The 20 June 1920 letter from the collection appears
in Cargill *et al,* above, p. 101.

Kinne, Wisner Payne. *George Pierce Baker and the American theatre.*
Cambridge, Mass., Harvard, 1954.
Contains 16 July 1914 application letter to Baker's English
47, also reprinted in Cargill *et al,* above, p. 19; and 9 May 1919
letter transmitting *Moon of the Caribbees, etc.,* also in Cargill,
p. 38. Both letters appear in chapter devoted to O'Neill, pp. 191-
198.

Quinn, Arthur Hobson. *A history of the American drama.* NY, Crofts,
revised ed., 1945, vol.2.
In Chapter XXI Eugene O'Neill, Poet and Mystic, and in
Chapter XXIV The New Decade, 1927-1936, Quinn makes considerable use of O'Neill letters, particularly the following two:
12 Dec. 1921 to New York *Times,* discussing the "happy
ending" of *ANNA CHRISTIE*, pp. 177-178.
1925 (no other date given) to Quinn, discussing critics' reaction to *DESIRE*, p. 199. Facsimile of original letter is reproduced
in part between pp. 198-199. This letter also published in Cargill,
p. 125.

Raleigh, John Henry. *Twentieth century interpretations of The Iceman Cometh*. Englewood Cliffs, Prentice-Hall, 1968. Excerpts from letter 17 July 1940 and 11 Aug. 1940 to Lawrence Langner on *ICEMAN*, pp. 19-20. Originally published as part of Langner's *The magic curtain*, NY, Dutton, 1951, pp. 397-398. Excerpt from Sept. 1943 letter to Barrett H. Clark on *ICEMAN*, originally published in Clark's *The man and his plays* (see above), p. 20.

All of the major biographies and critical studies of O'Neill, other than those listed above, by Frederic I. Carpenter, Arthur and Barbara Gelb, John Henry Raleigh, Louis Sheaffer and others, make use of various letters and excerpts, some having appeared in the volumes noted above, some of them unique to each individual study. Each of the biographies and other studies is listed and annotated in the main body of this bibliography.

The following letters appeared in the New York *Times:*
11 April 1920, VI, 2. Explanation of the origins of *HORIZON* through acquaintance with an old sea dog who continually cursed his foolishness for running away to sea twenty years before.
12 Dec. 1921, concerning the supposed "happy ending" of *ANNA CHRISTIE*. Published in *Times* of 18 Dec. 1921, VI, 1:8, and appearing also in Quinn's *History* (see above), pp. 177-178.
7 March 1926, VIII, 2:8. Praise for a production of Werfel's *Goat Song*.

The Boston *Transcript*, 31 Oct. 1925, III, 8, under title "Playwright and critic: The record of a stimulating correspondence," printed a group of fourteen letters between George Jean Nathan and O'Neill. These letters appear in Goldberg's *Theatre of George Jean Nathan*, above, pp. 143-165.

The New York *Post* on 6 April 1936, under item by critic John Mason Brown, "Eugene O'Neill salutes Mr. Anderson's Winterset," prints a letter praising the Drama Critics' Circle for their choice of *Winterset* for their annual prize. This is particularly interesting in view of the comparative coolness between these two writers of tragedy.

The New York *Herald-Tribune* on 19 June 1932 under title "O'Neill says Soviet stage has realized his dreams" reprints excerpts from letter to the Kamerny Theatre praising performances of *CHILLUN* and *DESIRE* in Paris. This item is also of particular interest in view of O'Neill's reluctance to attend the theatre at all, and his very rare attendance at a performance of one of his own plays. The letter is also reprinted in Cargill, *et al*, above, p. 123.

The *Yale University Library Gazette*, 35 (Oct. 1960) 87-93, prints an interesting exchange of correspondence in an item by John S. Mayfield entitled "Eugene O'Neill and the Senator from Texas." John Mayfield as a youth had written to O'Neill asking him to inscribe a copy of *CHILLUN* and *WELDED*. O'Neill's reply indicated a confusion of Mayfield's father, Senator Earle Mayfield, with a Col. Billy Mayfield, a Klansman, who had condemned *CHILLUN*. Five letters from O'Neill and one from the Senator included.

POEMS

Davenport, William H. "The published and unpublished poems of Eugene O'Neill." *Yale University Library Gazette* 38 (October 1963) 51-66.

Through special permission of Carlotta Monterey O'Neill, Davenport was able to read the poems in the Yale collection still marked "restricted" and withheld from publication. Poems include parodies of Kipling, Villon, Riley, and Burns, plus several "ballards" — or ballads — often in parody. Some thirty in total, in various conditions of typing and manuscript, mostly dated, were consulted, dating from 1910 through 1915. Davenport feels they merit recognition and that nobody who knows O'Neill as an artist can avoid reading the poems.

Sanborn, Ralph, and Barrett H. Clark. *A bibliography of the works of Eugene O'Neill, together with the collected poems of Eugene O'Neill*, NY, Random House, 1931. Reissued 1965 by Benjamin Blom, Inc., NY, by special arrangement with Random House. Part Three, pp. 109-161, publishes twenty-nine poems and one prose poem, and includes the title of one other, noted as "previously published in B. H. Clark's 'Eugene O'Neill.' " Dated from 1912-1917, mostly from the New London *Telegraph*, with one each from Pleiades Club Year Book for 1912, NY *Call* of 17 May 1914, "The Conning Tower" of 5 July 1915, and *The Masses*, Feb. 1917. Some were noted by Davenport, above. O'Neill objected to the publication, but permitted Clark to include them, though, as Clark reports, O'Neill was "extremely reluctant" to do so.

ESSAYS AND MISCELLANEOUS ITEMS

The following entries are listed chronologically in order to demonstrate how widely scattered were O'Neill's non-dramatic writing efforts during his lifetime, once he had ceased writing poetry and had undertaken the prolific production of plays in the 1920s and early 1930s. Most of these items reveal an effective, often informal writing style, though there are times, as in the "explanation of this explanation" included in his explanation of THE GREAT GOD BROWN when O'Neill loses his audience.

"Tomorrow." *The Seven Arts*, June 1917, pp. 147-170.
O'Neill's only published short story. Richard Dana Skinner in *Eugene O'Neill: A poet's quest*, states that O'Neill once wrote another story containing the germ of THE HAIRY APE, but it was never published.

"Eugene O'Neill's credo and his reasons for his faith." NY *Tribune*, 13 Feb. 1921, 1:4, 6:5. [Reprinted as "Damn the optimists" in Cargill *et al*, *O'Neill and his plays*, NY, NYU Press, 1961, p. 104.]

O'Neill's defense of *DIFF'RENT*, asserting the characters are ordinary people.

"Strindberg and our theatre." *Provincetown Playbill* No. 1, Season 1923-1924. Also in NY *Times*, 6 Jan. 1924, VII, 1:1. [Reprinted in Deutsch and Hanau, *The Provincetown*, NY, Farrar & Rinehart, 1931; Cargill *et al, O'Neill and his plays*, NY, NYU Press, 1961; and Frenz, *American playwrights on drama*, NY, Hill & Wang, 1965.]
    Widely quoted article in which O'Neill states his debt to Strindberg.

"Are the actors to blame?" *Provincetown Playbill* No. 1, Season 1925-1926. Also in NY *Times*, 8 Nov. 1925, VIII, 2:1. [Reprinted in Deutsch and Hanau, and in Cargill *et al*, p. 113.]
    A plea for repertory acting which will enable modern actors to break restrictions of type casting and give playwright, director, and designer something to work with. Listed in Sanborn and Clark as No. 36.

"The Fountain." Greenwich Village Theatre program No. 3, Season 1924-1925.
    Explanation that the play represents O'Neill's ideas of what promoted Ponce de Leon to seek the Fountain of Youth, with solemn oath that the play is not "morbid realism." Listed in Sanborn and Clark as No. 41. (This program also contains a valuable list of O'Neill's destroyed plays.)

"The playwright explains." NY *Times*, 14 Feb. 1926, VIII, 2:1, and other newspapers of 13 and 14 Feb. [Reprinted in Quinn, *The American drama from the Civil War to the present day,*, NY, Crofts, revised ed. 1936, pp. 192-194; Durham and Dodds, *British and American plays, 1830-1945*, NY, Oxford, 1947, pp. 536-537; Cole, *Playwrights on playwriting*, 1960; and Meserve, *Discussions of American Drama*, Boston, Heath, 1965, pp. 130-131.]
    Explanation of the meaning behind the characters in *THE GREAT GOD BROWN*. It is not always clear, and the "ex-

planation of this explanation'' does little to help. Sanborn and
Clark No. 50.

"Author's foreword." In Valgemae, Mardi, "Eugene O'Neill's preface to The Great God Brown." *Yale Univ. Library Gazette* 43
(July 1968) 24-29.
    This appears to have been written in the 1920s, but it did
not appear in any regular edition of the play, nor is it the explanation so frequently quoted from the *Times* and elsewhere (see entry
immediately above). This article goes into considerable exploration of the subconscious. Original written version and subsequent
typescript from Yale collection are reproduced. The exact date
of composition is not precisely established.

Foreword to *Anathema: Litanies of negation*, by Benjamin De Casseres. NY, Gotham Book Mart, 1928.
    O'Neill's almost vicious attack on the public for their ignor-
ance of his good friend De Casseres was probably no help in
selling his unsuccessful volume limited to 1,250 copies. It was
undertaken at De Casseres' personal request, the first and last
thing of its type which O'Neill ever wrote. He consistently
refused thereafter to undertake anything else like it.

"O'Neill's own story of Electra in the making." NY *Her-Trib.*, Th.
Sec., 8 Nov. 1931, p. 2. [Reprinted in Clark's *European theories
of the drama*, NY, Brown, 1946; and in Frenz, *American playwrights on drama*, NY, Hill & Wang, 1965.]
    Important excerpts from the working diary for *ELECTRA*.

"Memoranda on masks." *American Spectator*, 1 (Nov. 1932) 3.
[Reprinted in Cargill *et al*, p. 116.]
    Plea for a masked drama to indicate true inner psychological
forces, the only way to see the true meanings as in *Hamlet*, etc.

"Second thoughts." *American Spectator*, 1 (Dec. 1932) 2.
    A desire expressed to add many more masks to all his plays,
including all those which originally contained them.

"A dramatist's notebook." *American Spectator*, 1 (Jan. 1933) 2.
Further defense of masks for crowd effects as aid to the "imaginative" theatre and as an improvement for acting techniques.

"Prof. George Pierce Baker." NY *Times*, 13 Jan. 1935, IX, 1:2.
Brief tribute upon Baker's death. Baker's inspiration and encouragement made O'Neill believe in himself.

"We owe him all the finest we have." *Emerson Quarterly* (Emerson College of Oratory, Boston), 15 (Jan. 1935) 1-2.
Brief tribute to the inspiration that Baker supplied.

"Prof. G. P. Baker, a note and some communications." In *George Pierce Baker: A memorial*. NY, Dramatists Play Service, 1939.
Praise for O'Neill's erstwhile teacher.

"The last will and testament of Silverdene Emblem O'Neill." New Haven, Yale University Library, 1956.
O'Neill wrote this on the death of a favorite dog. It was presented in published form to Mrs. O'Neill upon the publication of *LONG DAY'S JOURNEY*.

Inscriptions: Eugene O'Neill to Carlotta Monterey. New Haven, Yale University Library, 1960.
A privately printed limited collection of about a dozen poems and poetic prose passages taken in the main from fly leaves of plays.

Critical Bibliography

This Bibliography is designed as a comprehensive guide to the American critical reception given Eugene O'Neill from his earliest days as a dramatist until 1971, and to the limited but valuable biographical material found in American books and periodicals. It is arranged in the following three main divisions, each with its own individual pattern explained by an appropriate introduction:

BOOKS. All references from individually published volumes, other than periodicals.

PERIODICALS. All *general* references, as distinct from specific reviews and criticism of individual plays, from all forms of periodicals, including magazines, scholarly journals, and newspapers.

INDIVIDUAL PLAYS. All individual references, whatever the source, to produced and published versions of the separate plays.

Each main entry is briefly annotated by means of a short summary of its central idea, providing the user an estimate of its usefulness without having to seek it out. Annotations of entries of particular critical or historical interest may often contain the editor's own evaluation of the material.

No bibliography of this type can hope to be absolutely "complete." Limits must be set and lines must be drawn if the end product is to have practical use in a practical form. Furthermore, there are bound to be omissions, if for no more reason than simple oversight.

The following restrictions have been applied in the compilation of these more than 2,000 entries:

1. Only those items relating directly to Eugene O'Neill have been included. This embraces items of all kinds about his life and plays: critical, biographical, or merely informational. Books of criticism, such as Richard Dana Skinner's widely quoted *Eugene O'Neill: A Poet's Quest*, or biographies by Clark, the Gelbs, Sheaffer, and others, are listed, but subsequent reviews and criticism of the books themselves are not normally included.

2. O'Neill did not write for the screen or the musical stage. Consequently, reviews and criticism of all motion picture and musical versions of his works, the products of other hands, have been eliminated.

3. Because this bibliography is concerned with O'Neill's domestic reputation, no foreign references, save those few items written by British or Continental critics especially for publication in this country, have been listed. A few exceptions do appear from time to time, notably as in the case of the quarterly *Scandinavian Studies*, a periodical devoted to Scandinavian literature and criticism which often included important items on O'Neill. Prof. Horst Frenz of Indiana University has made a study of O'Neill's foreign reputation, and his work on that subject fills the gap.

Each of the three main divisions contains its own introduction for fuller explanation of the limitations and arrangements of the material contained therein.

A NOTE ON CROSS REFERENCES. Many of the items within this bibliography were reprinted in anthologies or periodicals of one kind or another. All such reprintings are given separate complete entries. The entry of the *original* item contains cross references to source of reprint and date. Fuller information may then be secured by consulting the reprint entry either under the original author's name, if the reprint appeared in a periodical, or under the name of the author of the volume in which the reprint appeared.

ABBREVIATIONS USED IN THIS BIBLIOGRAPHY

Amer. - American

Am. Lit. - *American Literature*
Am. Mag. - *American Magazine*
Am. Merc. - *American Mercury*
Am. Quar. - *American Quarterly*
Am. Rev. - *American Review*
Am. Schol. - *American Scholar*
Am. Speech - *American Speech*
Ariz. Quar. - *Arizona Quarterly*
Arts & Dec. - *Arts and Decoration*

Bk. - Book
Brook. - Brooklyn

Cath. Wld. - *Catholic World*
Ch. - Chapter
Christ. Cent. - *Christian Century*
Class. Jour. - *Classical Journal*
Coll. Eng. - *College English*
Coll. Lang. Assoc. Jour. - *College Language Association Journal*
Comp. Dr. - *Comparative Drama*
Comp. Lit.- *Comparative Literature*
Contemp. Rev. - *Contemporary Review*
Cur. Op. - *Current Opinion*

Dram. Cal. - *Drama Calendar*
Dram. Mir. - *Dramatic Mirror*
Dr. Surv. - *Drama Survey*

ed. - editor; edition
Ed. Th. Jour. - *Educational Theatre Journal*
Eng. Jour. - *English Journal*
Eng. Rev. - *English Review*
Eng. Stud. - *English Studies*

Her-Trib. - *Herald Tribune*
Holt, R & W - Holt, Rinehart and Winston

illus. - illustrated

Ind. & Week R. - *Independent and Weekly Review*
Ind. Quar. for Bookmen - *Indiana Quarterly for Bookmen*

Jour. - *Journal*
Jour-Am. - *Journal American*
Jour. Comm. - *Journal of Commerce*
Jour. Pop. Cul. - *Journal of Popular Culture*

Ky. For. Lang. Quar. - *Kentucky Foreign Language Quarterly*

L I - Long Island
Lit. & Psych. - *Literature and Psychology*
Lit. D. - *Literary Digest*
Liv. Age - *Living Age*

mag. - magazine
Mich. Alum. Quar. Rev. - *Michigan Alumni Quarterly Review*
Mod. Dr. - *Modern Drama*
Mod. Lang. Notes - *Modern Language Notes*
Mod. Lang. Q. - *Modern Languages Quarterly*

Nat. R. - *National Review*
New Rep. - *New Republic*
New States. - *New Statesman*
No. - Number
North Am. Rev. - *North American Review*
ns - new series
NY - New York
NYPL - New York Public Library

p. - page
pp. - pages
Phila. - Philadelphia
Pitt. - Pittsburgh
PMLA - *Publications of the Modern Language Association*
prod. - production
pub. - publishing; publisher

quar. - quarterly
Quar. Jour. Sp. - *Quarterly Journal of Speech*

Rev. - *Review*
rev. ed. - revised edition
Rev. of Rev. - Review of Reviews

Sat. R. Lit. - Saturday Review of Literature. Also indicated as *Sat. R.* after magazine dropped the "literature."
Scan. Stud. - *Scandinavian Studies*
sec. - section
South Atl. Bull. - *South Atlantic Bulletin*
South Atl. Quar. - *South Atlantic Quarterly*
South. Sp. Jour. - *Southern Speech Journal*
Sports Ill. - *Sports Illustrated.*

Theatre - *Theatre Magazine*
Th. Arts - *Theatre Arts*, including all of its many titles such as *Theatre Arts Magazine, Theatre Arts Monthly,* etc.
Th. Guild Mag. - *Theatre Guild Magazine*
Th. World - *Theatre World*
Tulane Dr. Rev. - *Tulane Drama Review* (subsequently, after move to New York University, *The Drama Review*)

Univ. - University
Univ. of Cal. Chron. - *University of California Chronicle*

v. - volume
Va. Quar. Rev. - *Virginia Quarterly Review*
Van. F. - *Vanity Fair*
vol. - volume

Week End R. - *Week End Review*
Weekly Rev. - *Weekly Review*
Wor-Tel. - *World-Telegram*
W.W. Daily - *Women's Wear Daily*

Yale Univ. Lib. Gaz. - *Yale University Library Gazette*

General References—Books

Introduction

It is virtually impossible to discuss contemporary drama without mention of Eugene O'Neill, and his name receives extended consideration in nearly every kind of dramatic history. References are also frequent in the broader literary histories, in collections of essays, books of literary criticism, and in similar volumes. There is also a limited but important library devoted exclusively to O'Neill as man and artist. This portion of the bibliography is a compilation of these references, arranged as explained below.

I. CONTENTS. Certain restrictions have been made in the type and treatment of the material.

1. No item has been entered unless it has been considered worthy of the effort to seek it out. This eliminates a considerable number of merely passing references to O'Neill contained in a wide variety of books. College and school textbooks are normally omitted.

2. As a general rule, introductions to plays contained in standard drama anthologies have been omitted. Most of them, even in the finer collections, are so short and routine that they contribute nothing to O'Neill scholarship. Only a few of these prefaces are important enough for inclusion.

3. Articles in other anthologies are listed independently, or under the title of the volume that includes them, depending upon the type of book, the familiarity of its editor, or the importance of the original author. For instance, the introduction by Joseph Wood Krutch to the familiar Modern Library *Nine Plays by*

Eugene O'Neill is listed under "Krutch." The book itself is not listed. On the other hand, an essay by Alan Reynolds Thompson published in a collection by Norman Foerster appears twice, under Thompson and Foerster, because of the reputation of each man. In all cases, cross references are included, but annotations appear only with the main entry.

4. All items *reprinted* from other sources are handled in this manner:

a. Essays from other books are included without annotation under the title of the volume in which they are reprinted if the book's author and/or the title are of recognizable importance. Again, Krutch's "Introduction" is an appropriate example. It appears not only by itself under "Krutch," but is also listed under Moses and Brown's *The American Drama as Seen by Its Critics,* a well-known collection of critical essays. Cross references are included, but all items receive full annotation only under their main entry.

b. Reprints of essays of a general nature (excluding individual play reviews) which first appeared in periodicals or newspapers are listed without comment under the title of the volume in which they appeared, with appropriate cross reference to the main entry included under Periodicals.

c. Reprints of individual play reviews are listed without annotation under the title of the volume in which they appear, with appropriate cross references to the main entry under Individual Plays.

II. MECHANICS. This bibliography is patterned after standard bibliographic practices, but departs on occasion as shown below. The order of information for each entry is as follows:

1. Author or editor in alphabetical order. Title is used if author is unknown; no entry appears under "Anonymous."

2. Book title, in *italics*. Library of Congress catalogue card procedure is followed by capitalizing only first words and proper nouns.

3. City of publication (New York is NY throughout); publisher's name, abbreviated but easily recognizable; publication

year; pertinent information about all subsequent editions.
immediately.

4. Specific chapter or page reference to those sections dealing with American drama and/or O'Neill, if separate from main body of book.

5. Information, included in brackets [ ], concerning all subsequent reprintings of the material in other publications.

6. Brief annotation, primarily designed to furnish a concise picture of the contents of each entry. Occasionally, significant references will be criticized or evaluated.

NOTE: Entries of special significance are marked with an asterisk (*). O'Neill's plays are spelled in *CAPITAL LETTERS*. An abbreviated form is often used to save space: e.g., *ICEMAN* for *THE ICEMAN COMETH; DESIRE* for *DESIRE UNDER THE ELMS*, and so on.

AIKEN, Conrad. *Reviewer's ABC*. NY, Meridian Books, 1958.
Reprints Aiken's *INTERLUDE* book review from NY *Post*, 21 July 1928, pp. 315-318.

*ALEXANDER, Doris, *The tempering of Eugene O'Neill*. NY, Harcourt, Brace, World, 1962.
This important biography covers O'Neill's life and career from the beginnings to the award of the first Pulitzer Prize for *ANNA CHRISTIE*. Opening with several chapters devoted to O'Neill's parents and brother, the book proceeds through a discussion of life in Greenwich Village and Provincetown, together with important consideration of those individuals who most influenced him, and concludes with marriage to Agnes Boulton and the initial financial and critical rewards of early successes. Covering the same general time span as Sheaffer's later *O'Neill: Son and Playwright,* Miss Alexander's volume treats this part of O'Neill's life as the process of development and eventual tempering of the artist and his talents. There is considerable involvement with the major personal and experiential influences, together with the rebellion and despair so constantly evident

in O'Neill's life and plays. A significant contribution to O'Neill scholarship.

ALTSHULER, Thelma, and Richard Paul Janaro. *Responses to drama: An introduction to plays and movies.* Boston, Houghton Mifflin, 1967. Ch. 12, "Modern currents," pp. 245-260.
Discussion of modern realism, "deterministic tragedy," and "The family theme in modern drama," with some discussion of *JOURNEY*.

ANGOFF, Charles, ed. *The world of George Jean Nathan.* NY, Knopf, 1952.
Reprints the following essays by Nathan:
"Eugene O'Neill," from *Intimate notebooks*, pp. 30-42.
Review of *ICEMAN*, from *Theatre book of the year 1946-1947*, pp. 395-411.

ATKINSON, Brooks. *Broadway scrapbook.* NY, Theatre Arts, 1947.
Reprints these two essays:
"O'Neill gets the Nobel prize," originally, "Ennobel-ing O'Neill," NY *Times,* 22 Nov. 1936, pp. 52-55.
"The Iceman Cometh," originally, "Four-hour O'Neill," NY *Times,* 20 Oct. 1946, pp. 241-246.

BARNET, Sylvan, with Morton Berman and William Burto, eds. *Aspects of the drama: A handbook.* Boston, Little, Brown, 1962.
Reprints "The American realist playwrights," by Mary McCarthy, from her *On the contrary,* 1961, pp. 80-97.

BENTLEY, Eric. *The dramatic event: An American chronicle.* NY, Horizon, 1954.
Reprints Bentley's "Eugene O'Neill's Pieta," *New Rep.,* 4 Aug. 1952, pp. 30-33.

*————. "Eugene O'Neill." In Miller, Perry, ed., *Major writers of America,* NY, Harcourt, Brace, World, 1962, vol. 2, pp. 557-575.

This introduction to the text of *ICEMAN* in this collection of American literary works is written by one who could never quite accept O'Neill as the great American dramatist (see Bentley's "Trying to like O'Neill"). Nonetheless, it is a highly significant essay on the whole aspect of O'Neill's background, personality, artistic outlook, and so on, including mention of all important plays from the beginnings to *JOURNEY*.

————. In search of theater. NY, Knopf, 1953; Vintage, 1954. Part Two, No. 9, "Trying to like O'Neill."
The opening chapter, "The Broadway Intelligentsia," discusses the inferiority of *ICEMAN*. The essay "Trying to Like O'Neill" was originally published in *Kenyon Review*, July 1952.

————. The playwright as thinker. NY, Reynal & Hitchcock, 1946; Harcourt, Brace, 1949; London, R. Hale, 1949.
Chapter Two, "Tragedy in Modern Dress," discusses the new *genre* of the tragedy of modern life. Section V and appended notes discuss Wedekind and O'Neill as representative of the aftermath of Ibsenesque bourgeois tragedy, of which *ELECTRA* is a "grotesque" example. O'Neill's seeming profundity turns into "silliness," says Bentley, taking issue with Krutch's attitudes voiced in *The American drama since 1918* or his introduction to O'Neill's *Nine plays*. Interesting comparisons and contrasts can be made with Geddes' *Melodramadness* approach and with Skinner's *Poet's quest*.

BLANKENSHIP, Russell. *American literature as an expression of the national mind.* NY, Holt, 1931. "Eugene O'Neill," pp. 710-717.
Mostly facts about the plays. The criticism finds *LAZARUS* and *BROWN* at top of O'Neill's works.

BLOCK, Anita. *The changing world in plays and theatre.* Boston, Little, Brown, 1939, pp. 137-193.
Plot detail and dialogue passages from all of O'Neill's plays. Miss Block considers O'Neill a great genius and has only praise for his work. Interesting comparison can be made with Eleanor Flexner's left wing approach.

*BOGARD, Travis. *Contour in time: The plays of Eugene O'Neill.* NY, Oxford, 1972.

The first significant study of O'Neill since the Sheaffer. biography, but devoted to a study of the O'Neill canon rather than to the playwright's life. However, considerable discussion revolves around the biographical nature of the plays, culminating in *LONG DAY'S JOURNEY*, as well as the recurring themes. An important volume in that it represents the first comprehensive critical study of O'Neill's plays since such efforts as Long's study of nemesis in 1968 and Tiusanen's study of scenic images in the same year.

————, and William I. Oliver, eds. *Modern drama: Essays in criticism.* NY, Oxford, 1965.

Reprints John Henry Raleigh's "O'Neill's Long Day's Journey and New England Irish-Catholicism" from *Partisan Review*, Fall 1959.

*BOULTON, Agnes. *Part of a long story.* NY, Doubleday, 1958.

This is the first half of a proposed two volume account of O'Neill's eleven-year marriage to Miss Boulton. It begins with her arrival in New York and first meeting with the 29-year old playwright in 1917 and carries through the birth of their first child, Shane, in October, 1919. The story is told without emotion or recrimination as a romance between two lonely people seeking desperately to find themselves amid their hard drinking, hard living Bohemian friends. It is curiously erratic in precise detail. Many important dates and other facts we would like to know are frequently omitted or noted as "forgotten"; yet it is filled with minute descriptions of long alcoholic binges or the items of food at a particular meal. Nonetheless, it is a rewarding book. For instance, it reveals O'Neill's own version of his first marriage and his suicide attempt as told to his wife, and there is considerable opportunity to become acquainted with the elder brother, James. More important, perhaps, is Miss Boulton's re-creation of O'Neill's early struggles for artistic recognition in Greenwich Village and Provincetown while submitting periodically to complete alcoholic paralysis. The entire story seems to emerge from an atmosphere that can only be termed nightmarish.

*BOWEN, Croswell, assisted by Shane O'Neill. *The curse of the misbegotten: A tale of the house of O'Neill.* NY, McGraw-Hill, 1959. [Cargill *et al*, *O'Neill and his plays,* 1961, reprints brief section on *ICEMAN* rehearsals as "Rehearsing the Iceman Cometh," and Raleigh reprints same passage in *Twentieth century interpretations of The Iceman Cometh,* 1968.]

Extensively assisted by O'Neill's younger son, Bowen has attempted to tell the story of O'Neill's life and artistic career in terms of the apparent "curse" upon the "house"; namely, the inability of its members successfully to communicate to each other their deep capacity for love, with the resulting doom to a lonely isolated life in the midst of material and artistic plenty. It is not, however, merely a book of critical analysis or philosophical interpretation, but is by far the most complete factual account of O'Neill's personal history to be published through 1959. Its early chapters provide specific detail helpfully supplementing Miss Boulton's account, and the entire volume gives more insight into O'Neill's vastly complex inner nature and outer character manifestations than any other work up to this time. Still, it is not a true biography; it is, as Bowen states, a "tale" —highly readable, vastly interesting, and, like Miss Boulton's report, terrifying in the darkness it reveals but cannot successfully explain. Its major drawback is Bowen's many pauses to discuss the merits of individual plays as they appeared, thus slowing down the interesting story he is telling.

BOYD, Alice K. *The interchange of plays between London and New York, 1910-1939.* NY, King's Crown Press, 1948.

This detailed study of plays that crossed the Atlantic discusses the comparative success and failure of each. Includes all of O'Neill's plays staged in England, with complete statistical data. An extremely valuable document for a comparative study of British and American writers and audiences.

BROCKETT, Oscar G., and Robert R. Findlay. *Century of innovation: A history of European and American theatre and drama since 1870.* Englewood Cliffs, Prentice-Hall, 1973, pp. 511-516.

Sec. VII of Chapter 13 is devoted to 6-page discussion of most of O'Neill's major works, emphasis being upon the innovative character without any specific criticism. The book itself is an important well-illustrated history of the last century, even though O'Neill comes in for only routine treatment.

BROOKS, Cleanth, and Robert B. Heilman. *Understanding drama: Twelve plays*. NY, Holt, 1948.
Appendix A compares the *Oresteia* with *ELECTRA*.

BROOKS, Van Wyck. *The confident years*. NY, Dutton, 1952. "Eugene O'Neill: Harlem," pp. 539-553.
Brooks reviews O'Neill's plays and career, with emphasis upon treatment of the Negro. He determines that perhaps O'Neill is "all the more American because he was uncertain, tentative, puzzling, and groping."

BROUSSARD, Louis. *American drama: Contemporary allegory from Eugene O'Neill to Tennessee Williams*. Norman, Univ. of Okla. Press, 1962. "Eugene O'Neill," pp. 9-38.
APE is seen as America's first morality play. *APE, DYNAMO, DAYS WITHOUT END* discussed as modern allegories of man's attempt to return to innocence.

BROWN, John Mason. *Dramatis personae*. NY, Viking, 1963.
Reprints the following:
"American tragedy," *Sat. R. Lit.*, 6 Aug. 1949, pp. 23-30.
"Eugene O'Neill," from Brown's *Upstage*, 1930, as "O'Neill and God's angry eye," pp. 39-53.
"Mourning Becomes Electra," from NY *Post*, 27 Oct. 1931, pp. 53-57.
"Moaning at the bar," originally "All O'Neilling," review of *ICEMAN*, from *Sat. R. Lit.*, 19 Oct. 1946, pp. 57-62.

————. *Letters from greenroom ghosts*. NY, Viking, 1934. "Cristopher Marlowe to Eugene O'Neill," pp. 69-116.
An original and clever book, incorporating much of Brown's dramatic criticism in the form of letters from great artists of the past. Marlowe finds similarity between himself and O'Neill and praises the tragic view, but warns that O'Neill is beyond himself in Freud. Having

come this far, he is expected to go further, and mere recollection, as in *AH, WILDERNESS!*, will not suffice.

―――. *Seeing more things.* NY, Whittlesey House, 1948. "Moaning at the bar," pp. 257-265.
Reprint of "All O'Neilling," review of *ICEMAN*, *Sat. R. Lit.*, 19 Oct. 1946. [Reprinted in Brown's *Dramatis personae,* 1963.]

―――. *Still seeing things.* NY, McGraw-Hill, 1950.
Reprints "American tragedy," *Sat. R. Lit.*, 6 Aug. 1949, pp. 185-195. [Reprinted in Brown's *Dramatis personae,* 1963.]

―――. *Two on the aisle.* NY, Norton, 1938. "Mr. O'Neill's Mourning Becomes Electra," pp. 136-142.
Reprint of review in NY *Post*, 27 Oct. 1931. [Reprinted in Brown's *Dramatis personae,* 1963.]

―――. *Upstage: The American theatre in performance.* NY, Norton, 1930. "Eugene O'Neill," pp. 60-77. [Reprinted as "O'Neill and God's angry eye" in Brown's *Dramatis personae,* 1963.]
O'Neill is ironic instead of tragic, say Brown. *DESIRE* is the nearest approach to Thebes. Brown finds O'Neill an "unsatisfactory genius" whose plays are "peaked with greatness rather than sustained by it"; his mysticism may be his undoing.

*BRUSTEIN, Robert. *The theatre of revolt.* Boston, Little, Brown, 1964. VIII. "Eugene O'Neill," pp. 319-359. [Extended review of *ICEMAN* reprinted in Raleigh, *Twentieth century interpretations,* 1968.]
In this major book by a major critic, O'Neill is discussed in terms of his emergence from a writer of "messianic" rebellion, seen in nearly all major plays through *DAYS WITHOUT END*, into a writer of existential rebellion in the last plays, particularly *ICEMAN* and *JOURNEY*, which are considered major masterpieces.

BRYER, Jackson R. *Checklist of Eugene O'Neill.* Columbus, Charles E. Merrill, 1971.
Basic checklist of O'Neill material in a series issued by this publisher.

*————, ed. *Fifteen modern American authors: A survey of research and criticism.* Durham, N.C., Duke Univ. Press, 1969.

"Eugene O'Neill," by John Henry Raleigh, pp. 301-322, is a summary of the status of O'Neill criticism by an important O'Neill scholar.

BUCK, Philo M., Jr. *Directions in contemporary literature.* NY, Oxford, 1942. "The new tragedy: Eugene O'Neill," pp. 125-147.

Review of O'Neill's accomplishments, seeing great hopes for future after seeing his willingness to undertake new doctrines, adopt tragic style, etc. Question is raised: "Has he now suddenly, without the discipline of crossing the Bar, entered upon the richness of the promised land?"

BUITENHUIS, Peter. *Five American moderns.* Toronto, Roger Ascham Press, 1968.

An extremely rare, Canadian-published volume (90 copies with hand water-colored designs) which discusses "The enigma and challenge of O'Neill," pp. 61-72. Despite the many drawbacks, O'Neill proved great drama can be written without great language.

CANBY, Henry Seidel. *Seven years' harvest: Notes on contemporary literature.* NY, Farrar and Rinehart, 1936. "Scarlet becomes crimson," pp. 139-146.

Reprint of Canby's article on *ELECTRA, Sat. R. Lit.,* 7 Nov. 1931.

CARGILL, Oscar. *Intellectual America: Ideas on the march.* NY, Macmillan, 1941. Ch. IV, "The primitivists," pp. 332-340; Ch. VI, "The Freudians," pp. 685-720. [Reprinted as "Fusion point of Jung and Nietzsche," in Cargill *et al, O'Neill and his plays,* 1961.]

O'Neill is treated in two categories. The early works of *JONES, APE* and others are regarded as "primitivist," *INTERLUDE* and *ELECTRA* as Freudian. Good analysis of most of the plays, finding *ELECTRA* in many ways superior to the Greek.

*————, N. Bryllion Fagin, and William J. Fisher, eds. *O'Neill and his plays: Four decades of criticism.* NY, NYU Press, 1961.

Reprints over ninety items by and about O'Neill, including his own "Memoranda on masks," "Are the actors to blame?" and certain significant letters, thirty-five play reviews from *EXORCISM* to *HUGHIE*, and a wide variety of critical essays, including Bentley's "Trying to like O'Neill," de Voto's "Minority Report," and many others. Appendices include checklist of plays and chronology of production, plus a selected bibliography. An outstanding collection, the single best volume of its type. Combined with Gassner's *Twentieth century views* 1964, and Miller's *Playwright's progress* 1965, this provides the reader with virtually everything of significance written through 1960.

CARPENTER, Frederic I. *American literature and the dream.* NY, Philosophical Library, 1955. "The romantic tragedy of Eugene O'Neill," pp. 133-143.

A review of the more important plays in terms of their dramatizing O'Neill's contrast between dream and reality. Carpenter feels that O'Neill has always known the impossibility of achieving the romantic dream, and feels the result is resignation and quiescence.

———. Eugene O'Neill. NY, Twayne, 1964.

Short (179 pages of text) but excellent study of O'Neill's life and works, avoiding much of the sensational and all too familiar aspects of his life. The treatment of O'Neill as a writer developing a pattern of tragedy unique in our stage literature is revealed without sentiment or emotion, completely avoiding discussion of the genuinely bad plays. Strengths and weaknesses are recognized with considerable objectivity, making this slim volume among the best analyses of O'Neill as an artist to be found anywhere.

CHENEY, Sheldon. *The art theatre.* NY, Knopf, 1925.

This book is not about plays but about the development of art theatres. Some excellent illustrations include pictures of the Guild Theatre, Neighborhood Playhouse, and Pasadena Playhouse, all directly associated with major O'Neill plays. O'Neill is mentioned only in connection with the Provincetown and other groups.

*CLARK, Barrett H. *Eugene O'Neill.* NY, Robt. M. McBride, 1926.

Subsequent editions entitled *Eugene O'Neill: The man and his plays*, NY, McBride, 1929; London, Jonathan Cape, 1933; NY, McBride, 1936; Dover, 1947. [Excerpts printed in *Theatre Arts*, May 1926.] The 1926 edition was the first book published anywhere to be devoted entirely to Eugene O'Neill. The same general plan of the original was maintained in all subsequent editions: a brief life history and· a short analysis of each play from *WIFE FOR A LIFE* to date of publication. Each edition contains passages from letters and articles by O'Neill, plus various bibliographical material. O'Neill never quite understood Clark's motives for writing the book in the first place; but, while expressing his plain disapproval, never interfered. The 1947 edition is, of course, the most valuable of all and includes *MOON FOR THE MISBEGOTTEN*. Although it is the best single book about O'Neill up to 1947, it is not a complete biography nor a detailed criticism. The material, however, still has its place on any reference shelf.

*————. *European theories of the drama, with a supplement on the American drama*. NY, Crown, 1947, pp. 529-536.
    Prints excerpts from O'Neill's working diary for *ELECTRA*. (See Non-Dramatic O'Neill.)

————. *A study of the modern drama*. NY, Appleton, 1925, 1928, 1936, 1938, pp. 404-410 (same in all editions).
    Statistics and data on O'Neill's life and plays; appropriately changed with each new edition.

————, and George Freedly, eds. *A history of modern drama*. NY, Appleton-Century, 1947. Ch. XIII, "Eugene O'Neill," pp. 682-691.
    General review of O'Neill's life and works. The book itself is dedicated to O'Neill.

CLURMAN, Harold. *Lies like truth*. NY, Macmillan, 1958. "Eugene O'Neill," pp. 24-33. [Essay on *JOURNEY* is reprinted in Cargill *et al, O'Neill and his Plays*, 1961.]
    Three short essays on O'Neill's artisty, the published version of *MOON FOR THE MISBEGOTTEN* and production of *LONG DAY'S JOURNEY*. Clurman finds O'Neill our greatest dramatist because of his consistent writing as an aritst.

―――. *The naked image: Observations on the modern theatre.* NY, Macmillan, 1966.
O'Neill included, specifically. *BROWN*, pp. 98-100.

COHEN, Henning, ed. *Landmarks of American writing.* NY, Basic Books, 1969.
Contains Gerald Weales' "Eugene O'Neill: The Iceman," pp. 353-367.

COHN, Ruby. *Dialogue in American drama.* Bloomington, Univ. Indiana Press, 1971.
Full chapter on O'Neill, together with chapters on Williams, Miller, Albee.

COLE, Toby. *Playwrights on playwriting.* NY, Hill & Wang, 1960.
For contents, involving O'Neill's own comments, see Non-Dramatic O'Neill, Letters.

COMBS, George H. *These amazing moderns.* St. Louis, The Bethany Press, 1933. "Eugene O'Neill," pp. 248-270.
A prejudiced view which finds ignorance of O'Neill's plays to be bliss, not loss. The critical comment makes no effort to go below O'Neill's surface violence.

COMMAGER, Henry Steele. *The American mind: An interpretation of American thought and character since the 1800's.* New Haven, Yale, 1950, p. 110.
O'Neill discussed in connection with Faulkner, Hemingway, and Jeffers as spokesmen for a new determinism, taking away from the conscience of men the responsibility for social and human evils.

COOLIDGE, Olivia. *Eugene O'Neill.* NY, Scribner's, 1966.

CORRIGAN, Robert W., ed. *Theatre in the twentieth century.* NY, Grove, 1963.
Reprints the following:
Hofmannsthal, Hugo von. "Eugene O'Neill," *Freeman,* 21 Mar. 1923, pp. 125-130.

Gassner, John, "The possibilities and perils of modern tragedy," from Gassner's Amos Taylor, Jr. Memorial Lecture, Johns Hopkins, 20 Jan. 1957, pp. 215-228. [Also printed in *Tulane Dr. Rev.* June 1957.]

COWLEY, Malcolm, ed. *After the genteel tradition: American writers since 1900.* NY, Norton, 1937.
   Reprints Lionel Trilling's "Eugene O'Neill, a revaluation," *New Rep.*, 23 Sept. 1936, pp. 127-140.

*DEUTSCH, Helen, and Stella Hanau. *The Provincetown: A study of the theatre.* NY, Farrar & Rinehart, 1931. [Prepublication excerpts printed in *Theatre Guild Mag.*, Aug. 1930, and Sept. 1930. Passages from Ch. 1 are in *Drama*, June 1931.]
   This informal and interesting history is the definitive text concerning the Provincetown Players. No study of O'Neill is complete without it. Contains a complete list of all productions, with casts, from 1915 through 17 Nov. 1929. Also valuable for publishing the only existing account of the first production of *BEFORE BREAKFAST,* Dec. 1916, and the inclusion of O'Neill's "Are the Actors to Blame?" from the Provincetown Playbill No. 1, Season 1925-1926 (see Non-Dramatic O'Neill), which is also reprinted in Cargill *et al, O'Neill and His Plays*, 1961.

*DE VOTO, Bernard. *Minority report.* Boston, Little, Brown, 1943. "Monte Cristo in modern dress," pp. 190-197.
   Reprint of "Minority report," *Sat. R. Lit.*, 21 Nov. 1936.

*DICKINSON, Thomas H. *Playwrights of the new American theatre.* NY, Macmillan, 1925. "The playwright unbound," pp. 56-123.
   The 67 pages of this essay represent the longest article about O'Neill in a book of criticism up to this time. It reviews each play in the light of O'Neill's creative vitality and imagination, unbound by the confines of criticism and definition.

DOWNER, Alan S. *American drama and its critics.* Chicago, Univ. of Chicago Press, 1965.
   Chapter VII consists of numerous excerpts and full-length pieces

by George Jean Nathan criticizing O'Neill plays from *CHILLUN* to *DYNAMO*. Reprints in part or in full such items as "The case of O'Neill," *Am. Merc.*, Apr. 1928, pp. 90-94, and "A nonconductor," review of *DYNAMO*, *Am. Merc.*, March 1929, pp. 102-114.

————. *The American theatre today*. NY, Basic Books, 1967.
Passing references to O'Neill's contribution during development of the American theatre and, in *JOURNEY*, to the post-World War II drama.

————. *Fifty years of American drama, 1900-1950*. Chicago, Regnery, 1951.
General review of American plays by type. O'Neill discussed in relation to his various contributions.

DUKES, Ashley. *Youngest drama: Studies of 50 dramatists*. London, Benn, 1923; Chicago, Charles H. Sergel, 1924, pp. 70-76.
A discussion of modern drama since Ibsen. Favorable comment on O'Neill plays through *ANNA CHRISTIE*.

DURHAM, Willard H., and John W. Dodds, eds. *British and American plays, 1830-1945*. NY, Oxford, 1947. "Eugene O'Neill," pp. 535-538, introducing *BROWN*.
The essay on O'Neill in this anthology is brief, but these two items are also reprinted:
O'Neill's own explanation of the play. (See Non-Dramatic O'Neill.)
Brooks Atkinson's opening night review, NY *Times*, 25 Jan. 1926.

DUSENBURY, Winifred L. *The theme of loneliness in modern American drama*. Gainesville, Univ. of Fla. Press, 1960, pp. 113-134.
APE, *ICEMAN*, *ELECTRA*, and *INTERLUDE* get major treatment among O'Neill's plays in this overall survey of the theme, an adaptation of Dusenbury's 1956 Florida dissertation *q.v.*

EASTMAN, Fred. *Christ in the drama*. NY, Macmillan, 1947. "Eugene O'Neill," pp. 92-103.

Because of his lack of spiritual insight, O'Neill lacks the sense of tragedy found in Euripides, to whom Eastman compares O'Neill in *ELECTRA. DAYS WITHOUT END* shows O'Neill realizes redemption in God's grace.

EATON, Walter Prichard. *The drama in English*. NY, Scribner's, 1930, pp. 331-343.

Brief disscussion, mainly about O'Neill's experiments.

————. *The theatre guild: The first 10 years*. NY, Brentano's, 1929.

Eaton's informal history of the Guild is interesting and valuable, but discussion of O'Neill, whom the Guild did not produce until 1928, is somewhat incidental. Includes some excellent pictures of Guild productions and the Guild Theatre itself, and a list of all casts of Guild plays for the first ten years. A good non-critical reference.

*ENGEL, Edwin A. *The haunted heroes of Eugene O'Neill*. Cambridge, Mass., Harvard, 1953.

One of the most complete volumes devoted to a study of the entire O'Neill canon. It specifically avoids bibliography and biography, holding closely to the plays in a concentrated attempt to analyze them and to determine their over-all worth and central themes. Various sections, bearing interesting titles like "Only God's Chillun Got Wings," "Everywoman," and "Everymannon," discuss important items from all plays in chronological order. Engel feels that O'Neill's early plays, up to about 1925, are best, and will in the long run survive. The detailed synopses and the many excerpts from the plays can be legitimately criticized, but to anyone not familiar with O'Neill's works, they will be helpful and revealing.

*————. "Ideas in the plays of Eugene O'Neill," in Gassner, John, *Ideas in the drama*, NY, Columbia U. Press, 1964, pp. 101-124.

In this collection of papers from the English Institute Conference of 1962-1963, Engel maintains that O'Neill's "single reality, the source of all nourishment, emotional and intellectual" was adolescence, the period between 1900-1912.

*FALK, Doris V. *Eugene O'Neill and the tragic tension.* New Brunswick, NJ, Rutgers Univ. Press, 1958. [Chapter "The way out" reprinted in Cargill *et al, O'Neill and his plays,* 1961, as "The way out: The many endings of Days Without End." Chapter "Fatal balance" reprinted in Raleigh, *Twentieth century interpretations of The Iceman Cometh,* 1968, as "The Iceman Cometh."]

A 200-page study, expanding a doctoral dissertation, which takes all of the plays in order of their appearance and carefully analyzes them as the cumulative development of a single theme—expressing and assuaging "the lifelong torment of a mind in conflict." A valuable companion to Engel's treatment in *The haunted heroes of Eugene O'Neill,* 1953.

*FLEXNER, Eleanor. *American playwrights, 1918-1938.* NY, Simon & Schuster, 1938. Ch. V, "Eugene O'Neill," pp. 130-197.

A left wing outlook which deplores O'Neill's insistence on dealing with man's relation to God instead of taking into account that the main trouble in society today is man's relation to man. Interesting, if biased, account, especially in the light of O'Neill's initial welcome from socialist groups.

FOERSTER, Norman, ed. *Humanism and America: Essays on the outlook of modern civilization.* NY, Farrar & Rinehart, 1930.

See Thompson, Alan Reynolds, "The dilemma of modern tragedy," this section.

FREEDMAN, Morris. *American drama in social context.* Carbondale, So. Ill. U. Press, 1971

Chapter on O'Neill, with others on Eliot, Miller.

————.ed. *Essays in the modern drama.* Boston, Heath, 1964.

Reprints the following:

Krutch, Joseph Wood, "Eugene O'Neill's claim to greatness," from NY *Times Bk. Rev.,* 22 Sept. 1957, pp. 91-95.

Trilling, Lionel, "Eugene O'Neill: A revaluation," *New Rep.,* 23 Sept. 1936, pp. 96-103.

FRENCH, Warren, ed. *The fifties: Fiction, poetry, drama.* Deland, Fla., Everett/Edwards, 1970.

See Bryer, Jackson R., " 'Hell is other people': Long Day's Journey Into Night" under Individual Plays, *LONG DAY'S JOURNEY.*

———. *The forties: Fiction, poetry, drama.* Deland, Fla., Everett/Edwards, 1969.

See Kahn, Sy, "O'Neill's legion of losers in The Iceman Cometh" under Individual Plays, *ICEMAN.*

———, and Walter E. Kidd, eds. *American winners of the Nobel literary prize.* Norman, Univ. of Okla. Press, 1968.

See Miller, Jordan Y., "Eugene O'Neill," this section.

FRENZ, Horst, ed. *American playwrights on drama.* NY, Hill & Wang, 1965.

Reprints O'Neill's "Strindberg and our theatre" and working notes and fragments from the *ELECTRA* diary (see Non-Dramatic O'Neill).

———. *Eugene O'Neill.* NY, Frederick Ungar, 1971.

Brief introduction to O'Neill in this series of volumes of dramatic criticism. Contains important aspects of O'Neill's life and plots of the important plays.

GAGEY, Edmond M. *Revolution in American drama.* NY, Columbia, 1947. "Eugene O'Neill" pp. 39-70.

Brief review of each major play. Lists nine important contributions O'Neill has made to the stage. He is best remembered for plays which show "ideal fusion of realism and imagination."

*GASSNER, John. *Dramatic soundings.* NY, Crown, 1968.

Reprints in its entirety the Univ. of Minnesota pamphlet noted below, pp. 254-281. Also contains among other many passing references to O'Neill in this very large collection of essays on drama brief comments on Lincoln Center Repertory production of *MARCO* and Actors Studio production of *INTERLUDE.*

————. *Eugene O'Neill*. Minneapolis, Univ. of Minn. Press, 1965.
This booklet of less than fifty pages, one of a series of pamphlets on American writers, provides brief but complete summary of life and works. It is reprinted in its entirety in Gassner's *Dramatic soundings*, 1968.

————. *Form and idea in modern theatre*. NY, Dryden, 1956.
Occasional mention of O'Neill in an excellent study of the structure of modern drama.

————. *Ideas in the drama*. NY, Columbia Univ. Press, 1964.
See Engle, Edwin A., "Ideas in the plays of Eugene O'Neill," under Periodicals.

————. *Masters of the drama*. NY, Random House, 1940; Dover, 1945, 1954. "The voyages of O'Neill."
One of the standard comprehensive histories of world drama. Its 16 pages on O'Neill review all the plays with plot outlines and fairly routine comment.

*————. *O'Neill: A collection of critical essays*. Englewood Cliffs, N.J., Prentice-Hall, 1964.
This volume in the Twentieth Century Views series includes an introduction by Gassner summarizing O'Neill's career, and the following articles:
Bentley, Eric, "Trying to like O'Neill," abbreviated, from Bentley's *In search of theater*, 1952, pp. 89-98.
Bogard, Travis, "Anna Christie: Her fall and rise."
Day, Cyrus, "*Amor Fati:* O'Neill's Lazarus as superman and savior," *Mod. Dr.*, Dec. 1960, pp. 72-81.
Driver, Tom F., "On the late plays of Eugene O'Neill," *Tulane Dr. Rev.*, Dec. 1958, pp. 110-123.
Gassner, John, "The nature of O'Neill's achievement: A summary and appraisal," revised and abbreviated version of "Eugene

O'Neill: The course of a major dramatist" in Gassner's *Theatre at the crossroads*, 1960, pp. 165-171.

Hayes, Richard, "Eugene O'Neill: The tragic in exile," *Th. Arts*, Oct. 1963, pp. 52-56.

Hofmannsthal, Hugo von, "Eugene O'Neill," *Freeman*, 21 Mar. 1923, pp. 23-28.

Lawson, John Howard, "Eugene O'Neill," from *Theory and technique of playwriting*, 1936, pp. 42-51.

Muchnic, Helen, "Circe's swine: Plays by Gorky and O'Neill," *Comp. Lit.*, Spring 1951, pp. 99-109.

Racey, Edgar F., Jr., "Myth as tragic structure in Desire Under the Elms," *Mod. Dr.* May 1962, pp. 57-61.

Raleigh, John Henry, "Eugene O'Neill and the escape from the Chateau d'If," paper presented at English Institute, Columbia Univ., Sept. 1963, pp. 7-22.

————. "O'Neill's Long Day's Journey into Night and New England Irish-Catholicism," *Partisan Rev.*, Fall 1959, pp. 124-141.

Whitman, Robert F., "O'Neill's search for a 'language of the theatre,'" *Quar. Jour. Sp.*, April 1960, pp. 142-164.

Young, Stark, "Eugene O'Neill's New Play," (review of *ELECTRA*), *New Rep.*, 11 Nov. 1931, pp. 82-88.

Volume also contains a brief life chronology. Though somewhat limited in scope by nature of the series, this is a significant collection of O'Neill criticism, fitting in well with Cargill *et al*, *O'Neill and his plays*, 1961, and Miller, *Playwright's progress*, 1965.

————. *Theatre at the crossroads*. NY, Holt, R & W, 1960.

Prints the following:

"Eugene O'Neill: The course of a major dramatist," pp. 66-76. This is taken from an essay of the same title in *Critique*, Feb. 1958. Revised and abbreviated version entitled "The nature of O'Neill's achievement: A summary and appraisal," appears in Gassner's Twentieth Century Views volume, *Eugene O'Neill*, 1964.

"The latter-day O'Neill," pp. 232-241, briefly reviewing *ICEMAN, MISBEGOTTEN, JOURNEY, TOUCH OF THE POET*.

*————. *The theatre in our times*. NY, Crown, 1954. "O'Neill in

our time," pp. 249-256; "The Electras of Giraudoux and O'Neill," pp. 257-266.

A major collection of essays on all phases of modern theatre by this tireless compiler of drama anthologies and theatre histories. An excellent companion to *Masters of the Drama*. The two fairly brief articles on O'Neill are very good. The first, written before the revival of the mid-fifties, expresses concern for O'Neill's unwarranted neglect by the newer theatrical generation; the second compares and contrasts two modern interpretations of the perennial Electra theme. (Gassner erroneously calls O'Neill's Aegisthus "David Mannon" instead of the correct Adam Brant.) The frontespiece is Gorelik's design for *DESIRE UNDER THE ELMS*.

———, ed. *A treasury of the theatre.*

First edition, 1935, and revised edition, 1940, were edited by Gassner together with Philo M. Buck, Jr., and H. S. Alberson. Subtitle: "An anthology of great plays from Ibsen to Odets." Gassner's brief essay, "Eugene O'Neill," pp. 245-248, precedes *ANNA CHRISTIE*. Publisher: Simon and Schuster. Distributor: The Dryden Press.

Next edition, 1950, edited by Gassner alone. Subtitle: "From Henrik Ibsen to Arthur Miller," but spine prints "Ghosts to Death of a Salesman." Two essays on O'Neill, pp. 786-789 and 817-818, precede *ANNA CHRISTIE* and *THE HAIRY APE*. Publisher: Simon and Schuster. Distributor: The Dryden Press.

Later edition, 1960, "Third College Edition," also by Gassner, bears subtitle on title page and spine, "From Henrik Ibsen to Eugene Ionesco." Includes the same plays by O'Neill and the essays bear same pagination. Publisher: Simon and Schuster. Distributor: Henry Holt.

Fourth edition, 1970, includes Bernard F. Dukore as co-editor. (Gassner died in 1967.) Subtitle on title page, cover, and spine now states "From Henrik Ibsen to Robert Lowell." *APE* remains but *ANNA CHRISTIE* has been dropped for *MISBEGOTTEN*. The general introductory essay, pp. 640-643, is essentially the same as in the other editions, except for certain updating of factual information. It also includes most of the comments on *APE* found in other editions.

Introduction to *MISBEGOTTEN* (pp. 664-665) discusses *ICEMAN*, *POET*, and *JOURNEY* as well. Publisher: Simon & Schuster. Distributor: Holt, Rinehart and Winston.

The O'Neill essays are general summaries much in the same style as Gassner's discussion in *Masters of the Drama* but conclude that O'Neill's works are "surely the most Cyclopean dramatic enterprise in the English language."

———— and Ralph G. Allen. *Theatre and drama in the making*. Boston, Houghton, Mifflin, 1964.

Reprints the following:

Gassner, John. "The possibilities and perils of modern tragedy," *Tulane Dr. Rev.*, June 1957, pp. 817-829.

Young, Stark. "Eugene O'Neill's new play," *New Rep.*, 21 Oct. 1946 (review of *ELECTRA*), pp. 985-991.

*GEDDES, Virgil. *The melodramadness of Eugene O'Neill*. The Brookfield Pamphlets, No. 4, Brookfield, Conn., The Brookfield Players, Inc., 1934.

This 48-page pamphlet uses most of O'Neill's plays to prove that O'Neill is not truly a man of the theatre because he does not actually contribute to what the new American drama and theatre demand. He lacks a comic spirit, a realistic understanding of women, and a true art; his tragedy is more like melodrama, lacking any philosophy. Geddes' attack is not violent, like Salisbury's, but it is heavily one-sided. As one of the few early books devoted to O'Neill alone, however, it is well worth reading.

————. *The theatre of dreadful nights*. The Brookfield Pamphlets, No. 3. Brookfield, Conn., The Brookfield Players, Inc., 1934.

A somewhat violent attack on theatrical producers for their inability to present worthwhile plays. O'Neill is included among the writers which prove the point.

*GELB, Arthur, and Barbara Gelb. *O'Neill*. NY, Harper's, 1962.

Five years of study by this critical husband and wife team of the NY *Times* went into this truly monumental volume of over 1,000 pages. All of O'Neill's life and works is treated in considerable detail, and when it appeared, this was the definitive biography. The appearance of the first half of Sheaffer's biography has altered the picture somewhat, but the Gelb effort must remain among the most significant undertakings of its type. Somewhat distracting are critical opinions of the plays introduced somewhat gratuitously from time to time, but the overall effect is excellent, if a little overwhelming.

GILDER, Rosamond, and others, eds. *Theatre Arts anthology: A record and a prophecy.* NY, Theatre Arts Books, 1950.
Reprints the following from *Theatre Arts:*
Gilder, Rosamond, "Each in his own way," (review of *ICEMAN*), Dec. 1946. [Reprinted as "The Iceman Cometh" in Cargill *et al, O'Neill and his plays,* 1961.]
Hutchens, John, "Greece to Broadway," Jan. 1932.
Isaacs, Edith, "Meet Eugene O'Neill," Oct. 1926.
Macgowan, Kenneth, review of *JONES*, Jan. 1921.

GILMAN, Richard. *Common and uncommon masks.* NY, Random House, 1971.
Reprints the following Gilman items:
"Between anger and despair," (*STRANGE INTERLUDE*), from *Commonweal*, 12 Apr. 1963, pp. 68-71.
"Epitaph for Lincoln Center," (*MARCO MILLIONS*), from *Commonweal*, 10 Apr. 1964, pp. 259-261.
"Mr. O'Neill's very last curtain call," (*MORE STATELY MANSIONS*), NY *Her-Trib.*, 31 May 1964, pp. 72-75.

GLASPELL, Susan. *The road to the temple.* London, Benn, 1926; NY, Frederick A. Stokes, 1927.
This biography of George Cram Cook (Miss Glaspell's husband) recounts the development of the Provincetown Players, with the group's early realization of how important O'Neill was to become. The description of the first reading of *CARDIFF* is reprinted as "O'Neill's first reading" in Cargill *et al, O'Neill and his plays,* 1961.

*GOLDBERG, Isaac. *Drama of transition*. Cincinnati, Stewart Kidd, 1922. "Eugene O'Neill," pp. 457-471. [Excerpt entitled "At the beginning of a career" reprinted in Cargill *et al*, *O'Neill and his plays*, 1961.]

The first extended discussion of O'Neill in a book of criticism. Prints list of destroyed plays later to appear on Greenwich Village Playbill for THE FOUNTAIN (see Non-Dramatic O'Neill). Goldberg finds O'Neill unable to fuse his elements perfectly, with the "traps of melodrama" evident in his "realism."

*————. *The theatre of George Jean Nathan*. NY, Simon & Schuster, 1926. "Eugene O'Neill to George Jean Nathan," pp. 143-165.

Unique because of its fourteen letters from the young playwright to Nathan, revealing his own attitudes toward his work, the producers, and the critics. Letter of 20 June 1920 from Provincetown appears as "Playwright and critic" in Cargill *et al, O'Neill and his plays*. 1961.

*GOLDEN, Joseph. *The death of Tinker Bell: The American theatre in the twentieth century*. Syracuse, Syracuse Univ. Press, 1967. Ch. 11 "O'Neill and the passing of pleasure," pp. 30-51.

Although O'Neill is treated in but a score of pages, this breezily written personal view of the American theatre and its ultimate failure at "reawakening our half-forgotten potential for sharing universal dreams and experiences," *i.e.*, the death of Tinker Bell, is well worth study. O'Neill is regarded not as one who helped American drama to mature but as a substantial contributor to Tinker Bell's death through his destruction of pleasure.

GORELIK, Mordecai. *New theatres for old*. NY, Samuel French, 1940. "O'Neill," pp. 230-236.

This volume belongs on every drama reference shelf as the finest account of twentieth century stage techniques. Gorelik discusses O'Neill's "inherited weakness of the will," and other aspects, such as a lack of clear statement of purpose. He agrees with Shaw's opinion that O'Neill is "banshee Shakespeare."

GOULD, Jean. *Modern American playwrights.* NY, Dodd, Mead, 1966.

Discussion of thirteen major writers from Glaspell to Albee. O'Neill receives usual biographical treatment; minimal attention to plays.

HALIO, Jay L. "Eugene O'Neill: The long quest." In Taylor, William E., ed., *Modern American drama: Essays in criticism.* Deland, Fla., Everett/Edwards, 1968, pp. 13-27.

Extensive review of major plays from *CARDIFF* to *MANSIONS* in terms of hopeless search by protagonists for "a home of your own." Compare with Skinner's "quest."

HAMILTON, Clayton. *Seen on the stage.* NY, Holt, 1920.

Reprints review of *BEYOND THE HORIZON, Vogue,* 1 April 1920.

HAMILTON, William Baskerville. *Fifty years of the South Atlantic Quarterly.* Durham, NC, Duke University Press, 1952.

Reprints "Eugene O'Neill," by Homer E. Woodbridge, *South Atl. Quar.,* Jan. 1938, pp. 258-271.

*HEILMAN, Robert B. *The iceman, the arsonist, and the troubled agent: Tragedy and melodrama on the modern stage.* Seattle, Univ. of Washington Press, 1973.

Companion and supplement to *Tragedy and melodrama* (below), asking whether or not tragedy is dead in the technological age. O'Neill included in depth with substantial treatment of such as Williams, Miller, Brecht, Frisch, and Durrenmatt.

*———. *Tragedy and melodrama: Versions of experience.* Seattle, Univ. of Washington Press, 1968.

First volume in two-part study of the tragic form, discussing differences of and causes for confusion between tragedy and melodrama. Western drama from Sophocles to Williams with O'Neill's tragedies as an important part is discussed in demonstration that tragic and melodramatic experiences are found in all ages.

HELBURN, Theresa. *A Wayward quest*. Boston, Little, Brown, 1960. Ch. 17. "Eugene O'Neill, playwright extraordinary." Personal reminiscenses of this prime mover in the Theatre Guild. Excerpts of correspondence with O'Neill and discussion of problems of working with him.

*HERRON, Ima Honaker. *Small Town America: The dramatization of a provincial world*. Dallas, Southern Methodist Univ. Press. 1968. Ch. X. "O'Neill's lost townsmen," pp. 273-337.
A complete rundown of O'Neill's plays from earliest to *JOURNEY*, plus several page account of his life. Discussion centers around "lost" nature of the small town inhabitant. Conclusion: O'Neill provides relatively little realization of the towns themselves, choosing instead the psychological and psychoanalytical approach to his characters. "No other native playwright has equalled his preoccupation with haunted provincials whose mental and physical suffering and frustration drive them to tragedy."

HEWITT, Barnard. *Theatre USA, 1688 to 1957*. NY, McGraw-Hill, 1959.
A unique history tracing the development of American theatre and drama through contemporary critical opinion. Reprints the following:
Gassner, John, review of *ICEMAN, Ed. Th. Jour.*, Oct. 1956, pp. 279-281.
Kerr, Walter, "Long Day's Journey into Night," NY *Her-Trib.*, 8 Nov. 1956, pp. 481-482.
Krutch, Joseph Wood, "The god of stumps," *Nation*, 26 Nov. 1924, pp. 333-335.
———, "The tragedy of masks," *Nation*, 10 Feb. 1926, pp. 363-364.
Lewisohn, Ludwig, "An American tragedy," *Nation*, 21 Feb. 1920, pp. 332-333.
Macgowan, Kenneth, review of *ANNA CHRISTIE, Th. Arts*, Jan. 1922, pp. 337-338.
———, review of *JONES, Th. Arts*, Jan. 1921, pp. 333-335.
Motherwell, Hiram, "Mourning Becomes Electra," *Th. Guild Mag.*, Dec. 1931, pp. 387-390.

Seldes, Gilbert, "The Hairy Ape," *Dial*, May 1922, pp. 338-340.

Skinner, Richard Dana, "Strange Interlude," *Commonweal*, 22 Feb. 1928, pp. 371-374.

HICKS, Granville. *The great tradition: An interpretation of American literature since the Civil war.* Rev. ed., NY, Macmillan, 1935. Ch. VII, "Two roads," pp. 253-256.
O'Neill is treated briefly as one of the literary pessimists of his age.

HOFFMAN, Frederick J. *The twenties: American writing in the post-war decade.* NY, Viking, 1955.
An astute and original discussion of the various types of literary expression during this ten-year period. Each section uses some literary work of particular significance for its "text." O'Neill's inclusion is noteworthy because of its brevity. In "Forms of Experiment and Improvisation" he receives two pages (221-223) only because of his innovations. He is then summarily dismissed as a failure because of the failure of expressionism itself.

HUGHES, Glenn. *History of the American theatre, 1700-1950.* NY, Samuel French, 1951, pp. 399-402.
Quick review of O'Neill's career, which brought our dramatic literature to "maturity." A fact-crammed history of the American theatre with excellent pictures of theatres and actors.

ISAACS, Edith J. R. *The Negro in the American theatre*, NY, Theatre Arts, 1947. Ch. 5, "Bright lights on Broadway," Ch. 6, "Plays and players."
Full page picture of Gilpin's Jones; *CHILLUN* regarded as unsuccessful.

JONES, Robert Edmond. *Dramatic imagination.* NY, Duell, Sloan & Pearce, 1941.
This outstanding book by the designer who worked as O'Neill's partner should be read by all serious students of the theatre, though there is little mention of O'Neill except *INTERLUDE*, a "brilliant

exception'' to Jones' generalization that the present theatre is essentially one of prose and journalism.

KARSNER, David. *Sixteen authors to one*. NY, Lewis Copeland, 1928. Ch. VI, "Eugene O'Neill," pp. 101-122.

Karsner, who spent some time with O'Neill in the Maine woods (see his article in NY *Her-Trib.*, 8 Aug. 1926), feels the playwright's mystic quality cannot be conveyed in words.

*KAUCHER, Dorothy J. *Modern dramatic structure*. Univ. of Missouri Studies, Columbia, Univ. of Missouri Press, 1 Oct. 1928. Ch. VI, "Eugene O'Neill," pp. 125-158.

A detailed study of the dramatic structure of Eugene O'Neill's major plays. Considerable dialogue and stage directions show the use of sound, action, etc., in the development of the individual play. The progress of insanity in *GOLD* is diagrammed by two interesting charts. This is a valuable contribution to O'Neill scholarship from the dramatic and theatrical point of view, rather than the critical. The entire work of 183 pages is well worth close study, as it represents an interesting if highly technical analysis of modern playwrights and their techniques. A better O'Neill play might have served more aptly for Miss Kaucher's elaborate graph, but otherwise she treats all the plays with equal emphasis.

KENTON, Edna. "Provincetown and Macdougal street." Preface to Cook, George Cram, *Greek coins*, NY, George H. Doran, 1925. [Reprinted in Cargill *et al, O'Neill and his plays,* 1961.]

Miss Kenton's main tribute is to Cook's efforts with the Provincetown group in its formative days and his insistence that the world would some day know the plays of O'Neill. The rest of the volume is a collection of Cook's poetry.

KERR, Walter. *Pieces at eight*. NY, Simon & Schuster, 1957, pp. 120-125.

Kerr reviews *LONG DAY'S JOURNEY* as an exorcism of O'Neill's past. In summary, he feels that for all O'Neill's many weaknesses, the great strength in the plays is an overwhelming sense of the melodramatic.

*KINNE, Wisner Payne. *George Pierce Baker and the American theatre*. Cambridge, Mass., Harvard, 1954. Ch. XXXVII, "Beauty vs. Broadway—Enter Eugene O'Neill," pp. 191-198.

No student of the American theatre can neglect this book, which recounts the work of the man who "epitomized the lay forces at work in the evolution of twentieth-century American drama." O'Neill's name, of course, reappears constantly throughout the book, along with many illustrations of playbills and scenes from the O'Neill plays produced at Yale. The short chapter devoted to O'Neill is significant because it prints for the first time the letter to Baker in which O'Neill seeks admittance to the 47 Workshop at Harvard, stating "I want to be an artist or nothing." [The letter, together with one other under title "A yowl at fate," is printed in Cargill *et al, O'Neill and his plays*, 1961.]

KREYMBORG, Alfred. *Troubadour: An autobiography*. NY, Boni & Liveright, 1925. "The Provincetown players," pp. 303-311.

A discussion of O'Neill's association with the Provincetown by one who was there.

*KRUTCH, Joseph Wood. *The American drama since 1918*. NY, Random House, 1939; George Brazillier, 1957. Ch. III, "Tragedy: Eugene O'Neill," pp. 73-133, both editions. [Excerpt entitled "Postwar" reprinted in Meserve, *Discussions of modern American drama*, 1965.]

This "Informal History" is the best single-volume treatment of the major aspects of modern American drama and those who wrote it. The essay on tragedy includes other dramatists, but O'Neill occupies the major position. Krutch consolidates several of his earlier comments, including his introduction to *Nine Plays* into a penetrating and lucid analysis of all of O'Neill's major works. Two central themes are O'Neill's sense of "belonging" and his attempt to bring the grandeur and elevation of tragedy into modern times and temper. This should be a standard reference in any American drama library, especially in its revised version.

*————. Introduction to O'Neill, Eugene, *Nine Plays*, NY, Horace Liveright, 1932; Random House, 1936, 1939 (as Modern Library

Giant). [Reprinted in Moses and Brown, *The American theatre as seen by its critics,* 1934; in Thorp and Thorp, *Modern writing,* 1944; and in Oppenheimer, Louis, *The passionate playgoer,* 1958.]

Krutch sets forth his consistently held tenet that O'Neill's tragedy is modern in every sense, feeling the view of its audiences as did all great tragedies. The height and depth of passion puts them in the class of those plays that "purge" by pity and terror, despite our lack of clear definition of the phrase. O'Neill's large weakness is lack of great language to accompany his tragic approach.

————. *Modernism in modern drama.* Ithaca, NY, Cornell, 1953.

A few general references to O'Neill's regard for tragedy and the man-God theme, which is seen as essentially anti-modernistic, along with views of Maxwell Anderson.

*LAMM, Martin. *Modern drama.* Translated by Karlin Elliott. Oxford, Blackwell's, 1952; NY, Philosophical Library, 1953. "Eugene O'Neill," pp. 315-333.

The essay is mainly a routine review of O'Neill's life and plays, finding him a great writer, with faults, but certainly along with Synge the greatest in the twentieth century. This study of modern drama from the Scandinavian view is worth close attention.

LANGFORD, Richard E., Guy Owen, and William E. Taylor. *Essays in modern American literature.* Deland, Fla., Stetson Univ. Press, 1963. "Eugene O'Neill: The mask of illusion," by Richard E. Langford, pp. 65-75.

The plays affirm man's meaning in life and are positive expressions of "one man's understanding of the human dilemma."

*LANGNER, Lawrence. *The magic curtain.* NY, Dutton, 1951.

This director of the Theatre Guild, O'Neill's major producer from *MARCO MILLIONS* through the unsuccessful *MOON FOR THE MISBEGOTTEN*, writes of his years in this distinguished producing group, including information about his many contacts as a personal friend of O'Neill. An important document in the study of O'Neill the man and artist. Letters of 17 July 1940 and 11 Aug. 1940 from

O'Neill to Langner regarding *ICEMAN* are reprinted in Raleigh, *Twentieth Century Interpretations of The Iceman Cometh*, 1968.

*LAWSON, John Howard. *Theory and technique of playwritings*. NY, Putnam's, 1949. Part II, Ch. V., "Eugene O'Neill," pp. 75-120. [Reprinted in Gassner, *Twentieth Century Views of Eugene O'Neill*, 1964.]

An interesting discourse on O'Neill's confused philosophy and his attempts to display it in later plays. Nina and Hedda help compare O'Neill's and Ibsen's last phases.

LEECH, Clifford. *Eugene O'Neill*. NY, Grove, 1963.

Brief (120 pages) and fairly sketchy account of O'Neill's life and works. Designed as inexpensive and handy introduction to O'Neill the book has some merit, but it provides little that is not available in a variety of sources elsewhere.

LEWISOHN, Ludwig. *Expression in America*. NY, Harpers, 1932, pp. 534-553.

Strongly unfavorable review, concerned with O'Neill's faults. There is hope O'Neill may "amount to something" some day.

*LONG, Chester Clayton. *The role of nemesis in the structure of selected plays by Eugene O'Neill*. The Hague, Paris, Mouton & Co., 1968.

O'Neill canon from *ABORTION* and *THIRST* to *JOURNEY* is examined in terms of "Nemesis" as the idea of justice-in-action, seen in four aspects: "natural law" over which characters have no control, social nemesis, ultimate nemesis derived from previous individual choices and the divine, and tragic nemesis. One of the few volumes devoted exclusively to development of a single artistic point of view. Avoids usual biography; terms established and well defined, though one may not always agree. This is an important book of O'Neill scholarship.

LUCCOCK, Halford E. *Contemporary American literature and religion*. Chicago, Willet, Clark, 1934.

ELECTRA is a direct contrast to the ideas of Hebrew and Christian religions.

LUMLEY, Frederick. *New trends in twentieth century drama: A survey since Ibsen and Shaw*. NY, Oxford, 1967.

Originally published some years earlier only in England as *Trends*, etc., the work of this British critic included a brief item on *AH, WILDERNESS!* The 1967 edition is included here because of publication in this country by Oxford and inclusion of comments on *ELECTRA* and *JOURNEY*.

McCARTHY, Mary T. *On the contrary*. NY, Farrar, Strauss & Cudahy, 1961. "The American realist playwrights," pp. 293-312. [Reprinted in Barnet, *Aspects of the drama*, 1962; in Meserve, *Discussions of modern American drama*, 1965; and in McCarthy, *Theatre chronicles*, 1963.]

O'Neill included in broad discussion of realism along with Miller, Williams, and others. *JOURNEY* is "surely the greatest realist drama since Ibsen."

————. *Sights and spectacles 1937-1956*. NY, Farrar and Strauss, 1956.

Reprints the following:

"Eugene O'Neill: Dry ice," from *Partisan Rev.*, Nov-Dec. 1946, pp. 81-85.

Review of *MISBEGOTTEN*, originally "The farmer's daughter," from NY *Times*, 31 Aug. 1952, pp. 86-88.

————. *Theatre chronicles 1937-1962*. NY, Farrar, Strauss, 1963.

Reprints the following:

"Eugene O'Neill: Dry ice," from *Partisan Rev.*, Nov.-Dec. 1946, pp. 81-88.

"The American realist playwrights," from *On the contrary*, pp. 209-229.

McCOLE, C. John. *Lucifer at large*. NY, Longmans, Green, 1937, pp. 112-115.

In this somewhat narrow attack on modern literature's treatment of mankind as less than human, O'Neill is mentioned because of his insistence on Freudian interpretations.

MacGowan, Kenneth, and William Melnitz. *The living stage.* NY, Prentice-Hall, 1955. "Eugene O'Neill-Dramatic pioneer," pp. 487-490.
    A comprehensive stage history designed for popular reading. It is somewhat disappointing because of the cheapening effect of its illustrations, which are all drawings instead of plates or photographs. It is, however, a good text, edited by O'Neill's one-time producing partner. O'Neill's original sketches for the setting of *DESIRE* are included.

Mackay, Constance D'Arcy. *The little theatre in the United States.* NY, Holt, 1917. "The Provincetown players," pp. 46-53.
    Written when O'Neill's plays had been appearing less than a year, this brief history of the Provincetown group mentions the "signal power" of its writers, among them O'Neill and his original themes.

Madden, David, ed. *American dreams, American nightmares.* Carbondale & Edwardsville, Ill., So. Ill. Univ. Press, 1970. Contains "Focus on Eugene O'Neill's The Iceman: The Iceman hath come," by Frederic I. Carpenter, pp. 158-164.

Maier, Norman R., and H. Willard Reninger. *A psychological approach to literary criticism.* NY, Appleton, 1933, pp. 101-104.
    This interesting book, devoted to a somewhat different approach to literary criticism, terms *INTERLUDE* successful because it follows a successful literary technique, *i.e.*, the direction of the reader is clearly indicated and the precise meaning attained.

Mais, Stuart P. B. *Some modern authors.* Originally published 1923 by Richards, but now available as reprint, published 1960, Freeport, NY, by Books for Libraries Press.
    A very early essay on O'Neill as an evolving American writer, with brief (six page) discussion entitled simply "Eugene O'Neill," covering plays through *APE*.

MANTLE, Burns. *Contemporary American playwrights.* NY, Dodd, Mead, 1938. "Eugene O'Neill," pp. 62-73.
Factual account of O'Neill's life and works, with play list.

MAYORGA, Margaret. *A short history of the American drama.* NY, Dodd, Mead, 1932. "Eugene O'Neill," pp. 317-337.
While mainly discussing playwrights before 1920, Miss Mayorga does review most of O'Neill's plays. Her main criticism is O'Neill's lack of knowledge about the real behavior of obsessed characters.

MERSERVE, Walter. *Discussions of modern American drama.* Boston, Heath, 1965.
Reprints the following:
Krutch, Joseph Wood. Excerpts from *American drama since 1918,* 1957, concerning O'Neill revival, pp. 67-73.
McCarthy, Mary, "The American realist playwrights," from *On the contary,* 1961, pp. 113-127.
O'Neill, Eugene, Explanation of *BROWN*, pp. 130-131.
Parks, Edd Winfield, "Eugene O'Neill's quest," *Tulane Dr. Rev.,* Spring 1960, pp. 96-105.
Quinn, Arthur Hobson. "Eugene O'Neill," excerpts from "The American spirit in comedy and tragedy," *Eng. Jour.,* Jan. 1924, pp. 5-7.
Trilling, Lionel. Excerpts from "Eugene O'Neill," *New Rep.,* 23 Sept. 1936, pp. 18-25.

*MICKLE, Alan D. *Six plays of Eugene O'Neill.* NY, Horace Liverright, 1929.
The title is misleading. The book reviews but does not reprint *CHRISTIE, APE, BROWN, FOUNTAIN, MARCO* and *INTERLUDE*. Its complete and unqualified praise of O'Neill places him with Shakespeare, Ibsen, Goethe and Blake. Amidst all of Mickle's assertions that O'Neill could do no wrong, the most remarkable point is his "proof" that all the characters in *STRANGE INTERLUDE* are perfectly normal. None of O'Neill's most avid supporters in America ever admitted this. The lyric adoration is interesting but of limited value, especially in view of the fact that Mickle bases all his criticism on having read but not seen the plays.

MIDDLETON, George. *These things are mine: The autobiography of a journeyman playwright.* NY, Macmillan, 1947, pp. 118-119.
Contains a letter from O'Neill replying to congratulations sent to him on the success of *HORIZON*.

MILLER, Jordan Y. *American dramatic literature.* NY, McGraw-Hill, 1961.
The general introduction of this anthology discusses the historical perspective of O'Neill in American drama. *DESIRE* discussed in separate essay as tragedy.

————. "Eugene O'Neill," in French, Warren G., and Walter E. Kidd, eds., *American winners of the Nobel literary prize.* Norman, Univ. of Okla. Press, 1968, pp. 54-84.
In this volume on American prize winners from Lewis to Steinbeck the O'Neill essay attempts to summarize the apparent reasons for the award, tracing the development from uncertain early plays to the Nobel award itself.

*————. *Playwright's progress: O'Neill and the critics.* Chicago, Scott, Foresman, 1965.
Through reprints of 67 play reviews and other essays on O'Neill and his works, this volume traces the critical reception of O'Neill from his first New York newspaper review (Heywood Broun, *Times*, on *CARDIFF*) to revivals of *MARCO* and *INTERLUDE* in 1964. The following major items are included:
Bentley, Eric, "Trying to like O'Neill," *Kenyon Rev.*, July 1952, pp. 146-158.
"Counsels of despair," *Times* (London) *Lit. Supp.*, 10 Apr. 1948, pp. 137-146.
de Casseres, Benjamin, "The triumphant genius of Eugene O'Neill," *Theatre*, Feb. 1928, pp. 88-91.
de Voto, Bernard, "Minority report," *Sat. Rev.*, 21 Nov. 1936, pp. 108-113.
Hofmannsthal, Hugo von, "Eugene O'Neill," *Freeman*, 21 Mar. 1923, pp. 44-48.
Kemelman, H. G., "Eugene O'Neill and the highbrow melodrama," *Bookman*, Sept. 1932, pp. 94-105.

Krutch, Joseph Wood, "Eugene O'Neill, the lonely revolutionary," *Th. Arts,* Apr. 1952, pp. 158-161.
————, "Why the O'Neill star is rising," NY *Times Mag.,* 19 Mar. 1961, pp. 174-179.
Nathan, George Jean, "The case of O'Neill," *Am. Merc.,* Apr. 1928, pp. 91-94.
Quinn, Arthur Hobson, "Eugene O'Neill, poet and mystic," *Scribner's,* Oct. 1926, pp. 82-88.
Trilling, Lionel, "Eugene O'Neill," *New Rep.,* 23 Sept. 1936, pp. 113-119.

MILLER, Perry. *Major writers of America.* NY, Harcourt, Brace, World, 1962, vol. 2. "Eugene O'Neill," by Eric Bentley, pp. 557-575. See comment under Bentley.

MOREHOUSE, Ward. *Just the other day.* NY, McGraw-Hill, 1953.
Random mention of O'Neill in connection with Morehouse's life as a New York dramatic critic. Brief discussion of his stay with O'Neill in France.

————. *Matinee tomorrow.* NY, Whittlesey House, 1949. Ch. 11, "The drama's revolt—and O'Neill," pp. 180-193.
General discussion of the new drama and O'Neill's influence. This is a very interesting popular history of 50 years of American drama and theatre by one who witnessed and criticized much of it.

MORRIS, Lloyd R. *Postscript to yesterday. America: The last fifty years.* NY, Random House, 1947. "All man's blundering unhappiness," pp. 177-184.
A general review of O'Neill's major plays and their treatment of the "sickness of today" in a chapter devoted to American playwrights from Fitch to Behrman.

MOSES, Montrose J. *The American dramatist.* Boston, Little, Brown, 1925. Ch. 20, "Eugene O'Neill and the new drama," pp. 415-434.
Moses views the early plays rather narrowly, especially *ALL*

GOD'S CHILLUN, and finds O'Neill's view too dark and uncompromising.

————, and John Mason Brown. *The American theatre as seen by its critics, 1752-1934.* NY, Norton, 1934.
Reprints the following articles:
Anderson, John, review of *DAYS WITHOUT END*, NY *Journal*, 9 Jan. 1934.
Benchley, Robert, review of *MOURNING BECOMES ELECTRA*, *New Yorker*, 7 Nov. 1931.
Broun, Heywood, review of *BEYOND THE HORIZON*, NY *Tribune*, 4 Feb. 1920.
Krutch, Joseph Wood, Preface to *Nine plays*, 1933 ed.

MUCHNIC, Helen. *From Gorky to Pasternak.* NY, Random House, 1961.
Reprints portions of Muchnic's article "Circe's swine: Plays by Gorky and O'Neill," originally appearing in *Comp. Lit.* Spring 1951. Deals mainly with *ICEMAN*.

MULLER, Henry J. *The spirit of tragedy.* NY, Knopf, 1956. "Tragedy in America: O'Neill," pp. 311-315.
In a volume devoted wholly to tragedy as a dramatic art from Greek to modern, O'Neill is seriously and "respectfully" treated as one who, like others, had great but unrealized tragic potential. *ELECTRA* briefly reviewed as his best play.

MYERS, Henry Alonzo. *Tragedy: A view of life.* Ithaca, NY, Cornell, 1956. V. "Macbeth and the Iceman Cometh: Equivalence and ambivalence in tragedy," pp. 98-109.
O'Neill's tragic view of our time is the sickness of an age. While O'Neill is *ambivalent* in his finding mankind at once attractive and repulsive, Shakespeare shows *equivalence*, *i.e.*, joy and sorrow, guilt and remorse, and the justice of human destiny. An interesting and original approach to evaluating O'Neill's tragic idea.

MYERS, J. Arthur. *Fighters of fate*. Baltimore, Williams & Wilkins, 1927. "Eugene O'Neill," pp. 306-318.
   This book is subtitled, "A story of men and women who have achieved greatly despite the handicaps of the great white plague." It briefly reviews O'Neill's life and his accomplishments because of and despite his fight with tuberculosis.

NATHAN, George Jean. *Art of the night*. NY, Knopf, 1928, pp. 160-164.
   Nathan discusses O'Neill's sense of humor in *MARCO MILLIONS*. It is not a regular kind of humor, but is sardonic and bitter, and can be seen in most of O'Neill's plays.

————. *Encyclopedia of the theatre*. NY, Knopf, 1940.
   Not actually an "encyclopedia," but a series of items in alphabetical order showing Nathan's extensive theatre knowledge. Four pages on O'Neill recount Nathan's personal acquaintance with the man to whom he dedicated this book.

————. *House of Satan*. NY, Knopf, 1926. "A few footnotes on O'Neill," pp. 199-207.
   General discussion of what O'Neill has brought to the stage. Contains a number of interesting comments on the public reaction to *ALL GOD'S CHILLUN*, which Nathan sees basically as no different from many plays treating similar problems.

————. *The intimate notebooks of George Jean Nathan*. NY, Knopf, 1932. "Eugene O'Neill," pp. 21-38. [Reprinted in Van Doren, Carl, *Borzoi reader*, 1938; and in Angoff, Charles, *The world of George Jean Nathan*, 1952; and as "Portrait of O'Neill," in Cargill *et al*, *O'Neill and his plays*, 1961.]
   Intimate notes on O'Neill's personality, with interesting quotations from a letter in which O'Neill sums up his feelings on the completion of *ELECTRA*.

————. *Materia critica*. NY, Knopf, 1924. "Certain dramatists," pp. 122-123.

Discussion of O'Neill's failure in Strindbergian drama like *WELDED* and *FIRST MAN*.

————. *The morning after the first night*. NY, Knopf, 1938.
Chapter III discusses O'Neill and Anderson.

————. *Passing judgments*. NY, Knopf. 1935. Ch. VIII, "O'Neill," pp. 112-126.
General discussion; includes *AH, WILDERNESS!*, *DYNAMO*, *DAYS WITHOUT END*.

————. *Theatre book of the year, 1946-1947*. NY, Knopf, 1947.
Reprints review of *ICEMAN*, originally entitled "The Iceman cometh, seeth, conquereth," NY *Jour-Am.*, 14 Oct. 1946, plus additional material, pp. 93-111.

————. *The theatre in the fifties*. NY, Knopf, 1953.
Bits of personal reference here and there. Mentions some of O'Neill's ideas about newer playwrights.

*————. *The theatre of the moment*. NY, Knopf, 1936. Ch. XI, "The recluse of Sea Island," pp. 196-207. [Original article in *Redbook*, Aug. 1935.]
Nathan was O'Neill's close personal friend and here tells some highly interesting "inside" stories, dispelling some of the previous misconceptions about his personality. These ten pages and the other "intimacies" of which Nathan writes elsewhere offer some of the best material obtainable on O'Neill the man.

————. *The theatre, the drama, and the girls*. NY, Knopf, 1921.
"Eugene O'Neill," pp. 181-185.
Nathan championed O'Neill's cause in *The Smart Set* and elsewhere as early as 1917 (see Chronology of Publication), but here mentions him in a book for the first time. Contains plot review of *HORIZON* and short discussion of "the most distinguished young man of the American theatre."

————. *The world in falseface*. NY, Knopf, 1923, pp. 79-80; 141-143.
Two brief attacks on the shortsightedness of O'Neill criticism.

NICOLL, Allardyce. *World drama*. London, Harrap, 1949; NY, Harcourt, Brace, 1950. Ch. VIII, "Eugene O'Neill," pp. 880-893.
Concise review of each major play. O'Neill is the representative of American drama as a whole, full of vitality and strength, lacking refinements of greatness or sense of relationship with his times, but with no true literary ability. (Nicoll was Chairman of the Department of Drama at Yale when the University awarded O'Neill an honorary LLD.)

O'HARA, Frank Hurburt. *Today in American drama*. Chicago, Univ. of Chicago Press, 1939.
This short review of modern American plays includes frequent references to O'Neill, but mainly discusses *APE* and its left-wing atmosphere.

OLSON, Elder. *Tragedy and the theory of drama*. Detroit, Wayne St. Univ. Press, 1961. Ch. X, "Modern drama and tragedy," pp. 237-243.
ELECTRA is not a tragedy mainly through O'Neill's lack of comprehension of genuine tragic quality. Passing references to *MARCO*.

OPPENHEIMER, George. *The passionate playgoer*. NY, Viking, 1958.
Reprints the following:
Benchley, Robert, "Mourning Becomes Electra," (originally, "Top") from *The New Yorker*, 7 Nov. 1931, p. 580.
Chapman, John, introduction to *LONG DAY'S JOURNEY* as originally printed in his 1957 *Broadway's Best*, p. 281.
Krutch, Joseph Wood, Introduction to *Nine plays*, p. 268.

PARKS, Edd Winfield. *Segments of Southern thought*. Athens, Univ. of Georgia Press, 1938. Ch. XVI, "Eugene O'Neill's symbolism," pp. 293-313.
Broad discussion of O'Neill's symbols. Despite his apparent turn

to the cross in *DAYS WITHOUT END*, says Parks, O'Neill is merely using another symbol to express the same thoughts he always has.

PELLIZZI, Camillo. *English drama: The last great phase.* Translated by Rowan Williams, NY, Macmillan, 1936, pp. 253-262. [Reprinted in Cargill *et al, O'Neill and his plays,* 1961, as "Irish Catholic anti-Puritan," pp. 353-357.]
    Whether or not he is aware of it, O'Neill is the Irish-Catholic rebel against Puritanism, very aware of the existence of evil and divine grace, according to this Italian critic.

*QUINN, Arthur Hobson. *A history of the American drama from the Civil War to the present day.* NY, F. S. Crofts, 1927,1936, vol. 2, Ch. XXI, "Eugene O'Neill, poet and mystic," pp. 165-206; Ch. XXIV, "The New Decade, 1927-1936," pp. 252-260.
    This standard history of the American drama received a fourth printing in 1945, which date appears on title page, but covers plays only until 1936, although certain additions at the end of some chapters and the bibliography contain material into the 1940's. This edition is a consolidated single volume with separate pagination for the two originally separate volumes. The essay on O'Neill remains essentially identical through all editions and printings, but the final chapter on the "New Decade" carries through *DAYS WITHOUT END.* The "Poet and Mystic" chapter originally appeared in *Scribner's* in Oct. 1926 but was considerably expanded for the book. [The *Scribner's* article also appears in Miller, *Playwright's progress,* 1965, pp. 82-88.] Quinn's view is that O'Neill's Celtic background makes him a mystic, and the plays are analyzed in this light.
    The chapter includes O'Neill's explanation of *BROWN*, which appeared in most New York newspapers in Feb. 1926 (see Non-dramatic O'Neill). There is also a personal letter from O'Neill, partly reproduced in facsimile, explaining his artistic philosophy. [Reprinted in Cargill *et al, O'Neill and his plays,* 1961, pp. 125-126.]
    Although Quinn's book dwells heavily upon American drama before O'Neill, it is a popular and easy-reading history which is a basic reference text in any drama library.

————. *The literature of the American people.* NY, Appleton-Century-Crofts, 1951. Ch. 49, "Vitalizers of the drama," pp. 928-934.

A few pages devoted to O'Neill's plays in this survey of American literature. The book is on a level with the three volumes by Spiller *et al,* but bibliography is not as complete.

————. *Representative American plays.* NY, Appleton-Century-Crofts, 1953. Seventh edition. "Beyond the Horizon," pp. 929-937.

This anthology has gone through seven editions, 1917, 1920, 1925, 1928, 1930, 1938, and 1953. It has always relied heavily on early American drama, and is not truly "representative" since 1918. *HORIZON* has always been the choice for O'Neill, and it has several pages of introduction in the last two editions.

*RALEIGH, John Henry. "Eugene O'Neill," in Bryer, Jackson R., *Fifteen modern American authors: A survey of research and criticism.* Durham, Duke Univ. Press, 1969, pp. 301-322.

An invaluable guide to matters of bibliography, editions of works, manuscripts, letters, biography, criticism, including material in books, theatre reviews, scholarly articles.

————. "Eugene O'Neill and the escape from the Chateau d'If." Paper presented at the English Institute, Columbia University, September 1963. [Reprinted in Gassner, *O'Neill,* 1964, pp. 7-22.]

The influence of James O'Neill's version of *Monte Cristo* on O'Neill's "first" career (up to *DAYS WITHOUT END*) demonstrated in detail, including character, style, incident, theme, climaxes, etc. Escape from this influence did not occur until the later plays.

————. *"The plays of Eugene O'Neill.* Carbondale, So. Ill. Univ. Press, 1965.

All O'Neill plays covered in this substantial (300 page) study of his artistry and position as an American writer. O'Neill held to be a giant figure in American literature. [Discussion of *ICEMAN* reprinted in Raleigh's *Twentieth century interpretations,* 1968.]

*————. *Twentieth century interpretations of The Iceman Cometh.* Englewood Cliffs, Prentice-Hall, 1968.

In the usual format of this series, volume contains general biographical and critical introduction, followed by variety of essays, letters, interviews etc., expressing Viewpoints and Interpretations of the play. Brief chronology and bibliography included. The following major items are reprinted:

Alexander, Doris M., "Hugo of the Iceman Cometh: Realism and O'Neill," *Am. Quar.*, Winter 1953, pp. 63-71.

Bentley, Eric, "Trying to like O'Neill," *Kenyon Rev.*, July 1952, pp. 37-49.

Brustein, Robert, review of *ICEMAN* from *Theatre of revolt*, 1965, pp. 92-102.

Day, Cyrus, "The iceman and the bridegroom: Some observations on the death of O'Neill's salesman," *Mod. Dr.*, May 1958, pp. 79-86.

Falk, Doris, "The Iceman Cometh," (originally "Fatal Balance") from *Eugene O'Neill and the tragic tension,* 1958, pp. 87-91.

McCarthy, Mary, "Eugene O'Neill: Dry Ice," *Partisan Rev.*, Nov-Dec. 1946, pp. 50-53.

Muchnic, Helen, "The irrelevancy of belief: The Iceman and the Lower Depths," (original title "Circe's swine: Plays by Gorky and O'Neill), *Comp. Lit.*, Spring 1951, pp. 103-112.

Raleigh, John Henry, "The historical background of The Iceman Cometh," from Raleigh's *Plays of Eugene O'Neill,* 1965, pp. 54-62.

Winther, Sophus Keith, "The Iceman Cometh: A study in technique," *Ariz. Quar.*, Winter 1947, pp. 72-78.

*REAVES, J. Russell. *An O'Neill concordance.* Detroit, Gale, 1969, 3 vol.

This giant computerized effort at a complete concordance of most of O'Neill's works overwhelms in its detail and disappoints in its usefulness. Entire plays are arbitrarily omitted without explanation, which at once limits the scholarly value. If O'Neill has reached the level of Shakespeare and the Bible, thereby meriting this effort, well and good, but one might seriously question, especially because of the limited nature of this undertaking. If one really wishes to find out when and where O'Neill wrote "God," "Gawd," or "b'God," here's the source.

*SALEM, James M. *A guide to critical reviews: Part I: American drama from O'Neill to Albee*. NY & London, Scarecrow Press, 1966.

Listing sources of critical reviews in NY *Times* and US and Canadian magazines.

*SALISBURY, William. *A dress suit becomes Hamlet. Why not, if Mourning Becomes Electra?* New Rochell, NY, The Independent Publishing Co., 1933.

Subtitle: "A dissertation upon the comedies of Eugene O'Neill, addressed to the author." This small pamphlet is a violently prejudiced attack upon all of O'Neill's major plays, full of ridicule based on superficialities of story form. Racial prejudice is injected without warrant in the form of vicious anti-Semitism; and there is name calling with no point. A low water mark in dramatic criticism.

SALZMAN, Maurice. *Plagiarism, the "art" of stealing literary material*. Los Angeles, Parker, Stone and Baird, 1931.

Includes a factual report of the Georges Lewys plagiarism case against O'Neill and *STRANGE INTERLUDE*.

*SANBORN, Ralph, and Barrett H. Clark. *A bibliography of the works of Eugene O'Neill*, NY, Random House, 1931. Reissued in offset, NY, Benjamin Blom, 1965.

Careful collation of all texts to and including *DYNAMO*, with numerous plates illustrating variations. Contains limited references to periodical, newspaper, and book articles (including separate books on O'Neill) and also a collection of little-known poems which O'Neill reluctantly gave permission to publish.

SAYLER, Oliver M. *Our American theatre*. NY, Brentano's, 1923. Ch. III, "Eugene O'Neill, the American playwright," pp. 27-43.

Sayler regards O'Neill as the personification of the current American drama. Brief life sketch and review of plays. Excerpts from Hugo von Hofmannsthal's widely quoted criticism. Also includes O'Neill's own statement concerning his credo of leaving social ideas behind. [This statement reprinted in Cargill *et al*, *O'Neill and his plays*, 1961.]

SERGEANT, Elizabeth Shepley. "O'Neill: The man with a mask," in *Fire under the Andes*, NY Knopf, 1927.
>Reprinted from *New Rep.*, 16 March 1927.

*SHEAFFER, Louis. *O'Neill, son and playwright*. Boston, Little, Brown, 1968; *O'Neill, son and artist*, Boston, Little, Brown, 1973. By far the most significant biography of O'Neill yet to appear. The combined volumes are probably the definitive work. Representing some sixteen years of detailed research into every possible corner of O'Neill's life, through documents, personal interviews with many individuals who have since died, and personal letters now available, particularly from the O'Neill collection at Yale, these books carry O'Neill from his family backgrounds even before his birth through his entire career and death. As the titles imply, the aspect of O'Neill's position as the son of James O'Neill and as the surviving son of the tortured family gets continual emphasis throughout the biographical and critical discussions. There is no attempt to make any journalistic exposé of a "real" or "secret" individual, but a better picture of many of O'Neill's personal and artistic motivations beyond the simplistic "curse" of something like Bowen's approach does emerge through Sheaffer's extensive research. Critical evaluation of the plays is minimal, but to the point. These volumes give the playwright and his family a fully-rounded portrait, placing O'Neill the man and artist in the clearest, most understandable perspective yet available.

*SHIPLEY, Joseph T. *The art of Eugene O'Neill*. Univ. of Washington Chapbooks, Seattle, Univ. of Washington Bookstore, 1928.
>This 34-page pamphlet is the second small book (Clark's *Eugene O'Neill* was the first) devoted exclusively to O'Neill. Shipley finds that O'Neill's theme of life as a vale of tears is too restrictive. The booklet's value is limited by Shipley's emphasis on O'Neill's lack of humor.

————. *Guide to great plays*. Washington, Public Affairs Press, 1956.

All important plays from sea plays of Glencairn cycle to *ICEMAN* (*DIFF'RENT* thrown in for some reason) are included in this volume which reviews plots and some of the critical comments from the press.

*SIEVERS, W. David. *Freud on Broadway*. NY, Hermitage House, 1955. Ch. VI, "Freud, Jung and O'Neill," pp. 97-133.

General review of O'Neill's plays in light of accepted and assumed influence of psychoanalysis. *A MOON FOR THE MISBEGOTTEN* is found to be one of the best. The entire book treats the Freudian theme in considerable detail as reflected on the New York stage during this century, often roaming far afield to include works one would normally not consider appropriate. An intriguing, if not always convincing, book.

*SIMONSON, Lee. *The stage is set*. NY, Harcourt, Brace, 1932.

This excellent book treats most aspects of theatrical production from the viewpoint of one of our most successful designers. No specific section on O'Neill, but he is often mentioned, particularly in the very fine discussion of language and dramatic poetry. Simonson's hilarious parody of Hamlet's soliloquies as O'Neill would write them shows precisely what Krutch and others have meant in their deploring O'Neill's lack of poetic grandeur. *DYNAMO* is discussed in detail relative to its setting and O'Neill's emphasis upon sound effects. [Portion on *DYNAMO* reprinted in Cargill *et al, O'Neill and his plays,* 1961.]

SINCLAIR, Upton. *Money writes!* NY, A. & C. Boni, 1927. Ch. XXXV, "The springs of pessimism," pp. 175-177.

Sinclair's study of American literature from the economic point of view briefly mentions O'Neill, whose pessimism is regarded as part of the same disease afflicting art in a dying capitalism.

*SKINNER, Richard Dana. *Eugene O'Neill: A poet's quest*. NY, Longmans, Green, 1935.

O'Neill's entire career is recreated as a poet's quest, comparable to a saint's pilgrimage. An interesting study, carefully drawn, but effective only if the reader accepts Catholic doctrine. Otherwise, an able discussion of the positions the plays occupy in O'Neill's life, based on a chronology of compostion supplied by O'Neill himself. Although Skinner realizes other plays are yet to come, his conclusions would indicate O'Neill has "arrived" at the goal of his quest in *DAYS WITHOUT END*. The chronology, allowing for some inaccuracies in O'Neill's memory, is the most valuable item in the book.

————. "A note on Eugene O'Neill," in Skillin, Edward S., ed., *The Commonweal reader*. NY, Harpers, 1949, pp. 80-83.
   Reprints Skinner's review of *AH, WILDERNESS!*, *Commonweal*, 27 Oct. 1933.

————. *Our changing theatre*. NY, Dial Press, 1931. Ch. III, "The song in tragedy," pp. 43-47; Ch. IV, "Tragedy without song," pp. 76-96.
   Skinner believes that O'Neill will be a true poet of tragedy if he recaptures the vision of *BROWN*. The discussion of other plays, such as *INTERLUDE, DYNAMO, DESIRE*, forms the approach to Skinner's later book, *Eugene O'Neill: A poet's quest*.

*SLOCHOWER, Harry. *No voice is wholly lost: Writers and thinkers in war and peace*. NY, Creative Age Press, 1945. "In quest of everyman: Eugene O'Neill & James Joyce," pp. 248-254. [Reprinted as "Eugene O'Neill's lost moderns," in Cargill *et al*, *O'Neill and his plays*, 1961.]
   This book deals with various literary and artistic reactions to the social and cultural instability of today. The brief analysis of O'Neill is excellent, going to the center of his philosophy more directly than many other extensive treatments of the subject. Compare Slochower's essay with Krutch's opinion of O'Neill's tragic characters, or Flexner's social viewpoint.

SPILLER, Robert E. *The cycle of American literature*. NY, Macmillan, 1955. Ch. XI, "Full circle: O'Neill and Hemingway," pp. 243-274.
   O'Neill is discussed with Hemingway, Dos Passos, Wolfe, and others as part of the post-war generation literature of social protest, symbolism, and so on. O'Neill is clearly identified as apart from the "lost" generation.

*————, and others. *Literary history of the United States.* NY, Macmillan, 1949. Vol. II, No. 73, "Eugene O'Neill," by Joseph Wood Krutch, pp. 1237-1250.

This two-volume compendium and its third volume of bibliography (containing extended references to O'Neill) is the outstanding work in the field of American literary history. Krutch's essay again summarizes most of the views which he has expounded in other articles. There is a brief account of the development of the little theatre movement and O'Neill's position therein. In discussing *DESIRE, BROWN, INTERLUDE,* and *ELECTRA*, Krutch considers that O'Neill's plays "are not so much summary of an era as a new mode and a new theme for the American stage."

*STAMM, Rudolf. *The shaping powers at work: 15 essays on poetic transmutation.* Heidelberg, Carl Winter Universitätsverlag, 1967. IX. The achievement of Eugene O'Neill, pp. 236-276.

In forty pages devoted to O'Neill, Stamm includes three major essays:

"The dramatic experiments of Eugene O'Neill," from *Eng. Stud.*, Feb. 1947.

"The Iceman Cometh," written in 1948 (source at present unidentified).

"Faithful realism: Eugene O'Neill and the problem of style," from *Eng. Stud.*, Aug. 1959.

STARK, Harold. *People you know.* NY, Boni and Liveright, 1923. "The hairy ape," pp. 244-247.

Interview between "Young Boswell" (Stark) and O'Neill, discussing O'Neill's basic dramatic theories.

*STRAUMANN, Heinrich. *American literature in the twentieth century.* London, Hutchinson's University Library, 1951. Ch. V, "The great conflict: The rise of American drama."

Written by a professor of English literature at University of Zurich. An interesting study which finds O'Neill the "most complete and powerful symbol" of the conflicts between determinism and pragmatism, and the acceptance of reality on the one hand and the search for values beyond the world of experience as an offshoot of the old moral and religious tradition on the other. This approach should certainly be considered in comparison with many domestic attitudes toward O'Neill's tragic view.

————. *American literature in the 20th century.* NY, Harper, 1965. Six-page treatment of O'Neill in very general terms.

STUART, Donald Clive. *The development of dramatic art.* NY, Appleton-Century, 1928, pp. 644-650.
LAZARUS and BROWN discussed as expressionism, *STRANGE INTERLUDE* as "super-naturalism."

SUTTON, Graham. *Some contemporary dramatists.* NY, Geo. H. Doran, 1925; Port Washington, NY, Kennikat Press, 1967.
Routine account of O'Neill's career through *APE*.

TAUBMAN, Howard. *The making of the American theatre.* NY, Coward, McCann, 1965. Ch. XVI. "Eugene O'Neill," pp. 168-176.
Quick review of major plays, concluding that, though O'Neill is the best we have, he does not rank with the great masters.

TAYLOR, Walter F. *A history of American letters.* Boston, American Book Co., 1936. Ch. V, "The rise of the drama: Eugene O'Neill," pp. 406-418.
O'Neill's work is divided into four categories called "explorations." *ELECTRA* does not suffer in comparison with *Lear* and *Macbeth*, though O'Neill is in the tradition of Webster and Ford, more than Shakespeare.

TAYLOR, William E. *Modern American drama: Essays in criticism.* Deland, Fla., Everett/Edwards, 1968.
See Halio, Jay L. "Eugene O'Neill: The long quest," this section.

THOMPSON, Alan Reynolds. *The anatomy of drama.* Berkeley, Univ. of California Press, 1942, pp. 298-306; 1946, pp. 303-312.
Thompson downgrades O'Neill as a romanticist relying too heavily upon psychopathology.

*————. "The dilemma of modern tragedy," in Foerster, Norman, ed., *Humanism and America: Essays on the outlook of modern civilization.* NY, Farrar & Rinehart, 1930, pp. 127-148.

The dilemma: a modern naturalist poet cannot be both honest and sublime. The elevation of tragedy cannot achieve its goal by modern naturalistic or even romantic means. The essay is a careful analysis of the tragic concept and treatment by modern writers. O'Neill seeks nobility in man and the answer to life in life itself without resort to romantic escape, but he does not exalt to elevation of heroic tragedy, finding life muddled and leaving it that way.

THORP, Willard, and Margaret Thorp. *Modern writing.* NY, American Book, 1944.

Contains Krutch's introduction to *Nine plays.*

*TIUSANEN, Timo. *O'Neill's scenic images.* Princeton, Princeton Univ. Press, 1968.

A significant piece of O'Neill scholarship, giving careful consideration to the trademark of "revolutionary" scenic effects from stage settings to the aside-monologue-soliloquy. Rarities such as *BREAD AND BUTTER, NOW I ASK YOU,* and *SHELL SHOCK* are included. One of the few book-length studies of O'Neill as an artist of the theatre rather than as a writer of dramatic literature.

TOOHEY, John L. *A history of the Pulitzer prize plays.* NY, Citadel, 1967.

Plot summaries, limited critical comments in popular illustrated history.

*TORNQVIST, Egil. *A drama of souls: Studies in O'Neill's super-naturalistic technique.* New Haven, Yale, 1969.

One of the most valuable studies of O'Neill's techniques in print. Using the term "super-naturalism" coined by O'Neill to define the type of realism practiced by Strindberg, the book covers all of O'Neill's plays in detail under chapter headings such as "Human setting," "Visualized soul," "Verbalized soul," and so on. Includes some O'Neill sketches for scene design and plans of action, and publishes the most complete chronology of O'Neill's works (plays only) now available, including dates of various drafts and of final versions, with information on locations where O'Neill composed the plays, producing companies, and cities involved with first productions.

TRILLING, Lionel. Introduction to O'Neill, Eugene, *The Emperor Jones, Anna Christie, The Hairy Ape. NY, The Modern Library, 1937, pp. vii-xix.
Trilling discusses these three plays as a part of O'Neill's over-all philosophical pattern. O'Neill is uncopied because he is in the tradition of *Lear* and *Faust*, and nobody else is interested in the same thing.

UNTERMEYER, Louis. *Makers of the modern world*. NY, Simon & Schuster, 1955. "Eugene O'Neill," pp. 662-668.
Brief biography in a collection of 92 biographies of men and women "who formed the pattern of our century."

VALGEMAE, Mardi. *Accelerated grimace: Expressionism in the American drama of the 1920s*. Carbondale, So. Ill. Univ. Press, 1972.
From Pound's "The Age demanded an image/Of its accelerated grimace" comes the title, with expressionism held to be the grimace of American drama of the 1920s. *JONES* and *APE* important factors, together with *MARINER, CHILLUN, BROWN*.

VAN DOREN, Carl, ed., *The Borzoi reader*. NY, Garden City, 1938.
Reprints "Eugene O'Neill," by George Jean Nathan, from *Intimate Notebooks* pp. 590-603.

————, and Mark Van Doren. *American and British literature since 1890*. NY, Century, 1925; 1939, pp. 102-107.
The first edition of this volume was one of the first American literature surveys to consider O'Neill worthy of discussion. The treatment, however, is very broad.

VORSE, Mary Heaton. *Time and the town*. NY, Dial, 1942.
Reminiscences by the owner of the Wharf Theatre, Provincetown, where *CARDIFF* had its first performance in 1916.

WALTER, Erich A., ed. *Essay annual*. NY, Scott, Foresman, 1933.

Reprints "O'Neill and Aeschylus," by John Corbin, *Sat. R. Lit.*, 30 April 1932, p. 159.

———. *Essay annual.* NY, Scott, Foresman, 1936. Reprints "O'Neill: what next?" by Hiram Motherwell, *Stage,* Aug. 1935, p. 202.

*WATON, Harry. *The historic significance of Eugene O'Neill's Strange Interlude.* NY, Worker's Educational Institute, 1928. Originally a lecture delivered at the Rand School, NY, May 18, 1928. It is truly an astonishing document, showing the play to reflect "great, historic changes taking place in the life of mankind." The soliloquies show our double lives—that shown to the world, and that suppressed unhealthily—as well as how man has suppressed woman. Every character is a symbol of profound social significance. Nina is revolutionary woman; Leeds is the fossil priest-professor; Gordon is revolutionary hero who, like Jesus, dies young; the crippled soldiers are downtrodden masses; Darrell is modern science and crude materialism; and so on and on.

WEISSMAN, Philip. *Creativity in the theatre: A psychoanalytical study.* NY, Basic Books, 1965. This practicing psychologist, who has written lengthy works on American dramatic subjects, notably Tennessee Williams' female characters, includes *ELECTRA* and *JOURNEY* in this provocative study.

WHIPPLE, Thomas K. *Spokesmen: Modern writers and American life.* NY, Appleton, 1928. XI, "Eugene O'Neill," pp. 230-253. The essay is based on Whipple's *New Republic* article of 21 January 1925. O'Neill is seen as a writer of tragedy based on his own attitude that life is a matter of spiritual frustration—probably the tragedy of America as well. *BROWN* is his best play because it is not a tragedy of desolation, but of great poetry.

WHITE, Arthur Franklin. *The plays of Eugene O'Neill.* Cleveland, Western Reserve Univ., Studies by Members of the Faculty, Bulletin Vol. 26, No. 8, August, 1923. A pamphlet of historical interest as the first scholarly study of

O'Neill's plays. It is rare, and not readily available in most libraries.

WILDE, Percival. *The craftsmanship of the one-act play.* NY, Crown, 1951.
Comprehensive guide to the creation of successful one-act plays through all the elements of composition. O'Neill's short plays are frequently used to illustrate pertinent points.

WILLIAMS, Raymond. *Modern tragedy.* Stanford, Stanford Univ. Press, 1966.
This important volume on modern tragic drama includes *ELECTRA* and *JOURNEY* in the overall discussion.

WILSON, Edmund. *Shores of light.* NY, Farrar & Strauss, 1952. "Eugene O'Neill and the naturalists," pp. 99-104. [Reprinted in Cargill *et al, O'Neill and his plays,* 1961, as "Eugene O'Neill as a prose writer."]
Two brief essays discussing mainly *APE* and *CHILLUN.* He finds O'Neill at home most when he is writing in the vernacular.

WILSON, Garff B. *Three hundred years of American drama and theatre from Ye Bare and Ye Cubb to Hair.* Englewood Cliffs, Prentice-Hall, 1973. "Eugene O'Neill," pp. 423-429.
These six pages devoted to quick survey of major works in an outstanding volume of American theatre and drama history.

*WINTHER, Sophus Keith. *Eugene O'Neill: A critical study.* NY, Random House, 1934.
An excellent study of O'Neill's dominant ideas in relation to the modern industrial age, written when he was still considered a practicing playwright. Highly favorable without eulogy. The whole O'Neill canon is considered as a unit, and discussed in terms of moral and social philosophy. It bears comparison with Skinner's *Poet's quest* and contrast with Geddes' *Melodramadness.*

WOOLLCOTT, Alexander. *The portable Woollcott.* NY, Viking, 1946.
Reprints Woollcott's review of *ELECTRA* from *While Rome burns.*

*————. *Shouts and murmurs*. NY, Century, 1922. Ch. XI, "Eugene O'Neill," pp. 144-170.

Woollcott was not an O'Neill admirer, but steers a neutral ground in his first major article about the playwright. He finds O'Neill the "most interesting playwright of the new generation," always vigorous, always somber, but undisciplined. Included is Woollcott's review of *HORIZON*.

————. *While Rome burns*. NY, Viking, 1934, 1940, pp. 288-291. Prints a review of *ELECTRA*.

YOUNG, Stark. *Immortal shadows*. NY, Scribner's, 1948.

Reprints these essays:

"The Great God Brown," *New Rep.*, 10 Feb. 1926.

"Eugene O'Neill's new play," *New Rep.*, 11 Nov. 1931 (review of *ELECTRA*).

"O'Neill and Rostand," *New Rep.*, 21 Oct. 1946 (review of *ICEMAN*).

ZABEL, Morton D., ed. *Literary opinion in America*. NY, Harper's, 1937, 1951.

Reprints the following essays:

Fergusson, Francis, "Eugene O'Neill," *Hound and Horn*, Jan-Mar. 1930.

Young, Stark, review of *ELECTRA*, *New Rep.*, 11 Nov. 1931.

General References—Periodicals

Introduction

This section lists important articles about Eugene O'Neill the man and the artist which have appeared in domestic periodicals at least through June 1972. It is arranged within certain limits as explained below.

I. CONTENTS. Certain restrictions have been made in the type and treatment of the material.

1. Only articles of substantial critical or biographical value have been included. This eliminates numerous items in which O'Neill is mentioned merely in passing, or which otherwise contribute little or nothing to O'Neill scholarship.

2. All items are concerned with O'Neill and/or his works in general. All references dealing primarily with the individual plays, such as opening night reviews and subsequent discussions in newspapers, periodicals, and books, are included in the next section, INDIVIDUAL PLAYS.

3. Because of the sheer impossibility of assembling every single item about O'Neill from every possible newspaper or magazine, sources are limited as follows:

a. Only domestic publications, with rare exception, have been consulted.

b. Because of comparative ease of access through the New York Public Library, only New York newspapers have been directly consulted. Important articles from newspapers of other cities found in various clipping collections of the New York Public Library or at Yale, for instance, or in special bibliographies, may occasionally appear. However, no effort has been made to conduct any systemized search of newspaper files outside New York.

    c. Primary sources for periodical references have been the several indexes, general and specialized, found in most reference libraries, plus special indexes, such as the Dramatic Index, and special bibliographies. Library clipping collections have frequently yielded loose articles from periodicals not regularly indexed.

II. MECHANICS. The general pattern follows standard bibliographical practices, but departs on occasion as shown below. The order of information for each entry is as follows:

    1. Author in alphabetical order. Titles are used if authors are unknown; no entry appears under "Anonymous."

    2. Article title in "quotation marks." Library of Congress catalogue card procedure is followed by capitalizing only first words and proper nouns.

    3. Periodical title, often abbreviated, *in italics*.

    4. Volume, date, and page.

    a. Periodicals other than newspapers include, wherever possible, full information in this manner:

48 (21 Oct. 1946) 71

Please Note: If periodical reference covers more than one page, inclusive pages are indicated only if they are consecutive.

    b. Except for the *New York Times,* newspaper references indicate only the date. Frequent differences among various editions of the same paper and the limited availability of newspapers other than the *Times* render impractical any indication of column or page. The *Index* to the *Times* and the paper's uniform library edition permit references of date, section (Sunday edition only), page and column in this manner:

25 Jan. 1921, II, 1:3

    5. Cross reference information. This includes reprints in books and other publications. Most of the cross references are listed elsewhere in this bibliography.

6. Brief annotation concerning the contents of the entry, occasionally including an evaluation of the item as a piece of O'Neill scholarship. Frequent cross references are made to other items within the bibliography for comparison and contrast.

NOTE: Entries of more than routine interest or of special significance are marked with an asterisk (*). All of O'Neill's plays are spelled out in italic *CAPITAL LETTERS*. An abbreviated form is often used to save space: *e.g.*, *ICEMAN* for *THE ICEMAN COMETH*; *DESIRE* for *DESIRE UNDER THE ELMS*, and so on.

ABEL, Lionel. "O'Neill and his critics." *New Leader*, 61 (6 Jan. 1958) 25-26.
Discussion of some of the good and some of the erroneous points included in reviews of *POET* by Krutch, McCarthy, Bentley, others.

AGEE, James. "Ordeal of Eugene O'Neill." *Time*, 48 (21 Oct. 1946) 71.
Review of O'Neill's life and works upon opening of *ICEMAN*. Agee sees O'Neill as our greatest craftsman, rather than a dramatist.

ALEXANDER, Doris. "Eugene O'Neill and Charles Lever." *Mod. Dr.*, 5 (Feb. 1963) 415-520.
Demonstration that Cornelius Melody of *POET* is closely patterned after leading figure in Charles Lever's 1894 novel *Charles O'Malley, the Irish Dragoon*.

———. "Eugene O'Neill and *Light on the Path*." *Mod. Dr.*, 3 (Dec. 1960) 260-267.
Explanation of origins of O'Neill's mysticism in terms of volume of philosophy given him at Provincetown during winter of 1915-1916 by Terry Carlin.

———. "Eugene O'Neill as social critic." *Am. Quar.*, 6 (Winter 1954) 349-363. [Reprinted in Cargill *et al*, *O'Neill and his plays*, 1961.]

An extended analysis of O'Neill's criticism of modern society, including facts from earliest plays like *SERVITUDE* and *APE*, through *BROWN, MARCO, INTERLUDE,* and *DAYS WITHOUT END*, as well as *AH, WILDERNESS*. Miss Alexander finds O'Neill's criticism cancels itself out because of his condemnation of all society and his rejection of all solutions to make it better.

————. "Eugene O'Neill: The Hound of Heaven and the Hell Hole." *Mod. Lang. Q.,* 20 (Dec. 1959) 307-314.

Well documented thesis that *SERVITUDE, WELDED,* and *DAYS WITHOUT END* are all based on O'Neill's fear of love and his fascination with Thompson's "Hound of Heaven," which he delighted in reciting to all comers in Greenwich Village's Golden Swan bar, known as the Hell Hole.

Anderson, John. "Eugene O'Neill." *Th. Arts,* 15 (Nov. 1931) 938-942.

An appreciation of O'Neill's powers. He is first important dramatist to contend with shifting values of modern life.

ANDREWS, Kenneth. "Broadway, our literary signpost." *Bookman,* 53 (July 1921) 407-417.

JONES is the best argument against those who lament the passing of the "palmy days and their great tragedians." *JONES, DIFF'RENT,* and *HORIZON* show we are beginning to think in the theatre.

————. "Broadway, our literary signpost." *Bookman,* 57 (April 1923) 191.

O'Neill and the Guild are encouraging producers to give better plays. O'Neill makes us think, which is something new.

ANSHUTZ, Grace. "Expressionistic drama in the American theatre." *Drama,* 16 (April 1926) 245.

O'Neill is the best expressionistic writer in his welding of the external and internal—the body and the spirit—so harmoniously.

ATKINSON, Brooks. "After all these years." NY *Times,* 12 Oct. 1941, IX, 1:1

Atkinson wonders why more of O'Neill is not revived, though he realizes that many plays are beyond revival.

————. "Dramatist of the sail and the sea." NY *Times*, 3 May 1931, VIII, 1:1.
The earthy, emotional characters of *APE, JONES, DESIRE,* are better than those of O'Neill's recent confused experimentation.

————. "Ennobel-ing O'Neill." NY *Times*, 22 Nov. 1936, XI, 1:1.
[Reprinted as "O'Neill gets the Nobel prize," in Atkinson's *Broadway scrapbook,* 1947.]
The award is one of the most cheering things of otherwise depressing theatre season. It was awarded fairly, to a man whose accomplishments merited it.

————. "Eugene O'Neill." NY *Times*, 20 Jan. 1952, II, 1:1.
Atkinson praises the revivals of *ANNA CHRISTIE* and *DESIRE* and expresses sorrow for O'Neill's 25-year limbo.

————. "Eugene O'Neill." NY *Times*, 13 Dec. 1953, II, 5:1.
Eulogy to a giant who has been dropped from earth, a great spirit and a great dramatist. No one like him before, none like him now.

*————. "Feuding again." NY *Times*, 25 Apr. 1948, II, 1:1.
Reply to the anonymous "Counsels of Despair" from London *Times*. Atkinson attempts to point out O'Neill's greatness, showing how this "peevish" London writer lost sight of what was behind the plays. Atkinson successfully attacks the obvious weakness in the article by pointing out that the writer's prejudice and illogical reasoning are not based on what O'Neill has done, but on the critic's own ideas of what he should have done.

————. "Head man in the drama." NY *Times*, 19 Aug. 1951, II, 1:1.
Only an improvident theatre such as ours today would neglect this man who has written the finest dramatic literature we have.

————. "King of tragedy." NY *Times*, 28 Mar. 1954, II, 1:1.

Inquires why America does not recognize its own great master whose plays, regardless of one's personal opinion, have become accepted as the works of a man struggling with higher things.

———. "O'Neill's finale." NY *Times*, 12 May 1957, II, 1:1.
A brief look at the current revival with especial reference to *JOURNEY* and *MISBEGOTTEN*.

———. "O'Neill off duty." NY *Times*, 8 Oct. 1933, X, 1:1.
Informal interview finds O'Neill a different, more human person, relaxed and capable of laughing "without brilliant provocation," apparently having abandoned much of his earlier style of tragedy.

"Author." *New Yorker*, 31 Dec. 1927.
Brief discussion of the "quiet young man" sitting alone at rehearsals of his plays. Some "intimate notes" designed to alter the picture of O'Neill's morose pessimism.

BAB, Julius. "Eugene O'Neill—as Europe sees America's foremost playwright." *Th. Guild Mag.*, 9 (Nov. 1931) 11-15. [Reprinted in Cargill *et al, O'Neill and his plays*, 1961.]
O'Neill is the most vigorous personality among all playwrights known to Europe, says Bab, and deserves at least some immortality for his tragedy of the proletariat.

BAKER, George Pierce. "O'Neill's first decade." *Yale Rev.*, ns, 15 (July 1926) 789-792. [Reprinted in Cargill *et al, O'Neill and his plays*, 1961.]
Review of O'Neill's first ten years by his erstwhile teacher. Now at middle of his career, says Baker, O'Neill should develop his material more imaginatively.

BAND, Muriel S. "O'Neill is back." *Mayfair*, Oct. 1946., p. 66.
Report of the press conference before *ICEMAN*, with O'Neill's views concerning America's failings.

*BASSO, Hamilton. "The tragic sense." *New Yorker*, 24 (28 Feb. 1948) 34; 24 (6 Mar. 1948) 34; 24 (13 Mar. 1948) 37.

The most extensive item to appear in any periodical, this typical *New Yorker* "profile" is written in straightforward reportorial style, without criticism or evaluation of O'Neill or his work. Part I gives a good account of the playwright's background, in many ways better than what Clark supplies in his several editons of *The Man and His Plays.* Part II lists and discusses all the plays. Part III deals with O'Neill's more recent life and closes with an interview expressing many of his personal views about his own work and the theatre. Basso makes the first announcement that the multi-play cycle, *A TALE OF POSSESSORS SELF-DISPOSSESSED,* had been destroyed.

*BENTLEY, Eric. "Trying to like O'Neill." *Kenyon Rev.,* 14 (July 1952) 476-492. [Reprinted in Bentley's *In search of theatre* and in the following: Cargill *et al, O'Neill and his plays,* 1961; Gassner, *O'Neill* (Twentieth Century Views series), 1964; Miller, *Playwright's progress,* 1965; and Raleigh, *Twentieth century interpretations of the Iceman Cometh,* 1968.]

Having been asked to assist in directing the German language version of *ICEMAN,* Bentley thought he began to see some good points in O'Neill's work. But the period of "liking" was soon over, for O'Neill's great intentions are never realized, says Bentley, and he achieves less the more he attempts, with his characters blown up in size by cultural and psychological gas. The final conclusion is, however, that if one dislikes O'Neill he actually dislikes our age, of which O'Neill is the representative. This essay, together with Krutch's introduction to *Nine plays* is a widely quoted criticism.

"Big run for O'Neill plays." *Life* 42 (24 June 1957) 108.

Illustrations from the many revivals and adaptations in current popularity, such as *LONG DAY'S JOURNEY, MISBEGOTTEN, POET,* and the musical version of *ANNA CHRISTIE, New Girl in Town.*

BIRD, Carol. "Eugene O'Neill—the inner man." *Theatre,* 39 (June 1924) 8.

This interview at the Provincetown Playhouse has particular interest because of its extended presentation of O'Neill's defense of his continued writing of the down-and-out.

BJORK, Lennart A. "The Swedish critical reception of O'Neill's post-humous plays." *Scan. Stud.*, 38 (Aug. 1966) 231-250.
Detailed review of Swedish acceptance of *JOURNEY, POET, HUGHIE, MANSIONS*.

BLACKBURN, Clara. "Continental influences on Eugene O'Neill's expressionistic drama." *Amer. Lit.*, 13 (May 1941) 109-133.
If "expressionistic drama" had been left out of the title the article would become clearer. Miss Blackburn finds many of O'Neill's plays have considerable Swedish and German influence. Carl Dahlstrom's "norms" for expressionism are used as points of departure, often much too literally. For instance, the simple battle of the sexes desplayed by Nina and Darrell in *INTERLUDE* is seen as "expressionism." Miss Blackburn frequently mistakes mere similarity for influence.

BODENHEIM, Maxwell. "Roughneck and romancer." *New Yorker*, 3 (6 Feb. 1926) 17-18. [Reprinted in Cargill *et al, O'Neill and his plays*, 1961.]
The first *New Yorker* "profile" (see Basso's 3-installment version) regrets O'Neill's apparent change from the prober of lower world rowdies and adventurers to more "highbrow" world of Mencken and Nathan.

BOWEN, Croswell. "The black Irishman." *PM*, 3 Nov. 1946. [Reprinted in Cargill *et al, O'Neill and his plays*, 1961.]
The main discussion centers around O'Neill's loss of faith early in life and his failure to regain it. Some good pictures of New London home and the O'Neill family. Most of the material here is available in earlier articles elsewhere. (See also Bowen's *Curse of the misbegotten*.)

————. "The greatest tragedy of Eugene O'Neill." *Look*, 23 (12 May 1959) 57.
Extensive passages, with photographs concerning O'Neill's family life, taken from Bowen's *Curse of the misbegotten*.

BOWLING, Charis C. "The touch of poetry: A study of the role of poetry in three O'Neill plays." *Coll. Lang. Assoc. Jour.*, 12 (Sept. 1968) 43-45.

Study of O'Neill's use of poetry in plot, character, development of theme in *POET, AH,WILDERNESS*, and *JOURNEY*. His use of quotations from Swinburne, Wilde, Kipling is regarded as important. Not a discussion of O'Neill as a poet.

BOYD, Ernest. "A great American dramatist." *Freeman*, 3 (6 July 1921) 404-405.

O'Neill's great ability is to create mood and atmosphere and great characters at expense of plot.

BOYNTON, Percy H. "American authors of today: X. The drama." *Eng. Jour.*, 12 (June 1923) 407-415.

This long treatment of the history of American playwriting concludes with a discussion of O'Neill as the man who embodies so much of modern theatrical and dramatic history in his own story.

BRASHEAR, William R. "O'Neill and Shaw: The play as will and idea." *Criticism*, 8 (Spring 1966) 155-169.

Interesting contrasts between treatments of themes found in Nietszche and Schopenhaur with Shaw emerging as great comic intellect, with O'Neill closer to tragedy in his ideas of hope in hopelessness.

————. " 'To-morrow' and 'Tomorrow': Conrad and O'Neill." *Renascence*, 20 (Autumn 1967) 18-21, 55.

Conrad's 1903 "To-morrow" and O'Neill's 1917 short story "Tomorrow" compared, but differences are considerable. Much speculation but little establishment of any close relationship between the two authors.

*BREESE, Jessie M. "Home on the dunes." *Country Life in America*, 45 (Nov. 1923) 72-76.

Detailed description of O'Neill's unique residence on Cape Cod's Peaked Hill Bars, including five excellent photographs of its interior and exterior.

BROCK, H. E. "O'Neill stirs the gods of the drama." NY *Times*, 15 Jan. 1928, V, p. 9.
Discussion of this amazing young man who commands audiences to do as he likes.

BROWN, Ivor. "American plays in England." *Am. Merc.*, 33 (Nov. 1934) 315-322.
An attempt to explain why O'Neill is not generally accepted in England. The English have an idea of America which O'Neill does not present, and he is therefore ignored.

BROWN, John Mason. "All O'Neilling." *Sat. R. Lit.*, 29 (19 Oct. 1946) 26. [Reprinted as "Moaning at the bar," in Brown's *Seeing more things*, 1948, and in his *Dramatis personae*, 1963.]
Combined review of *ICEMAN* and discussion of O'Neill's past work, which has always shown unmistakable courage and the single theme of the relationship of man to the universe.

————. "American tragedy." *Sat. R. Lit.*, 32 (6 Aug. 1949) 124-127. [Reprinted in Brown's *Still seeing things*, 1950, and his *Dramatis personae*, 1963.]
The need for tragedy today, in its exaltation of Man, is great. O'Neill sensed it, and despite shortcomings and lack of language, did exalt man, finding happiness not in the happy ending but in the tragic concept of the greater nobility of man. All of his plays have been in the Greek and Elizabethan concept of tragedy.

————. "Eugene O'Neill, 1888-1953." *Sat. R.* 36 (19 Dec. 1953) 26-28. [Reprinted in Brown's *Dramatis personae*, 1963, as "O'Neill in retrospect."]
Regardless of how high he aspired and how low he fell, O'Neill was never afraid to face and attack any theme he felt would forward his tragic theme. Wonder expressed that America, the land of laughter, should put forth the only major modern tragic writer.

————. "The present day dilemma of Eugene O'Neill." NY *Post*, 19 Nov. 1932.
In his greatest victories, O'Neill has met defeat in his inability

to keep in contact with the type of play he originally conceived, turning now from rough life of sea to the drawing room of Freud and Jung. Brown finds O'Neill's essay on masks in the *Spectator* (see Non-Dramatic O'Neill) hard to take. It seems to mark the decline of a great original power.

BRUSTEIN, Robert. "Why American plays are not literature." *Harpers*, 219 (Oct. 1959) 167-172.

O'Neill is included in a discussion of the serious shortcomings of American literary drama, including such aspects as O'Neill's own "inarticulacy."

BUNZEL, P. "O'Neill: A tragic epilogue to the drama." *Life*, 53 (26 Oct. 1962) 70B-72.

Popular account of the tragic family life of the O'Neills, with special attention to Eugene O'Neill, Jr., who was the writer's teacher at Princeton.

BURRILL, Edgar W. "Eugene O'Neill." *Drama Calendar*, 10 (3 Apr. 1928) 2.

A review of significant plays to this date, praising the tragic view and O'Neill's "ring of eternal verities."

BURTON, Katherine. "Aldous Huxley and other moderns." *Cath. Wld.*, 139 (Aug. 1934) 552-556.

This article on *Brave new world* includes discussion of O'Neill's ideas about machine worship.

CALDWELL, Marguerite J. "Teaching reading through a play: Ah, Wilderness!" *Jour. of Reading*, 11 (Nov. 1967) 105-110.

Use of this play to demonstrate how to teach high school students literary expression and appreciation.

CARB, David. "Eugene O'Neill." *Vogue*, 68 (15 Sept. 1926) 100.

O'Neill's position as our first dramatist comes from his daring to be himself and a sense of theatre unequalled by contemporaries.

CARPENTER, Frederic I. "Eugene O'Neill, the Orient, and American

transcendentalism." *Trancendentalism*, 60 (1966) 204-214.
(Search of three major university libraries and the New York Public failed to secure copy of this issue.)

————. "The romantic tragedy of Eugene O'Neill." *Coll. Eng.*, 6 (Feb. 1945) 250-258.
Carpenter regards O'Neill's belief in the unattainably perfect life as basically romantic. *LAZARUS, INTERLUDE, ELECTRA* discussed as a trilogy showing the development in O'Neill's attitude from the assertion of romantic perfection, through the inability to gain it, to the tragic despair in failure.

CERF, Bennett. "Three new plays." *Sat. R. Lit.*, 29 (23 Feb. 1946) 26.
Discussion of some of O'Neill's projected plays.

*CERF, Walter. "Psychoanalysis and the realistic drama." *Jour. of Aesthetics & Art Criticism*, 16 (Mar. 1958) 328-336.
Taking Laurents' *A Clearing in the woods* and O'Neill's *JOURNEY*, Cerf attempts to show that modern realism cannot successfully convey "psychoanalytically guided retrospection" and that the impact of a play like *JOURNEY* is not good drama because in this retrospect there is no place for Aristotle's "peripity," or sudden turn, so essential to good drama.

CHAITIN, Norman C. "The power of daring." *Mod. Dr.*, 3 (Dec. 1960) 231-241.
Eulogy to an artist who dared to experiment, to abandon conventional tricks, to fly through the air. "The most American of our playwrights, and the most universal."

CHASE, R. "English elective: O'Neill: A journey into light." *Eng. Jour.*, 61 (May 1972) 649-652.

CHEN, David Y. "Two Chinese adaptations of Eugene O'Neill's Jones." *Mod. Dr.*, 9 (Feb. 1967) 431-439.
Demonstration of O'Neill's strong and direct influence on the

Yama Chao 1922 and *The Wild* 1937, two distinctly expressionistic Chinese plays.

CHIAROMONTE, Nicola. "Eugene O'Neill (1958)." *Sewanee Rev.*, 68 (Summer 1960) 494-501.

Summarizing O'Neill's artistic achievements finds that despite the many weaknesses he emerges as the "most original playwright after Pirandello."

CHURCHILL, Allen. "Portrait of a Nobel prize winner as a bum." *Esquire* 47 (June 1957) 98-101.

Popular review of the influences behind O'Neill from the earliest days as a waterfront derelict until his death.

CLARK, Barrett H. "Eugene O'Neill, a chapter in biography." *Th. Arts*, 10 (May 1926) 325-326.

Excerpts from Clark's first edition of *Eugene O'Neill*.

CLURMAN, Harold. "At odds with gentility." *Nation*, 194 (7 Apr. 1962) 312.

In discussion of Alexander's *Tempering of Eugene O'Neill* and the Gelbs' biography O'Neill is discussed as man and artist attempting to understand himself, his family, his time, and his country.

————. "O'Neill revived." *New Rep.* 126 (4 Feb. 1952) 22-23.

O'Neill is an artist of deep personal feeling and a playwright of high order, despite certain lacks as a writer.

COHN, Ruby. "Absurdity in English: Joyce and O'Neill." *Comp. Dr.*, 3 (Fall 1969) 156-161.

HUGHIE dramatizes the "prototypical absurdist situation—man's confrontation with mortality."

COLE, Lester, and John Howard Lawson. "Two views on O'Neill." *Masses and Mainstream*, 7 (June 1954) 56-63.

Discussion of whether or not O'Neill has merit in view of Marxist criticism.

COLEMAN, Alta M. "Personality portraits: No. 3. Eugene O'Neill." *Theatre*, 31 (April 1920) 264.

This is the first acknowledgement given this "suddenly acclaimed" young writer by Arthur Hornblow's *Theatre* magazine, the "prestige" stage publication of its day. The article is a review of facts about O'Neill's life and writings.

COLUM, Mary M. "Drama of the disintegrated." *Forum*, 94 (Dec. 1935) 358.

O'Neill brings his characters to life; they have disintegrated, but cling to sanity. Compared to these, Shaw's characters are mere abstractions.

CONRAD, Lawrence H. "Eugene O'Neill." *The Landmark*, 11 (July 1929) 413-416.

Whatever it is O'Neill is trying in theatre, it is of tremendous significance.

*COOK, Jim. "A long tragic journey." NY *Post*, 2 Dec. 1956.

The important part of this brief sketch of O'Neill's life is an interview with his first wife, the former Kathleen Jenkins, Mrs. George Pitt-Smith of Little Neck, L.I. She lived with O'Neill for only a few days and in this article cannot recount much of their brief life together, although she does wonder why she is not even mentioned in *LONG DAY'S JOURNEY*. The article also includes some material on O'Neill's son Shane, whose dissolute life in many ways paralleled that of his father.

COOPER, Grace. "Laurel wreaths." NY *Telegraph*, 9 Oct. 1927.

Review of pertinent but well-known facts of O'Neill's life and some comments on *DYNAMO* and *INTERLUDE*.

CORBIN, John. "The one-act play." NY *Times*, 19 May 1918, IV, 8:1.

This is the earliest "critical " reference to O'Neill in the *Times*. Discussing the demise of the Washington Square Players, Corbin states that one of their "highest results" was the introduction of O'Neill's one-act plays.

―――. "O'Neill and Aeschylus." *Sat. R. Lit.*, 8 (30 Apr. 1932) 693-695. [Reprinted in Walter, Erich A., ed., *Essay annual*, NY, 1933, p. 159.]

Corbin believes a possible reason for O'Neill's decline of creative powers can be found in his increased interests in technical stunts and morbid psychology. *ELECTRA* is not Aeschylus, and even Freud would disapprove of this exploration of the mental underworld.

*"Counsels of despair." *Times Lit. Supp.* (London), 10 Apr. 1948, pp. 197-199. [Reprinted in Cargill *et al*, *O'Neill and his plays*, 1961, and in Miller, *Playwright's progress*, 1965.]

Written after publication of *ICEMAN* in London. One of the most bitter and devastating attacks on O'Neill's plays ever to be published, ranking far beyond Geddes' "melodramadness" or Kemelman's "highbrow melodrama." The anonymous author finds O'Neill juvenile, puerile, contemptuous of fellow man, of church and society, obsessed with undisciplined emotions and jejune opinions, regarding human beings without love. The award of the Nobel Prize was "capricious."

COWLEY, Malcolm. "Eugene O'Neill, writer of synthetic drama." *Brentano's Book Chat*, 5 (July-Aug. 1926) 17-21.

Account of O'Neill's Hell Hole days, of which Cowley himself knew. Review of O'Neill's attempts to break from the conventional forms. Does not approve of these later tendencies as in *BROWN*.

―――. "A weekend with Eugene O'Neill." *Reporter*, 17 (5 Sept. 1957) 33-36. [Reprinted in Cargill *et al*, *O'Neill and his plays*, 1961.]

Intimate glimpses of O'Neill's domestic life at Brook Farm, Ridgefield, Conn., in 1923.

CRAWFORD, Jack. "Eugene O'Neill: A Broadway philosopher." *Drama*, 12 (Jan. 1922) 117.

O'Neill is shown as a man with a philosophy, literary courage and originality. Crawford does not seem quite sure whether or not O'Neill's philosophy is intentional.

CRICHTON, Kyle. "Mr. O'Neill and the iceman." *Collier's*, 118 (26 Oct. 1946) 18.

A popular entertaining interview in O'Neill's NY apartment prior to *ICEMAN*. Writer finds O'Neill "less like a ghost than would be imagined."

CUMMINGS, Ridgley. "Hail, sailor, and farewell." *Am. Mer.*, 78 (May 1954) 45-46.

Upon hearing of O'Neill's death, this writer tells how it felt when he himself was a bum on the waterfront and how he enjoyed reading O'Neill's plays.

CURLEY, Thomas. F. "The vulgarity of Eugene O'Neill." *Commonweal*, 83 (14 Jan. 1966) 443-446.

Much of the exhilaration experienced from O'Neill's plays comes from the vulgarity itself. Central characters are not heroes or villains, but they are representatively vulgar people, shown in speech and action by which they suffer and endure.

DAICHES, David. "Mourning becomes O'Neill." *Encounter*, 16 (June 1961) 74-78.

DALE, Alan. "On the rebound back to Broadway, with its bad plays, from 'cult' pieces." NY *American*, 12 Mar. 1922.

Dale strongly attacks plays like *FIRST MAN* and *STRAW*, with their "slice of life, birth, death, and tuberculosis. Why not portray cirrhosis of the liver, or stage a post-mortem?"

DAWBER, Thomas C. "Strindberg and O'Neill." *Players*, 45 (Apr.-May 1970) 183-185.

Citing studies of Strindberg's influence by Winther, Hayward, and Fleisher, this critic concludes most influence lies in style and expressionistic techniques. Very little discussion of Strindberg's battle of the sexes so apparent in the early plays.

*DE CASSERES, Benjamin. "Eugene O'Neill—from Cardiff to Xanadu." *Theatre*, 46 (Aug. 1927) 10.
O'Neill's friend and vigorous champion outlines several aspects of O'Neill's ideas. De Casseres' praise is highly eulogistic and must be taken with reservation.

*_____. "Eugene O'Neill—a vignette." *Popular Biography*, 1 (April 1930) 31-38.
A eulogy, rather than a vignette, showing O'Neill as a man who has been to hell, whose life is an epic of will.

_____. "The psychology of O'Neill." *Arts & Dec.*, 35 (Oct. 1931) 82.
A summation of O'Neill's apparent psychological themes. The most moving and lasting are to be found in *LAZARUS*, while all are summed up in *ELECTRA*.

*_____. "The triumphant genius of Eugene O'Neill." *Theatre*, 47 (Feb. 1928) 12. [Reprinted in Miller, *Playwright's progress*, 1965.]
Extravagant, hysterical praise for *INTERLUDE, MARCO, LAZARUS*. "The genius of O'Neill evolves naturally, rhythmically, and masterfully like a colossal symphony."

DE POLO, Harold. "Meet Eugene O'Neill, fisherman." *Outdoor America*, 6 (May 1928) 5-8.
Informal account of Maine fishing trip with O'Neill and wife.

DE PUE, Elva. "The tragedy of O'Neill." *The Figure in the Carpet*, No. 4, May 1928, pp. 18-25. (Known as *Salient* after this issue.)
The shortcomings of recent O'Neill plays come from a deficient language, a proneness to repetition, and a lack of the real unexpectedness, richness and glamor of life.

DEUTSCH, Helen, and Stella Hanau. "Flashlights of theatrical history—The old Provincetown." *Th. Guild Mag.*, 8 (Aug. 1931) 20-21; 8 (Sept. 1931) 30.

Brief passages concerning early days at MacDougal Street from the book, *The Provincetown.*

————. "When the Provincetown group began." *Drama*, 21 (June 1931) 3.

Excerpts from first chapter of *The Provincetown.*

*DE VOTO, Bernard. "Minority report." *Sat. R. Lit.*, 15 (21 Nov. 1936) 3. [Reprinted as "Monte Cristo in modern dress" in De Voto's *Minority report*, 1943; in Cargill *et al*, *O'Neill and his plays*, 1961; and in Miller, *Playwright's progress*, 1965.]

Sharp disagreement not only with the Nobel award but with the recognition of O'Neill as a great dramatist. By DeVoto's standards, O'Neill has given us only great theatre, never great drama.

DOBREE, Bonamy. "The plays of Eugene O'Neill." *Southern Rev.*, 2 (Winter 1937) 435-446.

This English critic analyzes O'Neill's style and finds the playwright unable to overcome adolescent emotions. Despite great powers, fate is never inevitable, and too obviously man-made.

DONOGHUE, Denis. "The human image in modern drama." *Lugano Rev.*, 1 (1965) 155-168.

DOWNER, Alan S. "Eugene O'Neill as poet of the theatre." *Th. Arts*, 35 (Feb. 1951) 22-23.

Poetry of theatre is not necessarily the poetry of the printed word, as evidenced by the patterns and rhythms of O'Neill.

DOYLE, Louis F. "The myth of Eugene O'Neill." *Renascence*, 17 (Winter 1964) 59-62.

A broad generalized attack on O'Neill's competence as a writer and a theatre artist. Critic finds very little of worth, noting that the various prizes awarded meant nothing at all. The myth that O'Neill restored tragedy to the American drama will "die hard," since what he really restored was melodrama in false whiskers. This brief but intense attack bears comparison with Geddes' *Melodramadness* and the anonymous London *Times* "Counsels of Despair."

————. "O'Neill redivius." *America* 98 (2 Nov. 1957) 137-138.
Reviewing O'Neill's past in view of his popular revival, Doyle finds only *JONES* and *APE* great drama. He deplores the later autobiographical plays, defends the elder James O'Neill as one who really knew theatre, which the son did not. Finds O'Neill's final critical status, like Shaw's, undecided.

*DRIVER, Tom F. "On the late plays of Eugene O'Neill." *Tulane Dr. Rev.*, 3 (Dec. 1958) 8-20. [Reprinted in Gassner, *O'Neill* (Twentieth century views), 1964.]
Believing O'Neill does not write true tragedy as Krutch and Nathan see it, Driver chooses *JOURNEY, ICEMAN* and *POET* to show that O'Neill's later mood was a combination of Romanticism and Stoicism. He disagrees with O'Neill's assertion that life is merely an inevitable progression toward death, but he feels the grandeur and imagination of O'Neill makes the rest of our theatre "petite and timid."

DUNKEL, W. D. "Theology in the theatre." *Theology Today* 16 (Apr. 1959) 65-73.

EASTMAN, Fred. "Eugene O'Neill and religion." *Christ. Cent.*, 50 (26 July 1933) 955-957.
In Eastman's opinion, O'Neill will not become immortal as a great dramatist until he achieves a religious viewpoint. The preaching against sin and the devil never seems to recognize the help of higher grace.

EATON, Walter Prichard. "The American drama flowers: Eugene O'Neill as a great playwright." *World's Work*, 53 (Nov. 1926) 105-108.
With the publication of Clark's *Eugene O'Neill* Eaton believes O'Neill has achieved major status as the first contributor to a native dramatic literature.

*————. "The hermit of Cape Cod." NY *Her-Trib.*, 8 Jan. 1928.
    A highly favorable critical appraisal of O'Neill's "natural rebell-
ion" against theatrical convention. O'Neill is compared somewhat in
extravagance to Emerson and Thoreau.

*————. "O'Neill: New risen attic stream?" *Amer. Scholar*, 6
(Summer 1937) 304-312.
    A discussion of O'Neill's approach to good and evil and his plays
in the Greek tradition, especially *DESIRE*. Eaton makes the interesting
point that *ELECTRA*, most Greek in form, is possibly less Greek in
spirit than many others.

————. "Where is the American theatre going?" *World's Work*, 52
(Aug. 1926) 461-465.
    While American drama exhibits no special direction, O'Neill's
sincerity as a sensitive artist shows some indication of a tendency
toward the spiritual.

————. "Why America lacks big playwrights." *Theatre*, 32 (Dec.
1920) 346.
    Success of *HORIZON* shows our lack of playwrights of real
individualism, because the public generally approves only the
"popular" writer.

EDEL, Leon. "Eugene O'Neill: The face and the mask." *Univ. of
Toronto Quar.*, 7 (Oct. 1937) 18-34.
    The Nobel award is seen as belated crowning for past achieve-
ments, since O'Neill no longer writes for the present.

EMMANUEL, Sister Mary, RSM. "Why O'Neill?" *Eng. Journ.*, 55
(Sept. 1966) 710-713.
    A plea to include more drama beyond Shakespeare, and specifi-
cally O'Neill, in the secondary school study of drama.

ENANDER, Hilma. "Eugene O'Neill—his place in the sun." *Theatre*,
43 (Jan. 1926) 7.

This critic finds it difficult to evaluate the man and the plays separately, but has no doubt that O'Neill has elements of greatness which will put American drama in its proper place.

ENGEL, Edwin A. "Eugene O'Neill's long day's journey into light." *Mich. Alum. Quar. Rev.* 63 (1957) 348-354.

Taking *ICEMAN, JOURNEY* and *MISBEGOTTEN*, Engle shows how O'Neill has faced himself and his past in his last plays to show he has at last given "love an ascendancy over peace" (the peace of death) and reveals that the "sickness of today" at which he always stated his plays were digging was, in reality, his own sickness.

―――. "Ideas in the plays of Eugene O'Neill." *English Institute Essays,* n.v. 1964, 101-124.

STRANGE INTERLUDE, ICEMAN, and *JOURNEY* discussed in this essay on O'Neill's dramatic presentation of ideas.

―――. "O'Neill, 1960." *Mod. Dr.,* 3 (Dec. 1960) 219-223.

O'Neill held to be more alive today than a decade or two ago. Lasting fame lies in pattern of religious theme of earlier plays and greatness of *ICEMAN* and *JOURNEY*, the latter "his most genuine tragedy."

―――. "The theatre of today: Eugene O'Neill." *Chrysalis,* 6 (1953) No. 9-10, pp. 3-11.

A general review of O'Neill's entry into the writing of American drama.

ERVINE, St. John. "Is O'Neill's power in decline?" *Theatre,* 43 (May 1926) 12.

Ervine finds indications of decline in O'Neill's reduction of his people to absolute bestiality. (See rebuttal by Frank H. Freed.)

―――. "Literary taste in America." *New Rep.* 24 (6 Oct. 1920) 144-147.

An article on American poets, novelists and other writers by this famous Irish dramatist. O'Neill and the Cape Cod group are "trying to create an American drama that cannot be mistaken for any other than an American drama."

*————. "Mr. Eugene O'Neill." *Observer* (London) 31 Oct. 1926, p. 15.

Reviewing *BROWN* and others, along with Clark's *Eugene O'Neill*, Ervine states O'Neill will not be an accomplished dramatist and live up to his tremendous ability until he stops being a faddist and settles down to a definite style. Ervine's attitude differs markedly from those who praise O'Neill for *refusing* to be a faddist.

————. "Our playwrights as Europe sees them." *Theatre*, 43 (Feb. 1926) 12.

This discussion of the negligible influence of American plays in Europe shows that O'Neill has started no new movement in technique, despite his familiarity overseas.

"A Eugene O'Neill miscellany." NY *Sun*, 12 Jan. 1928.

An interview which gives a few of O'Neill's personal reactions to his own favorite plays.

"Eugene O'Neill, newest of the Guilders." *Van. F.*, 29 (Nov. 1927) 73.

Upon O'Neill's first production by the Guild, this article offers brief comment as he returns from Bermuda for the production of *MARCO*.

"Eugene O'Neill talks of his own plays." NY *Her-Trib.*, 16 Nov. 1924.

Anonymous interviewer tells of O'Neill's opinions on expressionism and his determination to use it in order to get his message across.

"Eugene O'Neill's teacher." NY *Times*, 12 Dec. 1936, 18:4.

Report of O'Neill's Nobel prize acceptance speech which gives credit to Strindberg. (O'Neill did not go to Stockholm himself.)

*FAGIN, N. Bryllion. "Eugene O'Neill." *Antioch Rev.*, 14 (March 1954) 14-26.

An evaluation of O'Neill shortly after his death looks at the over-exaggerated praise he received at first and the undervalued reputation of later years. Reviewing many of the plays, Fagin determines that O'Neill, while imperfect, can still be powerfully disturbing in this generation.

*———. "Eugene O'Neill contemplates mortality." *Open Court*, 45 (April 1931) 208-219. [Reprinted in Cargil *et al*, *O'Neill and his plays*, 1961.]

This periodical is devoted to "the science of religion, the religion of science, and the extension of the religious parliament idea." Fagin finds that O'Neill has a positive approach to the question of what life is; namely that it is a matter of endless continuity and no death. (Most critics, of course, are disturbed by O'Neill's *lack* of positive approach.)

———. " 'Freud' on the American stage." *Ed. Th. Journ.* 2 (Dec. 1950) 296-305.

Discussion of themes from *Suppressed Desires* to *Cocktail Party*. O'Neill found to be preoccupied with morbid psychological "obsession" from *DIFF'RENT* to *ICEMAN*.

*FALK, Doris. "That paradox, O'Neill." *Mod. Dr.*, 6 (Dec. 1963) 221-238.

Significant exploration of O'Neill's seeming paradoxes as seen in subject and treatment of major plays—the exhibitionist hiding behind masks to conceal himself, totally aware of all standard tricks and devices of the theatre, using them to scorn those writers who use and audiences who appreciate them.

FALK, Signi. "Dialogue in the plays of Eugene O'Neill." *Mod. Dr.*, 3 (Dec. 1960) 314-325.

Numerous examples from early one-acters to *JOURNEY* to show most of the shortcomings and successes of O'Neill's many varieties of dialogue.

FEDO, David. "In defense of Eugene O'Neill." *Boston Univ. Jour.*, 18 (1970) 30-35.

"Fellow student thought O'Neill 'very likable.'" NY *Her-Trib.*, 9 Jan. 1927.
Facts about O'Neill's early experience in Baker's class. Compare this with John Weaver's account.

*FERGUSSON, Francis. "Eugene O'Neill." *Hound and Horn,* 3 (Jan.-March 1930) 145-160. [Reprinted in Zabel, Morton, ed., *Literary opinion in America,* 1937, 1951 and in Cargil *et al, O'Neill and his plays,* 1961, as "Melodramatist."]
Fergusson criticizes O'Neill for his inability to make his characters a true part of the play alone, because of being too closely identified with O'Neill himself. This article is one of the most widely cited essays on O'Neill up to this time.

FINDLAY, Robert R. "The Emperor Jones: O'Neill as scene designer." *Players,* 45 (Oct-Nov. 1969) 21-24.
Scene by scene analysis, with eight line sketches of appropriate setting for each, noting O'Neill's acute sense of values and effects of line, color, light, and other theatrical devices.

FISKIN, A. M. "The basic unity of Eugene O'Neill." *Writers of Our Years,* Univ. of Denver Studies in Humanities, No. 1, 1950 (no further issues) p. 101.
An attempt to relate all of O'Neill's plays up to *ICEMAN* as parts of a consistent viewpoint, mainly that of Being and Becoming. Plays fall into three groups: obsession, view of the universe involving a naturalistic mysticism, and the human beings in action within the metaphysical system set up.

FLEISHER, Frederic. "Strindberg and O'Neill." *Symposium,* 10 (Spring 1956) 84-93.
Carefully documented account of Strindberg's influence on O'Neill in subject matter, dramatic style, themes, and so forth. Plays, dialogue compared to show resemblances. General conclusion, how-

ever, is that O'Neill was not as influenced by Strindberg as he was by Nietzsche.

―――――― and Horst Frenz. "Eugene O'Neill and the Royal Dramatic Theatre of Stockholm: The later phase." *Mod. Dr.*, 10 (Dec. 1967) 300-311.
 Review of Swedish productions beginning with *MISBEGOTTEN* in 1953 through *JOURNEY, POET, HUGHIE,* and *MANSIONS* in 1962.

FRANCIS, Eugene. "The O'Neill tragedy." *Am. Weekly,* 17 Dec. 1950, pp. 4-5.
 A comparison, shortly after his suicide, of the violent life of Eugene, Jr., with the father's tragedies.

FREED, Frank H. "Eugene O'Neill in the ascendant." *Theatre,* 44 (Oct. 1926) 30.
 A rebuttal to St. John Ervine's assertion of O'Neill's decline. Freed maintains that tremendous effect of *BROWN* has everything in it which Ervine desires in a good play.

FREEDMAN, Morris. "O'Neill and contemporary American drama." *Col. Eng.,* 23 (Apr. 1962) 570-574.
 Failure of modern American drama lies in "its uncomfortable relation to O'Neill" who reveals most of the failings of others. Seriousness and concern for theme and subject matter make O'Neill's drama important.

FRENZ, Horst. "Eugene O'Neill in France." *Books Abroad,* 18 (Spring 1944) 140-141.
 Brief review of O'Neill's success in France.

―――――. "Eugene O'Neill in Russia." *Poet Lore,* 49 (Autumn 1943) 241-247.
 Review of the popularity of American writers in Russia, such as Twain and O'Neill. O'Neill himself liked the Russian productions of *DESIRE, CHILLUN,* and others.

————. "Eugene O'Neill's plays printed abroad." *Col. Eng.*, 5 (March 1944) 340-341.

Frenz's list of foreign publication in *Bulletin of Bibliography* is better.

————. "A list of foreign editions and translations of Eugene O'Neill's dramas." *Bulletin of Bibliography*, 18 (1943) 33-34.

A listing of the major foreign editions of O'Neill's plays.

*————. "Notes on Eugene O'Neill in Japan." *Mod. Dr.*, 3 (Dec. 1960) 306-313.

Comprehensive review of the considerable quantity of critical material in Japan as far back as early 1920's. A valuable bibliographical reference.

GASSNER, John. "Eugene O'Neill: The course of a modern dramatist." *Critique: Critical Rev. of Th. Arts* 1 (Feb. 1958) 5-14. [Reprinted in Gassner's *Theatre at the crossroads*, 1960; and in revised version of his *O'Neill* (Twentieth century views), 1964.]

In light of the revived interest in O'Neill, Gassner reviews his artistic career in an attempt to evaluate his position as a modern dramatist. Gassner concludes that no other dramatist of this century has approached O'Neill's "dark and disturbing impressiveness."

————. "Homage to Eugene O'Neill." *Theatre Time*, 3 (Summer 1951) 17-21. [Reprinted in Cargill *et al*, *O'Neill and his plays*, 1961.]

Considerable disappointment at the lack of interest of the younger theatre generation in this man who wrestled with demons instead of pigmies. This survey of O'Neill's work attempts to give him the stature that Gassner thinks a writer of his passion deserves.

*————. "The possibilities and perils of modern tragedy." *Tulane Dr. Rev.*, 3 (June 1957) 3-15. [Reprinted in Corrigan, *Theatre in the twentieth century*, 1963, pp. 215-228; and in Gassner and Allen, *Theatre and drama in the making*, pp. 985-991.]

Originally an Amos Taylor, Jr., Memorial Lecture, Johns Hopkins Univ., 20 Jan. 1957. Although O'Neill is not considered individually, this is an important essay on the prospects of whether or not modern tragedy can be written. Many contemporary writers, including Eliot, Miller, Anderson, as well as O'Neill, are included. Conclusion: tragedies of one kind or another have contributed to the modern theatre, but perhaps we will have to "stress the perils rather than the possibilities."

————. "There is no American drama." *Th. Arts,* 36 (Sept. 1952) 24-25.

The "new critics" says Gassner, insisting on comparison of American dramatic effort to that of Europe, find little in our modern drama. This is a sterile approach, he concludes.

GEDDES, Virgil. "Eugene O'Neill." *Th. Arts,* 15 (Nov. 1931) 943-946.

A typical Geddes approach to O'Neill—strongly negative. The plays have no real dramatic sense but make use of the devices of the bad dramatist in tricks of the theatre which do not convey dramatic emotion.

GELB, Arthur. "O'Neill's hopeless hope for a giant cycle." *NY Times,* 29 Sept. 1958, II, 1:4.

Factual account of the development of the ideas for *TALE OF POSSESSORS* upon the opening of *POET,* the only play of the cycle to survive suitable for production.

————. "Onstage he played the novelist." NY *Times Book Rev.* 30 Aug. 1964.

In reviewing Yale edition of *MANSIONS* and Random House edition of *Lost plays,* Gelb discusses in some detail O'Neill's regard for the playscript as a piece of literature not unlike a novel, rather than merely an acting script.

———— and Barbara Gelb. "As O'Neill saw the theatre." NY *Times Mag.,* 12 Nov. 1961, p. 32.

Numerous excerpts from O'Neill letters and statements in interviews giving his opinion on drama and theatre.

*————. "Start of a long day's journey: The New London youth of Eugene O'Neill." *Horizon*, 2 (Mar. 1960) 25-40.

Lengthy and detailed account by these major biographers, with excellent illustrations of O'Neill's boyhood and youth in New London.

————. "Time out from tragedy." *Sports Ill.*, 16 (2 Apr. 1962) E7-E10.

Discussion of O'Neill the sports enthusiast, including six-day bicycle racing, baseball, boxing, and his own excellent swimming.

GIEROW, Karl-Ragnar. "Eugene O'Neill's posthumous plays." *World Th.*, 7 (Spring 1958) 46-52. [Reprinted in Cargill *et al, O'Neill and his plays*, 1961.]

The director of the Stockholm Royal Theatre discusses the Cycle and its contents and O'Neill's plans which never materialized. Also revealed for the first time are facts concerning O'Neill's nervous trembling which had afflicted him most of his life and which was definitely not Parkinson's disease, as commonly assumed.

GRANGER, Bruce Ingham. "Illusion and reality in Eugene O'Neill." *Mod. Lang. Notes*, 73 (March 1958) 179-186.

Extended evidence from most of the plays to show how O'Neill consistently discussed his belief that the dilemma of modern man involves his inability to get order out of chaos without illusion, which in turn incapacitates him for meaningful action.

GRANT, Neil F. "The American theatre in England." *Atlantic*, 137 (Feb. 1926) 418-423.

O'Neill is mainly responsible for the rise in literary value of American plays in England. Grant sees American influence increasing, a somewhat different view from St. John Ervine who finds no influence whatever.

GRAUEL, George E. "A decade of American drama." *Thought*, 15 (Sept. 1940) 398-419.

In a review of the 1930's O'Neill is discussed as one who "sees conjunction of spiritual forces in the problem of evil," with *DAYS WITHOUT END* as climactic in its stormy, emphatic final assertion.

GROFF, Edward. "Point of view in modern drama." *Mod. Dr.*, 2 (Dec. 1959) 268-282.

O'Neill briefly discussed with Miller in section entitled "Point of View in the Drama of the Inner Life."

HALASZ, George. "Crowds fame into 40 years." *Brook. Eagle*, 25 March 1928.

Newspaper supplement article on O'Neill's life and fame, acquired in so short a time.

HALL, Philip G., "Dramatic irony in Mourning Becomes Electra." *South. Sp. Jour.*, 30 (1965) 42-55.

HALLINE, Allan Gates. "American dramatic theory comes of age." *Bucknell Univ. Studies*, 1 (June 1949) 1-11.

O'Neill leaves something to be desired in proportion and comprehensiveness.

HALMAN, Doris F. "O'Neill and the untrained playwright." *Writer*, 40 (July 1928) 215-217.

Miss Halman gives firm warning to aspiring writers that O'Neill's genius transcends, rather than benefits by, theatrical tricks. They cannot be used to cover a shoddy plot.

*HAMILTON, Clayton. "A shelf of printed plays." *Bookman*, 41 (Apr. 1915) 182. [Reprinted in Cargill *et al, O'Neill and his plays*, 1961.]

Under "Playwrights of Promise" Hamilton writes the only known review of O'Neill's first book, *THIRST and Other One Act Plays*. He finds the favorite mood is horror. (Hamilton, a friend of the O'Neill family, had urged James O'Neill to finance publication of this book.)

*HAMILTON, Gladys. "Untold tales of Eugene O'Neill." *Th. Arts*, 40 (Aug. 1956) 31-32. [Reprinted in Cargill *et al, O'Neill and his plays*, 1961, as "O'Neill's debt to Clayton Hamilton".]

Recollections of the youthful O'Neill written by Mrs. Clayton Hamilton. She describes him at New London in 1914-1915 as the inarticulate, unobstrusive young man who did not wish his silences disturbed. Quotations from O'Neill's letters to Hamilton show gratitude for his help and guidance, especially because Hamilton urged James O'Neill to send his son to Harvard.

*HANSFORD, Montiville M. "O'Neill as the stage never sees him." Boston *Transcript*, 22 March 1930.
Hansford lived with O'Neill for several years during the writing of *BROWN, INTERLUDE,* and *LAZARUS.* He admits the almost impossible task of presenting the man on paper. His report is one of the better personal recollections and avoids the pitfalls of "explaining" O'Neill through childhood influences and social backgrounds.

HARTMAN, Murray. "Strindberg and O'Neill." *Ed. Th. Jour.,* 18 (Oct. 1966) 216-223.
Discussion of similar intellectual background, childhood feeling of rejection, Oedipal obsessions, love-hate between men and women, etc.

*HASTINGS, Warren H., and Richard F. Weeks. "Episodes of Eugene O'Neill's undergraduate days at Princeton." *Princeton Univ. Library Chron.,* 29 (Spring 1968) 208-215.
Reminiscences by two classmates from 1910 desiring to clear the inaccuracies and misconceptions concerning O'Neill at Princeton. Seen as a loner who did not squander all his time, much spent in reading. Stone-throwing episode explained (it was neither President's house nor station-master's house, but just a house), for which he was not expelled, but merely suspended. Friends note a streak of genius, even madness.

"Haunting recollections of life with a genius." *Life,* 45 (25 Aug. 1958) 55-56.
Ten pictures of O'Neill and his family from Agnes Boulton's own collection, printed at time of publication of *Part of a long story.* Comments by Miss Boulton make this a valuable collection hitherto unavailable.

HAWTHORNE, Hildegarde. "The art of Eugene O'Neill." NY *Times*, 13 Aug. 1922, III, 7:1.

Miss Hawthorne is impressed by O'Neill's originality and power, although she sees a note of hysteria in his work. He has been too long with sick people.

HAYES, Richard. "Eugene O'Neill: The tragic in exile." *Th. Arts*, 47 (Oct. 1963) 16-17. [Reprinted in Gassner, *O'Neill* (Twentieth century views), 1964.]

Discussion of why the plays, in words of C. S. Lewis, are "the tragic in exile," "rejected by cultured people and abandoned to the masses."

*HAYWARD, Ira N. "Strindberg's influence on Eugene O'Neill." *Poet Lore*, 39 (Winter 1928) 596-604.

Comparison of styles in language, character, technique between the two playwrights. The language of *BROWN* and *FOUNTAIN* is poetic, according to Hayward, a view not widely shared with others.

HELBURN, Theresa. "O'Neill: An impression." *Sat. R. Lit.*, 15 (21 Nov. 1936) 10.

Personal impressions by this Guild member who places O'Neill on a parallel with Lindbergh in his courage, conviction and strength, and desire to be alone, the "lone eagle" in his profession.

HENDERSON, Archibald. "Two moderns." *Va. Quar. Rev.*, 5 (Jan. 1929) 133-136.

Discussion of Shaw, past his zenith; O'Neill, the emotional adventurer; and Pirandello, the fantastic intellectual, as top men in the drama today.

HERBERT, Edward T. "Eugene O'Neill: An evaluation by fellow playwrights." *Mod. Dr.*, 6 (Dec. 1963) 239-240.

Paul Green, Thornton Wilder, Sean O'Casey, Arthur Miller, Clifford Odets all quoted briefly concerning O'Neill's influence on their works, ranging from "a lot" by Green to none in particular by Wilder.

HICKS, Granville. "From a black abyss, a man and artist." *Sat. Rev.*, 45 (7 Apr. 1962) 16.

Reviewing the Gelbs' biography, this critic finds it enables us to realize how O'Neill, who in many ways was not an admirable man, was able to "look steadily into the black abyss of his inner life" which became his triumph as man and artist.

*HIGHSMITH, James Milton. "The Cornell letters: Eugene O'Neill on his craftmanship to George Jean Nathan." *Mod. Dr.*, 15 (May 1972) 68-88.

Extensive excerpts and discussion of exchange of letters as found in O'Neill-Nathan collection in Rare Book Department at Cornell University. A significant contribution toward increasing awareness of the important relationship between this important critic and the playwright.

————. "O'Neill's idea of theater." *South Atl. Bull.*, 33 (Nov. 1968) 18-21.

Determination through letters, conversations, interviews, and informal articles of O'Neill's four-fold idea of theatre: 1) drama to approximate life but 2) to transform life into art; 3) theatre to present this aesthetic transformation; and 4) presentation itself acquiring ritualistic value.

*HOFMANNSTHAL, Hugo von. "Eugene O'Neill." *Freeman*, 7 (21 Mar. 1923) 39-41. Translated by Barrett H. Clark. [Reprinted in *Tulane Dr. Rev.*, 5 (Sept. 1960) 169-173, and in the following books: Cargill *et al*, *O'Neill and his plays*, 1961; Freedman, *Essays in modern drama*, 1964; Gassner, *O'Neill* (Twentieth century views), 1964; and Miller, *Playwright's progress*, 1965.]

An important article by a distinguished Viennese poet and playwright who presents some strong indictments against much of O'Neill's material. He finds first acts good and last acts weak, heading toward a climax that is already expected.

HOLTAN, Orley I. "Eugene O'Neill and the death of the 'covenant.' " *Quar. Jour. Sp.*, 56 (Oct. 1970) 256-263.

In a study of *POET* and *MANSIONS* O'Neill is seen to be "dealing with the contradictions of the American experience, with the dream of pastoral innocence, equality and simplicity as opposed to the reality of urban corruption, greed and complicity."

"Ideas of good and evil in the plays of Eugene O'Neill." *Chrysalis,* 12, No. 5-6. 1959, pp. 3-10.

This review of a number of later plays upon opening of *POET* finds that the characters do not necessarily do the right thing, but audiences can learn a lot through the vicarious experience.

ISAACS, Edith J. R. "Meet Eugene O'Neill." *Th. Arts,* 30 (Oct. 1946) 576-587. [Reprinted in Gilder, Rosamond, *Theatre Arts anthology,* 1950.]

Mrs. Isaacs reflects on the present interest in O'Neill after 12 years. His early plays were the "trumpet blare" that broke the walls of resistance.

————. "The Negro in the American theatre." *Th. Arts,* 26 (Aug. 1952) 492-543.

The entire issue is devoted to this topic. Includes illustrations and general remarks about *JONES* and *CHILLUN.*

JANNEY, John. "Perfect ending." *Am. Mag.,* 117 (Apr. 1934) 38. Popular account of O'Neill's life and personality.

JONES, Carless. "A sailor's O'Neill." *Revue Anglo-Americaine,* 12 (Feb. 1935) 226-229.

Portrayal of the working seaman is accurate and real, if at times restrained. Atmosphere is much better than character.

KALONYME, Louis. "O'Neill lifts curtain on his early days." *NY Times,* 21 Dec. 1924, IV, p. 7.

Report of O'Neill's life as reflected in plays of the sea.

*KARSNER, David. "Eugene O'Neill at close range in Maine." *NY Her-Trib.,* 8 Aug. 1926.

In his interview at O'Neill's summer home in Maine, Karsner finds it impossible to describe what is behind the man and his work.

This is an interesting and valuable account of a personal visit, which does not become sentimental in the manner of Merrill's account.

KATZIN, Winifrid. "The great God O'Neill." *Bookman,* 68 (Sept. 1928) 61-66.

Imaginary conversation between Eustace Jones, American critic, and Achille Pasivite, New York correspondent of a French journal. Jones worships O'Neill, finds little fault. Pasivite finds no masterpieces, and seems to get the better of the argument.

*KEMELMAN, H. G. "Eugene O'Neill and the highbrow melodrama." *Bookman,* 75 (Sept. 1932) 482-491. [Reprinted in Miller, *Playwright's progress,* 1965.]

An extremely hostile and ill-conceived attack on all of O'Neill's plays as "violent and unbalanced melodrama." Kemelman sets up and annihilates O'Neill's characters, action, dialogue and experimentation as the work of a writer lacking any dramatic talent whatsoever. Kemelman is in a forest-trees predicament, as he makes little effort to find any value whatever in O'Neill's work. Instead he violently attacks many of the obvious shortcomings which, in themselves and out of context, are admitted faults. Mere tabulating of deaths and murders, or listing the number of loose women is not valid criticism. Compared to this broadside, the opinions of Geddes and Salisbury are mild dissensions.

*KEMP, Harry. "Out of Provincetown: A memoir of Eugene O'Neill." *Theatre,* 51 (April 1930) 22-23.

Harry Kemp, a "vagrom poet" and an original Provincetown Players member, wrote this recollection of the early days on Cape Cod and at MacDougal Street. O'Neill is painted as a very human and entertaining friend. Main shortcoming of the article is its lack of specific dates to identify important events.

KERR, Walter. "He gave it to 'em boy." NY *Her-Trib.,* 14 April 1957.

An attempt to determine what made O'Neill great, assuming Pulitzer prize will go to *LONG DAY'S JOURNEY.* (Similar item in Kerr's *Pieces at eight,* NY, Simon and Schuster, 1957.)

————. "The test of greatness." NY *Her-Trib.*, 25 Aug. 1957.
Kerr attempts to determine if O'Neill is permanent, and gives
a reluctant "No." It is only his personal power that still holds us.

KINNE, Wisner Payne. "George Pierce Baker and Eugene O'Neill."
Chrysalis, 7 (1954) No. 9-10, pp. 3-14.
A report of Baker's position as O'Neill's teacher at Harvard. Re-
prints three letters from O'Neill to Baker: two application letters of
July, 1914, and a letter of 1919, before production of *HORIZON*,
thanking Baker for past help.

KLAVSONS, Janis. "O'Neill's dreamer: Success and failure." *Mod.
Dr.*, 3 (Dec. 1960) 268-272.
O'Neill's dreamers such as Don Juan, Dion Anthony, John Loving, often seem to resemble O'Neill physically. The failures come
from locales O'Neill himself knew: ships, saloons, family. Successes
such as Lazarus and Marco Polo come from books.

KOMMER, Rudolf.. "O'Neill in Europe." NY *Times*, 9 Nov. 1924,
VIII, 2:1. [Reprinted in Greenwich Village Playbill No. 2, Season
1924-1925; and in Cargill *et al, O'Neill and his plays*, 1961.]
A valuable article on the poor reception of *ANNA CHRISTIE* in
Berlin, condemning some of the inexcusable blunders such as the
insertion of Anna's suicide.

*KRUTCH, Joseph Wood."Eugene O'Neill's claim to greatness." NY
Times Book Rev., 22 Sept. 1957, p. 1. [Reprinted in Freedman,
Essays in modern drama, 1964.]
While inferior in literary style to other great names, O'Neill wrote
not "to get a style" but to say what he had to say.

*————. "Eugene O'Neill, the lonely revolutionary." *Th. Arts*, 36
(Apr. 1952) 29-30. [Reprinted in Miller, *Playwright's progress*,
1965.]
Like many American greats—Poe, Hawthorne, Melville
—O'Neill is alone in his work, apart from the "spirit of the age."
O'Neill's work with tragedy, which no one else attempted, kept him
from successful communication with the mass of his audience.

————. "Long day's journey into greatness." NY *Times Book Rev.*, 8 Apr. 1962, p. 1.
Mainly a review of the Gelbs' book, but article contains large amount of Krutch's views on O'Neill's life and artistic greatness.

————. "The meaning of the modern drama. III—The American tradition." *Nation*, 141 (18 Sept. 1935) 320-323.
In this series of four articles, Krutch discusses the "classical" and "revolutionary" plays as developed in his *American drama since 1918*. The public is now ready for the "liberal point of view" represented by Rice, Howard, Anderson, and O'Neill.

————. "O'Neill the inevitable." *Th. Arts*, 38 (Feb. 1954) 66-69.
In Krutch's opinion, whatever you may think of O'Neill you cannot discuss American drama in the 20th century without him. As the drama had its obligatory scene, O'Neill is the obligatory subject.

*————. "O'Neill's tragic sense." *Amer. Schol.*, 16 (Summer 1947) 283-290.
Kurtch discusses the outstanding shortcomings and the equally outstanding merits of O'Neill's works in an effort to see why, after 30 years of writing, O'Neill can still command an audience to do as he wishes. Matters of intuition, sincerity, and skills as tragic writer are mentioned to show how this man is either praised or damned, never considered in between.

*————. "The rediscovery of Eugene O'Neill." NY *Times*, 21 Oct. 1956, VI, pp. 32-34.
After two decades of neglect, O'Neill may now be in the position to be rediscovered and reappraised by a new generation. No artist can be accurately evaluated in his own time, and if O'Neill survives this test, he will have the marks of permanent greatness.

————. "Ten American plays that will endure." NY *Times*, 11 Oct. 1959, VI, pp. 34-35.
INTERLUDE and *LONG DAY'S JOURNEY* are chosen along with

Streetcar Named Desire, Green Pastures, Oklahoma! and others as likeliest American plays to last through posterity.

*————. "Why the O'Neill star is rising." NY *Times Mag.,* 19 March 1961, pp. 36-37. [Reprinted in Miller, *Playwright's progress,* 1965.]

O'Neill's sense of tragedy with capital T is in classic sense of the word, more optimistic and cheerful than that of Williams or Miller. A welcome revival.

KUTNER, Nanette. "If you were daughter to Eugene O'Neill." *Good Housekeeping,* 115 (Aug. 1942) 26.

An "intimate glimpse" of O'Neill as a father, told by daughter Oona, age 17, whose cafe society life was intensely disliked by the parent.

LANDAUER, Bella C. "The international O'Neill." *Am. Book Collector,* 2 (1932) 55-56.

Gives complete list of foreign performances from Moscow to Berlin and Tokyo.

LARDNER, John. "O'Neill's back." *Look,* 16 (26 Feb. 1952) 4.

Brief, admiring welcome to the revivals of *DESIRE* and *CHRISTIE,* plus a report of O'Neill's love of sports during his stay in south of France.

LEE, Robert C. "Eugene O'Neill's approach to playwriting." *Drama Critique,* 11 (Winter 1968) 2-8.

Fairly extensive outline of O'Neill's methodology, pointing out that O'Neill was never able to remold his plays despite many revisions into the polished work admired by critics.

————. "Eugene O'Neill's remembrance: The past is the present." *Ariz. Quar.,* 23 (Winter 1967) 293-305.

Later plays show how "beastly incidents" from the past made up O'Neill's highest artistic achievement, but "selective recall" of the plays could not bring the self-understanding he sought in art.

————. "The lonely dreams." *Mod. Dr.*, 9 (Sept. 1966) 127-135.
Demonstration of how the artist or sensitive being so often central in O'Neill's plays is an extension of O'Neill himself, a figure of alienation who "pines for a plateau of peace."

LEECH, Clifford. "Eugene O'Neill and his plays." *Critical Quarterly*, 3 (1961) 242-256, 339-353.
APE, ELECTRA, INTERLUDE and *ICEMAN* receive major emphasis.

LEWISOHN, Ludwig. "Eugene O'Neill." *Nation*, 113 (30 Nov. 1921) 626.
Lewisohn was never one to praise O'Neill. In this accurate evaluation of the writer's early faults, he states that O'Neill must learn to stop interfering with fate if he is to create memorable plays and not merely memorable fragments.

LINDLEY, Ernest K. "Exile made him appreciate U.S., O'Neill admits." NY *Her-Trib.*, 22 May 1931.
Interviewed on his return from France, O'Neill gives some personal viewpoints on the European theatre.

LOVELL, John, Jr. "Eugene O'Neill's darker brother." *Th. Arts*, 32 (Feb. 1948) 45-48.
By presenting the Negro on equal terms with white, O'Neill portends of a brighter future for stage treatment of the Negro.

*LOVING, Pierre. "Eugene O'Neill." *Bookman*, 53 (Aug. 1921) 511-520.
This is one of the earliest long journalistic treatments of the rising O'Neill. It is a generally favorable account, written by a personal friend. Each play briefly analyzed in an attempt to discover influences of Conrad, Strindberg, etc., and possible trends.

McANENY, Marguerite. "Eleven manuscripts of Eugene O'Neill."

Princeton Univ. Library Chronicle, 4 (Feb.-Apr. 1943) 86-89.

Discussion of the original MS of *STRAW, GOLD, ANNA CHRISTIE, JONES, DIFF'RENT, APE, FOUNTAIN, WELDED, CHILLUN, FIRST MAN* and *DESIRE* given by O'Neill to the Princeton library. Facsimile of plans for *STRAW* stage setting included. Early titles mentioned—*The Silver Bullet* for *JONES*, *The Mirage* for *THE STRAW*, *Thirty Years* for *DIFF'RENT*.

McCARDELL, Roy L. "Eugene O'Neill: Son of Monte Cristo born on Broadway." NY *Telegraph Sunday Mag.*, 19 Dec. 1920.

A long article about O'Neill's life and early plays. The first important item to appear in a New York Sunday supplement.

McCLAIN, John. "O'Neill cometh back." NY *Jour-Am.*, 12 Oct. 1956.

With the current revival in interest, McClain reviews O'Neill's background and early stage experiences.

McDONNELL, Thomas P. "O'Neill's drama of the psyche." *Cath. Wld.*, 197 (May 1963) 120-125.

The great power of O'Neill himself and his plays on stage comes from the portrayal of his own agonies and the lost identity of Self.

MacGOWAN, Kenneth. "O'Neill as stage director." NY *Post* 18 Dec. 1926.

O'Neill's producing partner gives examples of the demands which most O'Neill plays make on stage effects.

———. "O'Neill in his own plays." NY *Times*, 9 Jan. 1927, VII, 2:7.

Brief discussion by O'Neill's partner concerning matters of O'Neill's life as reflected in the plays.

———. "The O'Neill soliloquy." *Th. Guild Mag.*, Feb. 1929. [Reprinted in Cargill *et al*, *O'Neill and his plays*, 1961.]

A discussion of the evolution of the O'Neill technique from the earliest plays like *WELDED* through *INTERLUDE*.

MAYO, Thomas F. "The great pendulum." *Southwest Rev.*, 36 (Summer 1951) 190-200.

Tracing the swing from romance to rationalism and back in the history of western civilization, Mayo finds O'Neill's early "ruthless dissection of emotions" part of the rationalism of 20's, and *DAYS WITHOUT END* and *ICEMAN* part of the swing to romanticism of 30's and 40's.

*MERRILL, Charles A. "Eugene O'Neill." *Equity Mag.*, Aug. 1923, pp. 26-29.

An interesting report of an interview at O'Neill's Cape Cod home, which presents a sentimental picture of cozy domesticity and of peaceful isolation from the world. Merrill creates an image of a man extraordinarily eager to return to Ireland, a facet of O'Neill's personality no other commentator ever seems to have discovered. Compare with Karsner's interview in Maine and Cowley's report of a weekend in Connecticut.

MERRILL, Flora. "Fierce oaths and blushing complexes find no place in Eugene O'Neill's talk." NY *World*, 19 July 1925.

Account of personal conversation.

MILLER, Jordan Y. "Eugene O'Neill's long journey." *Kansas Mag.*, 1958, pp. 77-81.

O'Neill's enigmatic character and his reluctance to be anything but a devoted playwright discussed in a general review of his life and plays in view of the revived interest in his works.

―――. "The Georgia plays of Eugene O'Neill." *Georgia Rev.*, 12 (Fall 1958) 278-290.

O'Neill's decline into romanticism and ultimate disappearance from the American stage for more than a decade are traced through the two plays sent to NY from Georgia, *AH, WILDERNESS!*, and *DAYS WITHOUT END*.

―――. "Myth and the American dream: O'Neill to Albee." *Mod. Dr.*, 7 (Sept. 1964) 190-198.

The myth of Youth and its ability to achieve all things is attacked and exploded in *BROWN* and *MARCO*, together with Miller's Salesman, Williams' Kilroy, and Albee's walking young Dream.

MOLLAN, Malcolm. "Making plays with a tragic end; an intimate interview with Eugene O'Neill, who tells why he does it." Phila. *Public Ledger*, 22 Jan. 1922.
One of the most widely quoted articles of its type. O'Neill asserts he will write happy endings only when he finds the right kind of happiness.

MOREHOUSE, Ward. "The boulevards after dark: Four hours from Paris in his French chateau Eugene O'Neill is writing American drama." NY *Sun*, 14 May 1930.
Report of O'Neill's life in France, including description of his love for speed in a 100 mph French sports car.

*MORRILL, M. M. "Eugene O'Neill's shack." *Drama*, 20 (Apr. 1930) 203.
An overdramatic discussion of O'Neill's home at Peaked Hill Bars. This writer is firmly convinced its desolation is the only kind of atmosphere O'Neill could happily live in (a view obviously disproven within a short time). Three pictures of the home are included.

MOSES, Montrose J. "A hopeful note in the theatre." *North Am. Rev.*, 234 (Dec. 1932) 528-535.
O'Neill is one of those who is bringing new hope to the theatre.

———. "The 'new' Eugene O'Neill." *North Am. Rev.*, 236 (Dec. 1933) 543-549.
The O'Neill legend is shattered somewhat by *AH, WILDERNESS!*. Does it represent a new O'Neill? Moses is not sure.

———. "New trends in the theatre: IV. American." *Forum*, 73 (Jan. 1925) 83-87; 73 (Feb. 1925) 231-237.
Moses observes that O'Neill's treatment of the Negro was formerly impossible on the commercial stage. O'Neill also has the quality

of soul which is not detected in other modern American playwrights.

MOTHERWELL, Hiram. "O'Neill—what next?" *Stage*, 12 (Aug. 1935) 28-30. [Reprinted in Walter, *Essay annual*, 1936.]
    After a year's silence from O'Neill, Motherwell speculates if he will emerge as perhaps the diagnostician and prophet of individualism in the social order.

*MULLET, Mary B. "The extraordinary story of Eugene O'Neill." *Am. Mag.*, 94 (Nov. 1922) 34.
    The best article to appear in a popular magazine up to this date, discussing O'Neill's plays and personal philosophy. It recognizes O'Neill's successes as a new force in the theatre.

NATHAN, George Jean. "The American dramatist." *Am. Merc.*, 17 (Aug. 1929) 500-505. [Reprinted in Downer, *American drama and its critics*, 1965.]
    In a review of the accomplishments of all modern American dramatists, Nathan finds O'Neill the leader, a first rate dramatist, despite his failures.

————. "The American prospect." *Am. Merc.*, 15 (Oct. 1928) 248-249. [Reprinted in Downer, *American drama and its critics*, 1965.]
    O'Neill has done much to bring American drama to better standards, but there is still a long way to go.

————. "The bright face of tragedy." *Cosmopolitan*, 143 (Aug. 1957) 66-69.
    More personal recollections, designed to remove the idea that O'Neill was always gloomy. Many stories of his youth. Nathan reveals that O'Neill fought all his life against the nervous trembling which eventually incapacitated him. (See Gierow's explanation of this affliction.)

————. "The case of Eugene O'Neill." *Am. Merc.*, 13 (Apr. 1928) 500-502. [Reprinted in Downer, *American drama and its critics*, 1965; and in Miller, *Playwright's progress*, 1965.]

Stinging attack in the Nathan manner on the critics who praise O'Neill's early amateur works and condemn the later ones, like *MARCO* and *INTERLUDE*.

————. "The Cosmopolite of the month." *Cosmopolitan*, 102 (Feb. 1937) 8.

As a close friend for 20 years, Nathan attempts to debunk the common idea of the gloomy introvert by giving facts about O'Neill's personal life which show him the happiest most contented practitioner of *belles-lettres*.

————. "Eugene O'Neill—Intimate portrait of a Nobel prizewinner." *Rev. of Rev.*, 95 (Feb. 1937) 66-67.

O'Neill shown as lover of detective stories, sports, garden work, as opposed to the common depressing picture of him.

————."Eugene O'Neill." *Smart Set*, July 1920.

Having introduced readers of this magazine to O'Neill's early one-act *LONG VOYAGE HOME* and review of *HORIZON*, Nathan writes one of first items about the man.

————. "Many are called and two are chosen for the dramatic hall of fame." *Cur. Op.*, 69 (Aug. 1920) 201-202.

George Jean Nathan chooses George Ade and O'Neill as top American playwrights. O'Neill chosen not for what he has done, but for what he has tried and failed to do. Nathan was the earliest important critic to recognize O'Neill's potential. *LONG VOYAGE HOME* and *ILE* had already been published in Nathan and Mencken's *Smart Set* magazine.

————. "O'Neill." *Van. F.*, 41 (Oct. 1933) 30.

After years of restiveness O'Neill has found calm and tranquility. Nathan also shows how he has been a severe O'Neill critic while remaining a close friend.

————. "O'Neill: A critical summation." *Am. Merc.*, 63 (Dec. 1946) 713-719.

Critical appraisal of O'Neill as writer, taking all plays in chronological order. Nathan cites some of Eric Bentley's criticism from *Playwright as thinker* to show lukewarm British reception.

————. "The recluse of Sea Island." *Redbook*, 65 (Aug. 1935) 34. [Reprinted in Nathan's *The theatre of the moment*, 1938.] More of Nathan's revelation of intimate facts about O'Neill as a man. Many pictures from the plays.

NETHERCOT, Arthur H. "The psychoanalyzing of Eugene O'Neill." *Mod. Dr.*, 3 (Dec. 1960) 242-256. Detailed tracing of history of O'Neill criticism as it involves his psychoanalytical aspects. Includes references to and quotations from all major O'Neill criticism from the 1920's to 1960.

————. "The psychoanalyzing of Eugene O'Neill: Postscript." *Mod. Dr.*, 8 (Sept. 1965) 150-155. Based on Gelbs' book and other studies of O'Neill, this gives fairly convincing proof that O'Neill knew much more about Freudian psychology than he cared to admit.

NEUBERGER, Richard L. "O'Neill turns west to new horizons." *NY Times*, 22 Nov. 1936, VIII, p. 6. Purely reportorial account of an interview, relating well-known facts about his life, etc. Portrait and scenes from *APE, CHRISTIE, AH, WILDERNESS* and *INTERLUDE*.

NORTON, Elliot. "Conscience and a touch of the poet." Boston *Post*, 2 May 1954. An attempt to show why O'Neill uses New England almost exclusively for settings, mainly because of the "laconic, volcanic, soul searching people" whose conscience is "uneasy, accusing, and relentless."

"Notes on rare books." *NY Times*, 18 Nov. 1928, IV, 29:1. An attempt to review Benjamin De Casseres' poem, "Anathema! Litanies of Negation" to which O'Neill wrote the introduction.

O'Neill is out of his element in this introduction, says the anonymous critic, who finds himself unable even to finish the poem itself.

O'CASEY, Sean. "Tribute to O'Neill." NY *Times*, 9 Nov. 1959. [Reprinted in Cargill *et al, O'Neill and his plays*, 1961.]
   Letter to Lester Osterman, owner of Eugene O'Neill Theatre, upon renaming of the Coronet Theatre in O'Neill's honor.

"O'Neill as actor is recalled by one who saw him in '17." NY *Her-Trib.*, 17 Mar. 1929.
   Report of O'Neill's few stage appearances in early Provincetown days.

*"O'Neill goes mildly pirate, etc." *House & Garden,* 65 (Jan. 1934) 19-21.
   Description and six excellent photographs of Casa Genotta, Sea Island Beach, Georgia.

"O'Neill in Paris." NY *Times*, 18 Nov. 1923, VIII, 2:8.
   This report of O'Neill's Paris failures, especially *JONES*, gives some interesting examples of the complete misunderstanding of the French critics.

"O'Neill, 'shy, dark boy' bold master of modern drama." *Newsweek*, 2 (19 Aug. 1933) 16-17.
   A general news report concerning O'Neill's life and current activities upon completion of *DAYS WITHOUT END* and *AH, WILDERNESS!*

"O'Neill talks about his plays." NY *Her-Trib.*, 16 March 1924. [Reprinted in Cargill *et al, O'Neill and his plays*, 1961.]
   In an interview with staff members of this paper, O'Neill states he is through with the one-act form and discusses *APE* as expressionism.

"O'Neill's future." *Drama*, Oct.-Nov., 1921.
   O'Neill may become spoiled by the praise heaped upon him, but

so far he has not. He occupies a "seat which has long been empty."

*PALLETTE, Drew B. "O'Neill and the comic spirit." *Mod. Dr.*, 3 (Dec. 1960) 273-279.
An attempt to show how the comic plays an organic part in O'Neill's works. Two types seem to be the mocking satirical social ridicule and the more "organic" humor arising from agony, meant to divert pain. Not quite absurdist in the Beckett style, O'Neill's humor is meant to intensify the portrayal of man's position.

————. "O'Neill's A Touch of the Poet and his other last plays." *Ariz. Quar.*, 13 (Winter 1957) 308-319.
All of the later plays, starting with *AH, WILDERNESS!*, are reviewed as parts of O'Neill's changed approach of more individualized characters instead of Freudian representatives and a tone of compassion for the "damaged" human being. *POET* is a synthesis of the various elements of all the others.

*PARKS, Edd Winfield. "Eugene O'Neill's symbolism." *Sewannee Rev.*, 43 (Oct.-Dec. 1935) 436-450.
Attempting to analyze the poor critical reception of *DAYS WITHOUT END*, Parks goes into a complex explanation of O'Neill's symbols and philosophy. Parks' main theme, apparent amidst frequently unclear digressions, is that O'Neill has consistently overused symbols, employing them as the reason for the play itself. An interesting contrast to Skinner's viewpoint in "poet's quest," because Parks sees no continuity of philosophy at all.

————. "Eugene O'Neill's quest." *Tulane Dr. Rev.*, 4 (Spring 1960) 99-107.
Major plays analyzed as part of the familiar quest for fulfillment, the "last harbor," which always eluded the artist as he witnessed mankind and his characters stumbling on toward nowhere.

*PECK, Seymour. "Talk with Mrs. O'Neill." NY *Times*, 4 Nov. 1956, II, 1:6. [Reprinted in Cargill *et al, O'Neill and his plays*, 1961.]
A rare interview with O'Neill's widow, in which she describes

RALEIGH, John Henry. "Eugene O'Neill." *Eng. Jour.*, 56 (Mar. 1967) 367-377.

Extensive review of O'Neill's dramatic and theatrical contributions toward making American drama a part of world drama.

*————. "Eugene O'Neill." *Ramparts*, 2 (Spring 1964) 72-87.

This essay covers many of the usual aspects—arresting personality, tragic life, his simultaneous loves and hates. Raleigh's most interesting point is that unlike so many modern artists, O'Neill did not "go to pot" late in his life and career such as Hemingway, Fitzgerald and others, but developed his greatest works later after becoming a teetotaller with his past behind him. There are many affinities between O'Neill and Melville, according to Raleigh.

*————. "O'Neill's Long Day's Journey and New England Irish-Catholicism." *Partisan Rev.*, 26 (Fall 1959) 573-592.

Extended and detailed study of Irish-Catholic traditions, inhibitions, fantasies, etc., evident in the characters, situations, and actions of this play, together with some reference to others such as *DESIRE* and *MISBEGOTTEN*.

RANDEL, William. "American plays in Finland." *Am. Lit.*, 24 (Nov. 1952) 291-300.

This brief factual review starts with 1900 and indicates that O'Neill is a "most respected" dramatist in Finland.

REARDON, William R. "O'Neill since World War II: Critical reception in New York." *Mod. Dr.*, 10 (Dec. 1967) 289-299.

Summary of critical reception of new and revived plays between 1946 and 1967.

REDFORD, Grant H. "Dramatic art vs. autobiography: A look at Long Day's Journey into Night." *Coll. Eng.*, 25 (April 1964) 527-535.

Though admittedly autobiographical, to regard the play solely in that light is to neglect it as art. It is "one of the best plays written within the realistic convention in the United States."

RENIERS, Percival. "If I were you." *Theatre*, 41 (Apr. 1925) 12.

"A dialogue between Eugene O'Neill and Owen Davis —overheard in the imagination." They discuss writing about the hard New England life.

RIDDELL, John. "Strange interview with Mr. O'Neill." *Van. F.*, 30 (May 1928) 86.
Parody of O'Neill's style in a dialogue between O'Neill and his own inner voice.

Ross, Don. "New O'Neill." NY *Her-Trib.*, 28 Sept. 1958.
A pre-opening night review of POET and discussion of prospects of further O'Neill works.

*ROTHENBERG, Albert. "Autobiographical drama: Strindberg and O'Neill." *Lit. & Psych.*, v. 17, nos 2 & 3, 1967, pp. 95-114.
Well-documented study of similarities and differences, noting that Strindberg wrote early and admitted autobiographical aspects, while O'Neill, particularly in *JOURNEY*, held back until after his death.

*ROY, Emil. "The archetypal unity of Eugene O'Neill's drama." *Comp. Dr.*, 3 (Winter 1969-1970) 263-274.
Pervasive thrust, non-realistic and negative, sadistic and melodramatic define O'Neill's plays. He uses archetypal motifs in contexts that amplify their ironic implications. O'Neill's heroes are on a quest of lost innocence or peace, a circular journey away from his origin, then trial by ordeal, and back.

ROYDE-SMITH, Naomi. "Eugene O'Neill." *Forum*, 76 (Nov. 1926) 795-796.
It is time O'Neill stops being a Conrad and Maupassant and starts being "our one and only Eugene O'Neill."

SALEM, James M. "Eugene O'Neill and the sacrament of marriage." *Serif*, 3 (June 1966) 23-35.
Demonstration that O'Neill maintained a very proper attitude toward marital fidelity and illicit sex. Everybody who violates proper precepts suffers.

SARLOS, Robert K. "Producing principles and practices of the Provincetown players." *Theatre Research*, 10 (1969) 89-102.
A paper delivered on Sept. 27, 1967, at the Fifth International Congress on Theatre Research in Budapest. While O'Neill himself is not specifically singled out, this is a valuable item on his first producing company.

————. "Wharf and dome: Materials for the history of Provincetown players." *Theatre Research* 10 (1970) 163-178.
Further material, with the title referring to Mary Heaton Vorse's tiny Wharf Theatre, home of first production of *CARDIFF* in 1916, and the plaster dome, built especially for *JONES*, the first of its kind in America, used for varieties of effects with backlighting, projections, etc.

SAYLER, Oliver M. "The artist of the theatre." *Shadowland*, 49 (Apr. 1922) 66. [Reprinted in *Theatre Arts*, 41 (June 1957) 23-24.]
"A colloquy between Eugene O'Neill and Oliver M. Sayler." Discusses playwright as an artist not only *in* but *of* the theatre.

————. "Our awakening theatre." *Century*, 102 (Aug. 1921) 514-524.
O'Neill may yet be able to blend the old realism and the new theatre into a successful combination.

————. "The real Eugene O'Neill." *Century*, 103 (Jan. 1922) 351-359. [Statement by O'Neill entitled "What the theatre means to me," taken from this article, is reprinted in Cargill *et al, O'Neill and his plays*, 1961.]
Sayler attempts to explain this man who is already a kind of legend. It is too early, says Sayler, to mark him as our greatest, but his background enables him to bring forth essential tragedy of life.

————. "Seeking a common denominator to Andreieff, Pirandello, O'Neill." NY *Her-Trib.*, 26 Apr. 1931.
The native writing of these 3, says Sayler, transcends national limits.

SEARS, William P., Jr. "O'Neill begins another marathon." *Lit. D.*, 119 (27 Apr. 1935) 28.

Discussion of *TALE OF POSSESSORS*, although not actually named as such.

*SERGEANT, Elizabeth Shepley. "O'Neill: The man with a mask." *New Rep.*, 50 (16 Mar. 1927) 91-95. [Reprinted in *Fire Under the Andes*, 1927.]

An attempt to analyze the mask O'Neill wears in life. Compare this discussion with O'Neill's revelation of his own family life in *LONG DAY'S JOURNEY*. This critic explains O'Neill's plays in terms of childhood rebelliousness against parental autocracy and the need for the "lovely distant mother" who was never there when wanted. Many of the interpretations of O'Neill's later behavior are much closer to the truth than was probably recognized at the time. No other contemporary critic pursued this line of thinking.

SHIPLEY, Joseph T. "Eugene O'Neill and the critics." *Venture*, June 1961, pp. 118-124.

Review of much adverse criticism from early plays to *JOURNEY*, demonstrating how O'Neill became a "storm center" in the "dead calm" of the American theatre. Conclusion: he writes melodrama. with great American writer of tragedy yet to come.

SISK, Robert F. "Eugene O'Neill disgusted with opposition to stage art." NY *American*, 29 May 1927.

Admiration expressed that O'Neill has maintained his ideals and has written what he wanted, despite opposition of those who would discourage true stage art.

SKINNER, Richard Dana. "O'Neill and the poet's quest." *North Am. Rev.*, 240 (June 1935) 54-67.

Excerpts from Skinner's book, *Eugene O'Neill: A poet's quest*.

SLOCHOWER, Harry. "Eugene O'Neill's lost moderns." *Univ. Rev.*, 10 (Autumn 1943) 32-37.

His characters often being "masochistic products of modern

rationalistic self-probings" they never find any release or resting place, live in a closed world, their doom foreshadowed.

SMITH, Winifred. "Mystics in the modern theatre." *Sewanee Rev.*, 50 (Jan.-Mar. 1942) 35-48.
General discussion of all mystics, including O'Neill, Sherwood, and Hemingway.

SMYSER, William L. "A temporary expatriate again views Broadway." NY *Times,* 1 July 1928, VIII, 1:4.
A returning traveler points out that much of O'Neill's technique is really gleanings from what Europe long since discarded.

*STAMM, Rudolph. "The dramatic experiments of Eugene O'Neill." *Eng. Stud.*, 28 (Feb. 1947) 1-15. [Reprinted in Stamm's *The shaping powers at work,* 1967.]
Interesting survey covering O'Neill's main phases from one-acts to *DAYS WITHOUT END.* To one unfamiliar with O'Neill it is somewhat misleading because the "phases" of atmosphere, emotional struggle, and split personality do not follow in chronological order. Conclusion is that most plays are admirable experiments.

————. " 'Faithful realism': Eugene O'Neill and the problem of style." *Eng. Stud.*, 40 (Aug. 1959) 242-250. [Reprinted in Stamm's *The shaping powers at work,* 1967.]
This European critic is convinced that after rejecting the unsatisfactory experiments of his plays before 1934, O'Neill at last found his own consistent style in *ICEMAN, JOURNEY,* and *MISBEGOTTEN*; *i.e.,* a belief in a Puritanical view of life as worse than death, portrayed in a style of "faithful realism" in scene and language.

————. "The Orestes theme in three plays by Eugene O'Neill, T. S. Eliot and J. P. Sartre." *Eng. Stud.*, 30 (Oct. 1949) 244-255.
ELECTRA, Family Reunion, and *The Flies* diagnosed carefully in terms of the concept of guilt and sin in Orestes story. O'Neill finds no purification or liberation therein, which the others definitely do.

STEELE, Robert. "A new film on the genius of Eugene O'Neill." *Film Comment*, 4 (Summer 1968) 18-21.

Detailed discussion of success and failure of "the face of genius," a TV film aired 14 March 1966 on life of O'Neill.

STEINHAUER, H. "Eros and Psyche: A Nietzschean motif in Anglo-American literature." *Mod. Lang. Notes*, 64 (Apr. 1949) 217-228.

Convincing partial explanation of *BROWN* and meaning of *LAZARUS* in terms of Nietzschean philosophy on evils of sex-repression, plus certain aspects of *ELECTRA* in the same vein.

STEVENS, Thomas W. "How good is Eugene O'Neill?" *Eng. Jour.*, 26 (Mar. 1937) 179-186.

Attempt to evaluate O'Neill in light of his Nobel prize. The contribution of each major play is discussed as seen by Puff and Sneer of Sheridan's *Critic*. The decision determines that he cannot be judged from literary standards, and many no better than he have received the award.

*STRAUMANN, Heinrich. "The philosophical background of the modern American drama." *Eng. Stud.*, 26 (June 1944) 65-78.

A brief but excellent analysis of O'Neill's place in modern American literature from an objective European viewpoint. American drama is classified into three schools: empirico-pragmatic, historical, and ethico-religious. O'Neill achieves greatest success in combination of all in *ELECTRA*. Straumann finds all of these groups evident to varying degrees in all O'Neill's plays.

STROUPE, John H. "Eugene O'Neill and the problem of masking." *Lock Haven Review* (Lock Haven St. Coll., Pa.), 12 (1971) 71-80.

SULLIVAN, Frank. "Life is a bowl of Eugene O'Neills." *Golden Bk.*, 18 (July 1933) 60-62.

A parody on O'Neill's style, presenting the struggles of the General Baddun family.

SWEENEY, Charles P. "Back to the source of plays written by Eugene O'Neill." NY *World*, 9 Nov. 1924.

Report of brief interview with O'Neill before production of *DESIRE*, revealing where he got the ideas of many of his plays.

TAPPER, Bonno. "Eugene O'Neill's world view." *Personalist* (Univ. of So. Cal. School of Philosophy), 18 (Winter 1937) 40-48.
INTERLUDE and *ELECTRA* taken as examples of O'Neill's world view, determining the manner in which he has diagnosed the "sickness of today."

TAYLOR, Joseph R. "The audacity of Eugene O'Neill." *Jour. of Expression*, 3 (Dec. 1929) 209-212.
A run-down of O'Neill's "rule-breaking" that brought him success.

THROCKMORTON, Juliet. "As I remember Eugene O'Neill." *Yankee*, 32 (Aug. 1968) 84.
Reminiscences of one who knew O'Neill at Provincetown in the 1920's.

THURMAN, William R. "Journey into night: Elements of tragedy in Eugene O'Neill." *Quar. Jour. Sp.*, 52 (Apr. 1966) 129-145.
Evidence from the major plays to show that O'Neill's consistent emphasis upon the denial of life is against the real concept of tragedy which should be a positive affirmation and a "journey into light."

TÖRNQVIST, Egil. "Ibsen and O'Neill: A study in influence." *Scan. Stud.*, 37 (Aug. 1965) 211-235.
A discussion of Ibsen's influence in aspects of character as well as in all areas of dramatic craftsmanship.

————. "Jesus and Judas: On biblical allusions in O'Neill's plays." *Etudes Anglaises*, 24 (1971) 41-49.

*————. "Personal addresses in the plays of Eugene O'Neill." *Quar. Jour. Sp.*, 55 (Apr. 1969) 126-130.
Highly interesting look at O'Neill's forms of direct address by a variety of characters to indicate various moods and personal relation-

ships, particularly in view of the lack of the second-person familiar pronoun in English.

*————. "Personal nomenclature in the plays of O'Neill." *Mod. Dr.*, 8 (Feb. 1966) 362-373.

Detailed study of the names of O'Neill's characters in relation to their dramatic qualities. A surprisingly convincing argument that O'Neill, through his career, "baptized" his stage "children" with "right" names which contribute to our understanding of them and the world in which they live.

TOWSE, J. Ranken. "A word of warning to Eugene O'Neill." NY *Post*, 18 Mar. 1922.

Towse's opening night reviews of *FIRST MAN, APE, STRAW* were not particularly favorable, and *APE* was roundly condemned. He therefore warns O'Neill that he must not give way to the broad and easy "path of sensationalism" or use the abnormal merely to point up general propositions.

TRASK, C. Hooper. "Eugene O'Neill in Berlin." NY *World*, 4 Jan. 1925.

Discussion of minimum success of *APE, JONES* and *ANNA CHRISTIE*.

*TRILLING, Lionel. "Eugene O'Neill, a revaluation." *New Rep.*, 88 (23 Sept. 1936) 176-179. [Reprinted in Cowley, *After the genteel tradition*, 1937; Cargill *et al, O'Neill and his plays*, 1961, as "The genius of Eugene O'Neill"; Freedman, *Essays in the modern drama*, 1964; Meserve, *Discussions of modern American drama*, 1965; and Miller, *Playwright's progress*, 1965.]

Although Trilling is no great admirer of O'Neill, he regards the playwright's artistic efforts worthy of attention and therefore of criticism. In this excellent survey he contrasts the "surrender" of *DAYS WITHOUT END* to O'Neill's more typical great force in affirming the power and hope of life by saying "O'Neill has crept into the dark womb of the mother church and pulled the universe in with him."

"Trouble with Brown." *Time*, 62 (7 Dec. 1953) 77-78.

Obituary, review of life and works. He may not have achieved his tragic view, but few tried so hard as he.

VALGEMAE, Mardi. "Eugene O'Neill's preface to The Great God Brown." *Yale Univ. Lib. Gaz.*, 43 (July 1968) 24-29.
See "Author's foreword," Essays and Miscellaneous items, Nondramatic O'Neill.

————. "Expressionism and the new American drama." *Twentieth Cent. Lit.*, 17 (1971) 227-234.
This item on expressionistic movement in America expanded into book form, *Accelerated grimace*, 1972, *q.v.*

————. O'Neill and German expressionism." *Mod. Dr.*, 10 (Sept. 1967) 111-123.
Influences, or lack of them, in discussion of *JONES, APE,* and *BROWN.*

*VENA, Gary A. "The role of the prostitute in the plays of Eugene O'Neill." *Drama Critique,* 10 (Fall 1967) 129-137; 11 (Winter 1968) 9-14; 11 (Spring 1968) 82-88.
As far back as *THE WEB* O'Neill was interested in the streetwalker who is warm, elegant, spiritually virginal. O'Neill's most successful common streetwalkers are found in *ICEMAN.* O'Neill moved his picture of the mother and the whore together until in the end he suggests that "they join hands in a shameful conspiracy to destroy the soul with love."

VERNON, Grenville. "Our native dramatist comes into his own." *Theatre,* 41 (May 1925) 20.
O'Neill is not yet the great American dramatist, says Vernon, but in imagination and courage he represents the great hope in native playwriting. This article contains an interesting photograph of O'Neill at age 8, sitting on a rock, pad and pencil in hand.

*VORSE, Mary Heaton. "O'Neill's house was shrine for friends." *NY World,* 11 Jan. 1931.

Written by the owner of the famous wharf which saw the first production of an O'Neill play, *BOUND EAST FOR CARDIFF* in 1916, Miss Vorse relates in detail the collapse of the Peaked Hill Bars cottage during a storm.

*WAITH, Eugene M. "Eugene O'Neill: An exercise in unmasking." *Ed. Th. Jour.*, 13 (Oct. 1961) 182-191. [Reprinted in Gassner, *O'Neill* (Twentieth century views), 1964.]

Discussion of techniques, methods of use, themes developed through masks. Frequent reference to "Memoranda on masks" (see Non-dramatic O'Neill). Even in plays using no masks there is progressive "unmasking" and the plays themselves are a kind of unmasking of the author.

WALKER, Roy. "The right kind of pity." *Twentieth Century*, 155 (1954) 79-86.

WATTS, Richard, Jr. "Can O'Neill do wrong or not?" NY *Her-Trib.*, 17 Mar. 1929.

Criticism which condemns O'Neill for lack of "intellect" and use of "tricks" is invalid, says Watts, who argues that good use of theatrical tricks is a perfectly valid step for any playwright.

————. "Difficulty in staging plays is no concern of Mr. O'Neill." NY *Her-Trib.*, 8 Jan. 1928.

A catalogue of the almost impossible demands O'Neill makes on actor and stage designer with his written directions, but admitting they come from a knowledge of the theatre and a desire to blend all the arts into one.

————. "Realism doomed, O'Neill believes." NY *Her-Trib.*, 5 Feb. 1928.

Quotes O'Neill's belief that realism as we know it is doomed, though not necessarily in the style of *INTERLUDE*.

————. "A visit to Eugene O'Neill, now of Arcady." NY *Her-Trib.*, 8 June 1930.
Report of an interview at O'Neill's chateau at Villa Mimosas, France. Watts wonders how the lovely home and easy life will affect O'Neill works yet to come. Compare this with Morrill's view concerning O'Neill's home on Cape Cod.

WEAVER, John V. A. "Eugene O'Neill and Pollyanalysis." *Van. F.*, 16 (July 1921) 43.
Weaver maintains that the "Pollyannas" who attack O'Neill have only one real complaint—his lack of pity for his characters.

*————. "I knew him when. . ." NY *World*, 21 Feb. 1926. [Reprinted in Cargill et al, *O'Neill and his plays*, 1961.]
Weaver was O'Neill's classmate in Baker's English 47 at Harvard. This informative report is one of the few such personal reminiscences in existence. Weaver is unhappy to find that the "swashbuckling" O'Neill he knew has now disappeared.

WEISSMAN, Philip. "Conscious and unconscious autobiography in the dramas of Eugene O'Neill." *Jour. of Am. Psychoanalytic Assoc.*, 5 (July 1957) 432-460.
This long item by a professional analyst (he has written extensively on Tennessee Williams as well) goes into detail concerning the biographical aspects of all important O'Neill plays.

WELCH, Mary. "Softer tones for Mr. O'Neill's portrait." *Th. Arts*, 41 (May 1957) 67-68. [Reprinted in Cargill et al, *O'Neill and his plays*, 1961.]
The actress who played the original Josie in the first abortive production of *MISBEGOTTEN* writes of her experiences trying out for the part and acting under O'Neill's supervision. Some interesting glimpses into O'Neill's personality not long before his death.

WELSH, Robt. G. "Behind the scenes." NY *Telegram*, 24 Feb. 1922.
Some interesting background material on O'Neill's life.

WENNING, T. H. "Dead man triumphant." *Newseek*, 49 (17 June 1957) 65-68.

General review of life and works by the magazine's theatre editor in view of the widely popular O'Neill revival.

WHIPPLE, Thomas K. "The tragedy of Eugene O'Neill." *New Rep.*, 41 (21 Jan. 1925) 222-225.

This writer sounds a different note in his analysis. While most critics observe that O'Neill's characters are far beyond the identity of the audiences which view them, Whipple believes their tragedy of frustration in modern society is ours as well.

*WHITMAN, Robert F. "O'Neill's search for a 'language of the theatre.' " *Quar. Jour. Sp.*, 46 (Apr. 1960) 153-170. [Reprinted in Gassner, *O'Neill* (Twentieth century views), 1964.]

Each play reviewed to show attempts to find a "language." Later plays are not a return to past "realism," but a progesssion toward a last device which uses liquor as escape. O'Neill has said the same thing all along, but now saying it better.

WEIGAND, Charmion von. "The quest of Eugene O'Neill." *New Theatre*, Sept. 1935. p. 12.

Lengthy detailed analysis of all plays, showing that O'Neill's quest for his "long lost innocence" has gotten him nowhere. Strongly leftish article condemns O'Neill as the "poet" of the decadent American petty bourgeois, whose audience is fast dwindling.

WILSON, Edmund. "Two young men and an old one: Eugene O'Neill as a prose writer." *Van. F.*, 19 (Nov. 1922) 24. [A portion reprinted in Cargill *et al*, *O'Neill and his plays*, 1961.]

While O'Neill often writes dreary and flat dialogue, when he enters the vernacular he becomes a poet as in *JONES*, *APE*, first act of *ANNA CHRISTIE*.

WINCHELL, Walter. "Portrait of a playwright." NY *Mirror*, 13 June 1957.

Facts and information about O'Neill's life and personality, quoting Nathan and others.

WINTHER, Sophus Keith. "Eugene O'Neill: The dreamer confronts his dream." *Ariz. Q.,* 21 (Autumn 1965) 221-233.
While in rebellion against romantic ideal, *POET* and *MANSIONS* most carefully develop the romantic dreamer.

*————. "Strindberg and O'Neill: A study of influence." *Scand. Stud.,* 31 (Aug. 1959) 103-120.
The best study of Strindberg's influence on O'Neill, going much farther in matters of artistry and philosophy than either Hayward or Fleisher. Winther is convinced that Strindberg and Nietzsche were far more important to O'Neill than Freud and Jung throughout his entire creative life.

WOLFSON, Lester M. "Inge, O'Neill, and the human condition." *South. Sp. Jour.,* 22 (Summer 1957) 221-232.
Comparison of Inge's "often deftly slick" treatment of the isolated, lonely individual with O'Neill's "deadly earnest" portrayals in *ICEMAN, MISBEGOTTEN,* and *JOURNEY.* Wolfson finds *JOURNEY* a tragedy of near-Shakespearean quality.

WOODBRIDGE, Homer E. "Eugene O'Neill." *South Atl. Quar.,* 37 (Jan. 1938) 22-35. [Reprinted in Hamilton, *Fifty years of the South Atlantic Quarterly,* 1952; and in Cargill et al, *O'Neill and his plays,* 1961, as "Beyond melodrama."]
A tendency toward melodrama, and an inability successfuly to mix symbol, naturalism, and melodrama deprive much of O'Neill's work of great success. An interesting analysis of each play in light of this opinion.

WOOLLCOTT, Alexander. "The rise of Eugene O'Neill." *Everybody's,* 43 (July 1920) 49.
Mainly a review of his life and explanation of strength of plays.

YOUNG, Stark. "Eugene O'Neill." *New Rep.,* 32 (15 Nov. 1922) 307-308.
Young hopes O'Neill gets out from the burden of the fairly limited world he has created and goes on to find his own truth in the complex nature of life.

————. "Eugene O'Neill: Notes from a critic's diary." *Harper's,*
214 (June 1957) 66.

Some interesting facts about Young's personal acquaintance with
O'Neill revealed in notes from 1923 to 1956.

Individual Plays

Introduction

This section has been designed to present a clear picture of the tenor of O'Neill criticism as seen in reviews and essays devoted exclusively to the individual plays. For best effect, the entries have been arranged in a somewhat arbitrary fashion.

In order to establish the precise pattern of criticism throughout O'Neill's lifetime and during his posthumous revival, a straight alphabetical listing by author would be impractical. The most practical system would seem to be to group all critical references under the titles of the individual plays and, for ease in using the bibliography, to list the plays in alphabetical, rather than chronological, order. A strict alphabetical listing by author or title under each individual play would not successfully trace the interesting pattern of developing criticism which can be seen in a chronological listing. In the hope that a satisfactory compromise has been found to meet the objective for which this entire bibliography was designed, the entries in this section are listed in the following order:

First - BOOK REVIEWS. In a very few instances, as in the case of *LONG DAY'S JOURNEY* or *MARCO MILLIONS*, the published version appeared before the play was actually staged in New York or elsewhere. These volumes were reviewed somewhat irregularly, generally by literary rather than drama critics. Those book reviews that have been located are therefore presented as the *first* series of entries, listed in alphabetical order by author or title, with periodical volume and page numbers included when known. The year of publication appears in the heading as follows:

219

LONG DAY'S JOURNEY INTO NIGHT
Book - 1956

Second - ROAD TRYOUTS. O'Neill would not ordinarily permit his plays to be given road tryouts and preferred to open "cold" in New York. A few, however, did open out of town. Reviews of these tryouts form the *second* group of entries, listed in alphabetical order by author or title. Periodical titles, almost without exception newspapers, are indicated; dates appear in the heading as follows:

AH, WILDERNESS!
Opening night reviews - Pittsburgh Tryout
Newspapers of 26 Sept. 1933

Third - NEW YORK OPENINGS. This *third* group of entries is the first to be listed under most of the play titles. Once again, the periodicals are almost without exception newspapers. Their number has been purposely restricted. Reviews of New York openings are generally limited to New York City (*i.e.,* Manhattan Island) dailies plus the Brooklyn *Eagle*. While many clipping collections of O'Neill material in major libraries contain reviews from around the country, most of them were taken from wire service releases, and the impracticality of listing all of them is clearly apparent. Upon occasion, and particuiarly as New York newspapers declined in number, reviews from such papers as the Long Island *Newsday* and others may be included. *Women's Wear Daily, The Wall Street Journal,* and the *Morning Telegraph,* highly specialized newspapers which ran regular drama columns, are included.

In the case of the early one-act and a few full-length plays, reviews in the daily press often appeared some days after the opening night. In such instances, reviews are noted under the following heading:

DESIRE UNDER THE ELMS
Opening run reviews - New York
Newspapers of November 1924

When the plays began to receive regular coverage, the opening night review appeared in newspapers of the following day. They are listed under this heading:

AH, WILDERNESS!
Opening night reviews - New York
Newspapers of 3 Oct. 1933

Please Note: The newspaper date is always the day *following* the first performance. Newpaper titles are given, but dates are not included because of the designation in the heading.

Fourth - OTHER REVIEWS. Subsequent reviews in trade papers such as *Variety* or specialty papers such as *The Wall Street Journal,* often appearing several days after opening night, and discussions in magazines and quarterlies, as well as in Sunday supplements, are included in the *fourth* listing, once more in alphabetical order by author or title. Groupings are by year, under headings as follows:

ANNA CHRISTIE
Other reviews and criticism
1933

Fifth - REVIVALS. Entries are treated in the same manner as other opening nights, under appropriate headings.

Sixth - FURTHER REVIEWS. Subsequent reviews and criticism are treated in the same manner as those following the opening night listings.

The general mechanics of this section follow the same system used in the listing of general references in periodicals in the preceding section. Only the New York *Times* entries contain page and column number; other newspaper entries show date only. Magazine and quarterly publications are given volume, date, and page if known, but there may be rare cases in which the entire information was unavailable.

AH, WILDERNESS

GAUL, Harvey. "O'Neill, Cohan share spotlight in world premiere at Nixon." Pitt. *Post Gazette.*
It is Cohan's piece; long arid stretches need trimming.

PARRY, Florence F. "Wherein the boy Penrod grows older under the new and nostalgic pen of Eugene O'Neill." Pitt. *Press*
Negative report; not a play, but a series of unmatched scenes strung together; old O'Neill is much preferred.

SEIBEL, George. "O'Neill world premiere of Ah, Wilderness! hit at Nixon." Pitt. *Sun Telegraph.*
Praise for O'Neill's ability to restrain and condense.

ALLEN, Kelcey. "Ah, Wilderness! O'Neill play, is bright comedy." *W. W. Daily.*
The play shows that O'Neill can write in a lighter vein.

ANDERSON, John. "Humor flows from O'Neill pen." NY *Jour.*
High praise for charm and vivacity, "affectionate, indulgent, and tear-stained humor."

ATKINSON, Brooks. "In which Eugene O'Neill recaptures the past . . ." NY *Times,* 28:2. [Reprinted in Miller, *Playwright's progress,* 1965.]
O'Neill now on level where he can talk to all of us; highest recommendation, even if commonplace and hackneyed.

BROWN, John Mason. "George M. Cohan in Eugene O'Neill's comedy." NY *Post.*

Praise for cast, production, and O'Neill's laying aside the tragic mask.

COHEN, Julius. "Ah, Wilderness! new O'Neill success." *Jour. Comm.*
Happiest and most entertaining of Guild's offerings in some time. Cohan makes his role more tolerant than O'Neill's pen could have.

GABRIEL, Gilbert. "Ah, Wilderness!" NY *Amer*. [Reprinted in Cargill et al, *O'Neill and his plays*, 1961; and in Miller, *Playwright's progress*, 1965.]
Comedy of recantation as well as recollection; the play is "paradise enow."

GARLAND, Robert. "Laughs, tears in Ah, Wilderness!" NY *Wor-Tel.*
Enthusiastic praise for all elements of play and production.

HAMMOND, Percy. "Ah, Wilderness!" NY *Her-Trib.*
Dismissed as little more than sentiment; Cohan is better than the script.

LOCKRIDGE, Richard. "Ah, Wilderness! . . . is offered by the Theatre Guild." NY *Sun.*
O'Neill is just plain folks after all.

MANTLE, Burns. "Ah, Wilderness! — and George Cohan." NY *News*.
Praise for Cohan; play fits the groove of American family life as it is currently being presented in drama.

POLLOCK, Arthur. "Eugene O'Neill writes a gentle, kindly play." Brook. *Eagle.*
O'Neill has gone through his own revolution and likes the world a bit more.

WINCHELL, Walter. "Cohan triumphs at Guild theatre in O'Neill hit." NY *Mirror*.

Eventful night, abundance of delight; "chords of emotion played with skill, dignity and good taste."

Other reviews and criticism
1933

ADAMS, Franklin P. "The conning tower." NY *Her-Trib.*, 2 Oct.
Best O'Neill play ever seen; worth "50 Interludes and dozen Electras."

"Ah, Wilderness!" *Variety*, 10 Oct.
Admirable start for Guild; helps enliven new season.

"Ah, Wilderness!" NY *Wor-Tel.*, 13 Oct.
This editorial regards O'Neill's experiments as a good thing, but the writer is delighted with this play's turn toward gentleness and simplicity.

BOLTON, Whitney. "Geo. M. Cohan is THE THING in O'Neill's Ah, Wilderness!" NY *Morn. Teleg.*, 4 Oct.
Not great, but extremely satisfying, the skilled trickery of good theatre. Cohan is a better actor than O'Neill is a playwright.

BOWEN, Stirling. "E. O'Neill and G. Cohan." *Wall St. Jour.*, 5 Oct.
A folksy play, full of nostalgia, which brings together in O'Neill and Cohan two foremost virtuosi of observation and showmanship in this generation.

"Broadway boy." *Time*, 22 (9 Oct.) 26.
"Human, kindly, sure drawn" picture of home life.

BURR, Eugene. "Ah, Wilderness!" *Billboard*, 45 (14 Oct.) 16. [Reprinted in Miller, *Playwright's progress*, 1965.]
Strongly negative report; most of the play is trite, full of stage tricks. Written by anybody else it would have been thrown out. (Burr, however, finds the beach love scene one of the theatre's "most lovely," while many other critics condemned it.)

CALDWELL, Cy. "To see or not to se." *New Outlook*, 162 (Nov.) 42.
Charming, tender, thoroughly delightful.

CORBIN, John. "O'Neill backs and fills." *Sat. R. Lit.*, 10 (28 Oct.) 217.
A new facet of O'Neill's genius, but with the same preoccupation with deadly sin.

EATON, Walter Prichard. "Eugene O'Neill changes style and mood." NY *Her-Trib.*, 22 Oct.
O'Neill proves he can write a normal play and please the masses; smiling, tender, simple treatment of subject.

GABRIEL, Gilbert. "Personal element." NY *Amer.*, 5 Oct.
Gabriel draws some tenuous parallels between O'Neill's early life and the play's events.

GARLAND, Robert. "Finds subtle change in outlook of O'Neill." NY *Wor-Tel.*, 5 Oct.
Garland likes this best of any O'Neill.

———. "Hails O'Neill play for wit and daring." NY *Wor-Tel.*, 9 Oct.
Extensive quotes from Clayton Hamilton's high praise; the kind of play nobody previously dared write or produce in this "over-wearied world."

———. "Hokum that assays at humanity." NY *Wor-Tel.*, 3 Nov.
O'Neill and Mae West both use hokum and both succeed.

"Garment of repentance." *Lit. D.*, 116 (28 Oct.) 24.
"The family scenes strike one as things overheard rather than lived or truthfully imagined."

"Guild's new O'Neill play escapes dullness with Cohan." *Newsweek*, 2 (7 Oct.) 29.

"Moonlight and soft roses in old New England" which do not stand up very well without the stars and splendid supporting cast.

HAMMOND, Percy. "The theaters." NY *Her-Trib.*, 8 Oct.
Cohan keeps the play from being completely boring. He has been good in many bad plays, "among the worst of which is Ah, Wilderness!"

ISAACS, Edith J. R. "Good plays a plenty." *Th. Arts*, 17 (Dec.) 908-909.
Not much of a play, but merely conventional comedy.

JORDAN, Elizabeth. "Mr. O'Neill soft pedalled." *America*, 28 Oct., p. 89.
This critic does not admire O'Neill's usual plays and is happy to see this one. She concludes that if his recent marriage was the cause of his change, his wife is a public benefactor and should be awarded Pulitzer and Nobel prizes.

KRUTCH, Joseph Wood. "Mr. O'Neill's comedy." *Nation*, 137 (18 Oct.) 458-459.
Charming humor, pleasant entertainment, written about sentiment instead of passion.

LOCKRIDGE, Richard. "Requiescat in pace?" NY *Sun*, 7 Oct.
Hope expressed that the change in O'Neill will not remove one of the most exciting reasons for going to the theatre by becoming ordinary, unexciting, conventional.

MANTLE, Burns. "Mister O'Neill changes a few spots." NY *News*, 15 Oct.
Attempts to explain the change in O'Neill, tracing back some of his personal history. It is to O'Neill's credit that he should have written this play.

NATHAN, George Jean. "A turn to the right." *Van. F.*, 41 (Nov.) 66.

Proof O'Neill can write comedy as well as serious material. Nathan is glad he can work in a conventional medium.

"Old man O'Neill, and others." NY *Her-Trib.*, 5 Oct.
This review of published version warns that if this is a changed O'Neill, we may soon expect a satire on "serious young Freudian of yesteryear."

"O'Neill relaxes." *Stage*, 11 (Nov.) 7-9.
Large double page picture of dinner scene, with brief review. O'Neill has put people you are drawn to on stage just because you love them.

"O'Neill turns to simple folk." NY *Post*, 11 Oct.
Mainly discusses the ease with which the play was composed in six weeks.

SKINNER, Richard Dana. "Ah, Wilderness!" *Commonweal*, 18 (27 Oct.) 620. [Reprinted as "A note on Eugene O'Neill," in Skillin, *The Commonweal reader*, 1949.]
More than just Tarkington; O'Neill is looking into his own soul as he pauses on a difficult journey.

WYATT, Euphemia Van R. "A great American comedy." *Cath. Wld.*, 138 (Nov.) 214-215.
No more tender plea could be made for the Pope's Encyclical on Marriage than this play, written in keeping therewith by Catholic O'Neill. (In reality, O'Neill did not practice his religion after his childhood.)

YOUNG, Stark. "Variegated hits." *New Rep.*, 76 (18 Oct.) 280.
Some effect lost by O'Neill's lack of gift for true words and living speech rhythm. The basic appeal is still O'Neill.

1934-1936

"Ah, Wilderness!" *Newsweek*, 3 (12 May 1934) 23.

"Ah, Wilderness!" *Th. Arts*, 18 (May 1934) 390.
   The published version, while gracious, nostalgic, and trivial, loses much without Cohan.

BRANDT, George. "Ah, Wilderness!" *Rev. of Rev.*, 89 (Feb. 1934) 39.
   "Booth Tarkington sort of tenderness."

EATON, Walter Prichard. "The drama in 1933." *Am. Schol.*, 3 (Winter 1934) 96-101.
   Reviewing the season, Eaton hopes O'Neill has not departed from his gropings into the human spirit.

GILBERT, Douglas. "Did the Nobel judges consider O'Neill's Ah, Wilderness!?" NY *Wor-Tel.*, 14 Nov. 1936.
   Not to be taken lightly; more rational than any of O'Neill's others.

WYATT, Euphemia Van R. "O'Neill and his miracle." *Cath. Wld.*, 138 (Mar. 1934) 729.
   This play is a "sincere confession of faith" and forecasts the "miracle" of the later *DAYS WITHOUT END*.

*Opening night reviews—Revival—New York
Newspapers of 3 Oct. 1941*

"Ah, Wilderness!" *W. W. Daily.*
   Has lost none of its flavor and charm; excellent production.

ANDERSON, John. "Ah, Wilderness! revived by Guild." NY *Jour-Am.*
   Enduring comedy; never reaches the sentimental or slushy.

ATKINSON, Brooks. "Eugene O'Neill's Ah, Wilderness! restaged." NY *Times*, 26:2.

Welcomes return; still a play of great pleasure, "never more enchanting."

BROWN, John Mason. "Ah, Wilderness! remains tender and enjoyable." NY *Wor-Tel.*
Even better than the original, despite Cohan's absence.

COLEMAN, Robert. "Ah, Wilderness is again a hit." NY *Mirror.*
One of the best scripts from the master's pen. It has heart, decent sentiment, literate humor.

KRONENBERGER, Louis. "The Miller family stands the test." *P.M.*
More sentiment than Tarkington, without the gentility.

LOCKRIDGE, Richard. "O'Neill's Ah, Wilderness! is revived." NY *Sun.*
Better than the original.

MANTLE, Burns. "Ah, Wilderness! is happily revived." NY *News.*
Expertly written play, intelligently revived.

POLLOCK, Arthur. "O'Neill's Wilderness pleasingly revived." Brook. *Eagle.*
Still a pleasant comedy; O'Neill's insight into character is apparent.

WALDORF, Wilella. "Theatre Guild's revival series begins with Ah, Wilderness!" NY *Post.*
Measures up in every respect to the original, and there is even some improvement. Still provides a tender and amusing picture of family life.

WATTS, Richard, Jr. "O'Neill revival." NY *Her-Trib.*
Enchanting picture of a lost decade, despite some dawdling.

Other reviews and criticism
1941

"Ah, Wilderness!" *Commonweal*, 34 (17 Oct.) 613.
Fresh as the day it was written; Guild is to be thanked for reviving it when the theatre needs spiritual awakening.

"Ah, Wilderness!" *Variety*, 8 Oct.
"Least exciting" of Guild's proposed revivals.

"Ah, Wilderness! revival is season's best play." *Life*, 11 (3 Nov.) 59-61.
Mainly pictures of the revival, small amount of text.

BURR, Eugene. "Ah, Wilderness!" *Billboard*, 53 (11 Oct.) 15.
Occasionally sleazy, descends to obvious burlesque, but the production hides most of it.

COLBY, Ethel. "Ah, Wilderness! remains excellent play in revival." *Jour. Comm.*, 4 Oct.
More virile interpretation than the original; remains an enchanting comedy, one of the finest examples of playwriting.

COOKE, Richard P. "O'Neill revival." *Wall St. Jour.*, 4 Oct.
Refreshing reminder that there are still some good plays in existence, though its open and unabashed sentiment lacks what we call "pace" today.

FREEDLEY, George. "Guild presents poignant revival of Eugene O'Neill's Ah, Wilderness!" NY *Telegraph*, 4 Oct.
Eight years have not dimmed the success of this play.

GIBBS, Wolcott. "Ah, Wilderness!" *New Yorker*, 17 (11 Oct.) 47.
Full of cliches; less to believe in than even a Tarkington story.

GILDER, Rosamund. "Candles that light the way—Broadway in review." *Th. Arts*, 25 (Dec.) 867-868.

Mellowed with age; still has basic quality of Americana appropriate in these times.

KRONENBERGER, Louis. "Wanted: Six grade B playwrights." *P.M.*, 12 Oct.

A minor play, but not a false one. Kronenberger pleads for more plays of this type, about ordinary good people. The theatre should stop its search for new Ibsens and Chekhovs and concentrate on some good adult plays on a level with good magazine fiction.

KRUTCH, Joseph Wood. "The fires of spring." *Nation*, 153 (18 Oct.) 381.

Better than original. The play is typical of O'Neill in dealing with "hard virtues vs. the soft ones."

LOCKRIDGE, Richard. "Footnote on Ah, Wilderness! and the way of life it celebrates." NY *Sun*, 18 Oct.

Improved in quality; paints life as basically good and a way of life all but forgotten at this time.

WARNER, Ralph. "Theatre Guild revival reveals the true O'Neill." *Daily Worker*, 7 Oct.

Welcomes the revival of this lovable family.

WYATT, Euphemia Van R. "The drama." *Cath. Wld.*, 154 (Nov.) 212-213.

Thoroughly recommended revival.

Further Reviews

ADLER, Jacob H. "The worth of Ah, Wilderness!" *Mod. Dr.*, 3 (Dec. 1960) 280-288.

Defense of the play as a valuable example of domestic comedy, though one that "strains the genre." Rounded characters and serious treatment of love and passion make it distinguished within the genre.

GOING, William T. "O'Neill's Ah, Wilderness." *Explicator*, 29 (1970): Item 28.

HERRON, Ima Honaker. "O'Neill's 'comedy of recollection': A nostalgic dramatization of 'the real America.' " *CEA Critic*, 30 (Jan. 1968) 16-18.
Other plays are included in discussion of O'Neill's small town characters. This one is evocation of "real America" at turn of century.

SHAWCROSS, John T. "The road to ruin: The beginnings of Q'Neill's Long Day's Journey." *Mod. Dr.*, 3 (Dec. 1960) 289-296.
For comments on *AH, WILDERNESS!* as "source" of *JOURNEY*, see *JOURNEY* entry.

ALL GOD'S CHILLUN GOT WINGS

Opening night reviews—New York
Newspapers of 16 May 1924

"All God's Chillun Got Wings proves a poignant drama." *W.W. Daily.*
The more it is understood, the less virulent will be the criticism. Powerful, somber, and poignant, probing into the human soul. Probably better as a treatise than a play.

BROUN, Heywood. "All God's Chillun Got Wings." NY *World.*
A "downstroke" in O'Neill's uneven career; tiresome problem play about sanity and insanity.

CORBIN, John. "All God's Chillun Got Wings." NY *Times*, 22:3.
"A painful play" which, if left alone, would not have received the attention it got.

HAMMOND, Percy. "The mayor interferes a little bit with All God's Chillun Got Wings." NY *Her-Trib.*

Plays better than it reads, but without significance one way or another.

MANTLE, Burns. "Fitful fevers attack drama." NY *News.*
A dull drama, but sincere; sometimes exciting, but never inspiring. Nobody will go back twice.

"New O'Neill play and the mayor." NY *Post.*
It would be a good one-act play and does not rank with O'Neill's best. The second act climax is the O'Neill of *JONES*, going straight to the heart. The landscape is wreckage, but it is breathtaking.

POLLOCK, Arthur. "All God's Chillun." Brook. *Eagle.* [Reprinted in Miller, *Playwright's progress*, 1965.]
Not a play to arouse great enthusiasm. O'Neill can be heard explaining and expounding most of the evening, for it is mainly exposition. Affectation still persists in the Provincetown, and O'Neill is not free of it.

WELSH, Robert G. "James (*sic*) O'Neill Negro play." NY *Telegram and Eve. Mail.*
From the standpoint of a situation drawn out to its conclusion, one of the most "appealingly moral" plays.

WOOLLCOTT, Alexander. "All God's Chillun Got Wings." NY *Sun.*
Strange, wanton, largely unbelievable tragedy in which the antagonist is a taboo. The author is too much in evidence, pushing his characters into a trap and weeping for them. It is something tried, but missed.

Other reviews and criticism
1924

BJORKMAN, Edwin. "Plays and playmakers." *Outlook,* 137 (11 June) 238.
Reviewing published version of this and *WELDED*, finds both worth reading, with shortcoming hard to define.

CARB, David. "To see or not to see." *Bookman*, 59 (July) 582.
Many faults, but stabs "as only great tragedy can stab."

CORBIN, John. "Among the new plays." NY *Times*, 18 May, VII, 1:1.
In a rather surprisingly blunt assertion of white superiority over the Negro, Corbin pleads for a sane attitude toward the play, judgment of which will be by those who see it and by the play itself.

GRUENING, Ernest. "The wings of the children." *Th. Arts*, 8 (July) 497-498.
Has O'Neill poignancy, vigor, honesty, but race issue should be more clear-cut without the abnormalities.

HORNBLOW, Arthur. "Mr. Hornblow goes to the play." *Theatre*, 39 (July) 15.
The "tremendous theme" (which Hornblow does not define) lamely handled; Provincetown Players add nothing to their laurels.

KANTOR, Louis. "O'Neill defends his play of Negroes: All Gods Chillun." NY *Times*, 11 May, IX, 5:2.
Presents O'Neill's defense of this and *APE* as nothing but the treatment of problems of the individuals involved. He advocates nothing, merely presenting what is in the problem itself. Race prejudice is not O'Neill's concern.

LEWISOHN, Ludwig. "All God's Chillun." *Nation*, 118 (4 June) 664. [Reprinted in Miller, *Playwright's progress*, 1965.]
Race prejudice idea brings O'Neill new heights "hitherto inaccessible to him." Symbolic character, almost Greek.

METCALFE, J. S. "Stage miscegenation." *Wall St. Jour.*, 17 May.
The obvious strain of showing "realism" in relationship between white and Negro prevents the play from becoming real. Dramatic values are lost in the obvious racial basis of the play. (This critic makes the interesting suggestion that white actor in blackface, or Negro in whiteface would have eliminated much of the difficulty.)

NATHAN, George Jean. "The theatre." *Am. Merc.*, 2 (May) 113-114.
[Reprinted in Downer, *American drama and its critics*, 1965.]
Done with sincerity and intelligence, if overly sketchy. The violent attacks on the play all miss the point.

WILSON, Edmund. "All God's Chillun and others." *New Rep.*, 39 (28 May) 22. [Portions reprinted in Cargill *et al*, *O'Neill and his plays*, 1961.]
One of best things about race prejudice and one of best O'Neill.

WOOLLCOTT, Alexander. "All God's Chillun etc." NY *Sun*, 20 May.
Lesser O'Neill; compromises realism of the past with lack of persuasion; highly improbable situation in the first place.

1932

RICE, Elmer. "Sex in the modern theatre." *Harpers*, 164 (May) 665-673.
In a discussion of aspects of sex and sex taboos on the modern stage, Rice finds this play an "only moderately successful attempt" to deal honestly with the problem of miscegenation.

THE ANCIENT MARINER

Opening night reviews—New York
Newspapers of 7 Apr. 1924

ALLEN, Kelcey. "New plays at Provincetown Playhouse." *W. W. Daily..*
Impressively done. Flawless lighting, but drags terribly.

BROUN, Heywood. "The Ancient Mariner." NY *World*.
Base metal from a cracked test tube in the Provincetown lab. The ballad is now dreary recitation.

"Coleridge, Moliere and O'Neill on Provincetown bill." NY *Post*
Even with the O'Neill assist, Coleridge as theatrical entertainment
is under serious handicap. Neither narrative drama nor dramatic narrative. Weird imagery came through from time to time, but unsustained.

CORBIN, John. "A new Provincetown playbill." NY *Times*, 15:5.
Less grewsome and thrilling than the poem as read.

VREELAND, Frank. "Ancient Mariner made vivid even for schoolboys." NY *Her-Trib.*
It is so vivid, fresh and heart stirring that schoolboys will go
home and start memorizing it. The production has all the beauty one
has suspected of the poem. Dramatic fire has been drawn to it.

WELSH, Robert G. "Classics and Provincetown." NY *Telegram* &
Eve. Mail.
Skillfully arranged as sort of a dramatic monologue. Students of
the stage will find much to discuss here.

WOOLLCOTT, Alexander. "Coleridge and Eugene O'Neill." NY *Sun*.
More a charade than anything else; Coleridge comes out second
best.

Other reviews and criticism
1924

CANFIELD, Mary Cass. "The Provincetown Playhouse takes a
chance." *Ind. & Week. R.*, 112 (10 May) 259.
"Almost comes off," but offering no comment on O'Neill's contribution this critic states she does not know the amount of O'Neill's
own effort.

"The chorus as used in the Ancient Mariner." NY *Sun*, 23 Apr.
Anonymous critic comments on the part of the chorus, which
was used without any choral training.

"Coleridge and O'Neill." NY *Times*, 13 Apr., VIII, 1:4.

Reprints portion of MS to show the adaptation. Some stage directions are actual lines from the poem. A drawing of scenery is on p. 2.

CORBIN, John. "The playboys of Macdougal street." NY *Times*, 13 Apr., VIII, 1:2.
Force of the poem shrinks to the size of the Provincetown stage. The producers are fooling around, getting nowhere.

HORNBLOW, Arthur. "Mr. Hornblow goes to the play." *Theatre*, 39 (June) 19.
Ponderous and dull despite artistic background effects. The poem is destroyed; production wearisome, far from entertaining.

MACGOWAN, Kenneth. "Crying the hounds of Broadway." *Th. Arts*, 8 (June) 357-358.
A beautiful and significant form which is what is important, having nothing to do with the poem itself.

METCALFE, J. S. "Playing theatre." *Wall St. Jour.*, 8 Apr.
A strong suggestion of the kind of theatre children would put on at home before a curtain hung in a doorway; it is not art. Those who have forgotten the poem's dreariness will find it recalled here. "O'Neill's pretentious experiment seems hardly worth the hard work wasted on it."

"Moliere satire at Village playhouse." *Jour. Comm.*, 8 Apr.
Rather in the nature of experiment; vague and vacant.

NATHAN, George Jean. "The theatre." *Am. Merc.*, 2 (June) 243-244. [Reprinted in Cargill *et al*, *O'Neill and his plays*, 1961; and Downer, *American drama and its critics*, 1965.]
No scenery or lighting will remove the fact that this needs a writer. Too much an attempt at literal interpretation.

"Plays and players." *Town and Country*, 81 (1 May) 48.
A very thrilling experience.

POLLOCK, Arthur. "About the theatre." Brook. *Eagle,* 13 Apr.
    One of the most interesting of the week's productions. The
Provincetown players are always a step ahead of the Guild, being daring instead of dainty.

"Third Provincetown bill." *Drama Cal.,* 6 (7 Apr.) 1.
    Noteworthy experiment; "always beautiful, often stirring, some-
times thrilling, seldom convincing, never Coleridge."

WHYTE, Gordon. "George Dandin - Ancient Mariner." *Billboard,* 36
(19 Apr.) 34.
    Reminds one of an illustrated song. Too literally done; not a
happy experiment. A good idea if better worked out.

WOOLLCOTT, Alexander. "The Ancient Mariner." NY *Sun,* 12 Apr.
    Reminiscent of a charade by children in the back parlor.

ANNA CHRISTIE

    ANNA CHRISTIE was originally conceived as a play about the
old barge captain, Anna's father, and was entitled both *CHRIS
CHRISTOPHERSON* and *CHRIS.* Under the latter title it was given
a tryout tour in Atlantic City and Philadelphia before being withdrawn
for major revisions. It was never published.

Tryout reviews—CHRIS
Atlantic City and Philadelphia
Miscellaneous reviews of March 1920

BRONTE, C H. "Chris and the modernist school." Phil. *Pub. Ledger,*
21 Mar.
    O'Neill discussed in relation to modern ideas of realism. This
unsuccessful piece cannot be dismissed.

CASSEBOOM, Will, Jr. "A masterly play at the Apollo." Newspaper unidentified on NYPL clipping. Apparently Atlantic City 9 Mar.
Not a masterpiece, but masterly piece of writing; the tragedy of life.

"Chris." *Dram. Mir.*, 81 (27 Mar.) 577.
Slim plot, very little action.

"Chris." Phil. *Bulletin*, 16 Mar.
Hardly enough story for a good one-act.

"Chris." *The Stage*, 27 Mar. [Reprinted in Cargill *et al*, *O'Neill and his plays*, 1961.]
Slim plot, little action.

"Chris a new play by Eugene O'Neill." Phil. *Record.*, 16 Mar.
Worthy of serious attention in character and dialogue, but it is more of a short story expanded into a play than an original play.

"Chris a sea play, is Conrad on stage." Phil. *Eve. Ledger*, 16 Mar.
Little or no action or plot, like a staged Conrad story.

"Chris at Broad." Phil. *Inquirer*, 16 Mar.
Draggy, dreary play helped by excellent dialogue, though even that is tedious at times.

"Chris at the Apollo tonight." Apparently Atlantic City *Union*, 8 Mar., but source and date on NYPL clipping are not clear.
The story's climax is told with "unerring art."

"Chris sailor play at Broad." Phil. *Press*, 16 Mar.
Suggestions of Conrad. We should recognize the talent in this new writer.

"Lounger in the lobby." Phil. *Press*, 21 Mar.
The young writer is feeling his way, has defective sense of drama, but talent for character and atmosphere.

MARTIN, Linton. "Dramaless drama." Phil. *North American,* 22 Mar.
The overemphasis on art and atmosphere nearly omits the play.

————. "Novel note struck in Eugene O'Neill's Chris." Phil. *North American,* 16 Mar.
A novel note in playwriting. Everything is here for the success of a play but the play itself, which is a "colossal failure" because it is dramaless.

"Saline zephyrs blow through O'Neill's play." Atlantic City *Daily Press,* 9 Mar.
The play is a surprising comedy which everybody seemed to enjoy, but this critic lost interest in the conflict between the man and the sea after Act III.

"Sea story Chris by Monte Cristo's son." Phil. *Pub. Ledger,* 16 Mar.
Little feeling of theatre. Play is not engrossing; real drama comes too late.

"Seafaring folk as they really are." Phil *Record,* 21 Mar.
Loses intensity in happy ending, but play is the work of a "realist with poet's vision."

*Opening night reviews—New York
Newspapers of 3 Nov. 1921*

"Anna Christie at Vanderbilt." NY *Telegram.*
A hit, promising to repeat former O'Neill success.

"Anna Christie has its premiere." NY *Sun.*
Unconventional play dwindles to conventional happy ending, but still proves O'Neill can write 3-act play.

"Anna Christie is sordid and sad." *Journal of Commerce.*
Falls short of great play; dialogue far out of proportion to action.

"Anna Christie new triumph for O'Neill." NY *Journal.*
Great promise for future successes.

DALE, Alan. "Anna Christie is offered at the Vanderbilt." NY *American*. [Reprinted in Miller, *Playwright's progress,* 1965.]
Nothing comes through the oleaginous, permeating fog, and there's nothing worth coming through anyway. Better to have presented the fog without either O'Neill or Anna Christie.

DE FOE, Louis V. "Another grim O'Neill drama." NY *World*.
Performance makes this production worth seeing; shows keen imagination and ability of this yet immature artist.

"Drab life of the sea in O'Neill's Anna Christie." NY *Herald*.
Not worthy of O'Neill's ability. Too much "realism"; needs something more. Fantastic to have the sea as the protagonist.

HAMMOND, Percy. "Anna Christie, by the acrid O'Neill." NY *Tribune*.
Recommended for "veracious picture of some interesting characters in interesting circumstances."

KAUFMAN, S. Jay. "Round the town." NY *Globe*.
Good play, despite repetition and happy ending.

MACGOWAN, Kenneth. ". . . A notable drama notably acted." NY *Globe*. [Reprinted in Miller, *Playwright's Progress,* 1965.]
No American drama has searched its portion of life as this does. Power and humor; notable in vision, writing, acting.

MANTLE, Burns. "Anna Christie, vivid drama." NY *Mail*.
Whatever your opinion, it is finest piece of O'Neill writing, sheer realism "stripped to its ugly vitals."

MARSH, Leo A. "Anna Christie at the Vanderbilt." NY *Telegraph*.
O'Neill's claim to fame could rest with this alone. Continuing vitality despite apparent compromise in happy ending.

POLLOCK, Arthur. "Anna Christie." Brook. *Eagle*.
At last produced as O'Neill should be; a play of real persons. Happy ending comes naturally out of the plot.

Torres, H. Z. "Anna Christie a triple triumph." NY *Commercial*.
End result somewhat unhappy because of ugliness and morbidness of the story, despite brilliant writing.

Towse, J. Ranken. "Anna Christie." NY *Post*.
"Incredible" happy ending is "disastrous." The play promises more for the future than is presently achieved.

Woollcott, Alexander. "The new O'Neill play." NY *Times*, 22:1.
Mark of imagination. Much better than most current plays.

Other reviews and criticism
1921

Allen, Kelcey. "Anna Christie superbly played drama of the sea."
W. W. *Daily*, 4 Nov.
Ranks with the best of several seasons.

"Anna Christie." NY *Clipper*, 16 Nov.
Too literal a transfer from life; too much gloom, commonplace dialogue.

"Anna Christie." *Drama Calendar*, 21 Nov.
As fine a play as American theatre has yet produced.

"Anna Christie." *Variety*, 11 Nov.
While most critics are lyrical in praise of Pauline Lord, this one finds her very ordinary, using stock mannerisms.

"Anna Christie at the Vanderbilt Theatre." *Town Topics*, 10 Nov.
Does not cohere; more of shreds and patches than a unified whole.

Benchley, Robert. Untitled review. *Life*, 78 (24 Nov.) 18.
Miss Lord's performance better than the play, but it is still one of the season's most important productions.

Boyd, Ernest. "Mr. O'Neill's new plays." *Freeman*, 4 (7 Dec.) 304.

The ending is the worst anti-climax in the theatre, after one of the most tremendous third acts ever written.

CASTELLUN, Maida. "Anna Christie thrilling drama, perfectly acted, with a bad ending." NY *Call*, 4 Nov.
Ending not a blunder but a crime; 3-1/2 acts have the quality of greatness.

————. "The plays that pass—the season's climax." NY *Call*, 6 Nov.
Reiteration of praise; "the spark of divine fire."

DARNTON, Charles. "Anna Christie human flotsam." NY *World*, 4 Nov.
Chris is the main character, Anna merely a "barnacle on the paternal hulk." Treatment of character is the most important aspect.

DAWSON, N. P. "Books in particular." NY *Globe*, 23 Dec.
This writer, who "knows nothing about the theatre anyway," does not find the ending of the published version sentimental.

HACKETT, Francis. "After the play." *New Rep.*, 29 (30 Nov.) 20. [Reprinted in Cargill *et al*, *O'Neill and his plays*, 1961.]
Essentially a hoax, full of fantasy. To become great, O'Neill must use people for their effectiveness as they are.

"How Joseph Conrad influenced O'Neill." NY *Eve. Telegram*, 16 Nov.
This critic finds interesting parallels between O'Neill and Conrad by quoting their common idea toward the sea.

KAUFMAN, S. Jay. "Anna Christie." *Dram. Mir.*, 84 (12 Nov.) 701.
Simple story and theme played upon by a great artist; honest, not stooping to theatrical effect for its own sake.

"The O'Neill irony." NY *Herald*, 6 Nov.
"None of the works of the O'Neill theatre is so destitute of imagination as Anna Christie."

Parker, Robert Allerton. "An American dramatist developing." *Ind. & Week. R.*, 107 (3 Dec.) 235. [Reprinted in Miller, *Playwright's progress*, 1965.]
O'Neill is in the literary class of those who continually create anew. This has some of his most exalted moments.

————. "Deeper notes in the current drama." *Arts & Dec.*, 16 (Dec.) 110.
This play, despite its faults, is preferable to most of the technically perfect, but superficial, offerings.

POLLOCK, Arthur. "About the theatre." Brook. *Eagle*. 6 Nov.
Play not so significant as earlier works, but excellent staging brings out the best, more than in any other O'Neill play.

SELDES, Gilbert. "The theatre." *Dial*, 71 (Dec.) 724-725.
Conclusion and "happy ending" satisfactory; O'Neill surrenders to a certain amount of theatricality.

"A triumph for Eugene O'Neill and Pauline Lord." NY *Review*, 5 Nov.
Questionable ending; deep ethical significance in play.

WHITTAKER, James. "O'Neill has first concrete heroine." NY *News*, 13 Nov.
For the first time characters surmount environment; O'Neill denies the sea its prey as in earlier works.

WOOLLCOTT, Alexander. "Second thoughts on first nights." NY *Times*, 13 Nov., VI, 1:1.
Despite faults (last act) "hardened with theatrical alloy" and should be seen again and again.

————. "Second thoughts on first nights." NY *Times*, 25 Dec., VI, 1:1.
Comment on O'Neill's letter to editor (see Non-Dramatic O'Neill) defending the "happy" ending. Woollcott informs O'Neill

that he, O'Neill, should not have been surprised at the public reaction to it.

1922

"Anna Christie." *Cur. Op.*, 72 (Jan.) 57-66.
Retells the plot, with some critical comment from New York press. Well illustrated.

BONE, David W. "The sea across the footlights." NY *Times*, 15 Jan., III, p. 3.
This member of the British merchant marine finds that the character and atmosphere of the sea as the sailor knows it is now shown for the first time on the stage.

EATON, Walter P. Untitled comment. *Freeman*, 11 Jan.
The main aspects that puzzle the O'Neill audience are: sympathy for actually unsympathetic characters, poetry in brutal dialogue, grim naturalism that attracts.

HAMMOND, Percy. "The theaters." NY *Tribune*, 28 May.
Justifies the award of the Pulitzer Prize; the play meets the specifications.

HORNBLOW, Arthur. "Mr. Hornblow goes to the play." *Theatre*, 35 (Jan.) 29.
A youthful interest in tragedy is shown by this play. It blunders at times, but has some unforgettable scenes and good character delineation.

MACGOWAN, Kenneth. "Anna Christie." *Th. Arts*, Jan. [Reprinted in Hewitt, Barnard, *Theatre USA*, 1959.]
"The most searching and the most dramatically consistent study in realism that our playwrights have produced."

———. "Anna Christie." *Vogue*, Jan.

O'Neill's most mature play yet. Finest first act ever written by an American. Clear, vigorous pictures of life in the characters.

PEARSON, Edmund L. "New books and old." *Independent,* 109 (19 Aug.) 78.
    On reading the published version, this critic cannot understand the "extravagant praise" the play has received.

*Opening night reviews—City Center Revival—New York
Newspapers of 10 Jan. 1952*

ATKINSON, Brooks. "Anna Christie." NY *Times,* 33:1. [Reprinted in Miller, *Playwright's progress,* 1965.]
    Still a play of vitality. Tumultuous and elemental, with honest and dramatic characters. It is part of our American theatre heritage.

CHAPMAN, John. "A fine O'Neill play in a grand revival." NY *News.*
    After 30 years it still stands the test because "when it was made it was made right."

COLBY, Ethel. "Revival of Anna Christie reveals O'Neill still packs a potent punch." *Journal of Commerce.*
    One of the best O'Neill's, still has a fascination.

COLEMAN, Robert. "Anna Christie welcome revival at the City Center." NY *Mirror.*
    Comparison of Lord and Holm in the roles.

DASH, Thomas R. "Anna Christie." *W.W. Daily.*
    Because of valid, well drawn characters, play is not dated. It is basically a comedy.

HAWKINS, William. "Anna Christie back—why not sooner?" NY *Wor-Tel. & Sun.*
    Great stature and power; O'Neill's theme "crystal clear."

KERR, Walter. "Anna Christie." NY *Her-Trib.*

Still "seaworthy," but "shipping light" because characters not presented as O'Neill demanded; too much comic emphasis.

McCLAIN, John. "Anna Christie." NY *Jour-Am.*
  Celeste Holm is as good as Garbo or any of the rest.

SHEAFFER, Louis. "Only 'Anna' herself disappoints in City Center O'Neill revival." Brook. *Eagle.*
  Still effective; flavorsome, true dialogue.

WATTS, Richard. "Revival of O'Neill's Anna Christie." NY *Post.*
  Still has emotional power and atmosphere, "brute intensity."

Other reviews and criticism
1952

"Anna Christie." *Time,* 59 (21 Jan.) 73.
  This production stresses the age and O'Neill's "adolescence." Wasn't one of his good plays anyway.

"Anna Christie." *Variety,* 16 Jan.
  "Somewhat dated" but still of power and "compelling drama."

BEYER, William H. "The state of the theatre: Classics revisited." *School & Society,* 75 (16 Feb.) 107.
  "An unfortunate production."

BOLTON, Whitney. "An interesting, vigorous version of Anna Christie." NY *Telegraph,* 11 Jan.
  Still touching and at times witty; age has affected it a little.

BROWN, John Mason. "Dat ole Davil and a hard God." *Sat. R. Lit.,* 35 (16 Feb.) 32-34.
  Irony rather than tragedy; still moving and effective.

GIBBS, Wolcott. "Two from way back." *New Yorker,* 27 (2 Feb.) 48.

"One of the most engagingly absurd works in the English language" but still effective theatre, on a "primary level."

KERR, Walter. "New generation gets two looks at O'Neill." NY *Her.Trib.*
Revaluation of the revival (including *DESIRE*) finds *ANNA CHRISTIE* the more real and genuine play.

————. "The stage—Anna Christie." *Commonweal*, 55 (25 Jan.) 399.
Still has a strong ring.

KRUTCH, Joseph Wood. "Anna Christie." *Nation*, 174 (26 Jan.) 92.
While "dated" as any play of another time is "dated" this still has strength of its own.

————. "The strange case of Anna Christie." NY *Her.-Trib.*, 6 Jan.
Explanation of why the public liked and O'Neill disliked this early play, clearly indicating the completely opposite views of playwright and playgoer.

NATHAN, George Jean. "Mr. Nathan goes to the play." *Th. Arts*, 36 (Mar.) 70.
Better than the original, which is not saying much.

"O'Neill shines again." *Life*, 32 (4 Feb.) 82.
Pictures of Celeste Holm in City Center revival and June Havoc on Celanese Theatre TV performance.

WATTS, Richard, Jr. "Those two plays by Eugene O'Neill." NY *Post*, 27 Jan.
Praise for revival of this and *DESIRE*.

WYATT, Euphemia Van R. "Anna Christie." *Cath. Wld.*, 174 (Mar.) 462-463.
Agrees this is not one of O'Neill's best.

Further Reviews

*BOGARD, Travis. "Anna Christie: Her fall and rise." In Gassner, John, *O'Neill* (Twentieth Century Views), 1964. An original essay published here for the first time.

Original *CHRIS CHRISTOPHERSON* and *OLE DAVIL* compared with and contrasted to the final version of *ANNA CHRISTIE*, tracing O'Neill's eventual abandonment of Chris as central figure and the problems surrounding making Anna and Burke the eventually "happy" protagonists. (See Flory, below.)

*FLORY, Claude R. "Notes on the antecedents of Anna Christie." *PMLA*, 86 (Jan. 1971) 77-83.

Determined to discover the original play, Flory found the complete text of early *CHRIS* and *CHRIS CHRISTOPHERSON* on microfilm at the Univ. of California. *THE OLD DAVIL* [variations: *OLE DEVIL, OLE DAVIL. Ed.*] shown to be virtually another title for the later *ANNA CHRISTIE,* with about 95% of text intact. The original *CHRIS* was reduced by nine characters and some 10,000 words, making a study of the manuscripts "an enlightening study of O'Neill's maturation." (See Bogard, above.)

FRAZER, Winifred L. "Chris and Poseidon: Man versus God in Anna Christie." *Mod. Dr.,* 12 (Dec. 1969) 279-285.

Interesting examination of mythic sea god theme (Chris' awe and fear; Matt as son of Poseidon) plus other notes on O'Neill's feeling for myth.

*MCALEER, John J. "Christ symbolism in Anna Christie." *Mod. Dr.,* 4 (Feb. 1962) 389-396.

Using a well-known medieval prayer, the Anina Christi, McAleer traces many parallelisms, concluding that fairly literal symbols may have resulted from O'Neill's acquaintance at the time with Sherwood Anderson, whose use of such symbolism and attitude toward pointless suffering appeared in *Winesburg, Ohio.*

BEFORE BREAKFAST

Search through the files of major New York newspapers could not reveal a single report of the Provincetown's third bill, 1 December 1916, which included this play. The first references appear after the revival of 5 March 1929, when *BEFORE BREAKFAST* was given on the same bill with Vergil Geddes' *The Earth Between*. Cargill *et al, O'Neill and his plays*, reprints the account of the first production of the play as reported in *The Provincetown*, 1931, by Helen Deutsch and Stella Hanau.

Opening night reviews—Revival—New York
Newspapers of 6 March 1929

ALLEN, Kelcey. "Before Breakfast." *W. W. Daily.*
Evidence even in this apprentice work that O'Neill would develop into the incorrigible experimenter.

ANDERSON, John. "Before Breakfast." NY *Journal.*
Flimsy and artificial; so tedious as to seem longer than *INTERLUDE*.

ATKINSON, Brooks. "The McDougal street blues." NY *Times*, 33:1.
O'Neill a glutton when he composed this interlude of domestic horror.

"Before Breakfast, short O'Neill play, produced in Village." NY *Her-Trib.*
The least of all O'Neill plays currently showing.

"The Earth Between in the Village." NY *News.*
"Mary Blair played Eugene O'Neill's *Before Breakfast* as a curtain raiser. She played it for half an hour."

GABRIEL, Gilbert. "Incest and other dark drama down MacDougal street way." NY *American.*
Little service is rendered O'Neill in doing this.

GARLAND, Robert. "Before Breakfast." NY *Telegram*.
Miss Blair "did wonders with a role which called for no less a star than Harpo Marx with a skirt on."

LITTELL, Robert. "The play." NY *Post*.
Moderately effective. Does not like the intrusion of the disembodied hand.

LOCKRIDGE, Richard. "Some dramatic episodes." NY *Sun*.
This critic's hair stood on end only mildly.

POLLOCK, Arthur. "The theatre." Brook. *Eagle*.
No need to see this twice.

Other reviews and criticism
1929

"Before Breakfast." *Arts and Dec.*, 81 (May) 104.
Powerful, but tricky in construction.

CLARK, Barrett H. "Eugene O'Neill and the Village experiment." *Drama*, 19 (29 Apr.) 200.
"It is not an impressive work."

"Earth Between." *Variety*, 20 Mar. 1929.
Brief note only. Mary Blair "makes much" of her opportunities.

ERVINE, St. John. "Greenwich gloom." NY *World*, 7 Mar.
A monologue misnamed a play; mostly bunk.

LITTELL, Robert. "Broadway in review." *Th. Arts*, 13 (May) 334.
Insistent, clumsy *tour de force*, not well written.

RILEY, Wilfred J. "Before Breakfast." *Billboard*, 41 (16 Mar.) 49.
Ineffective and incoherent; O'Neill at his worst.

BEYOND THE HORIZON

Opening matinee reviews—New York
Newspapers of 4 Feb. 1920

BROUN, Heywood. "Beyond the Horizon by O'Neill a notable play."
NY *Tribune*. [Reprinted in Moses and Brown, *The American theatre*
as seen by its critics, 1752-1934, 1934; and in Miller, *Playwright's*
progress, 1965.]
Signs of clumsiness because the young man has not mastered the
tricks of his trade, but deserves attention; significant and interesting.

DARNTON, Charles. "Beyond the Horizon close to life." NY *Eve.*
World.
"A real play with real people"; the writer should go far.

"Eugene O'Neill's tragedy played." NY *Herald*.
O'Neill's fame will be vastly increased. Profoundly moving and
human story, although unnecessarily long and formless.

MARSH, Leo A. "Beyond the Horizon stirring drama." NY *Tele-*
graph.
"This new American tragedy is one of the best New York has
been fortunate enough to see in many a season."

"O'Neill play is a tragedy of misery." *Journal of Commerce*.
Shouldn't be missed; one of season's great plays.

TOWSE, J. Ranken. "Beyond the Horizon." NY *Post*.
"Uncommon merit and definite ability" though shambling and
unnecessarily gloomy.

"Tragedy of great power at Morosco." NY *World*.
Great power from psychological study of character; much promise for this young writer. A real event in intellectual theatre.

WELSH, Robert G. "Bitter, ironic strength in Beyond the Horizon."
NY *Telegram*.

Masterpiece; because of its type and subject it may not be popular.

WOOLLCOTT, Alexander. "Beyond the Horizon." NY *Times*, 12:1 [Reprinted in Woollcott's *Shouts and murmurs*, 1922; in Cargill *et al*, *O'Neill and his plays*, 1961; and Miller, *Playwright's progress*, 1965.]
O'Neill is a gifted writer; the play is so full of meat the rest of season's offerings look like merest meringue.

Other reviews and criticism
1920

"An 'American tragedy'." *Lit. D.*, 64 (28 Feb.) 33.
This item summarizes other reviews, mainly NY *World*.

"Better days for the theatre." NY *Post*, 21 Feb.
Considerable accomplishment that so young a man could write such a play and draw audiences; the theatre is showing a healthy reaction.

"Beyond the Horizon." *Dram. Mir.*, 82 (14 Feb.) 258.
"Fine sense of the theatre," with much promise in the mood of Synge, Chekhov.

"Beyond the Horizon." *Independent*, 101 (13 Mar.) 382.
Powerful play, weak construction.

"Beyond the Horizon a frank tragedy, is very interesting." NY *Clipper*, 68 (11 Feb.) 21.
Strong in human appeal, frankly a tragedy. The writer has promise.

"Beyond the Horizon is presented at matinee." NY *News Record*, 6 Feb.
The essence of tragedy; we await further writings of this man.

"Beyond the Horizon one of the season's real successes." NY *Review*, 26 Feb.
Proof that American public will support a tragedy of their own soil.

BISHOP, John Peale. "At last an American tragedy." *Van. F.*, June.
Great, within narrowness of the *genre*. Perhaps it could be better as a novel.

"Broadway banter." *Town Topics*, 12 Feb.
Greatness is here; our first modern native tragedy, and it must not fail.

BROUN, Heywood. "Books." NY *Tribune*, 29 Mar.
The published version deserves much praise, but is is immature in spots, showing false tragedy.

————. "The heroine may die and the play still live." NY *Tribune*, 15 Feb.
A long discussion of "rule breaking" in modern drama (such as the death of the leading character) uses this play as a striking example.

DALE, Alan. "With Alan Dale at the new plays." NY *American*, 8 Feb.
The show acting pace is sharply criticized, but the play is of "sterling merit."

EATON, Walter Prichard. "Eugene O'Neill." *Th. Arts*, 4 (Oct.) 286-289.
Judging by this first major play and some of O'Neill's others, this young writer is spiritually thin, but with organic form so necessary to true works of art.

"Eugene O'Neill's Beyond the Horizon is one of the great plays of the modern American stage." NY *Call*, 5 Feb.
Overpowering with realism and naturalness, devoid of theatrical-

ism but great in drama. It is memorable drama; the writer has great promise for the future.

"Eugene O'Neill wins fame." NY *Telegraph*, 31 Mar.
An explanation of who this suddenly popular writer is.

FIRKINS, O. W. "Beyond the Horizon." *Weekly Rev.*, 2 (21 Feb.) 185-186.
O'Neill has slipped and fallen in the transfer from one act to three.

HAMILTON, Clayton. "Seen on the stage." *Vogue*, 1 Apr. [Reprinted in Hamilton's *Seen on the stage*, 1920.]
He will write better plays if he steers clear of theatres.

HORNBLOW, Arthur. "Mr. Hornblow goes to the play." *Theatre*, 31 (Mar.) 185.
A tragedy that could happen anywhere, but Hornblow wonders why the intelligent man married the clod of a woman.

JAMES, Patterson. "Beyond the Horizon." *Billboard*, 21 Feb.
Uncommonly fine play about real people; beauty, tenderness, faithfulness to artistic ideal.

KAUFMAN, S. Jay. "Round the town." NY *Globe*, 1 Mar.
If O'Neill keeps this up he will become the American Ibsen.

LEWISOHN, Ludwig. "An American tragedy." *Nation*, 110 (21 Feb.) 241-242. [Reprinted in Hewitt, *Theatre USA*, 1959.]
Establishes American kinship with the stage of the modern world.

MCELLIOT. "Eugene O'Neill's new tragedy is most pathetic." NY *Illus. News*, 11 Feb.
"It is art, and it is life, but it hurts intolerably."

MACGOWAN, Kenneth. "America's best season in the theatre." *Th. Arts*, 4 (Apr.) 91.

Just as powerful and sturdy as the one-acts were, but could be perhaps shorter, getting the doom "over with."

————. "Eugene O'Neill writes a fine, long play." NY *Globe,* 7 Feb.
Extraordinary ability in stretching the theme out; gets down to emotional roots, shows real power.

MANTLE, Burns. "A fine performance of a fine play." NY *Mail,* 5 Feb.
True sense of theatre; much promise for future in this tragedy, which should hearten those interested in serious drama.

METCALFE, J. S. "Beyond the Horizon." *Life,* 75 (19 Feb.) 332.
Before "placing the crown of greatness" on O'Neill's head, we had better wait to see if he can write further tragedy without the great gloom shown here.

NATHAN, George Jean. "Beyond the Horizon." *Smart Set,* April.
Praise from this magazine which first printed O'Neill's early works.

POLLOCK, Arthur. "About the theater." Brook. *Eagle,* 6 Feb.
Not as good as some of the one-acts, but at his worst O'Neill is far better than most current drivel and this is not his worst.

Untitled discussion in column on drama. *Freeman,* 17 Mar.
Not native in form and tone, because naturalism and tragedy are foreign to us, but the theme is universal.

WOOLLCOTT, Alexander. "The coming of Eugene O'Neill." NY *Times,* 8 Feb., VIII, 2:1.
One of the real plays of our time. At times impracticable and loose, but a tragedy of the misfit which in mood and austerity has seldom been written in America even half so good.

"Words versus situations." NY *Sun,* 19 Mar.

Richard Bennett, star of play, discloses great admiration for way O'Neill can use words alone to bring his idea.

"A 'worthwhile' drama." NY *Sun,* 5 Feb.

Discriminating theatregoers will put this bleak but poignant tragedy on their select list.

1921-1926

MacGowan, Kenneth. "1920 saw great progress in the American theatre both in plays and acting." NY *Globe,* 15 Jan. 1921.

This and *JONES* are two of the most important plays of an encouraging season.

Ridge, Lola. "Beyond the Horizon." *New Rep.,* 25 (5 Jan. 1921) 173-174.

The published version is good drama, but short of being a great play because of "theatre consciousness" of playwright. He is "too anxious a father to his brood."

Shipp, Horace. "Conviction and the drama." *Eng. Rev.,* 42 (May 1926) 701-703.

Despite "realism" the play fails because the writer seems to follow too many rules and predestines his characters.

Opening night reviews—Revival—New York
Newspapers of 1 Dec. 1926

Anderson, John. "The Actor's theatre revives O'Neill's Beyond the Horizon." NY *Post.*

It has withstood the years well; a rich and engrossing evening. Its early, naive approach in its strict sorrow is still vivid and compelling. For all its creakiness its blunt impact on the feelings is tremendous.

"Beyond the Horizon is seen here again." NY *Times.*

Still fine and engrossing; an almost perfect tragedy. It has lost none of its power.

"Beyond the Horizon staged in revival." NY *American.*
Its realism never tires; the intensity holds the audience. The revival is befitting the play's power and beauty.

GABRIEL, Gilbert. "Recalling the early O'Neill." NY *Sun.*
Still one of the great contributions to our American drama. It is full of vigor, simplicity, fierce sincerity.

GARRICK. "An O'Neill revival." NY *Journal.*
Still stands out as one of the finest American dramas of all time. Seems infinitely better than when first produced.

HAMMOND, Percy. "Beyond the Horizon revived skillfully by the Actors' Theatre." NY *Her-Trib.*
Even better in its production than the original.

MANTLE, Burns. "Beyond the Horizon food for the O'Neills." NY *News.*
Still an eloquent drama of frustration.

OSBORN, E. W. "Beyond the Horizon." NY *World.*
One of O'Neill's finest. There is a feeling of being cleansed rather than of sorrow on leaving the theatre.

ZIMMERMAN, Katharine. "Actors' Theatre revives Beyond the Horizon." NY *Telegram.*
Still strong and unimpaired by its age.

Other reviews and criticism
1926-1927

"Beyond the Horizon." Brook. *Eagle,* 2 Dec. 1926.
Distinguished production, although O'Neill's plays are "always something of a penance to witness." It is about average O'Neill.

"Beyond the Horizon, O'Neill's tragedy of soil, born at sea." NY *Her-Trib.*, 5 Dec. 1926.
  O'Neill explains how he came to create Robert.

BROWN, John Mason. "The gamut of style." *Th. Arts*, 11 (Feb. 1927) 86.
  One of our "starkest" plays, showing signs of age.

CLARK, Barrett H. "Dirty plays and dirty minds." *Drama*, 17 (Feb. 1927) 136.
  The season's review finds this one of O'Neill's minor efforts.

HARKINS, John. Untitled article. NY *Telegram*, 5 Dec. 1926.
  Still O'Neill's best; a play of great dramatic moments.

KRUTCH, Joseph Wood. "A note on tragedy." *Nation*, 123 (15 Dec. 1926) 646-647.
  After giving a clear definition of what tragedy is now and has been, Krutch then praises *HORIZON* because it comes closer to the real thing than other modern plays.

LELAND, Gordon. "Beyond the Horizon." *Billboard*, 38 (11 Dec. 1926) 9.
  Improved with age; shows O'Neill's great ability in tragic drama. It is not depressing; one actually feels refreshed.

STENGEL, Hans. "Beyond the Horizon." NY *Telegraph*, 5 Dec. 1926.
  Whatever else O'Neill has done he has never come nearer greatness. He is best in his love of soil, but loses much in flights of symbolism.

Further reviews

ROY, Emil. "Tragic tension in Beyond the Horizon." *Ball State Univ. Forum*, 8 (Winter 1967) 74-79.
  This early realistic play discussed in light of tensions inherent in concept of tragedy.

BOUND EAST FOR CARDIFF

The first production in New York of a play by Eugene O'Neill was this play, which appeared at 139 MacDougal Street on 3 November 1916. According to Louis Sheaffer in *O'Neill: Son and Playwright* four New York critics were subscribers to the Provincetown Players productions, but were not expected to attend in their professional capacity. However, two reviews did appear, noted below—the first professional critical notice of twenty-eight year old Eugene G. O'Neill, as he then signed his name.

BROUN, Heywood. "Bound East for Cardiff." NY *Trib.*, 30 Jan. 1917. [The full review appears in Cargill *et al, O'Neill and his plays*, 1961; and in Miller, *Playwright's progress*, 1965.]

The author strikes a rich vein in his successful approximation of the true talk of seamen. Of the Players: "A most efficient experimental theatre."

RATHBUN, Stephen. "Bound East for Cardiff." NY *Eve. Sun*, 13 Nov. 1916.

The play is real, "subtly tense" avoiding "a dozen pitfalls that might have made it 'the regular thing.' " Of the Players: "The world shall make a path to their door."

CHRIS (*See ANNA CHRISTIE*).

CYCLE PLAYS (*see A TALE OF POSSESSORS SELF-DISPOSSESSED*)

DAYS WITHOUT END

Opening night reviews—Boston Tryout
Newspapers of 28 Dec. 1933

CROSBY, Edward H. "Mr. O'Neill drama at Plymouth." Boston *Post*. A strange play.

EAGER, Helen. "Eugene O'Neill's new play in first performance at the Plymouth theatre." Boston *Traveler*.
A fascinating and absorbing evening with this sombre serious drama.

HOLLAND, George. "Eugene O'Neill's new play has masterpiece possibilities." Boston *American*.
More than a love story: that of the soul sold to the devil. Ridges as Loving should make New York critics "delirious."

HUGHES, Elinor. "ONeill play has world premiere here." Boston *Herald*.
On dangerous ground; O'Neill now the affirmer instead of the denier.

"In new vein the new play from O'Neill." Boston *Transcript*.
O'Neill's "Faust." He writes, reborn, out of his inner life.

"Premier performance of Days Without End." Boston *Globe*.
Typically O'Neill; a little more baffling than usual.

On 9 Jan 1934, the same date as the New York opening, *Variety* published a review of the Boston opening, calling it "heavy fodder" with "long and laborious exposition" with the ending as safe and flat as a Sunday School cantata.

Opening night reviews—New York
Newspapers of 9 Jan. 1934

ALLEN, Kelcey. "Days Without End, O'Neill's new play, here." *W. W. Daily*.
A work of exceptional strength and characterization; the speeches are vigorous and strikingly written, but it is mainly for the serious theatre goer.

ANDERSON, John. "Guild makes fine production of work in which author delves into religion." NY *Journal*. [Reprinted in Moses and

Brown, *The American theatre as seen by its critics, 1752-1934*. 1934;
and in Cargill *et al, O'Neill and his plays*, 1961.]
   Fundamental error in making faith an intellectual process that can
be touched through words. Confusing, florid, ornamentally phony.

ATKINSON, Brooks. "Days Without End." NY *Times*, 19:1.
   A bad play, written as if O'Neill had never written a play before.
Lacks size, imagination, vitality and knowledge of human character.

BROWN, John Mason. "The play." NY *Post*. [Reprinted in Miller,
Playwright's progress, 1965.]
   Tedious and aritificial, one of O'Neill's feeblest. Split infinitive
of a hero. Conclusion so trite that without the O'Neill name the play
would not have been tolerated.

COHEN, Julius. "Days Without End new O'Neill theme." *Jour.
Comm.*
   "Miracle" is O'Neill's reconversion—a confession of futility of
non-belief. O'Neill is out of place at the altar; might have been written
by Billy Sunday.

GABRIEL, Gilbert "Days Without End." NY *American*.
   Nothing can make it good; true miracle is that it got produced
at all.

GARLAND, Robert. "O'Neill's drama is certain to mean many things
to many people." NY *Wor-Tel*.
   Sophomoric; told in the most awkward manner possible.

HAMMOND, Percy. "Days Without End." NY *Her-Trib*.
   Signs of showmanship, but Hammond is not sure just what the
play is.

LOCKRIDGE, Richard. "O'Neill's miracle play." NY *Sun*.
   Not his best, but shows O'Neill as the poet seeking God.

MANTLE, Burns. "Back to the soul with O'Neill." NY *News*.
   "A thrill for the true religionist."

POLLOCK, Arthur. "Days Without End." Brook. *Eagle.*
Many audiences will listen devoutly. The Guild has a valuable piece of theatrical property.

SOBEL, Bernard. "Eugene O'Neill's new play." NY *Mirror.*
Outmoded theme; masks have lost poignancy and novelty.

Other reviews and criticism
1934

ANDERSON, John. "Defenders rally to O'Neill play." NY *Journal,* 20 Jan.
Having spoken twice against the play, Anderson reports on those who favor it, including the secular press. He still maintains, however, that it is not a matter of faith but of analyzing the playmaking itself.

———. "O'Neill's interest in religion." NY *Journal,* 12 Jan.
A review of the aspects of O'Neill's interest in religious themes from *FOUNTAIN* and *MARCO* through *DYNAMO* and *DAYS WITHOUT END.*

ATKINSON, Brooks. "On Days Without End." NY *Times,* 14 Jan. IX, 1:1.
This criticism is clear in its analysis of O'Neill's failure to reach exhilaration and spiritual exaltation needed for the theme. Language, expression and story all fail to gain the heights.

BOLTON, Whitney. "Mr. O'Neill has not taken holy orders, but new play misses fire." NY *Telegraph,* 10 Jan.
Befuddled concept of religion and sophomore philosophy. Diffuse, immature, completely lacking in O'Neill's usual authority.

BOWEN, Stirling. "The O'Neill drama." *Wall St. Jour.,* 11 Jan.
O'Neill has not changed, as *AH, WILDERNESS!* suggested, but in plays of this type he keeps alive the idea that drama can be art in the classic sense, infused with imagination.

BROWN, John Mason. "Mr. O'Neill and his champions." NY *Post*, 22 Jan.
This article prints quotations from some of the more violent attacks by the clergy on the lay critics. Brown tries to show that professional criticism was not against the theme but against O'Neill's presentation.

————. "O'Neill's interest in the agents controlling the fate of his characters in Days With End." NY *Post*, 15 Jan.
Brown reviews many plays in which God or Fate becomes a vitally interested, directly interfering personification in O'Neill's plays. *DAYS WITHOUT END* fails miserably to achieve any solution, and it is something that has bothered O'Neill since the days of *THIRST*.

BURR, Eugene. "Days Without End." *Billboard*, 46 (20 Jan.) 17.
The truly religious should be offended. The play has no real relation to fundamental realities. Blind, groveling faith; a bad play.

CALDWELL, Cy. "Days Without End." *New Outlook*, 163 (Feb.) 48-49.
Morbid inspection of the human soul. The weird and lugubrious "Siamese twins" are not real stuff. "Spiritual indigestion."

CORBIN, John. "Psyches without end." *Sat. R. Lit.*, 10 (20 Jan.) 419.
Much of theatrical value here.

"The critics and Days Without End." *Commonweal*, 19 (26 Jan.) 357-358.
Because critics are unable to recognize faith as a worthwhile subject they will not see this as a good play, although it is probably one of O'Neill's most important works.

"Critics out of their element." *Cath. Wld.*, 138 (Feb.) 513-517.
Lay critics are not qualified to criticize a play of this type without understanding the religious experience it portrays. This article is not, however, typical of the hysterical attack made by many of the clergy as shown in Brown's article.

"Days Without End." *Lit. D.*, 117 (10 Feb.) 17.
Summary of professional and clerical criticism.

"Days Without End." *Newsweek*, 3 (20 Jan.) 34.
The play suggests a high school debate.

"Days Without End." *Th. Arts*, 18 (May) 390.
Confused, pedestrian, no better as a book than as a play.

"Days Without End." *Variety*, 16 Jan.
This will test the drawing powers of O'Neill. Topic and religious fabric too heavy to click.

DONNELLY, Rev. Gerard B., S.J. "O'Neill's new Catholic play."
America, 50 (13 Jan.) 346..
Magnificently Catholic play in characters, story and mood. Priest is "noblest priest in the history of the modern theatre." Defies Broadway tradition; O'Neill at last heading toward the light.

EASTMAN, Fred. "O'Neill discovers the cross." *Christ. Cent.*, 51 (7 Feb.) 191-192.
O'Neill's greatness has begun. May they be Days Without End."

EATON, Walter Prichard. "Day Without End." NY *Her-Trib.*, 11 Feb.
This play dispels fears that O'Neill was becoming "normal." It is one of his weaker works.

FERGUSSON, Francis. "Mr. O'Neill's new play." *Am. Rev.*, 2 (Feb.) 491-495.
There is no more Christianity in this than in *DYNAMO* or *CHILLUN*. It is like all the others and has all the same faults. "It is not about a conversion; it is Mr. O'Neill's debate with himself about a man like Mr. O'Neill who is writing a novel about *another* man like Mr. O'Neill, who is toying with the Idea of the conversion of Mr. O'Neill."

GABRIEL, Gilbert. "As to Mr. O'Neill's latest Guild drama." NY *American,* 21 Jan.
Churchly in theme and well meant, but it is pretentious, wordy, and childishly indignant, like nursery blocks clumsily raised.

GARLAND, Robert. "Jesuit editor hails O'Neill miracle play." NY *Wor-Tel.,* 12 Jan.
Extended quotations from Donnelly's article.

————. "O'Neill miracle play of shopworn fabric." NY *Wor-Tel.,* 10 Jan.
A stingingly sarcastic review; doubts the play's sincerity, finds it a shoddy specimen, and "holy hokum."

HAMMOND, Percy. "Mr. O'Neill's experiment with masks and faces." NY *Her-Trib.,* 14 Jan.
Mainly a protest against the unnecessary alter-ego.

ISAACS, Edith J. R. "Parents and other people—Broadway in review." *Th. Art,* 18 (Mar.) 167.
Must not confuse bad play with religion. It is dull, pedestrian, unconvincing in every aspect.

KRUTCH, Joseph Wood. "The sickness of today." *Nation,* 138 (24 Jan.) 110-111.
After an unpromising first act, the play shows good theatre, but it is one of O'Neill's least successful plays. Does not solve today's sickness, but merely shows how "primitive religious instinct" survives.

LOCKRIDGE, Richard. "Quest Without End." NY *Sun,* 20 Jan.
A review of the play's religious aspects. The play challenges as it was meant to, but it is unsafe to assume O'Neill is now converted.

MANTLE, Burns. "An illuminating winter for the first dramatist." NY *News,* 21 Jan.
A serious and intelligent play.

MARCH, Michael. "A book critic disagrees with the drama critics." Brook. *Citizen,* 17 Jan.
Strong rebuttal to comments by the critics, whom March accuses of bigotry and prejudice. The play is of great importance, showing O'Neill's sincerity in his theme.

"The mask and the face." NY *Times,* 7 Jan., X, 2:5.
Mainly quotes from O'Neill "Memo on Masks." (See Non-Dramatic O'Neill.)

MOTHERWELL, Hiram. "Days Without End." *Stage,* 11 (Feb.) 16-18.
Not about religion, but about one man's experience in his own problem of personal salvation. Illustrated with four excellent pictures.

NATHAN, George Jean. "L'amour et—mondieu." *Van. F.,* 42 (Mar.) 42.
One of poorest and dullest things O'Neill has written.

―――. "Whither?" *Van. F.,* 42 (June) 49-50.
This O'Neill failure was notable among several others during the season.

SKINNER, Richard Dana. "Eugene O'Neill's next play." *Commonweal,* 19 (5 Jan.) 273.
It may be his most important play.

―――. "Can religious plays succeed?" *Commonweal,* 19 (23 Feb.) 469.
Skinner realizes other professional critics did not think the play truly dramatic, and he shows why he thinks it is. This is one of the most rational criticisms which appeared in a religious journal.

―――. "Days Without End." *Commonweal,* 19 (19 Jan.) 327-329.
Culmination of every play O'Neill has written, fitting the sequence of his work. John Loving's struggle will live among the great poetic and religious creations of world literature.

WYATT, Euphemia Van R. "A modern miracle play." *Cath. Wld.*, 138 (Feb.) 601-602.
Clumsy, and not his masterpiece, but "it is the cry of a man" with O'Neill baring his poet's soul to God.

YOUNG, Stark. "Days Without End." *New Rep.*, 77 (24 Jan.) 312.
Dramatic skeleton good; writing bad, though it does have theatrical and spiritual creation.

1935-1956

CAJETAN, Brother. "The pendulum starts back." *Cath. Wld.*, 140 (Mar. 1935) 650-656.
This play is one of the most outstanding examples of the swing back to Christian tradition in literature.

EASTMAN, Fred. "O'Neill's drama of Christian hope." *Christ. Cent.*, 73 (15 Aug. 1956) 950-951.
Eastman asks us to take note of the one play of hope which O'Neill wrote as we come to a reappraisal of his life in view of *LONG DAY'S JOURNEY*. (See Eastman's original review.)

GEIER, Woodrow. "O'Neill's Miracle play." *Religion in Life*, 16 (Autumn 1947) 515-526.
In Christian terms Loving's redemption is very pleasing.

DESIRE UNDER THE ELMS

Opening run reviews—New York
Newspapers of November 1924

BROUN, Heywood. "Desire Under the Elms." NY *World*, 12 Nov.
Despite some faults which he enumerates, Broun finds this towers high and could be O'Neill's best work.

DALE, Alan. "Desire Under the Elms." NY *American* 14 Nov.
Strenuous vein of morbidity presumably presented seriously. So much could be funny—and isn't.

"Desire Under the Elms an outspoken drama." *Journal of Commerce*, 12 Nov.
This review does little more than sketch out the story.

GABRIEL, Gilbert. "Desire Under the Elms." NY *Telegram*, 12 Nov.
Some vivid and great moments, such as bedroom scene, but play slumps into repugnance in last two scenes.

HABERSHAM, Stanton. "Another O'Neill offering at the Greenwich Village." NY *Graphic*, 13 Nov.
Unnecessary subject impressively handled. Crude vulgar dialogue.

HAMMOND, Percy. "Mr. O'Neill's Desire Under the Elms is the best of his pleasing tortures." NY *Her-Trib.*, 12 Nov. [Reprinted in Cargill *et al, O'Neill and his plays*, 1961.]
Hammond always leaves an O'Neill play glad he is not one of the people involved.

MANTLE, Burns. "O'Neill's new play is lustful and tragic." NY *News*, 14 Nov.
Should be seen by all who praise foreign drama and by all students of drama. Go prepared for lust, infanticide, sin.

METCALFE, J. S. "The slums of New England." *Wall St. Jour.*, 15 Nov.
O'Neill makes use of new freedom to create interesting drama, and this is faithful reproduction of New England at its most degraded. He is showing the daring for which he is known, but he will be admired only when he stops working in this field.

"Mr. O'Neill runs aground on a bleak New England farm." NY *Post*, 12 Nov.
Sterile bit of realism, mistaking crudity for power.

NIBLO, Fred, Jr. "New O'Neill play sinks to depths." NY *Telegraph*, 12 Nov. [Reprinted in Miller, *Playwright's progress*, 1965.]

"A gruesome, morbid" play, as real to life as a sewer. "Any one who cares anything about the theatre cannot approve . . . or disapprove in silence."

"O'Neill wins new somber laurels in latest drama." *W. W. Daily*, 12 Nov.

The gloom is deepened by pathos and horror and tragic irony. Its realism is lit by sympathy and a grim authentic poetry throughout.

OSBORN, E.W. "Desire Under the Elms." NY *World*, 14 Nov.

This play is very effective in its "relentless realism," making it better than the disliked *ANNA CHRISTIE* or *APE*.

"Shades of O'Neill." Brook. *Eagle*, 12 Nov.

Much of the material from the sea plays is now on a New England farm, which is not necessarily good. It is unentertaining; the more O'Neill's genius repeats itself, the more ingenious it appears. Nobody can paint yellow sin more gleaming white than O'Neill.

WOOLLCOTT, Alexander. "Through darkest New England." NY *Sun*, 12 Nov.

Criticizes the "fake" dialect and "ugly" climax.

YOUNG, Stark. "Eugene O'Neill's latest play." NY *Times*, 12 Nov., 20:7. [Reprinted in Miller, *Playwright's progress*, 1965.]

O'Neill has written nothing with more qualities of realism, poetry and terror than this.

Other reviews and criticism
1924

BENCHLEY, Robert. "Two ways." *Life*, 84 (11 Dec.) 18.

Up to a point O'Neill's finest, after which it becomes phony and ends in "a blaze of green fire."

"Desire Under the Elms." *Drama Cal.*, 7 (17 Nov.) 1.
Characters that live. A rare thing in being a tragedy which leaves spectator no unhappiness. Theatrically fine; finely conceived and worked out.

"Desire Under the Elms." *Time*, 4 (24 Nov.) 12.
People will object because they won't believe life can be so brutal.

EDBA. "Desire Under the Elms." *Variety*, 19 Nov.
Written in his best style; depth of story and characterization are typical O'Neill.

HOWARD, Sidney. Letter to the editor. NY *Times*, 14 Dec., VIII, 4:1.
A true tragedy, which can be compared only with *Macbeth* in practically every aspect.

KRUTCH, Joseph Wood. "The God of stumps." *Nation*, 119 (26 Nov.) 578. [Reprinted in Hewitt, *Theatre, USA,* 1959; and in Miller, *Playwright's progress*, 1965.]
This criticism attempts to get to the basis of O'Neill's plays; there is something in his nature that makes him "brother to tempest." If this quality is recognized and then overlooked, there are great compensations in this play.

NATHAN, George Jean. "The Kahn-Game." *Judge*, 87 (6 Dec.) 17.
May not be better than others he has done, but better than most being done nowadays.

"Plays and players." *Town and Country*, 81 (1 Dec.) 58.
A concentration of realism, rather than realism itself; elemental life and passion is presented in the spirit of blank verse.

RML. "Desire Under the Elms." *New Rep.*, 41 (3 Dec.) 44.
Exterior is stark and tragic, but interior, like the setting, is huddled and confused.

SKINNER, Richard Dana. "Decay 'under the elms.' " *Commonweal*, 1 (17 Dec.) 163.
Once the theme is accepted the play is worked out with often masterful intensity. The theme of decay, however, demands challenge.

WHYTE, Gordon. "Desire Under the Elms." *Billboard*, 36 (22 Nov.) 36.
Stark unmitigated tragedy. Horror done in O'Neill's best manner. O'Neill at his finest; will rank as one of his best.

YOUNG, Stark. "Acting in Eugene O'Neill." NY *Times*, 7 Dec., VIII, 5:1.
On the surface it may seem realistic, but it is actually on the edge of poetry and a tremendous task for the actor.

1925

BROMFIELD, Louis. "The New Yorker." *Bookman*, 60 (Jan.) 621.
This simple and terrible story on fine level of Greek tragedy is best analysis of witch-burning Puritans yet done; better than *Scarlet Letter*.

"The censored audience." *Nation*, 120 (1 Apr.) 346.
Attacks those who come to this to see a "dirty" play, or who go to one approved by the "play jury" because it must be "clean."

CRAWFORD, J. R. "Desire Under the Elms." NY *World*, 26 Apr.
Book review. "His creative passion almost sufficient to bridge those gaps of somewhat pedestrian writing."

"Desire Under the Elms." *Am. Rev.*, 3 (Mar.) 219-220.

EATON, Walter Prichard. "Desire Under the Elms." NY *Her-Trib.*, 24 May.
Book review. Crude and elemental tale elevated toward poetry. Fails as great work of art because of too much emotion and theaticality.

GARLAND, Robert. "Eugene O'Neill and this big business of Broadway." *Th. Arts,* 9 (Jan.) 3-16.

At his most "O'Neillian" and in ways one of his finest plays, going his own way completely apart from the big business of Broadway.

HORNBLOW, Arthur. "Mr. Hornblow goes to the play." *Theatre,* 41 (Jan.) 22.

Powerful enough by an ordinary writer, but must be judged differently because O'Neill demands different standards. Fails mainly because he gives in to the designer's art.

KRUTCH, Joseph Wood. "Drama—Summary I." *Nation,* 120 (10 June) 672-673.

Thanks to the producers, apart from the "commercial managers," we have such masterpieces as this.

————. "Drama—Summary II." *Nation,* 120 (24 June) 724.

Most "fundamentally important" of the season's major plays.

————. "Establishing a new tradition." *Nation,* 120 (7 Jan.) 22-23.

This play shows that writers no longer must have thesis plays but can proceed with the assumption that these subjects are already understood by audience.

NATHAN, George Jean. "By the dawn's early light." *Arts & Dec.,* 22 Jan.) 76.

The play lifts above all contemporary playwriting, but still lags after first half.

————. "The theatre." *Am. Merc.,* 4 (Jan.) 119.

Reads better than it acts. O'Neill does not define difference between real intensification and overexaggeration.

SELDES, Gilbert. "The theatre." *Dial,* 78 (Jan.) 82.

Outstanding fault is failure to make us believe in murder of baby.

SKINNER, Richard Dana. "Decay and flowing sap." *Ind. & Weekly R.*, 114 (10 Jan.) 51.
O'Neill will not be great until he is able to let light of finer things come into his soul; not a tragedy because nobody is on a height to fall, and everybody is on one level and rots there.

WHIPPLE, Leon. "Two plays by Eugene O'Neill." *Survey*, 53 (1 Jan.) 421-422.
Fails in its attempt to cross the abyss between realism and romanticism with bridge of symbolism.

WOOLLCOTT, Alexander. "Desire Under the Ellums." *Van. F.*, 23 (Jan.)27.
"A mad play, my masters," but still the kind that will be read long after other contemporary work has been forgotten.

WYATT, Euphemia Van R. "Eugene O'Neill on Plymouth rock." *Cath. Wld.*, 120 (Jan.) 519-521.
An unclean play and unhealthy scenes, with no healthy idea behind it.

1926-1928

"Desire Under the Elms." *Dial*, 80 (Jan. 1926) 70.
O'Neill is a much better dramatist than a literary man. Plays should carry their own emotion instead of having it written into them.

SEILER, Conrad. "Los Angeles must be kept pure." *Nation*, 122 (19 May 1926) 548-549. [Reprinted in Cargill *et al, O'Neill and his plays*, 1961.]
Step by step account of the legal involvements of the Los Angeles production from the initial arrest of the cast to the trial.

VAN DRUTEN, John. "The sex play." *Th. Arts*, 11 (Jan. 1927) 23-27.
Plea for treatment of sex as Elizabethans regarded it—incidental and universal. This play is a sex play in the theme of physical desire, which is unobjectionable enough.

WATTS, Richard. "Regarding Mr. O'Neill as a writer for the cinema." NY *Her-Trib.*, 4 Mar. 1928.
Presents a synopsis of O'Neill's own film scenarios for *DESIRE* and *APE*, neither of which were produced. They are much altered from the stage version.

Opening night reviews—ANTA Revival
New York—Newspapers of 17 Jan. 1952

ATKINSON, Brooks. "At the theatre." NY *Times*, 23:4. [Reprinted in Miller, *Playwright's progress*, 1965]
It may turn out to be the greatest play written by an American; the design of a masterpiece.

CHAPMAN, John. "Desire Under the Elms remains powerful, if just a leetle quaint." NY *News*.
A first class revival, but it seems a shade fancy and self-conscious.

COLEMAN, Robert. "ANTA puts on O'Neill's Desire Under the Elms." NY *Mirror*.
Makes a lot about people not worth it; a literary *Tobacco Road*.

HAWKINS, William. "Desire Under the Elms revived." NY *Wor-Tel.* & *Sun*.
Praise for this stark, hard play of elemental, overblown.passions.

KERR, Walter. "Desire Under the Elms." NY *Her-Trib.*
Well worth seeing.

McCLAIN, John. "A powerful drama, highly recommended." NY *Jour-Am.*
Still a good play, powerful drama.

SHEAFFER, Louis. "O'Neill's Desire soundly revived." Brook. *Eagle*.
A play of uncommon stature, with no show of age.

WATTS, Richard, Jr. "The tragic power of Eugene O'Neill." NY *Post*.

Play of overwhelming elemental power and almost embarrassing intensity, still one of the distinguished works of modern stage.

Other reviews and criticism
1952

BEYER, William H. "The state of the theatre: Classics revisited." *School & Society*, 75 (16 Feb.) 106-107.

Incredible that this powerful play has not been produced more.

BOLTON, Whitney. "Desire Under the Elms comes alive again as ANTA project." NY *Telegraph*, 18 Jan.

The original attitude that this was a play of strong and eloquent statement of man's fate still remains today.

BROWN, John Mason. "Dat ole davil and a hard god." *Sat. R. Lit.*, 35 (16 Feb.) 32-34.

Still retains its strength and intensity; achieves tragic grandeur.

COLBY, Ethel. "Carol Stone charms in O'Neill revival." *Jour. Comm.*, 23 Jan.

"Greatest living drama of this or any other season." A rare theatrical treat.

COOKE, Richard P. "Another O'Neill." *Wall St. Jour.*, 18 Jan.

It seems a bit heavy-handed, with a lack of conviction. Elemental passions often come close to parody, and O'Neill's "potent magic" does not come across.

"Desire Under the Elms." *Newsweek*, 39 (28 Jan.) 83.

Recognizable symbols of classic tragedy are here.

"Desire Under the Elms." *Th. Arts*, 36 (Apr.) 31-33.
Very brief account of the ANTA revival with three pages of excellent pictures.

"Desire Under the Elms." *Time*, 59 (28 Jan.) 44.
A play neither realistic nor tragic, but clumsily in between.

"Desire Under the Elms." *Variety*, 23 Jan.
A classic in its own right which years have failed to dim.

GIBBS, Wolcott. "Desire Under the Elms" *New Yorker*, 27 (26 Jan.) 53.
At times close to parody, it is still one of America's few classics.

KERR, Walter. "Desire Under the Elms." *Commonweal*, 55 (1 Feb.) 423.
A play that should be revived; characters so human it is difficult to present them.

————. "New generation gets two looks at O'Neill." NY *Her-Trib.*, 26 Jan.
A revaluation of the revival (including *ANNA CHRISTIE*) finds the characters in *DESIRE* are "mere figures," behaving in unnatural rhythms against a cosmic background.

NATHAN, George Jean. "Desire Under the Elms." *Th. Arts*, 36 (Mar.) 70-71.
Comes off pretty well, all considered.

"O'Neill shines again." *Life*, 32 (4 Feb.) 82-84.
Pictures from revival, text is generally approving.

WATTS, Richard. "Those two plays by Eugene O'Neill." NY *Post*, 27 Jan.
Praise for the revival. Possibly O'Neill's mightiest play.

WYATT, Euphemia Van R. "Desire Under the Elms." *Cath. Wld.*, 174 (Mar.) 464.
  Stylized form of this production better than original.

1958-1962

CONLIN, Matthew T. "The tragic effect in Autumn Fire and Desire Under the Elms." *Mod. Drama*, 1 (Feb. 1959) 228-235.
  Compares *DESIRE* with the successful *Autumn Fire* by T. C. Murray, both plays of 1924 concerning May-December marriages destroyed by father-son conflicts. *DESIRE* is less a tragedy because of its failure to evoke pity for the protagonist in the play's "painful nihilism."

GELB, Arthur. "At the roots of O'Neill's Elms." NY *Times*, 2 Mar. 1958. II, 5:3.
  In light of the coming motion picture version, Gelb shows how much of the original play came out of O'Neill's own background, including the "autobiographical" sketch of Cabot—taken in many points from his own life and that of his father, James O'Neill.

HARTMAN, Murray. "Desire Under the Elms in the light of Strindberg's influence." *Am. Lit.*, 33 (Nov. 1961) 360-369.
  Hardly a plot element that is not traced to Strindberg in some way. In this play O'Neill's "mystique of the Madonna" appears fully for the first time.

MILLER, Jordan Y. "Desire Under the Elms." In Miller's *American dramatic literature*, NY, McGraw-Hill, 1961, pp. 518-520.
  Presentation of the play as modern tragedy in an introduction to the text.

RACEY, Edgar F., Jr. "Myth as tragic structure in Desire Under the Elms." *Mod. Dr.*, 5 (May 1962) 42-46. [Reprinted in Gassner, *O'Neill*, 1964.]
  The Oedipal aspects, Old Testament references, and particularly

the Hippolytus myth shown as significant aspects of this play generally recognized as tragic in the classic sense.

WINTHER, Sophus Keith. "Desire Under the Elms: A modern tragedy." *Mod. Dr.,* 3 (Dec. 1960) 326-332.
    Reviewing early criticism of the play, this essay asserts the validity of the work as modern instead of classic tragedy with Cabot as its complete tragic hero.

Opening run reviews - Revival
Circle-in-the-Square
Newspapers of January 1963

On January 8, 1963, José Quintero presented a revival at the Circle-in-the-Square. Because of the New York newspaper strike at the time, no opening night reviews were published, save in miscellaneous area newspapers not affected by the news blackout. However, comments from a number of the regular critics were assembled and published separately. Those comments, and reviews published in all area newspapers outside of Manhattan, including the *Christian Science Monitor,* not normally included in this bibliography, are listed below.

COOKE, Richard P. "A need for elm trees." *Wall St. Jour.,* 11 Jan.
    Serious question as to whether or not the play can create the mood and power in arena staging, which is possible in proscenium staging for which it was written.

DORIN, Rube. "Desire Under the Elms revived: Colleen Dewhurst stands out." NY *Telegraph,* 10 Jan.
    Arena style does not seem to fit; difficult to go along with theme of consuming tragedy. Not as good as 1952 revival.

GOTTFRIED, Martin. "Revival of O'Neill play a letdown." *W.W. Daily,* 10 Jan.
    "Curiously ineffective." Soul of the play seems lost in a work that has the "drive and size of a production of genius."

"Desire Under the Elms." *Village Voice,* 17 Jan.
"The real thing. This is theatre." The play is the nearest thing
to an American classic, and this production shows why.

"Desire Under the Elms." *The Villager,* 10 Jan.
Nothing in New York equal to the impact of this play. The horror
is as fresh as if it were being staged for the first time.

KERR, Walter (NY *Her-Trib* critic)
Open style of arena production a distinct asset, giving intimacy,
bringing much more dimension to the O'Neill characters.

MADDOCKS, Melvin. "Desire in revival." *Christian Science Monitor,*
12 Jan.
The production helps rescue the play and O'Neill from caricature
and self-parody. Echoes of Greek tragedy are awkward; language is
studied.

NADEL, Norman (NY *Wor-Tel.* & *Sun* critic)
Good acting makes it "powerful and profoundly moving experience." The production style is right because "we should not be
shielded from O'Neill; we should be exposed to him."

OPPENHEIMER, George. "The great O'Neill." L.I. *Newsday,* 16 Jan.
Major tragedy 7/8 of the way; ending descends into lurid and
umbelievable melodrama which almost ruins it. The arena staging
becomes confusing, but the play looms large "after so many of the
pigmy efforts of recent seasons."

SHOWELL, Philip S., Jr. "Brilliant players rekindle Desire." *Newark
Eve. News,* 9 Jan.
Fine full-bodied revival—hot, hard, explosive as O'Neill must
have wanted it.

STERN, Harold. "Desire Under the Elms." NY *Standard,* 10 Jan.
Something is amiss, with blame to some degree on arena stage.
Perhaps the world no longer appreciates "simple pleasures like theft,
lust, adultery, and infanticide." The production "just sputters."

TAUBMAN, Howard. "New Desire." NY *Times*, 11 Jan. [Reprinted in Miller, *Playwright's progress*, 1965.]

Play has a "tension and passion rarely found in our frequently attenuated theatre." "elemental drama" with "granitic power."

WATTS, Richard. (NY *Post* critic).

Arena seems to be a mistake. "Inexorable tragedy" which needs the elms and the distance of the proscenium stage.

Other reviews and criticism
1963

"Bedrock O'Neill." *Newsweek*, 61 (21 Jan.) 57.

The production "captures not a fragile relic but a solid rock."

BRUSTEIN, Robert. "A buccaneer on Broadway." *New Rep.*, 14 (2 Feb.) 26.

Play has received its reputation "by default." Compared to *INTERLUDE* and *ELECTRA* it is a relief, but still full of tragic posturing and dreadful plotting.

CLURMAN, Harold. "Theatre." *Nation*, 196 (2 Feb.) 106-107.

One of the "most finely written and most powerfully conceived" American plays. A parable of the possession of the American continent, the drive of the Puritan that built it and the envy of hate of the younger generation. Classic, almost Greek nobility in construction.

"Desire Under the Elms." *Variety*, 30 Jan.

Memorable production, imaginative and effective staging.

GILMAN, Richard. "Revival time." *Commonweal*, 77 (15 Feb.) 543.

A good production, but the play seems to move "inexorably away from credibility or interest."

HEWES, Henry. "Less stately farmhouse." *Sat. R.*, 46 (26 Jan.) 32.

Probably O'Neill's best, requires no new revival to uncover its greatness. Emphasis on emotional responses rather than dramatic climaxes weakens the impact.

LEWIS, Theophilus. "Desire Under the Elms." *America,* 108 (23 Feb.) 275-276.
    Probably his most enigmatic play. Agitates your brain cells as well as your emotions.

OLIVER, Edith. "O'Neill on Bleeker street." *New Yorker,* 38 (19 Jan.) 62.
    No work was ever less suited to arena stage. Broad, explosive, often too explicit performance.

PRYCE-JONES, Alan. "Desire Under the Elms." *Th. Arts,* 47 (Feb.) 10.
    Keeps all its incandescence after forty years. Has power to move, and stage is used with skill, but the elms are missed. Echoes of Greek drama strong.

"Suffocated souls." *Time,* 81 (18 Jan.) 42.
    Seems "as familiar as inherited folklore." Demonstrates O'Neill's difficulty in failing to elevate man to tragic stature. O'Neill's heroes, instead of trying to be God, like the Classics, indict God "for failing to be god, or even to be." Objection to arena staging.

Further Reviews

*CATE, Hollis L. "Ephraim Cabot: O'Neill's spontaneous poet." *Markham Rev.,* 2 (May 1971) 115-117.
    If Cabot is to be regarded as the protagonist the genuinely poetic nature of his speech should be recognized. This critic makes good case for Cabot as much more than a tough rock-like individual, showing an inherent poetic and religious nature beyond the harshness so often emphasized.

HAYS, Peter L. "Biblical perversion in Desire Under the Elms." *Mod. Dr.,* 11 (Feb. 1969) 423-428.
    Harsh loveless Puritan religion of the play is shown as a perversion of religion that "cripples love and destroys men."

LAU, Joseph S. M. "Two emancipated Phaedras: Chou Fan-yi and

Abbie Putnam as social rebels." *Jour. Asian Studies,* 25 (Aug. 1966) 699-711.

Discussion of a heroine of popular 1933 Chinese tragedy in resemblance to Abbie as woman of passion, both resembling Racine Phaedra figure.

MEYERS, Jay Ronald. "O'Neill's use of the Phédre legend in Desire Under the Elms." *Revue de Litterature Comparée,* 41 (Jan.-Mar. 1967) 120-125.

O'Neill is closer to Racine than to Euripides with Abbie achieving tragic nobility through her illicit love in a tragedy of Aristotelian proportions.

REARDON, William R. "The path of a classic: Desire Under the Elms." *South. Sp. Jour.,* 31 (Summer 1966) 295-301.

Traces the rise of the play after its uneven initial reception to its position as a classic, mainly through shift in critical emphasis and increased acknowledgement in college text and books of criticism.

ROY, Emil. "O'Neill's Desire and Shakespeare's King Lear." *Neueren Sprachen,* 15 (1968) 1-6.

(Search of four major libraries, including New York Public, failed to reveal this reference, but included here because of Roy's extensive interest in O'Neill.)

TAYLOR, William E. "Six Characters in Search of an Author and Desire Under the Elms: What O'Neill did not learn from Europe." In Taylor's *Modern American drama: Essays in criticism,* Deland, Fla. Everett/Edwards, 1968, pp. 29-37.

Pirandello permits the domination of intellect (Father) over passion (Mother) and arrives at total catastrophe rather than tragedy. Passion however is the essence of O'Neill, and its victory leads to tragic affirmation unlike Pirandello.

DIFF'RENT

*Opening run reviews—New York
Newspapers of December 1920*

"A new O'Neill play." NY *Globe,* 31 Dec.

The conclusion is hard to stomach because it is brutal and bitterly nauseating but "true enough, God pity us." It is hoped O'Neill goes more toward the vein of *JONES* than continuing this way.

"New O'Neill play produced." NY *Tribune,* 28 Dec.

A brief notice of the opening, without comment.

"O'Neill's latest play presented by the Provincetown players." NY *Sun,* 31 Dec.

It is not a pleasant play, but written with the strength and subtlety that stamp O'Neill as a leading playwright. Well worth seeing; front rank O'Neill.

"Provincetown players offer second bill." NY *Commercial,* 31 Dec.

A reaction must have set in after success of *JONES* for this play and its companion piece represent a poor bill.

Towse, J. Ranken. "The play." NY *Post,* 29 Dec.

Relentless, ironic, sometimes gripping tragedy; intense drama.

"Two plays on programme." NY *World,* 28 Dec.

The play was warmly received. O'Neill is a fine drawing card for the Provincetown organization.

Woollcott, Alexander. "A new O'Neill play." NY *Times,* 29 Dec., 8:1.

Despite O'Neill's seeming lack of interest at the end, this will cause attention because of the great power of dramatic dialogue.

Other reviews and criticism
1921

BROUN, Heywood. "Diff'rent comes to Broadway at the Selwyn." NY *World*, 1 Feb.
O'Neill obviously does not know about what he is writing. O'Neill, a new Puritan of the theatre, finds man basically evil.

————. "Grey gods and green goddesses." *Van. F.*, 16 (Apr.) 33.
Broun complains against these "real" plays which are not art. True artist cannot be neutral and cannot be the scientist that O'Neill tries to be in this play of sex starvation.

CASTELLUN, Maida. " 'Diff'rent' . . . is true but not good drama." NY *Call*, 14 Jan.
Interesting sex psychology study; hero dies of "O'Neillitis" which is instinct for violent death rather than one from character or situation.

"Diff'rent." *Dial*, 70 (June) 715.
Brief book review.

"Diff'rent." *Drama Cal.*, 3 Jan.
The author again shows his versatility in this tragedy of character. "The grim outcome flows logically and inevitably from pshychological necessity." An "extraordinary play."

"Diff'rent." NY *Independent*, 105 (12 Feb.) 153.
A problem play "well written but amateurishly played."

"Diff'rent." *Th. Arts*, 5 (Oct.) 334-335.
Book review. "A backward step."

"Diff'rent." *Variety*, 4 Feb.
Should never have been written; until O'Neill gets restraint he should not be permitted to write again. Theatre should not be used as a chamber of horrors.

FIRKINS, O W. "Drama." *Weekly Rev.*, 4 (2 Mar.) 207-208.
Feeling of strangulation; curious rather than serious.

————. "Plays for the reader." *Weekly Rev.*, 4 (25 June) 406-407.
O'Neill is still not the master of the long play.

"Fresh horrors in Diff'rent brought from the Village." NY *Herald*,
1 Feb.
A clinical case; the move uptown is not successful.

"Greenwich Village cannot keep away from Broadway." NY *Review*,
5 Feb.
"Incisive study in the seamy side of human nature."

HORNBLOW, Arthur. "Mr. Hornblow goes to the play." *Theatre*, 33
(Apr.) 261.
Curious, if interesting.

JAMES, Patterson. "Diff'rent." *Billboard*, 33 (22 Jan.) 190.
Savage, true, brutal, told without faltering.

KAUFMAN, S. Jay. "Round the town." NY *Globe*, 17 Jan.
Greater than *JONES*; hope expressed it will move uptown.

KRUTCH, Joseph Wood. "Diff'rent." *Bookman*, 52 (Feb.) 565.
Brief book review along with *JONES*.

MACGOWAN, Kenneth. "The centre of the stage." *Th. Arts*, 5 (Apr.)
102.
"Utterly of the theatre in the best sense" but questions if O'Neill
is at his best here.

————. "Diff'rent." *Vogue*, 57 (15 Mar.) 80-82. [Reprinted in Cargill *et al*, *O'Neill and his plays*, 1961; and in Miller, *Playwright's
progress*, 1965.]
Disappointing, difficult to get same enthusiasm as for *JONES*,
despite some good characters. A "thriller" upon a sex topic.

"Provincetowners put on Diff'rent, a really great play." NY *Clipper*, 68 (5 Jan.) 19.
Best he has done to date; vitality far superior to *JONES*.

SAYLER, Oliver M. "Eugene O'Neill master of naturalism." *Drama*, 11 (Mar.) 189-190.
High, almost blind praise for a great naturalistic play, one of O'Neill's best and perhaps best of any American writer.

VSGL. "Diff'rent." *New Rep.*, 26 (25 May) 386.
Unfavorable review, together with *JONES* and *STRAW*.

Opening night reviews—Provincetown Revival
New York—Newspapers of 11 Feb. 1925

"Diff'rent." NY *World*.
It rings in a strange key "that will sound in your sleep."

"Diff'rent's revival at Provincetown players." NY *Telegram & Mail*.
Emma Crosby is probably the most enraging feminine creature ' a playwright ever conceived. O'Neill was not in a happy mood.

"Diff'rent revived." Brook. *Eagle*.
Passing notice that "Mary Blair is the starved old maid."

"Double bill excellently presented at the Provincetown." NY *Post*.
The acting is praised; the production is by-passed.

"O'Neill's Diff'rent revived." NY *Times*, 19:2.
Not in the best O'Neill tradition.

SIMON, Bernard. "O'Neill revival at Provincetown." NY *Telegraph*, 12 Feb.
An ill-advised revival. Effect of the theme almost obscene. O'Neill is now good enough not to confront his past.

"Triumph of the Egg played at Provincetown." NY *Her-Trib.*
Mary Blair effectively plays the lead in this specimen of O'Neill grimness.

Other reviews and criticism
1925

BROWN, John Mason. "Halfway theatre." *Th. Arts*, 9 (May) 291.
Brief mention of revival in a "discouraging" season.

"Diff'rent." *Drama Cal.*, 23 Feb.
This clinical analysis of abnormal people does not rise to the element of poetry as does some O'Neill.

"Diff'rent." *Time*, 5 (23 Feb.) 13.
One of the most unpleasant plays in our literature.

KRUTCH, Joseph Wood. Comment in Drama column. *Nation*, 120 (4 Mar.) 246.
Brilliant revival. When first seen in 1921 this critic thought it was the best American play to date, and nothing written since makes that position untenable. Extraordinary conciseness and force in dialogue.

LITTELL, Robert. "Three shades of black." *New. Rep.*, 42 (4 Mar.) 45.
The marionettes on strings never become individualized characters.

SKINNER, Richard Dana. "O'Neill and Anderson." *Commonweal*, 1 (4 Mar.) 466.
O'Neill a prisoner of his own feelings, and the gloom and decay deprive the tragedy of any power.

YOUNG, Stark. "Mary Blair in Diff'rent." NY *Times*, 1 Mar., VII, 1:2.

A "moving and unforgettable" performance.

Opening night reviews—Federal Theatre
Revival-New York—Newspapers of 26 Jan. 1938

BROWN, Herrick. "Diff'rent." NY *Sun.*
Worth doing. Full of closely knit action and well-drawn characters.

"Diff'rent." *W.W. Daily.*
Admirably directed and acted. Shows many of the unmistakable characteristics of later O'Neill work.

"Early O'Neill." NY *Times,* 26:4.
Worth study and revival, but O'Neill of 1921 is not the O'Neill of 1938.

"Eugene O'Neill's Diff'rent at Maxine Elliott theatre." NY *Wor-Tel.*
Theme seems old fashioned; does not ring true to contemporary dramatic reasoning.

FRANCIS, Robert. "O'Neill revival." Brook. *Eagle.*
Performance brings significance and power to this early work.

WALDORF, Wilella. "Federal theatre troupe in O'Neill's Diff'rent." NY *Post.*
Welcome relief from the more pretentious O'Neill of recent years.

Opening night reviews—Mermaid revival
New York—Newspapers of 18 Oct. 1961

BOLTON, Whitney. "Diff'rent showed O'Neill developing." NY *Telegraph,* 19 Oct.
Crude and rough hewn play, showing great powers to develop. A young writer's awkward attempt to devine human emotions.

COHEN, Richard. "Diff'rent O'Neill's first play, shows way to later work." *W.W. Daily.*
   Erroneously called "first play" by this critic who finds that it shows what would some day emerge.

COLEMAN, Robert. "Diff'rent has limited appeal." NY *Mirror.*
   Something of a copybook exercise. A kind of museum piece for those interested.

CRIST, Judith. "Diff'rent." NY *Her-Trib.*
   Seems to be a "latter-day collaboration" between Tennessee Williams and O'Neill. "The result is at best startling, at worst embarrassing." Melodrama borders on farce; a museum piece not enhanced by the production.

McCLAIN, John. "An early O'Neill play doesn't rate revival." NY *Jour-Am.*
   Not much of a play, which is why it isn't often resurrected.

TAUBMAN, Howard. "Diff'rent." NY *Times.* [Reprinted in Miller, *Playwright's progress,* 1965.]
   It has flaws, but is unsparing in its honesty. Remains valid in probing into the secret places of the mind.

WATTS, Richard, Jr. "An early play by Eugene O'Neill." NY *Post.*
   Despite weaknesses, a play of "dark and stubborn power" with "elemental strength" and monumental dramatic rigor. O'Neill could be a giant even in lesser phases.

Other reviews and criticism
1961

BLACK, Susan M. "Diff'rent." *Th. Arts,* 45 (Dec.) 70-71.
   Should have been allowed to rest in peace.

CLURMAN, Harold. "Theatre." *Nation,* 193 (2 Dec.) 459-460.

A crude play, but one is not irritated or bored by it. O'Neill's tragedy is powerfully personal; truth of the play is the truth of O'Neill's wounds.

"Diff'rent." *Cue*, 28 Oct.
Fascinating play, still appropriate in the America of 1961.

"Diff'rent." *Variety*, 25 Oct.
O'Neill's directness and simplicity are "like a breeze fresh off the water." A wallop in this revival, exposing the grimness of another age.

"Early O'Neill." L.I. *Newsday*, 25 Oct.
Perhaps a "milestone" in O'Neill's early days, but a "millstone" today. Some of O'Neill's "flattest and most unimpressive writing."

OLIVER, Edith. "Second runs." *New Yorker*, 37 (28 Oct.) 137.
A godawful early O'Neill melodrama. Most of the parts are one-dimensional as in a medieval morality in schoolboyish tone. Gawky irony.

TALLMER, Jerry. "Diff'rent." *Village Voice*, 26 Oct.
O'Neill's poverty as writer and thinker always undercut him, but the "raw Gothic strength" of the "uncluttered O'Neill" is "something to be experienced."

THE DREAMY KID

The following is the only review of the first performance of this play which the editor has discovered. It is reprinted in Cargill *et al*, *O'Neill and his plays*, 1961.

WOOLLCOTT, Alexander. "The Dreamy Kid." NY *Times*, 9 Nov. 1919.
Another good play from Eugene O'Neill. Induces complete sympathy and pity for an abhorrent character.

DYNAMO

Pre-production Comments

NATHAN, George Jean. Drama column in *Am. Merc.*, 15 (Dec. 1928) 505.
     Paragraph concerning the unstaged MS, telling what it's all about.

————. "The first of a trilogy." *Am. Merc.*, 16 (Jan. 1929) 119-120.
     Follow-up of Dec. 1928 comments, quoting O'Neill's letter to Nathan regarding the whole prospective *DYNAMO* trilogy. [This and previous comment are reprinted in Downer, *American drama and its critics*, 1965.]

Opening night reviews—New York
Newspapers of 12 Feb. 1929

ALLEN, Kelcey. "Whir of Dynamo electrifies audience of O'Neill admirers." *W. W. Daily.*
     A veritable anthology of O'Neill drama; everything so typical of him. Stirring and provocative, and actually reverent and pious; the most dynamic of O'Neill's plays.

ANDERSON, John. "Dynamo has premiere." NY *Journal.*
     Digs around roots of the big question about what is God with nothing more than a toothpick. No passionate sincerity and blazing vision. Too hysterical and sensational—no more important religious matter than that of Hottentot.

ATKINSON, Brooks. "God in the machine." NY *Times*, 22:1.
     The play is a center of controversy, but with much strength and breadth. "At last he seems to have gotten his drama in harmony with the universal theme he is freely developing."

BOLTON, Whitney. "O'Neill's machine-god." NY *Telegraph.*
     Incoherent disappointment. Nobody else could match thoughtful

and sympathetic first act—best part of the play. One cannot completely condemn on first visit because many overtones come out in later visits.

BROWN, George. "O'Neill's Dynamo leads town's dramatic fare." *Jour. Comm.*, 13 Feb.
    Truer, firmer, more lasting, more coherent, simpler than other of his plays. A giant, a great, grand voice. Tremendous surging drama, often majestic poesy. Some of his finest writing; real red meat; will send blood pressure soaring.

GABRIEL, Gilbert. "Eugene O'Neill salutes our god of the machine with new play, Dynamo." NY *American*.
    A disappointment; the scheme only intermittently comes alive. Settings more eloquent than the play.

GARLAND, Robert. "Eugene O'Neill's Dynamo displayed in 45th Street." NY *Telegram*. [Reprinted in Miller, *Playwright's progress*, 1965.]
    O'Neill "shook his fist at God and blew kisses in the general direction of electricity. Each of the gestures seemed a wee bit childish." Self consciously profound, phoney.

HAMMOND, Percy. "The Theatre Guild in Eugene O'Neill's slow and startling Dynamo." NY *Her-Trib*. [Reprinted in Miller, *Playwright's progress*, 1965.]
    This amusingly bitter criticism finds little to recommend. Asides are crutches, play at times ludicrous, "frequently raving."

LITTELL, Robert. "The Theatre Guild presents Dynamo." NY *Post*.
    Second-rate O'Neill. Goes into "often foolish neomysticism" with a "silly and dull" last act.

LOCKRIDGE, Richard. "Mr. O'Neill's Dynamo." NY *Sun*.
    Sophomoric, O'Neill fumbling whatever intentions he had.

MANTLE, Burns. "Dynamo throbs with mystery." NY *News*.
    An indeterminant drama meeting with mixed reception.

OSBORN, E. W. "Dynamo." NY *Eve. World*.
Applause sounded symbolically like a question mark. Not a satisfactory play—began better than it ended.

POLLOCK, Arthur. "Dynamo." Brook. *Eagle*.
A play of hardly any importance, sleazy and quick compared to *STRANGE INTERLUDE*.

WINCHELL, Walter. "In the Einstein manner." NY *Graphic*.
Incoherent, listless, a bore, will not survive.

Other reviews and criticism
1929

ANDERSON, John. "About Great God Gene, his new play and Mr. Broun." NY *Journal*, 16 Feb.
This is "unconscionable bunk" from one who takes himself so seriously he doesn't recognize how bad he is.

ATKINSON, Brooks. "Concluding a dramatic cycle." NY *Times*, 17 Feb., IX, 1:1.
In this play O'Neill has completed the cycle started by Ibsen; *i.e.*, the return to plays of a general instead of a specific nature.

BELLAMY, Francis R. "The theatre." *Outlook*, 151 (27 Feb.) 331.
Departs too far from reality, but O'Neill at his worst remains "more provocative and interesting than most others at their best."

BENCHLEY, Robert. "Dynamo." *Life*, 93 (8 Mar.) 24. [Reprinted in Cargill *et al*, *O'Neill and his plays*, 1961.]
"Nobody who could write this play is above being kidded." Now convinced that *BROWN* and *INTERLUDE* were as bad as they seemed.

BOLTON, Whitney. "By easy stages." NY *Telegraph*, 17 Feb.
A general review of the first O'Neill decade, including some of Heywood Broun's comments on O'Neill and on *DYNAMO*.

BOYD, Ernest. "Eugene O'Neill and others." *Bookman*, 69 (Apr.) 179-180.
O'Neill's capacity is projecting simple, elemental emotions, but in treating ideas he is dramatically lost.

BRACKETT, Charles. "Essays in the sublime and the ridiculous." *New Yorker*, 6 (23 Feb.) 27.
Pretentious rant.

BROUN, Heywood. "It seems to me." NY *Telegram*, 14 Feb.
This review sharply attacks the poor criticism which enables O'Neill to become more than he actually is. This play is not tragedy.

CARB, David. "Dynamo." *Vogue*, 73 (30 Mar.) 61.
Intemperate outpouring of adolescence; boring, flatulent, maudlin.

CLARK, Barrett H. "O'Neill's Dynamo and the Village experiments." *Drama*, 19 (Apr.) 201.
A refusal to write off O'Neill as "lost," despite his unimpressive result as thinker and prophet.

COLUM, Padriac. "Dynamo." *Dial*, 86 (Apr.) 349-350.
Whatever possessed O'Neill to write it? Insists on thinking in the philosophy of the day-before-yesterday.

DE CASSERES, Benjamin. "Broadway to date." *Arts & Dec.*, 30 (Apr.) 72.
If he had continued the play in the souls of his characters instead of the electric plant, would have been a different story to tell.

"DYNAMO." *Variety*, 13 Feb.
Not the best he has written, but the inspiration of a poet. Terrific, moving and agitating, will probably be a resounding success.

ERVINE, St. John. "The Greenwich Village atheist prepares to meet his God." NY *World*, 13 Feb.

O'Neill is killing the poet in himself determining to be intellectual. A plea to cease before it is too late.

————. "Mr. O'Neill takes a toss." NY *World*, 24 Feb.
O'Neill is a dramatic poet "who perversely imagines himself a
philosopher." This long column by a critic not given to O'Neill
praise discusses O'Neill's difficulties, and asks not to condemn him
in this piece alone, in view of his tremendous efforts otherwise.

GABRIEL, Gilbert. "Opening nights." NY *American*, 17 Feb.
Reviewing the play at a later date Gabriel admits that it is a bad
attempt on a mighty subject, although other critics have missed the
point of its drama of frustration.

GARLAND, Robert. "Eugene O'Neill's Dynamo and what the critics
say." NY *Telegram*, 14 Feb.
Summary of statements from major critics.

GOULD, Bruce. "O'Neill faw down, go boom!" *Wall St. News*, 14
Feb.
O'Neill has been living beyond his intellectual means and this
finds him bankrupt. He has redramatized a drama dramatized a
hundred times all ready.

HAMMOND, Percy. "Mr. O'Neill, an unfair iconoclast." NY *Her-
Trib.*, 17 Feb.
Unfair to electricity and public utilities—such things don't happen
in power houses. An amusing but telling attack against the artificial
uses to which O'Neill puts his power house and his people.

HANSEN, Harry. "Dynamo." NY *World*, 19 Oct.
Review of book.

HORNBLOW, Arthur. "The editor goes to the play." *Theatre*, 49
(May) 45.
Shocks O'Neill followers by intellectual ineptitude.

JORDAN, Elizabeth. "Plays of early spring." *America*, 30 Mar.

"Annoyingly childish," often ridiculous, most of it too unpleasant to discuss.

KRUTCH, Joseph Wood. "Epitaph I." *Nation*, 128 (29 May) 655-656.
Krutch admits that as a critic he was one of few who found this play interesting.

————. "The virgin and the dynamo." *Nation*, 128 (27 Feb.) 264.
An attempt to explain O'Neill's point, as a man on an individual quest for the meaning of existence.

LITTELL, Robert. "The land of the second best." *Th. Arts*, 13 (Apr.) 245-247.
When O'Neill makes mistakes he makes big ones. Full of crudity, unconscious caricature, muddy oratory.

————. "Two on the aisle." *NY Post*, 16 Feb.
In discussing O'Neill the Thinker and O'Neill the Artist, Littell finds a real issue in who is to rescue the artist from the thinker. O'Neill does not think through his profound thoughts. Passages from Adams' *Education* on "The Dynamo and the Virgin" are quoted to show O'Neill is not a thinker.

MACGOWAN, Kenneth. "Eugene O'Neill's new play." *Van. F.*, 31 (Feb.) 62.
If used often enough the asides may become standard in our theatrical conventions.

————. "O'Neill's new play Dynamo to be presented by the Theatre Guild." *NY Post*, 9 Feb.
In this preview, Macgowan warns that the play, though about religion, is not comforting, and would be banned in fundamentalist religious areas.

"Machines and motives." *Psychology Mag.*, Apr.
Obscurity need not enter—may be avoided by realizing O'Neill deals in symbols.

MANTLE, Burns. "The Messrs. O'Neill and Ibsen. Dynamo both irritates and mystifies." NY *News*, 17 Feb.
A plea not to judge the whole trilogy on basis of this play. No interested person can afford to miss it, especially those seeking what O'Neill actually is.

"Mr. O'Neill and the audible theatre." NY *Times*, 3 Mar., VIII, 4:6.
An explanation of O'Neill's viewpoints toward the use of the definite rhythm of sound as an important part of theatrical art.

MOSES, Montrose J. "Eugene O'Neill searches for God." *Rev. of Rev.*, 79 (Apr.) 158.
Nothing particularly new being said, but it is done "dynamically and with mad frenzy."

NATHAN, George Jean. "Judging the shows." *Judge*, 96 (9 Mar.) 18.
Crude, childish, trivial; a dud.

————. "A non-conductor." *Am. Merc.*, 16 (Mar.) 368-373. [Reprinted in Downer, *American drama and its critics*, 1965.]
Reprints complete stage directions from Act I, with some condensed dialogue, to show how ridiculous the play becomes. In science and philosophy O'Neill is lost.

"The new Dynamo as seen by O'Neill." NY *World*, 27 Jan.
Excerpts from some of O'Neill's letters to the Guild concerning his ideas, such as the emphasis upon sound and the insistence that the cast visit an actual power station.

"O'Neill wrestles with God." *Lit D.*, 100 (2 Mar.) 21-22.
Evidence from most reviews that O'Neill was "thrown in the first round."

POLLOCK, Arthur. "Mr. O'Neill gets excited again in Dynamo." Brook. *Eagle*, 17 Feb.
Under the impression he is to be taken seriously, O'Neill takes himself seriously. Mistakes excitement for thought.

RILEY, Wilfred J. "Dynamo." *Billboard*, 41 (23 Feb.) 47.
Must await the rest of the proposed trilogy before a decision is made.

RUHL, Arthur. "Second nights." NY *Her-Trib.*, 17 Feb.
A detailed review of the many symbols and the general approach O'Neill uses—aimed at showing how preposterous and outlandish the whole play is.

SHIPLEY, Joseph T. "Dyna-Might." *New Leader*, 15 Feb.
Distinct advance technically beyond *INTERLUDE*. The expressed thoughts are effective; a bold replacement of speech.

————. "Dynamolatry." *New Leader*, 1 Mar.
O'Neill can reach power, but perhaps his misdirection of aim keeps this from being poetry; he has gone astray.

SKINNER, Richard Dana. "Eugene O'Neill's Dynamo." *Commonweal*, 9 (27 Feb.) 389-390.
Not about world sickness, but about O'Neill's own.

WATTS, Richard. "Literary ancestor of Dynamo." NY *Her-Trib.*, 24 Feb.
Interesting review of other literary uses of the machine as in *Frankenstein, RUR, Processional*, and others.

WELLMAN, Rita. "In and out of town." *Town & Country*, 83 (15 Mar.) 58.
An arrogant experiment that does not come across.

WYATT, Euphemia Van R. "Plays of some importance." *Cath. Wld.*, 129 (Apr.) 80-82.
O'Neill is the loser in his clenching with a tremendous theme.

YOUNG, Stark. "Dynamo." *New Rep.*, 58 (27 Feb.) 43-44.
Significant as a "personal document" showing what can mean so much to O'Neill.

Further reviews

*DAHLSTROM, Carl E. W. L. "Dynamo and Lazarus Laughed: Some limitations." *Mod. Dr.*, 3 (Dec. 1960) 224-230.

Seeing science and religion as absolutes O'Neill does not adequately understand man's anguish and cannot bring artistic body to his materials. He cannot solve problems of man's fear of death by assuming some sort of immortality for Man, and he is "unable to give artistic treatment to the ferment in religion, science, and existence."

THE EMPEROR JONES

Opening run reviews—New York
Newspapers of November 1920

BROUN, Heywood. "Emperor Jones gives chance for cheers." NY *Tribune*, 4 Nov. [Reprinted in Cargill *et al*, *O'Neill and his plays*, 1961.]
Extreme praise for O'Neill's great value.

CASTELLUN, Maida. "O'Neill's Emperor Jones thrills and fascinates." NY *Call*, 10 Nov. [Reprinted in Miller, *Playwright's progress*, 1965.]
Provincetown players give the most thrilling evening of their theatrical lives. Vivid imagination, relentless power; a rare feast for lovers of the true drama.

MACGOWAN, Kenneth. "Emperor Jones an extraordinary drama of imagination." NY *Globe*, 4 Nov.
High praise for this new drama designed for the new stagecraft.

MANTLE, Burns. "Plays, players and playwrights." NY *Mail*, 6 Nov.
"A weird tragedy, this one." It does not cheer, because it leaves one cheerless, lacking O'Neill's promising distinction of text evident in other plays. Some traces of simple eloquence.

"Provincetown players stage remarkable play." Brook. *Eagle*, 9 Nov.
     "Admirable piece of dramatic craftsmanship."

RATHBUN, Stephen. "Provincetown players stage a brilliant bill." NY
Sun, 6 Nov.
     One of the noteworthy events of the season, both in depth and
power.

TOWSE, J. Ranken. "The play." NY *Post*, 3 Nov.
     O'Neill knows how to communicate the feelings of character to
the audience. Typical of little theatre experiments, and O'Neill took
the chance of being a trifle ridiculous in this one.

WOOLLCOTT, Alexander. "The new O'Neill play." NY *Times*, 7
Nov., VII, 1:3. [Reprinted in Miller, *Playwright's progress*, 1965.]
     The "as yet unbridled" O'Neill has strength and originality so
far unequaled in the American theatre.

     During November and most of December 1920 *THE EMPEROR
JONES* continued in the tiny Greenwich Village theatre of the Provincetown Players. By popular demand it was moved uptown into a
larger theatre, the Selwyn, on 27 December, and thence to the Princess
on 29 January 1921. Reviews continued to appear, and many critics
who had missed it downtown wrote their opinions after seeing it in
the Broadway house. Others, who had seen it earlier, reviewed it
again. Later in 1921 various publications of the play, in the same
volume with *DIFF'RENT* and *THE STRAW* and in separate editions,
were also discussed in periodical columns. To simplify matters, all
reviews and criticism after November 1920 and through 1921 are
placed together.

Other reviews and criticism
1920-1921

"Amusement notes." *W. W. Daily*, 28 Dec. 1920.
     The move uptown is an improvement because action flows more
quickly without the long waits between scenes.

CASTELLUN, Maida. "The Emperor Jones at the Selwyn repeats its success with Charles Gilpin." NY *Call*, 30 Dec. 1920.
Still unusual and thrilling.

DALE, Alan. "Emperor Jones artistically staged; appeals to fancy." NY *American*, 28 Dec. 1920.
Somewhat unique, somewhat impressive, somewhat artistic, could be improved with some comedy.

"The Emperor Jones." *Dial*, 70 (June 1921) 715.
Brief book review. *JONES* reads well, in spite of its essentially pictorial character.

"The Emperor Jones." *Independent*, 105 (8 Jan. 1921) 33.
A "sensation."

"The Emperor Jones." *Th. Arts*, 5 (Oct. 1921) 334-335.
Book review. *JONES* is "brilliant and forward looking."

"The Emperor Jones." *Variety*, 14 Jan. 1921.
Genuine tragedy, mixed with the "cynicism of youth."

"Emperor Jones at Selwyn." NY *Sun*, 28 Dec. 1920.
The transfer from Greenwich Village is an improvement.

"Emperor Jones uptown." NY *Herald*, 28 Dec. 1920.
Few pictures of terror are so engrossing as this.

FIRKINS, O. W. "Eugene O'Neill's remarkable play, The Emperor Jones." *Weekly Rev.*, 3 (8 Dec. 1920) 567-568.
Literary and theatrical, rather than dramatic; highly imaginative, possibly a profound piece of work.

————. "Plays for the reader." *Weekly Rev.*, 4 (25 June 1921) 606.
Book review. O'Neill is not yet the master of the long play. A sense of theatre and honesty should be helpful in the future.

GILLIAM, Florence. "The Emperor Jones." *Quill*, Nov. 1920, pp. 24-26.

The production could have been smoother.

HARRISON, Hubert H. "The Emperor Jones." *Negro World*, 4 June 1921.

It is aimless to criticize this play because it "does not elevate the Negro," since it could have been written about any race anywhere.

JAMES, Patterson. "The Provincetown players." *Billboard*, 32 (14 Dec. 1920) 19.

"One of the pitiably few compensations of the season."

LEWISOHN, Ludwig. "Native plays." *Nation*, 112 (2 Feb. 1921) 189.

Power and promise, though visions of the Negro seem to have been carefully selected rather than leaping from "creative necessity."

MACGOWAN, Kenneth. "The new season." *Th. Arts*, 5 (Jan. 1921) 5-7. [Reprinted in Gilder, *Theatre Arts anthology*, 1950; and in Hewitt, *Theatre USA*, 1959.]

A new and untheatrical power, with rhythmed beauty; genius and imagination are evident.

"More room improves The Emperor Jones." NY *World*, 28 Dec. 1920.

Vigor and charm of Gilpin stood out stronger and the characters are more convincing with the move.

MOSES, Montrose J. "O'Neill and the Emperor Jones." *Independent*, 105 (12 Feb. 1921) 158-159.

Mainly a discussion of the one-act play as a dramatic form and O'Neill's use of it, especially in this play.

"Not as others are, but still worth it." *Outlook*, 126 (22 Dec. 1920) 710-711.

Remarkable, despite severe shortcomings in drama and staging.

"Provincetown bill best thing they've done for long time." NY *Clipper*, 68 (24 Nov. 1920) 19.
Highly interesting, although O'Neill is not great. It is not certain whether he is better than Cohan or Walter.

Sᴀʏʟᴇʀ, Oliver M. "Delving into the sub-conscious." *Freeman*, 24 Nov. 1920.
Success is limited because of O'Neill's plunge into the field of Negro psychoanalysis.

VSGL "The Emperor Jones." *New Rep.*, 26 (25 May 1921) 420.
Book review. It is better not to read *JONES* if you liked it on the stage.

Wʜʏᴛᴇ, Gordon. "Provincetown players." *Billboard*, 32 (20 Nov. 1920) 190.
About the best of O'Neill so far.

*Opening night reviews—Paul Robeson revival
New York—Newspapers of 7-9 May 1924*

"The Emperor Jones." NY *World*, 7 May.
Robeson is almost as good as Gilpin.

"The Emperor Jones reappears at the Provincetown with a new emperor." NY *Post*, 7 May.
On the whole worthily presented. One comes away with a new respect for O'Neill's dexterity.

"The Emperor Jones revived." NY *Times*, 7 May, 18:1.
The play instead of the player seems to hold the audience.

"Paul Robeson wins fame in O'Neill play." NY *Telegram* & *Mail*, 7 May.
High praise for Robeson's interpretation.

Pᴏʟʟᴏᴄᴋ, Arthur. "The Emperor Jones." Brook. *Eagle*, 8 May.
The revival is praised, as is Robeson's interpretation.

"Provincetown theatre—The Emperor Jones." NY *American*, 9 May.
Completely satisfying, but there is a "bridge of difference" between Robeson and Gilpin.

VREELAND, Frank. "Bayoo they cry as Robeson rages in The Emperor Jones." NY *Her-Trib.*, 7 May.
High praise for the performance.

WOOLLCOTT, Alexander. "The Emperor Jones revived." NY *Sun*, 8 May.
Recommended without reservation.

THE EMPEROR JONES was revived twice in 1926, by the Provincetown Theatre, 15 February, and by the Mayfair Theatre, 10 November. Both starred Gilpin. Reviews still maintained high praise, and were so repetitive as to be of little value here. Moss Hart, who played Smithers in the Mayfair production, describes his experiences in some detail in *Act one*. One opinion, however, is worth noting, and is included below.

SHAND, John. "The Emperor Jones." *New Statesman*, 25 (19 Sept. 1925) 628-629. [Reprinted in Miller, *Playwright's progress*, 1965.]
O'Neill is basically a one-act dramatist and should not attempt something beyond his scope. This will never be a famous play because a good idea is spoiled by the wrong treatment.

Further reviews

KAGAN, Norman. "The return of The Emperor Jones." *Negro Hist. Bull.*, 34 (1971) 160-162.

*ROY, Emil. "Eugene O'Neill's The Emperor Jones and The Hairy Ape as mirror plays." *Com. Dr.*, 2 (Spring 1968) 21-31.
These most successful of O'Neill's experimental plays are seen as mirrors which complement each other. Both heroes are "messianic types," parodies of "hero myth," and both buried under the "historical layers of civilization" the "original form of society."

EXORCISM

The only known New York production of this play was on 26 March 1920. The professional critics were beginning to pay somewhat more attention to O'Neill's plays produced in Greenwich Village, particularly in light of the success of *BEYOND THE HORIZON* which had opened early the previous month. Still, reviews of *EXORCISM* were few. The following represent all that have been found to date.

BROUN, Heywood. Comment in NY *Trib.*, 1 April 1920.

Not quite up to previous O'Neill standards, but has "moments of blazingly real dialogue and intense poignancy." Lodging-house atmosphere is "powerfully successful," as is "the fierce depression and the fiercer hilarity in which depression is drowned by these derelicts."

JOLO. "Exorcism." *Variety*, 2 April 1920.

A "most depressing affair, devoid of uplift." Main character's observations on life "are of the most morbid kind, showing a depraved, degenerate mind which nothing can alter."

WOOLLCOTT, Alexander. "Exorcism." NY *Times*, 4 April 1920. Sec. 6, p. 6. [Reprinted in Cargill *et al*, *O'Neill and his plays*, 1961; and in Miller, *Playwright's progress*, 1965.]

"An uncommonly good" play, with original and distinctive characters having "the breath of life in them."

THE FIRST MAN

Opening night reviews—New York
Newspapers of 6 March 1922

ALLEN, Kelcey. "The First Man produced." *W. W. Daily*.
Well written, but far too morbid to succeed.

"Another O'Neill play on Grand Street." NY *Telegram*.
Distinct departure; keen satire, one of O'Neill's best.

"Convocation of woe in The First Man, O'Neill's new play." NY *Tribune*.
A murky play; it is hard to recognize O'Neill. "The name of Eugene O'Neill's star is Wormwood."

DALE, Alan. "The First Man, Eugene O'Neill's play staged." NY *American*. [Reprinted in Miller, *Playwright's progress*, 1965.]
The theatre is out of place in such painful and morbid exhibits.

DEFOE, Louis V. "Another play by O'Neill." NY *World*.
"Grimly humorous satire" on contemporary human traits; not O'Neill's best.

"Eugene O'Neill's study in morbid paternity." NY *Globe*.
A strain between O'Neill and theme; hardly an O'Neill play at all.

"First Man presented at Neighborhood Playhouse." NY *Sun*.
No glory here; should stick to the sea which is his best friend.

MANTLE, Burns. "O'Neill's The First Man." NY *Mail*.
Repetitious, lacks convincing detail.

MARSH, Leo A. "New O'Neill play a morbid drama." NY *Telegraph*.
Modern play with primitive theme; O'Neill still is able to write well about human frailties.

REAMER, Lawrence. "First Man . . . is a gloomy suburban story." NY *Herald*.
Should never have been produced; nothing new in the theme.

TORRES, H. Z. "Latest O'Neill opus a drama of gestation." NY *Commercial*.
No dramatic or literary excuse for this revolting and abhorrent treatment of gestation.

TOWSE, J. Ranken. "Eugene O'Neill's latest play." NY *Post*.
Signs of ability and inventive mind; what good is here is obstructed by violence and exaggeration.

WOOLLCOTT, Alexander. "The new O'Neill play." NY *Times*, 9:2.
Reiterative, clumsy, rubbishy language.

Other reviews and criticism
1922

ANDREWS, Kenneth. "Broadway, our literary signpost." *Bookman*, 52 (May) 284.
"Revives one's shaken faith in the author" after the *HAIRY APE*. Powerful and well rounded.

BAURY, Louis. "Mr. O'Neill's new plays." *Freeman*, 5 (3 May) 184-185.
O'Neill must learn responsibility and stop wallowing in words.

CASTELLUN, Maida. "Eugene O'Neill misses his mark." NY *Call*, 8 Mar. [Reprinted in Cargill *et al*, *O'Neill and his plays*, 1961.]
Badly constructed, overwritten, far from a good play. This critic points up the interesting fact that this is the first time in a play that a man instead of a woman has shown he does not want children.

"The First Man." Brook. *Eagle*, 7 Mar.
O'Neill on unfamiliar ground, but still a very good play.

"The First Man." *Drama Calendar*, 13 Mar.
Not up to O'Neill's best, but shows ability to write comedy scene and to handle more than two or three people in his dialogue.

"The First Man." *Town Topics*, 9 Mar.
Personal rancor, missing the form of art; ill-written melodrama.

"The First Man new O'Neill play at the Playhouse." NY *Clipper*, 15 Mar.
Distasteful, badly acted, worse O'Neill language than usual.

HOPKINS, Mary Alden. "First Man at the Neighborhood Playhouse."
Greenwich Villager, 11 Mar.
> This critic tries hard to find something to praise, but is not convincing. Says we must understand what O'Neill is doing, etc.

HORNBLOW, Arthur. "Mr. Hornblow goes to the play." *Theatre*, 35 (May) 308.
> Stretches to the straining point the obligation to be "truthful" about life. Some dramatic effectiveness, but not much more.

JAMES, Patterson. "The First Man." *Billboard*, 34 (8 Apr.) 19.
> Stupid reiterations, shoddy sentimentality. The offstage screams are "realism so extreme it is ludicrous." But O'Neill does push "remorsely to his conclusions"—a determination to be thankful for.

MACGOWAN, Kenneth. "Broadway at the spring." *Th: Arts*, 6 (July) 182.
> Shallow and arbitrary.

WHITTAKER, James. "O'Neill vents his gorge in The First Man."
NY *News*, 18 Mar.
> Rampant and arrogant pessimism.

THE FOUNTAIN

*Opening night reviews—New York
Newspapers of December 1925*

ALLEN, Kelcey. "O'Neill's The Fountain leaps to geyser heights of fantasy and romance." *W. W. Daily*, 11 Dec.
> Gushes, tumbles, and drops, like a fountain. Smothered with scenery, throwing sprays of condensed prose, colorful and dull. Reminds one of Rostand; Cyrano always seems to be peeking out somewhere.

ANDERSON, John. "New O'Neill play at the Greenwich Village theatre." NY *Post*, 11 Dec.
"Desire under the palms." Beautifully, often brilliantly written, lit with genuine poetic imagination and literary craftsmanship. Faults are poor construction, too many jerky tableaux, lack of cumulative interest.

COLEMAN, Robert. "Author explains play." NY *Mirror*, 14 Dec.
More pageant than play; feast for eyes, lean diet for ears.

DALE, Alan. "The Fountain." NY *American*, 12 Dec.
Without O'Neill's program notes it would have been impossible to gain the slightest idea what the play was meant to be.

GABRIEL, Gilbert. "De Leon in search of his spring." NY *Sun*, 11 Dec. [Reprinted in Miller, *Playwright's progress*, 1965.]
"Trial by scenery"; probably should not have been produced. Overly wordy, out-talking its aspirations.

HAMMOND, Percy. "Eugene O'Neill's The Fountain; a large romance done in a small way." NY *Her-Trib.*, 11 Dec.
Perhaps all right as a book, but it suffers from lack of elbow room in production. Needs too many of O'Neill's program explanations.

METCALFE, J. S. "The first Florida boom." *Wall St. Jour.*, 12 Dec.
O'Neill has discovered Ponce de Leon and embalmed him. One feels that George Cohan, Anne Nichols and others can claim rights as dramatists if O'Neill does so with this one. "A large section of Mr. O'Neill's most enthusiastic followers will be disappointed . . . It is a perfectly clean play."

"Mr. O'Neill seeking romance." NY *Times*, 11 Dec., 26:1.
Unwieldy; climactic scenes too brief. O'Neill is still brooding on human beings caught in the web of existence.

POLLOCK, Arthur. "Plays and things." Brook. *Eagle*, 11 Dec.
Structurally faulty, and O'Neill demands a Reinhardt production

in his scenery. Some scenes are fluent, but dogged, and the romance seems amateurish.

"Ponce de Leon a la Mr. O'Neill." NY *Telegraph*, 11 Dec.
If sharply pruned in last two scenes it may be the most distinguished drama of the year.

"Second thoughts on The Fountain." NY *Telegraph*, 13 Dec.
O'Neill has abandoned his acid etching and turned to water color, an allegory in pastel which has strength of Michalangelo mural. O'Neill is almost as effective as a poet as he has been a pathologist.

VREELAND, Frank. "Te Deum and tedium." NY *Telegram*, 11 Dec.
Too many pauses; it meditates too much. It is an obvious play which lays bare O'Neill's weaknesses.

WOOLLCOTT, Alexander. "The Fountain." NY *World*, 11 Dec.
Never uninteresting, but almost never alive. O'Neill fails for the first time to create real characters.

THE FOUNTAIN received only one production and was never revived. Many reviews did not appear until several weeks after the 11 December 1925 opening, so for this reason all reviews and criticism after 14 December are combined in a single group.

Other reviews and criticism
1925-1926

ATKINSON, Brooks. "New O'Neill aspects." NY *Times*, 20 Dec. 1925, VII, 3:1.
Attempting poetical history, O'Neill leaves his best medium of "morbid realism" behind. This is neither realism nor drama.

BARRETTO, Larry. "The New Yorker." *Bookman*, 62 (Feb. 1926) 704-705.
Fantasy is not O'Neill's forte. A fantastic, over-long tale.

BENCHLEY, Robert. "Art work." *Life*, 86 (31 Dec. 1925) 18.
O'Neill's morbid realism preferable to this boring play.

BROWN, John Mason. "The director takes a hand." *Th. Arts*, 10 (Feb. 1926) 77.
Full of inequalities; long winded and tiresome.

CARB, David. "Seen on the stage." *Vogue*, 67 (1 Feb. 1926) 60-61.
Maundering play, arousing no emotions. Here shuffles instead of strides.

CLARK, Barrett H. "The new O'Neill play and some others." *Drama*, 16 (Feb. 1926) 175.
The romantic is unfamiliar to O'Neill, but he surprises critics who do not realize he is an idealist and a poet.

EATON, Walter Prichard. "Masks and mysticism." NY *Her-Trib.*, 16 May 1926.
Published version reads extremely well despite failure as play.

FREEMAN, Donald. "A mid-season dramatic mixture." *Van. F.*, 25 (Feb. 1926) 118.
"Enriching and glamorous experience" despite certain failures in writing.

GILLETTE, Don Carle. "The Fountain." *Billboard*, 37 (19 Dec. 1925) 10.
"It interests but it does not stir; it pleases but it does not impress."

H.J.M. "The theatre." *New Yorker*, 1 (19 Dec. 1925) 17.
Questions how long O'Neill can be considered great with this and plays such as *WELDED* and *ALL GOD'S CHILLUN*.

HORNBLOW, Arthur. "Mr. Hornblow goes to the play." *Theatre*, 43 (Feb. 1926) 4a.
The scenery conceals much of what the play is about.

KALONYME, Louis. "Delectable mountain of current drama." *Arts & Dec.*, 24 (Feb. 1926) 66.
Shows some greatness in O'Neill, despite over-production.

M.W. "The play." *Commonweal*, 3 (23 Dec. 1925) 189.
Though a good portent that O'Neill may achieve his search for beauty and truth, the play itself is vague and dull.

NATHAN, George Jean. "O'Neill's latest." *Am. Merc.*, 7 (Feb. 1926) 247-249. [Reprinted in Downer, *American drama and its critics*, 1965.]
Much rewriting has ruined it, but it still shows O'Neill as our greatest native writer.

"Plays and players." *Town and Country*, 81 (1 Jan. 1926) 43.
Lusterless, formless and windy; prodigious, talky bore.

SELDES, Gilbert. "The theatre." *Dial*, 80 (Feb. 1926) 168-169.
Interesting play, produced with passion and beauty.

SISK. "The Fountain." *Variety*, 16 Dec. 1925.
Moments of dash killed by slow movement; not a success.

YOUNG, Stark. "The new O'Neill play." *New Rep.*, 45 (30 Dec. 1925) 160-161. [Reprinted in Cargill *et al*, *O'Neill and his plays*, 1961.]
A beautiful mood, new to O'Neill, but unequal to the demands the style places on words.

Further reviews

ANDREACH, Robert J. "O'Neill's use of Dante in The Fountain and The Hairy Ape." *Mod. Dr.*, 10 (May 1967) 48-56.
While not proving degree of O'Neill's acquaintance with Divine Comedy, critic shows interesting parallels. Discussion of O'Neill's development of female figure and the love-hate relationship.

GOLD

Opening night reviews—New York
Newspapers of 2 June 1921

ALLEN, Kelcey. "Eugene O'Neill's drama Gold acted at Frazee theatre." *W. W. Daily.*
Worth seeing if you like your drama strong.

BROUN, Heywood. "Gold at Frazee shows O'Neill below his best." NY *Tribune.* [Reprinted in Cargill *et al*, *O'Neill and his plays*, 1961.]
Slow, conventional beginning, with the O'Neill sign in last act.

DALE, Allen. "Artistic moments in Gold at the Frazee." NY *American.*
Curious symbolism, but too close to 10-20-30 melodrama.

DE FOE, Louis V. "New O'Neill play Gold is shown." NY *World.*
Moments of genuine drama, lacks effectiveness of his others.

"Eugene O'Neill's Gold tells a weird tale." NY *Times*, 14:2.
Interesting, but "curiously unconvincing" play; not up to standard.

"Eugene O'Neill's new play Gold not without alloy." NY *Herald.*
Too many "chunks of gloom" falling on the stage.

"Gold." NY *Sun.*
Over long; not among his best.

"Gold a triumph for Willard Mack." *Jour. of Comm.*
O'Neill seems unable to pen one light idea or pleasant thought.

MACGOWAN, Kenneth. "Eugene O'Neill's Gold disappoints in spite of many distinctions." NY *Globe*.

"Conceived in a bigger way than executed," but strength shows even in inadequate presentation.

MANTLE, Burns. "A new O'Neill tragedy." NY *Mail*.

Approaches *JONES* in study of conscience-driven fear, but with less of the novelty.

MARSH, Leo A. "Gold opens at Frazee theatre." NY *Telegraph*.

Looking for entertainment, don't go to this; full of O'Neill's "morbid vein" and shivers and shudders.

"O'Neill's Gold not glittering." NY *Telegram*.

Has power, but lines are blurred and uncertain; O'Neill deliberation becomes labored mannerism.

POLLOCK, Arthur. "Another O'Neill play." Brook. *Eagle*.

Hard to determine its aim; much of aimless nothingness.

TORRES, H. Z. "Willard Mack glitters in Gold." NY *Commercial*.

Thrilling tale of adventure and crime, suffers from repetition and halted action.

TOWSE, J. Ranken. "Gold." NY *Post*.

Crude melodrama; feeble play at best.

"Willard Mack scores in new drama." NY *Journal*.

Praise for acting, offers no criticism of play.

Other reviews and criticism
1921

ANDREWS, K. "Gold." *Bookman*, 53 (Aug.) 528-530.

O'Neill forgets his story between Acts I and IV, ends with his strange fire at his best.

BENCHLEY, Robert. "Gold—and some forty-niners." *Life*, 77 (16 June) 876.
Clumsy, resembles something Benchley (by own admission) might have written. Drought-provoking play.

"Eugene O'Neill's Gold is a drama of greed and gloom, plus symbolism." NY *Call*, 3 June.
Much repetition and discussion, enough to irritate the spirit.

FIRKINS, O. W. "Gold." *Weekly Rev.*, 4 (18 June) 584-585.
Two extraordinarily good first acts, but plot is abandoned and instead of Stevenson we have Conrad, the plot merely being towed into port.

"Gold." *Independent*, 105 (18 June) 633.
It is not up to O'Neill's best.

"Gold." *Lit. Rev. of NY Eve. Post*, 8 Oct., p. 74.
Gives hope of better things in the future.

"Gold." *Variety*, 10 June.
A big failure without merit; talky, balky, tiresome, impossible.

"Gold O'Neill's new play interesting but far from writer's best." NY *Clipper*, 69 (8 June) 19.
Almost 10-20-30 melodrama, but still more interesting than general run.

HORNBLOW, Arthur. "Mr. Hornblow goes to the play." *Theatre*, 35 (Aug.) 97.
Much force of expression but this is tedious, reiterative, banal.

JAMES, Patterson. "Gold." *Billboard*, 33 (18 June) 21.
Those wishing to profit at the boxoffice will categorize O'Neill as a "nut" author after this. Not a good play; a grisly picture of money craving. Everything is emptiness and desolation of spirit.

KAUFMAN, S. Jay. "Gold." *Dram. Mir.*, 83 (11 June) 1001.
Chaos when O'Neill writes conventional melodrama.

————. "Seen on the stage." *Vogue*, 15 Sept.
As vivid and vital a first act as any American has ever written;
play is ruined by acting and production.

LEWISOHN, Ludwig. "Drama." *Nation*, 112 (22 June) 902.
Seem to have heard all this before. Interesting comment by this
critic who places O'Neill second to Susan Glaspell as our leading
writer.

"O'Neill's Gold proves to be an impressive play." NY *Review*, 4
June.
In some ways O'Neill's most impressive play.

1922

BOYD, Ernest A. "Shorter notices." *Freeman*, 4 (4 Jan.) 406.
Book review. Prefers this to *WHERE CROSS IS MADE*, because
of more wild elemental force.

"Gold." *Cath. Wld.*, 114 (Jan.) 555.
More dramatic than literary value.

"The truth of O'Neill's technic." *Dramatist*, 13 (Jan.) 1095-1097.
O'Neill must learn the rules of playwriting like everybody else.

THE GREAT GOD BROWN

Opening night reviews—New York
Newspapers of 25 Jan. 1926

ALLEN, Kelcey. "Great God Brown by O'Neill unique." *W. W.*
Daily.
Personality transfer unacceptable, far-fetched. Expressionism and symbolism must have some relationship to the sphere of
logic; mask switching to the point of strangulation. A labora-
tory experiment not good for the theatre.

ANDERSON, John. "Another O'Neill play comes to town." *NY Post*.
[Reprinted in Miller, *Playwright's progress*, 1965.]
A superb failure, more than the stage can hold; O'Neill's fall from
heights of dramatic imagination is "brilliant and thrilling." They play
eventually drowns magnificently in the seething theories of the writer.

ATKINSON, Brooks. "Symbolism in an O'Neill tragedy." NY *Times*,
26:1. [Reprinted in Durham & Dodds, *British and American plays*,
1830-1945, 1947; and in Miller, *Playwright's progress*, 1965.]
Atkinson refuses to be bothered by the fact the play is not always
clear; what O'Neill does is more important that what he does not do.

COLEMAN, Robert. "God Brown tedious." NY *Mirror*.
Ineffective and tedious. Despairing dirge of puzzled pessimist.

GABRIEL, Gilbert. "All God's chillun got masks." NY *Sun*. [Reprint-
ed in Cargill *et al*, *O'Neill and his plays*, 1961.]
O'Neill does not write for popularity but for posterity. One will
remember the play, whatever he thinks of it. Gabriel's admiration is
"hot but troubled" for O'Neill's most poetic and penetrating play.

"Great God Brown ingenious concept, towers in dignity." *Jour.*
Comm.
Reveals the philosopher and poet. An epic without heroes,
abounding in fertility of genius. A great play. The pen is keen as a
scapel, dipped in wormword of reality. Rich portraiture; opulent
fancy; vision of a seer; strange and exciting. Towers in classic dignity.

"Great God Brown opens at Greenwich Village." NY *Graphic*.
Strength and beauty, but you will go home mystified and bored.

MARSH, Leo. "O'Neill's latest pure experiment." NY *Telegraph*.
A clinical experiment.

METCALFE, J. S. "A plea in defence." *Wall St. Jour*.
The masks hinder instead of help, making some speeches seem
laughable. O'Neill is no longer the great dramatist of realism and low-
life characters.

OSBORN, E. W. "The Great God Brown." NY *World*.
The unexpected is again introduced and spells wonderful, though
there is some symbolic running wild in the last act.

POLLOCK, Arthur. "The Great God Brown." Brook. *Eagle*.
Very little critical comment; mainly plot review.

VREELAND, Frank. "The masked marvel." NY *Telegram*.
O'Neill at both his best and his worst.

Other reviews and criticism
(With two exceptions all dates are 1926)

ANDERSON, John. "O'Neill the realist turns mystic." *Lit. Rev. of NY
Eve. Post*, 10 Apr., p. 2.
O'Neill is still handicapped by his tools of the theatre, but he
is also still an impressive dramatist.

ANSCHUTZ, Grace. "Masks, their use by Pirandello and O'Neill."
Drama, 17 (Apr. 1927) 201.
An interesting comparison of the two styles. Pirandello may do
better through character portrayal alone, than through use of actual
masks.

ATKINSON, Brooks. "Ibsen and O'Neill." NY *Times*, 31 Jan., VII,
1:1.

The two writers have much in common in emotional sensitiveness and philosophy, dealing with things that are not quite what they seem. Ibsen can be understood, but in this play O'Neill is on the verge of becoming unintelligible.

BARRETTO, Larry. "The New Yorker." *Bookman*, 63 (Apr.) 213.
"O'Neill has come a cropper while riding on a brave quest."

BENCHLEY, Robert. "So deep!" *Life*, 87 (11 Feb.) 20.
Last half unintelligible jumble, but it probably reads well.

BOGDANOFF, Rose. "Masks, their uses, past and present." *Drama*, 21 (May 1931) 21.
O'Neill's use of the mask is the finest in modern theatre, as much a part of the play as the lines themselves.

BROWN, John Mason. "Doldrums of midwinter." *Th. Arts*, 10 (Mar.) 145-146.
In an otherwise dull season, this comes as utterly different experiment. Fine for two acts, then confusion.

CARB, David. "The Great God Brown." *Vogue*, 67 (15 Mar.) 106.
"Subtly conceived symbolic tragedy, finely imagined, written with glowing loveliness. It fails to succeed only because of a physical device."

CLARK, Barrett H. "Fin de saison on Broadway." *Drama*, 16 (May) 289-290.
Hopes Pulitzer Prize is awarded to this play.

———. "High spots in a dull season." *Drama*, 16 (Mar.) 212.
Highest development of O'Neill's genius we have seen. Like all poets, he writes ahead of us.

EATON, Walter Prichard. "Masks and mysticism." NY *Her-Trib.*, 16 May.
The reading text may be clearer, but the absence of masks loses emotion.

GILLETTE, Don Carle. "The Great God Brown." *Billboard*, 38 (6 Feb.) 43.

Audiences must be educated to O'Neill more slowly; he is given in too big doses. This is "glorious confusion."

"The Great God Brown." *Drama Calendar*, 8 (1 Feb.) 1.

Has partly succeeded in "externalizing" the process of spiritual rebirth, and should be praised for it.

"The Great God Brown." *Outlook*, 143 (26 May) 151.

Tragic allegory. The characters attain stature.

"Great God Brown and other plays." *Dial*, 81 (Aug.) 175.

Most people over 40 would look at this with amused tolerance of the rebellion against life.

"Great God Brown—Another grotesque conundrum." *Dramatist*, 17 (July) 1307-1309.

This review is almost unbelievably narrow and unimaginative, calling the play a drama "for dumb Doras," about an architect who masquerades as his dead rival and fails.

G.W.G. "Goat Song, Great God Brown and other crashing symbols." *New Yorker*, 1 (6 Feb.) 26.

Some of the finest writing of O'Neill's career; underneath the "foam" of the masks lies the "nutritious fluid of a deeply digested idea."

HORNBLOW, Arthur. "Mr. Hornblow goes to the play." *Theatre*, 43 (Apr.) 18.

The mask exchange in late scenes is piffle. Nothing in the play outside of some utterly incomprehensible hocus-pocus.

KALONYME, Louis. "Dramatica Dionysiana." *Arts and Dec.*, 24 (Mar.) 62.

O'Neill's greatest achievement to date. This critic finds no confusion in mask switch, sees it as an "inevitable and integral step."

KRUTCH, Joseph Wood. "Review of the season." *Nation*, 122 (16 June) 675.
   One of O'Neill's most moving and most chaotic plays.

———. "The tragedy of masks." *Nation*, 122 (10 Feb.) 164-165. [Reprinted in Hewitt, Barnard, *Theatre USA*, 1959.]
   Never a more powerful or confused O'Neill play. Confusion perhaps because O'Neill is too close to subject; it masters him as much as he masters it.

MACGOWAN, Kenneth. "The mask in drama." Brook. *Eagle*, 30 Jan.
   Discussion of differences between O'Neill and the Greeks.

———. "The mask in drama." *Greenwich Playbill* No. 4, Season 1925-1926.
   Points out this is the first modern play making direct use of the mask, using it for character change instead of physical or emotional change.

MANTLE, Burns. "Great God Brown fascinating mystery." NY *News*, 26 Jan.
   Difficult play to follow, but one of most gripping tragi-comedies. Will stand as one of O'Neill's greatest messages.

NATHAN, George Jean. "The Theatre." *Am. Merc.*, 7 (Apr.) 503-504. [Reprinted in Downer, *American drama and its critics*, 1965.]
   Richly imagined, brilliantly articulated, has power of conviction and dialogue of profundity seldom equalled in native drama.

"Plays and players." *Town and Country*, 81 (15 Feb.) 60.
   Jerkily written, pretentious, masks clumsy and annoying, the theme better to be treated by European writers.

QUINN, Arthur Hobson. Letter to editor. NY *Times*, 21 Feb., VII, 2:6.
   Calls attention to this profound study as worthy of support.

SISK. "Great God Brown." *Variety*, 27 Jan.

He has hit on something almost great in the masks—but not quite.

SKINNER, Richard Dana. "Blossoms in arid dust." *Ind. & Weekly R.*, 116 (6 Mar.) 275.
Approval for masks, but audiences may not follow everything. O'Neill at his best. He is laying bare his own life, an opinion Skinner further develops in *Poet's quest*.

————. "The play." *Commonweal*, 3 (10 Feb.) 384.
O'Neill emerges from the swamp of despair and shows faith in resurrection. A notable play; O'Neill capable of "lofty vision."

SMITH, Geddes. "Three mirrors." *Survey*, 56 (1 Apr.) 43.
"Heavy with implications . . . sometimes clear, sometimes muddled, always insistent."

WYATT, Euphemia Van R. "Plays of some importance." *Cath. Wld.*, 122 (Mar.) 805-807.
If O'Neill is not a mystic, he is as close as any contemporary American. The play is a subtle study of the hide and seek men play with their lives and souls.

YOUNG, Stark. "The Great God Brown." *New Rep.*, 45 (10 Feb.) 329-330. [Reprinted in Young's *Immortal shadows*, 1948.]
Some unequal writing, but a feeling of great groping of life behind the play. Some effective use of masks.

Opening night reviews—Revival—New York
Newspapers of 7 Oct. 1959

ASTON, Frank. "Great God Brown reopens at the Coronet." NY *Wor-Tel. & Sun*.
Everyone deserves praise for courage in the revival; the difficulties of performance are beyond most people. Masks are clumsy, but play is harrowing, engrossing, rewarding.

ATKINSON, Brooks. "Theatre: O'Neill's Great God Brown." NY

Times, 48:1. [Reprinted in Miller, *Playwright's progress*, 1965.]

As avante garde as any play of Beckett or Ionesco. In form there is nothing today more modern; memorable characters in a fascinating fantasy. Whether or not it is a "success" is pedantic. O'Neill's power of introspection is magnetic, for he writes about permanent ideas.

CHAPMAN, John. "O'Neill's Great God Brown an impressive theatrical curio." NY *News*.

Nothing is any more clear now than ever. Perhaps a great work, but it seems now to be a curio.

COLBY, Ethel. "Entertainment on Broadway." *Jour. Comm.* 8 Oct.

Passing of time not noticeable; the theme is ageless. The masks are still electrifying. "The compulsion to think with O'Neill leaves one transfixed."

COLEMAN, Robert. "Great God Brown not O'Neill at best." NY *Mirror*.

O'Neill's mind and soul were in ferment. In seeking faith he had little interest in clarity. Appealing for students, not for regular playgoers.

DASH, Thomas R. "Great God Brown confusing but stirring." *W. W. Daily*.

Beckett & Ionesco are "rank amateurs" in the bewitched, bothered and bewildered kind of play compared to this. Still confusing after 33 years, the last scene being a "charade of fakery," fatuous and ludicrous.

KERR, Walter. "Great God Brown." NY *Her-Trib*.

Seems to have been written when O'Neill's energy was near exhaustion. Poor characters rob it of any cumulative force. Neither poetry nor people swell to any size. Seems dry as sand.

McCLAIN, John. "A well-acted puzzler." NY *Jour-Am*.

"A mess of dried shaving-cream" well performed, challenges anyone to dig out its meaning. McClain questions: "Why must good theatre be so oblique, so different?"

WATTS, Richard. "O'Neill's drama of men and masks." NY *Post*.
At times can be nothing short of maddening. Probably a failure,
but a failure of genius. Third act philosophy is too much. Disturbing
beauty, final confusion, but still a work of dramatic art.

Other reviews and criticism
1959

ATKINSON, Brooks. "Great God Brown." NY *Times*, 18 Oct., II,
1:1.
Absolute standards of excellence mark this a failure, although
O'Neill fascinates and enthralls with his attempt. The Phoenix production meets with high approval, but O'Neill is too far beyond his audience by the third act. Nonetheless, it is a major theatre work, full
of O'Neill's indomitability and tragic insight.

BERKELMAN, R. "O'Neill's everyman." *S. Atl. Quar.*, 58 (Fall) 609.
This is a 20th century Everyman's journey through life. Brown
and Dion are one person, and the women combine in Everywoman
as well. The play is not, however, O'Neill's best.

BOLTON, Whitney. "O'Neill play has areas of confusion." NY *Telegraph*, 8 Oct.
The last act can become clownish. We are never sure whether
the masks are good or bad, but the fact O'Neill tried is a tribute anyway.

BRUSTEIN, Robert. "O'Neill's adolescent talkathon." *New Rep.*, 141
(Oct. 19) 29.
Despite talk and abstractions, the play shows O'Neill's greatness
was in his probing of character instead of his hazy views of the universe. Too many undeveloped themes make it incoherent, and the play
cannot hold us now.

CLURMAN, Harold. "Theatre." *Nation*, 189 (24 Oct.) 259-260.
A crucial American tragedy in its portrayal of the incompleteness
of American civilization as it focuses on the individual. For all his

faults, O'Neill is our most important dramatist because he is more truly relevant to the American people.

COOKE, Richard P. "O'Neill's maskers." *Wall St. Jour.*, 8 Oct.
  Poetic jumble. Seems old fashioned and literary, still bearing the marks of an unsuccessful experiment.

GELB, Arthur. "An epitaph for the O'Neills." NY *Times*, 4 Oct., II, 1:1.
  A review of the play as an epitaph for his family of father, mother, and brother, all lost within the previous five years. This play therefore begins a lifelong evaluation of O'Neill's relationship to them, culminating in *LONG DAY'S JOURNEY*. The article points up interesting parallels between the play's characters and the real people O'Neill knew.

"The Great God Brown." *Th. Arts*, 43 (Dec.) 88.
  There is more immediacy and impact than in the original. The masks are not dated, and they illustrate more than ever O'Neill's anger and grief.

"Into the shadows again." *Newsweek*, 54 (19 Oct.) 80.
  It is still valid as an experiment. The philosophy is sometimes inspired, but confusing. A difficult but compelling play.

LEWIS, Theophilus. "The Great God Brown." *America*, 102 (31 Oct.) 139-140.
  It is not O'Neill's most impressive, but probably his most fascinating work. It is good to see a revival of this challenging play.

MORRISON, Hobe. "Great God Brown." *Variety*, 14 Oct.
  Remains one of O'Neill's important works; engrossing, challenging, uneven, a milestone in his career. The masks, while still novel, require more than most audiences will give.

"Old play in Manhattan." *Time*, 74 (19 Oct.) 56.
  Prolix and banal, as heavy with fog as it is lacking in flesh. The

production is not good. Some vivid tricks, but the "gaudy orchestration" merely emphasizes the music's hollowness.

RHODES, Robert E. "A brilliant revival." *Newsday*, 14 Oct.
Just as absorbing, stimulating, and effective as ever, regardless of time.

TYNAN, Kenneth. "O'Neill in embryo." *New Yorker*, 35 (17 Oct.) 131.
A fascinating evening. The end, however, is in the "soggy realm" of bad fantasy and cannot be accepted.

WATTS, Richard. "A maddening and fascinating play." NY *Post*, 18 Oct.
Still disturbing as it was when first produced. A magnificent failure because of the confusion. It is impossible to strike a balance between its great virtues and its great defects.

1965-1971

METZGER, Deena P. "Variations on a theme: A study of Exiles by James Joyce and The Great God Brown by Eugene O'Neill." *Mod. Dr.*, 8 (Sept. 1965) 174-184.
Though Joyce's approach demands "dramatic emotion of stasis" and the illuminating technique of "empathy," while O'Neill relies on traditional theatre fare of ecstasy and catharsis, this critic finds strong parallels between the plays.

ROSEN, Kenneth M. "O'Neill's Brown and Wilde's Gray." *Mod. Dr.*, 13 (Feb. 1971) 347-355.
Close parallels in character and theme between the play and the novel which O'Neill once admitted affected him considerably.

SOGLIUZZO, A. Richard. "The uses of the mask in The Great God Brown and Six Characters in Search of an Author." *Ed. Th. Jour.*, 18 (Oct. 1966) 224-229.
Exploration of the use of masks in the two plays, with Pirandel-

lo's mask used not as symbols but devices to show that life is illusion
and art reality.

*Opening night reviews—Revival—New York
Newspapers of 11-12 Dec. 1972*

BARNES, Clive. "Theatre: Phoenix revives Great God Brown." NY
Times, 11 Dec., p. 51.
   A "quite extraordinarily bad play" which seems to survive and
does make a rewarding evening. Symbolic "rigmarole" never quite
works, yet holds attention, with stylized masks "clever and adroit."

GOTTFRIED, Martin. "The Great God Brown." *W.W. Daily*, 12 Dec.
   As "patently nonsensical" as anything O'Neill wrote. No matter
how much we want a great playwright this "heavyhandedness of art
and sloppiness of craft" is unacceptable. Production, however, is
inventive, poised, and polished, and rescues the unfortunate
experimentation with masks. An oddity at best.

WATT, Douglas. "O'Neill's Great God Brown revived by the Phoenix
repertory." NY *News*, 11 Dec.
   "Sheer power of O'Neill's vision" transcends flaws and absurdities. Almost unplayable, unbelievably gauche, reaches point of absurdity, yet strange vision persists. An "uneasy production of an impossi-
bly difficult play."

WATTS, Richard. "O'Neill's world in falseface." NY *Post*, 11 Dec.
   One of the "strangest plays O'Neill or anyone else ever wrote."
Ambiguities and complexities do not work out successfully, but fascination cannot be denied. An O'Neill failure, but far more interesting
and important than most successes.

Further reviews

   By publication deadline for this volume, most periodicals had not
yet reviewed the play. The following two were, however, available.

GILL, Brendan. "Behind the masks." *New Yorker*, 48 (16 Dec. 1972) 86.

Because O'Neill never really felt that we could cast off the masks and be reborn, the play is "incoherent and often threatens to become absurd." O'Neill, unlike Molière (whose *Don Juan* appeared with this in repertory) thought mankind a bad joke, hence he was forever groaning while Molière, finding mankind a good joke, is forever laughing.

HUGHES, Catharine. "Picking up the pieces." *America*, 127 (30 Dec. 1972) 570-571.

More interesting in aspirations than in realization. Not O'Neill at his best, the expressionism far from convincing, with development of theme mechanical and often tedious and repetitious. "A really quite bad play" but the production makes it "palatable."

THE HAIRY APE

Opening night reviews—New York
Newspapers of 10 Mar. 1922

"Hairy Ape a logical tragedy." NY *World*.

Not as good as *JONES* because of less articulate human note.

HAMMOND, Percy. "Hairy Ape shows Eugene O'Neill in a bitter and interesting humor." NY *Tribune*.

An "interesting thing," the best since *ANNA CHRISTIE*.

MACGOWAN, Kenneth. "Eugene O'Neill sets a new mark in The Hairy Ape." NY *Globe*.

Welcome to a tremendous new drama form, "extraordinarily challenging."

MANTLE, Burns. "The Hairy Ape." NY *Mail*.

A better play than *JONES* because of better mood, more intimate contact with the modern world.

REAMER, Lawrence. "Hairy Ape, new O'Neill play, an impressive study of life." NY *Herald*.

General praise. Downfall of *JONES* more effective than fall of this "feeble giant."

TOWSE, J. Ranken. "Eugene O'Neill's latest effort." NY *Post*.

In his vigorous attack on the play's "juvenile appeal to ignorance and passion" Towse sees ominous foreboding for O'Neill's future. One of the strongest dissents among a minority of the critics who did not like the play. Towse finds the play worthless, and assigns it social and economic aspects which O'Neill probably never intended.

WELSH, Robert G. "Behind the scenes." NY *Telegram*.

Expressive and weird; does not do well in the shift from realistic beginning to "fantasy" of the second part.

WOOLLCOTT, Alexander. "Eugene O'Neill at full tilt." NY *Times*, 18:2. [Reprinted in Cargill *et al*, *O'Neill and his plays*, 1961; and in Miller, *Playwright's progress*, 1965.]

"Monstrously uneven" but O'Neill towers above the milling mumbling crowd of contemporary playwrights.

Other reviews and criticism
1922

THE HAIRY APE moved from the crowded Provincetown stage to the Plymouth theatre uptown on 17 April 1922. Several newspapers sent their critics to review it again, and their comments are included below.

ANDREWS, Kenneth. "Broadway our literary signpost." *Bookman*, 55 (May) 284.

The play is like a "badly written editorial in the 'Call.' "

"As to the Hairy Ape." NY *Star*, 22 Apr.

Ending is inevitable, very natural. A vivid play.

BAURY, Louis, "The Hairy Ape." *Freeman*, 5 (19 July) 449.
Baury replies to Kantor and denies that *APE* has been categorized as completely expressionistic.

————. "Mr. O'Neill's new plays." *Freeman*, 5 (3 May) 184-185.
This and *FIRST MAN* are failures. O'Neill must learn responsibilities of his art and cease "wallowing in mere words."

————. "On reply to Mr. Block." *Freeman*, 5 (14 June) 330.
Sharp reply to Block's letter. Baury shows respect for O'Neill but feels *APE* did not achieve greatness that modern drama is capable of.

BENCHLEY, Robert. "The Hairy Ape." *Life*, 79 (30 Mar.) 18.
His most powerful thing yet.

BLOCK, Ralph. "The old order changeth." *Freeman*, 5 (31 May) 281-282.
Letter protesting Baury's approach which seems to assume there are rules and responsibilities an artist must follow, which this writer believes do not exist.

BROUN, Heywood. "The Hairy Ape." NY *World*, 2 Apr.
Interesting and gallant attempt that does not come off.

————. "It seems to me." NY *World*, 25 Apr.
In reply to an accusation that he did not give the play justice as a social document, Broun states the artistic sense is lost when the artist adopts a cause, and this is the case with O'Neill.

————. "It seems to me." NY *World*, 3 May.
Cites a letter from Michael Gold attacking Broun and his "gang" for wanting sugar-coated stuff instead of this terrific kind of play.

CASTELLUN, Maida. "The plays that pass—O'Neill's Hairy Ape a powerful tragedy of today." NY *Call*, 12 Mar.
One of his finest achievements; a powerful and shattering play.

DALE, Alan. "Hairy Ape is presented at Plymouth." NY *American*, 19 Apr.
The audience should go to enjoy it for the new type play it is, and should forget the "bosh" about what it means.

DARNTON, Charles. "The Hairy Ape despair run amuck." NY *World*, 19 Apr.
Yank's bad liquor must be causing him bad dreams.

DAWSON, N. P. "Books in particular." NY *Globe*, 17 Apr.
O'Neill plows a very new and deep furrow in this one.

EATON, Walter Prichard. "The Hairy Ape." *Freeman*, 5 (26 Apr.) 160-161. [Reprinted in Miller, *Playwright's progress*, 1965.]
O'Neill is the writer of the future; no matter what one's opinion you cannot get away from it; whatever the symbols and interpretations, it is a tragedy.

"The Hairy Ape." *Drama Calendar*, 20 Mar.
A great play, but makes one wince. Beautiful in bold directness and stark reality.

"The Hairy Ape." NY *Post*, 22 Mar.
This editorial praises the play, which shows that the next decade in the theatre will be filled with admirable and surprising things.

"The Hairy Ape." NY *Tribune*, 20 Apr.
O'Neill is a young genius and our greatest playwright, completely lacking in superficiality.

"Hairy Ape at the Provincetown Playhouse." *Town Topics*, 16 Mar.
It should reach Broadway; if it does not it will be a disgrace.

"Hairy Ape is O'Neill at best." NY *Journal*, 19 Apr.
Tremendous force and imagination.

"Hairy Ape, O'Neill play, is dull and tiresome." NY *Clipper*, 70 (22 Mar.) 22.

Neither his best nor worst; interesting if you like O'Neill.

"Hairy Ape—Undramatized sensation." *Dramatist*, 13 (July) 1117-1118.
"Brute force that goes nowhere."

HOPKINS, Mary Alden. "Hairy Ape at the Provincetown Theatre." *Greenwich Villager*, 11 Mar.
Not a criticism; merely reviews matters of staging.

HORNBLOW, Arthur. "Mr. Hornblow goes to the play." *Theatre*, 35 (May) 305.
"Towering accomplishment" brilliant, vitally poetic, apocalyptic in message.

JAMES, Patterson. "Off the record." *Billboard*, 34 (15 Apr.) 18. [Reprinted in Miller, *Playwright's progress*, 1965.]
Violent, vitriolic attack comparing the play to swill wagons and slaughter houses in its "realism" of staging and language. This opinion is partner to Towse's and Robbins' in its purely surfacy attitude. The critic is so horribly offended that he makes little effort to offer worthwhile criticism.

KANTOR, Louis. "The Hairy Ape." *Freeman*, 5 (5 July) 402-403.
A letter to the editor differs with Baury's reply to Block's letter. Kantor says O'Neill is like the "modernist movement" in Germany, which he does not identify.

LEVICK, L. E. "Hairy Ape and the I.W.W. Marine transport workers turn dramatic critics and praise O'Neill." NY *Call*, 14 May.
Report of review in *Marine Worker*, which recommends the play to its members.

LEWISOHN, Ludwig. "The development of Eugene O'Neill." *Nation*, 114 (22 Mar.) 349-350.
O'Neill cannot work freely within established drama forms, but this is his best and approaches his own true form.

MacGowan, Kenneth. "Broadway at the spring." *Th. Arts*, 6 (July) 182.
    Our first expressionist play and quite successful.

————. "Curtain calls." NY *Globe*, 13 Mar.
    A sharp rebuttal to Towse, scolding "learned critics" who don't know a new form of drama when they see it.

————. "Hairy Ape uptown." NY *Globe*, 18 Apr.
    Improved with the move from the Village; the same surging and exciting piece.

————. "The theatrical callboard." *Van. F.*, 18 (Apr.) 16 d.
    This radically new play one of the big events of the season.

"Mr. Brady's view of the season." NY *World*, 30 Apr.
    It is part of a season that strives for the exceptional, bizarre, and shocking.

Pearson, Edmund L. "New books and old." *Independent*, 109 (19 Aug.) 78.
    Book review only. Gives feeling of being "deafening."

Pemberton, Brock. "Mr. Pemberton goes to The Hairy Ape." NY *Globe*, 15 Mar.
    Just back from Germany, writer finds "uncanny" similarities in comparison with Toller's *Masse Mensch*, though they are unlike in concept and execution.

"A play to see." *Commerce and Finance*, 15 Mar.
    "Not to see it is to have failed to have seen the best that American art has produced."

Pollock, Arthur. "About the theatre." Brook. *Eagle*, 21 May.
    Questions if we are to be confined to "sweet romances and banal detective plays" or if we will be permitted to encourage plays like *APE* so that America "may become articulate in the eyes of the artistic world."

————. "The Hairy Ape." Brook. *Eagle*, 12 Mar.

Enough realism ("imaginative realism") to make Belasco weep.

"A portrait play." NY *American*, 20 Apr.

Notes O'Neill's insistence that the play is only about a man who does not "belong."

RATHBUN, Stephen. "Eugene O'Neill's Hairy Ape is one of the most vital plays of the season." NY *Sun*, 11 Mar.

Opposes O'Neill's "negative philosophy," but finds there is something here to think about.

ROBBINS, R. "The I.W.W. on the stage." *Industrial Solidarity*, 8 Apr.

The critic of this labor periodical considers the play one of the most helpful and legitimate defenses of the I.W.W. position today. O'Neill has painted the inner tragedy of the proleterian soul.

SAYLER, Oliver M. "The Hairy Ape is a study in evolution of a play." NY *Globe*, 6 May.

This interesting account of the original idea for the play counts *JONES* as its "father."

————. "Our theatre at cross purposes." *Century*, 104 (Sept.) 748.

The season was a "patchwork of perversity," with O'Neill closest to whole garment.

SELDES, Gilbert. "The Hairy Ape." *Dial*, 72 (May) 548-549. [Reprinted in Hewitt, *Theatre USA*, 1959.]

Critic does not like shift from one framework to another.

TOWSE, J. Ranken. "The Hairy Ape in new conditions." NY *Post*, 18 Apr.

Initial view not changed; still a potboiler and melodramatic thriller without significance.

WHITTAKER, James. "That horrible gorilla crushed the Hairy Ape." NY *News*, 16 Mar.

JONES was dissection of a reverting type; this is vivisection. Yank never had a chance, and O'Neill is not fair to him.

WOOLLCOTT, Alexander. "Second thoughts on first nights." NY *Times*, 16 Apr., VI, 1:1.

General speculation on O'Neill's chances on Broadway in Plymouth Theatre, as opposed to success in Village.

YOUNG, Stark. "The Hairy Ape." *New Rep.*, 30 (22 Mar.) 112-113.

Whatever the opinion of the play or of O'Neill, this must be recognized as important in O'Neill's ability to free himself and carry through without impediment of event or convention.

Further reviews

ANDREACH, Robert J. "O'Neill's use of Dante in The Fountain and The Hairy Ape." *Mod. Dr.*, 10 (May 1967) 48-56.

While not able to prove how extensively O'Neill was acquainted with The Divine Comedy, this critic shows interesting parallels to and, particularly in APE, inversions of, Dante, whether intentional or not he cannot say. Discussion of the figure of the female and the love-hate relationship.

BAUM, Bernard. "Tempest and Hairy Ape: The literary incarnation of mythos." *Mod. Lang. Q.*, 14 (Sept. 1953) 258-273.

Interesting and provocative study of "displacement of world views." Caliban seen as natural man, while natural Yank appears as Man. An avatar of Caliban (with certain mutations) holds center stage in *APE*, with steel, not music, as the epitome of power.

CLARK, Marden J. "Tragic effect in The Hairy Ape." *Mod. Dr.*, 10 (Feb. 1968) 372-382.

Not necessarily tragic in classic Greek sense, but a little bit of each of Oedipus, Job, and Lear recognizing in the end his own humanity.

GUMP, Margaret. "From ape to man and from man to ape." *Ky. For. Lang. Quar.*, 4 (1957) 268-282.

APE discussed along with items by Huxley, Kafka, and others, as a part of literary comment on man's often ape-like qualities and tendencies.

"The Hairy Ape." *Cath. Wld.*, 116 (Feb. 1923) 714.

The ape is a *tour de force*, an artificial product; fails in primary quality of convincingness.

"The Hairy Ape." *Th. Arts*, 18 (Aug. 1934) 598.

O'Neill has caught the conflict of the individual and world around him more than anybody else.

JOHNSON, Annette T. "The Hairy Ape." *Ind. & Weekly R.*, 110 (28 Apr. 1923) 282-284.

Some reflections on civilization's responsibility to all the "hairy apes."

KEANE, Christopher. "Blake and O'Neill: A prophecy." *Blake Stud.*, 2 (Spring 1970) 23-34.

A unique study of THE HAIRY APE in terms of its fulfillment of Blake's vision in "The Tyger," in which he prophesied the world in which the hairy ape lives. Blake sees "an army of semi-conscious souls marching to the sound of a hammer pounding their human frames into robot-like tools on an assembly line." O'Neill realizes Blake's prophecy in Yank and his experiences as suffering under the forces of industry and capitalism, "which extinguish man's creativity and inspiration."

MACGOWAN, Kenneth. "Experiment on Broadway." *Th. Arts*, 7 (July 1923) 175-185.

A discussion of experimentation and expressionism includes this play.

ROBBINS, R. "The emperor O'Neill." *Industrial Pioneer*, 2 (Jan. 1925) 26-27.

Labor (I.W.W.) publication praises O'Neill for creating real characters in an age of dramatic sham and counterfeit.

ROLLINS, R. G. "O'Casey, O'Neill and the Expressionism in Within the Gates." *West Virginia Bulletin. Philological Papers*, 1961, vol. 13, pp. 76-81.

APE as O'Neill's example of the style in a comparison of expressionistic techniques.

ROY, Emil. "Eugene O'Neill's The Emperor Jones and The Hairy Ape as mirror plays." *Comp. Dr.*, 2 (Spring 1968) 21-31.

These successful experimental plays are seen as mirrors with complementing parallels. Both heroes are "messianic types" who parody the hero myth.

SCARBROUGH, Alex. "O'Neill's Yank: The Noble Ape." Marshall Univ. *Bulletin*, Spring 1972.

Yank's search for "belonging" demonstrated as striving to confer dignity upon his own life and to return to his own human significance.

WATTS, Richard. "Regarding Mr. O'Neill as a writer for the cinema." NY *Her-Trib.*, 4 Mar. 1928.

Synopsis of O'Neill's own film scenarios for *DESIRE* and *APE*, neither of which were produced. They are much altered from the stage versions.

HUGHIE

This single surviving play from the projected one-act cycle *BY WAY OF OBIT* was published by Yale in 1959 after its premiere in Stockholm in 1958. The book received comparatively little notice in the press, and the play was not produced in the United States until December 1964, when it received the usual critical coverage.

Early reviews

GELB, Arthur. "Dream and live." NY *Times*, 19 April 1959, VII, 5:3.

This reflects the same theme from many of the longer plays, namely that man must have his dreams in order to survive. The play, more of a short story, is a "compassionate, shattering character study."

HEWES, Henry. "Short night's journey into day." *Sat. R.*, 41 (4 Oct. 1958) 27. [Reprinted in Cargill *et al*, *O'Neill and his plays*, 1961.]
A report on the Stockholm production. "Top drawer O'Neill." The whole cycle of life has been put into forty-five minutes. The technique is Chekhovian.

KRUTCH, Joseph Wood. "And now—Hughie." *Th. Arts*, 43 (Aug. 1959) 14-15.
A real addition to the canon, and unlike most posthumous works, a good one, showing perhaps O'Neill was reaching maturity of his powers. It is restrained and more compact than the longer plays, and the dialogue is better.

WEALES, Gerald. "Variation on an O'Neill theme." *Commonweal*, 70 (15 May 1959) 187-188.
Another illustration of O'Neill's theme of the need for life illusion. Impressive because it says so briefly what *ICEMAN* developed in such detail.

Opening Night Reviews—New York
Newspapers of December 1964

BOLTON, Whitney. "Hughie is fascinating O'Neill; touching and compassionate." NY *Telegraph*, 24 Dec.
Not a major O'Neill work, but fascinating. Much praise for the performers in this play which "hits hard and evokes compassion."

CHAPMAN, John. "Robards in O'Neill's Hughie." NY *News*, 23 Dec.
Praise for the performances in this "remnant" of a play, quaint and lonesome in its character study. Hardly more than a curtain-raiser, "but a curtain-raiser to what?"

COOKE, Richard P. "O'Neill one-acter." *Wall St. Jour.*, 24 Dec.

Unfortunately not one of O'Neill's best. Honesty and power, but we are used to more "iron texture" from O'Neill. Lightweight, without the quality normally expected from Quintero productions of O'Neill.

GELB, Arthur, and Barbara Gelb. "Jason Robards returns in O'Neill's Hughie." NY *Times*, 20 Dec., Sec. 2, p. 1.
A two-part discussion "On the play" by Arthur Gelb and "On the player" by Barbara Gelb published prior to the New York opening. Little more than review of what the play is about, and a brief discussion of Robards as an actor.

GOTTFRIED, Martin. "Hughie." *W.W. Daily*, 23 Dec.
Not enough of a play for a full evening. O'Neill attempted a small play around a significant insight in special human needs, which does not succeed. Too slender, talky, "trundles along in rambling uninterest," a great disappointment.

KERR, Walter. "Hughie." NY *Her.-Trib.*, 23 Dec.
Some question as to why O'Neill returns to a "bluesy, blowsy" solo after having arranged for full orchestra in *ICEMAN*. Amid criticism for the director's overemphasis and dangers it presents, determination is that the play is a curiosity, "somewhat unrepresentative production for those who demand that drama carry its own weight."

MCCLAIN, John. "One-act O'Neill: A first." NY *Jour.-Am.*, 23 Dec.
Praise for Robard's performance which carries the long monologue, and the audience becomes fascinated by the tragic attempt of the central figure to "restore the tinsel which kept him alive."

NADEL, Norman. "O'Neill's Hughie is too limited." NY *Wor. Tel & Sun*, 23 Dec.
A superb production which does not overcome the limitation of the play itself, for the most part a dramatic monologue.

OPPENHEIMER, George. "Robards stars in Eugene O'Neill's Hughie." LI *Newsday*, 23 Dec.
An echo of *ICEMAN*, and could profit by cutting. The small scale

of the play fails to arouse emotion or empathy, despite its compassion and sharp characterization. Agrees that it is "less an acting piece than a short story with dialogue" as noted by the Gelbs in their biography.

TAUBMAN, Howard. "The theater: O'Neill's Hughie opens." NY *Times*, 23 Dec.
    Too small and spare to sustain a "sense of voyage and discovery." More like a mood piece, and O'Neill probably had grave doubts that it added anything beyond what he said in *ICEMAN*.

WATTS, Richard, Jr. "A late O'Neill character study." NY *Post*, 23 Dec.
    "Stretching a point to describe it as a play." Not a major play, with obvious weaknesses, but "the O'Neill spell is there."

Other reviews and criticism
1965

CLURMAN, Harold. Comments in Theatre column. *Nation,* 200 (18 Jan.) 65-66.
    "One of O'Neill's consummate creations."

HEWES, Henry. "Through the looking glass, darkly." *Sat. R.*, 48 (16 Jan.) 40.
    Should not be dismissed as a minor work because of length since it is a "complete theatre experience." The production realizes too little of the play's potential.

McCARTEN, John. "Bow bells jangled." *New Yorker*, 40 (2 Jan.) 58.
    A fine performance with a number of effective scenes even though the play flags upon occasion.

———. "Yes, yes." *Cue*, 2 Jan.
    Powerful, touching one-acter brilliantly performed. Not a major O'Neill work, but "beautiful, shimmering, haunting theatre-piece."

"Playwright as hedgehog." *Time*, 85 (1 Jan.) 63.

Old Greek saying "The fox knows many things but the hedgehog knows one big thing" applied here; O'Neill's one big thing is that truth kills and illusion nourishes life. Play is kind of an *ICEMAN*'s ice cube.

"Safe gamble." *Newsweek*, 65 (4 Jan.) 52.
Does not share power and assurance of O'Neill's last great period as in *ICEMAN*, *JOURNEY*, or *POET*. Worth seeing but only as a fragment. Thin stuff.

SHEED, Wilfred. "Late O'Neill." *Commonweal*, 81 (15 Jan.) 518-519.
Aggressively non-literary and a question as to whether or not it is a play. Because O'Neill could mount a "complete drama in a ten-minute speech" this is the most interesting play of the season.

Later reviews

ALEXANDER, Doris. "The missing half of Hughie." *The Drama Review* (formerly *Tulane Dr. Rev.*), 11 (Summer 1967) 125-126.
O'Neill had conceived of using certain screen techniques, showing, as in *JONES*, idea of "formless fears." This critic feels both Stockholm and New York failed to realize that much of the play was written as a stage-screen scenario.

THE ICEMAN COMETH

Opening night reviews—New York
Newspapers of 10 Oct. 1946

ALLEN, Kelcey. "The Iceman Cometh." *W.W. Daily*.
O'Neill's skilfull writing is here; it is vivid and dramatic, but has its dull moments. It's truthful dialogue seems unnecessarily profane, but the characters are real.

ATKINSON, Brooks. "Iceman Cometh has its world premiere." NY *Times*, 31:3. [Reprinted in Miller, *Playwright's progress*, 1965.]
One of O'Neill's best; over-long and garrulous, but he has heart of a poet.

BARNES, Howard. "O'Neill—at long last." NY *Her-Trib*.
Striking plot twist of characters facing their pipe dreams, but climax disappoints. Excellent production does not remove confusion.

CHAPMAN, John. "Eugene O'Neill's Iceman Cometh great drama, wonderfully acted." NY *News*.
Magnificent drama, cuts the ordinary commercial theatre down to size.

COLEMAN, Robert. "The Iceman Cometh a terrific hit." NY *Mirror*. [Reprinted in Miller, *Playwright's progress*, 1965.]
Everyone urged to hurry and buy tickets.

COOKE, Richard P. "New O'Neill play." *Wall St. Jour*.
A play more for people who think than for those who feel. Too long.

GARLAND, Robert. "Iceman Cometh at Martin Beck." NY *Jour-Am*.
Combination of *Lower Depths* and old time vaudeville being put on simultaneously. Cannot find why O'Neill felt called to write it.

HAWKINS, William. "O'Neill's Iceman here at last." NY *Wor-Tel*.
O'Neill can bring poetic grandeur to these little people he knows so well.

MOREHOUSE, Ward. "The Iceman Cometh is powerful theatre . . ." NY *Sun*.
Long winded, power with intensity, rich and vivid dialogue.

NORTH, Sterling. "Eugene O'Neill's turkey." NY *Post*.
Judging from reading version, "action draggeth, dialogue reeketh, play stinketh." North wonders how it ever got produced or published.

POLLOCK, Arthur. "The Iceman Cometh." Brook. *Eagle*.
Over-long and too much repetition.

WATTS, Richard, Jr. "Eugene O'Neill's new play is powerful and
moving." NY *Post*.
Too long and slow, still gives American theatre dignity and
importance; moving, powerful, beautiful, eloquent, passionate.

Other reviews and criticism
1946

"Applause in December." *Harper's Bazaar*, 80 (Dec.) 220-221.
Absorbing, disturbing, magnificently acted.

ATKINSON, Brooks. "Four hour O'Neill." NY *Times*, 20 Oct., II,
1:1. [Reprinted as "The Iceman Cometh" in Atkinson's *Broadway
scrapbook*, 1947.]
Our most dramatic dramatist; the play returns the theatre to its
high estate.

———. "To be or not to be." NY *Times*, 27 Oct., II, 1:1.
Disputes the O'Neill premise that illusions must be kept to remain
alive, but finds it one of O'Neill's best plays.

BARNES, Howard. "The Iceman Cometh." NY *Her-Trib.*, 20 Oct.
This critic, after a few days' study, dissents, finding much of
O'Neill's early power dissipated, and the curtain lines contrived.

BENTLEY, Eric. "The return of Eugene O'Neill." *Atlantic*, 178
(Nov.) 64-66. [Reprinted in Miller, *Playwright's progress*, 1965.]
O'Neill must be judged far above regular Broadway standards.
This evaluation by a critic not generally favorable toward O'Neill finds
him less "terrific" than in *ELECTRA*, and less emotional than
INTERLUDE, in many ways "cooler and steadier."

"Broadway goes highbrow." *Life*, 21 (28 Oct.) 109-111.
Imperfect, but absorbing; reaffirms man's struggle toward dignity. Six very good production pictures accompany the article.

BROWN, John Mason. "All O'Neilling." *Sat. R. Lit.*, 29 (19 Oct.) 26. [Reprinted as "Moaning at the bar" in Brown's *Seeing more things*, 1948, and in his *Dramatis personae*, 1963.]
Blue pencil and shears needed to make it a better play, but there are fine examples of compassion, insight and theatricality that only O'Neill can bring.

BULL, Harry. "The Iceman Cometh." *Town & Country*, Dec., p. 117.
This somewhat different review sees the theme as "the surviving need for violence in a peacetime world of artificial bourgeois convention."

CHAPMAN, John. "O'Neill brings new hope to the theatre." NY *News*, 20 Oct.
A frightening picture because it applies to all of us, drunk or sober. O'Neill's most profound work.

DOYLE, Louis F. "Mr. O'Neill's Iceman." *America*, 30 Nov., pp. 241-242.
This Catholic priest finds O'Neill a master playwright who falls short of being great because of his limitations in the field of thought. Keen disappointment that O'Neill's final solution is defeat.

EATON, Walter Prichard. "Habitués of Hope's saloon." NY *Her-Trib.*, 20 Oct.
Representative of nothing social or significant because the people are "self-made bums."

FRANCIS, Robert. "Time (4 hrs) goeth, as Iceman Cometh, reintroduces O'Neill." *Billboard*, 58 (19 Oct.) 46.
O'Neill has not lost touch—each character meticulously developed, lusty, salty. He still packs a wallop.

FREEDLEY, George. "Iceman Cometh proves O'Neill is America's greatest dramatist." NY *Telegraph*, 11 Oct.
First rate O'Neill.

————. "Many brilliant performances given in O'Neill's The Iceman Cometh." NY *Telegraph*, 16 Nov.
The published version emphasizes even more so the great writer in O'Neill.

GIBBS, Wolcott. "The boys in the back room." *New Yorker*, 22 (19 Oct.) 53-57.
Central theme of illusion very ordinary; ambiguity about ending shows O'Neill not the craftsman he should be. Not up to his best.

GILDER, Rosamond. "Each in his own way." *Th. Arts*, 30 (Dec.) 684. [Reprinted in Gilder's *Theatre Arts anthology*, 1950; in Cargill *et al, O'Neill and his plays*, 1961; and in Raleigh, *Twentieth century interpretations of The Iceman Cometh*, 1968.]
Despite unnecessary length and O'Neill's lack of humor, it still shows theatre is not just dumb show.

GOLD, Michael. "Eugene O'Neill's early days in the old Hell-Hole." *Sunday Worker*, 27 Oct.
A "party line" report of the play, which the author had not seen, which he says attempts to give our youth "musty flavor of our more recent literary past."

GREEN, E. Mawby. "Echoes from Broadway." *Th. World.*, 42 (Dec.) 31-32.
Work of a genius, not talent; heavy and ponderous, but still monumental in stature that is rare in the theatre.

HAWKINS, William. "Iceman is long, but acting is superior." NY *Wor-Tel.*, 12 Oct.
Review of the fine performances, with some comment on O'Neill's attitude in the play.

"The Iceman Cometh." *Variety*, 16 Oct.
"Bingo for the Theatre Guild"; a never to be forgotten play.

"The Iceman Cometh." NY *Times Mag.*, 13 Oct., pp. 22-23.

Very limited text concerning the opening, but two pages of excellent pictures.

KRONENBERGER, Louis. "Eugene O'Neill after 12 years." *PM*, 11 Oct.
O'Neill contributes nothing especially new to the dream idea.

KRUTCH, Joseph Wood. "Drama." *Nation*, 163 (26 Oct.) 481-482.
Comparable in many ways to *The Wild Duck*, and contains more of O'Neill's sincerity, which removes him from any other playwright.

MCCARTHY, Mary. "Dry ice." *Partisan Rev.*, 13 (Nov.-Dec.) 577-579. [Reprinted in McCarthy's *Sights and spectacles, 1937-1956*, 1956; in her *Theatre chronicles 1947-1962*, 1963; and in Raleigh, *Twentieth century interpretations of The Iceman Cometh*, 1968.]
O'Neill frankly cannot write. He is estranged from all influences and impressions, a man laughing in a square, empty room.

NATHAN, George Jean. "The Iceman Cometh, seeth, conquereth." *NY Jour-Am.*, 14 Oct. [Reprinted in Nathan's *Theatre book of the year, 1946-1947*, 1947; Angoff, *The world of George Jean Nathan*, 1952; and in Raleigh, *Twentieth century interpretations of The Iceman Cometh*, 1968.]
The theatre is once more dramatically alive. Play approaches essential tragedy, and is far above any attempts by others in the intervening 12 years.

"O'Neill's Iceman." *Newsweek*, 28 (21 Oct.) 92.
Too much of a good thing, though characters are developed with warmth and good humor.

"O'Neill speaks." *Cue*, 19 Oct.
Like a slow motion magic trick; almost, but not quite, comes off.

"The ordeal of Eugene O'Neill." *Time*, 48 (21 Oct.) 71.
As a drama, not much deeper than a puddle. This article is mainly

about O'Neill, finding him not a great dramatist but our greatest dramatic craftsman.

PEGLER, Westbrook. "Sinks his sharp tongs in O'Neill's Iceman." NY *Jour-Am.*, 8 Nov.
    The play never even starts—it is worse than a schoolgirl of 8 would write. Work is slapdash; nobody talks that much.

PHELAN, Kappo. "The Iceman Cometh." *Commonweal*, 45 (25 Oct.) 44-46.
    The play is daring on its esthetic level, but must be judged by its level of content. This critic wishes O'Neill would definitely choose his God or gods, Devil or devils.

POLLOCK, Arthur. "Edmond Rostand and Eugene O'Neill get the theater back on its feet." Brook. *Eagle*, 13 Oct.
    With *Cyrano* and *ICEMAN* now playing there is much to praise in the theatre. Still there are times when the O'Neill play is quite a bore, but it is something that makes you think.

SCHRIFTGRIESSER, Karl. "Interview with O'Neill." NY *Times*, 6 Oct., 11, p. 1. [Excerpts reprinted in Raleigh, *Twentieth century interpretations of The Iceman Cometh*, 1968.]
    Discussion of the characters as O'Neill knew them, and play's philosophy.

SHIPLEY, Joseph T. "Iceman cometh: Chill from the world of doom." *New Leader*, 19 Oct.
    It is too sprawling. O'Neill is constantly struggling to integrate his theme.

SINGLE, E. A. "Eugene O'Neill, our foremost dramatist, returns triumphantly in Iceman." *Jour. Comm.*, 11 Oct.
    O'Neill has lost none of his matchless skill in creating characters. Memorable experience in theatre going.

WATTS, Richard, Jr. "The controversies cometh over O'Neill's new play." NY *Post*, 19 Oct.

Watts takes sharp issue with North's book review and sees the play even more tremendous as a book. O'Neill's philosophy is not so important as the humanity.

WOOLF, S. J. "Eugene O'Neill returns after 12 years." NY *Times*, 15 Sept., VI, p. 11. [Reprinted in excerpt in Raleigh, *Twentieth century interpretations of The Iceman Cometh*, 1968.]
Informal account of interview with O'Neill before play opening.

WYATT, Euphemia Van R. "Who against hope believed in hope." *Cath. Wld.*, 164 (Nov.) 168-169.
Horrid, brutal, unflinching, yet with piercing analysis, truth, and insight. Bears mark of great playwright.

YOUNG, Stark. "O'Neill and Rostand." *New Rep.*, 115 (21 Oct.) 517-518. [Reprinted in Young's *Immortal shadows*, 1948.]
General review of plot, scenery, acting; very little criticism.

1947-1953

ALEXANDER, Doris M. "Hugo of The Iceman Cometh: Realism and O'Neill." *Am. Quar.*, 5 (Winter 1953) 357-366. [Reprinted in Raleigh, *Twentieth century interpretations of The Iceman Cometh*, 1968.]
Attempting to show that O'Neill's portrayal of Hugo was not the literary abstraction Bentley and others thought, Miss Alexander proves conclusively through document and photograph that Hugo was the nearly literal translation of an O'Neill acquaintance, Hippolyte Havel. In conclusion, she shows the basic deficiency of the play because of its portrayal of a series of static characters.

ARESTAD, Sverre. "The Iceman Cometh and the Wild Duck." *Scand. Stud.*, 20 (Feb. 1948) 1-11.
The two plays have much in common in exposing man's refusal to accept the truth as basis of life. Ibsen is optimistic, O'Neill pessimistic.

BURKE, Ed. "New York plays." *Player's Mag.*, 23 (Jan.-Feb. 1947) 58-59.
Some of the most penetratingly analytic writing on the stage in a long time.

DOBREE, Bonamy. "Mr. O'Neill's latest play." *Sewanee Rev.*, 56 (Jan.-Mar. 1948) 118-126.
This article, pursuing the question "Where is O'Neill taking us in this play?" concludes he uses more techniques of the novel than of the play.

GAYNOR, Leonard. "O'Neill's Iceman seen as ghost of Ibsen's Wild Duck." NY *Her-Trib.*, 2 Mar. 1947.
Comparison of many aspects of plot and theme. Ibsen is somewhat better because of the tragedy that he keeps pent up, while O'Neill's tragedy has occurred before the play begins.

GILDER, Rosamond. "Broadway laurels." *Th. Arts*, 31 (June 1947) 16.
Not sufficiently above other O'Neill plays to merit the Pulitzer prize.

HOPKINS, Vivian C. "The Iceman seen through The Lower Depths." *Coll. Eng.*, 11 (Nov. 1949) 81-87.
Interesting comparison, showing why O'Neill is more negative in his conclusion that death is the only solution. Gorki becomes far more dramatic, despite his errors regarding the perfect society and revolution.

MORGAŃ, Frederick. "The season on Broadway." *Sewanee Rev.*, 55 (Apr. 1947) 344-346.
O'Neill treats nothing beyond the most crude and general level because his characters have lost all humanity. The play lacks good dialogue.

MUCHNIC, Helen. "Circe's swine: Plays by Gorky and O'Neill." *Comp. Lit.*, 3 (Spring 1951) 119-128. [Reprinted as "The irrelevancy of belief: The Iceman and The Lower Depths,'' in Cargill *et al*, *O'Neill and his plays*, 1961, with some revision; in Gassner, *O'Neill* (Twentieth century views), 1964; and in Raleigh, *Twentieth century interpretations of The Iceman Cometh*, 1968. Parts have also appeared in Muchnic's *From Gorky to Pasternak*, 1961.]

Excellent analysis of *Lower Depths* and *ICEMAN*, showing their wide divergence. Gorki maintains man is in an evil society; O'Neill maintains man himself is evil.

SILVERBERG, William V. ''Notes on The Iceman Cometh.'' *Psychiatry*, 10 (Feb. 1947) 29.

(While several major libraries have holdings of this periodical, search of several collections failed to secure copy of this particular issue.)

*STAMM, Rudolph. ''Eugene O'Neill's The Iceman Cometh.'' *Scan. Stud.*, 29 (1948) 138-145.

A long and important review of details of the play. Conclusion is that O'Neill retains old passions for description of character and the milieu, with absorption in the psychological processes. His plays become more than case studies; they are poetic expressions of the dramatist's suffering.

WINTHER, Sophus. ''The Iceman Cometh: A study in technique.'' *Ariz. Quar.*, 3 (Winter 1947) 293-300. [Reprinted in Raleigh, *Twentieth century interpretations of The Iceman Cometh*, 1968.]

Detailed analysis of O'Neill's use of the paradox as an instrument of tragedy in character, action, settings.

Opening night reviews—Circle-in-the-Square Revival
New York—Newspapers of 9 May 1956

ATKINSON, Brooks, ''O'Neill tragedy revived.'' NY *Times*, 38:1. [Reprinted in Cargill *et al*, *O'Neill and his plays*; and in Raleigh, *Twentieth century interpretations of The Iceman Cometh*, 1968.]

Major production of a major theatrical work. O'Neill achieves value on level with Ibsen, Gorki, Strindberg.

COLEMAN, Robert. "O'Neill's Iceman deserveth revival." NY *Mirror*.
  Eminently deserves revival, an absorbing cavalcade of humanity on the rack. O'Neill at his most interesting in plays about people he knew.

DASH, Thomas R. "The Iceman Cometh." *W.W. Daily*.
  Anticipates Becket's *Waiting for Godot*. We cannot identify with these people, so it is not good tragedy.

HAWKINS, William. "Circle cast revives Iceman." NY *Wor-Tel. & Sun*.
  There is not one dull or indifferent moment. O'Neill is bitter but compassionate, and play reveals new, biting vividness.

KERR, Walter. "Iceman revived at Circle in the Square." NY *Her-Trib*.
  The author's compulsive conviction is our own. Play is verbose, but built "like a drunken, somnambulistic dance." O'Neill is ready for reexamination and this revival should do it.

McCLAIN, John. "Iceman's message too elusive." NY *Jour-Am*.
  O'Neill in one of his most depressed moods. Audience is in for a long haul.

WATTS, Richard, Jr. "The revival of O'Neill's Iceman." NY *Post*.
  A pleasure and honor to see it again, the work of titanic power, quite possibly is O'Neill's finest drama. Deep insight into human heart, closer to *Godot* than to Gorky.

Other reviews and criticism
1956

ATKINSON, Brooks. "Iceman returns." NY *Times*, 20 May, II, 1:1.
  O'Neill essentially romantic, driven by a romantic dream. His characters are romantic, and heroes to themselves. This play ranks with *DESIRE* and *ELECTRA* as O'Neill in his greatest form.

GASSNER, John. "Broadway in Review." *Ed. Th. Jour.*, 8 (Oct.) 224-225. [Reprinted in Hewitt, *Theatre, USA*, 1959.]
A devastating and exhilarating experience.

GIBBS, Wolcott. "Good old Hickey." *New Yorker*, 32 (26 May) 72-74.
The revival is better appreciated than the original because its great length is expected and not a hindrance. All modern tragedies seem like soap operas compared with this.

HATCH, Robert. "Theatre." *Nation*, 182 (26 May) 458.
O'Neill works with acid that eats deep. Leaves you glad you do not have to wrestle with a Hickey yourself.

HAYES, Richard. "Waiting for Hickey." *Commonweal*, 64 (24 Aug.) 515-516.
Pain and personal upheaval are made into art by some inexplainable process. Main shortcoming is lack of any sense of possibility or of reality.

HEWES, Henry. "Derelictical materialism." *Sat. R.*, 39 (26 May) 24.
In spite of obvious artificialities, it is a good production. The characters are "desperately real."

"The Iceman Cometh." *Variety*, 16 May.
A brilliant study of self-delusion.

"The Iceman returneth." *Th. Arts*, 40 (Oct.) 72-73.
Brief review with pictures of the production.

LEWIS, Theophilus. "The Iceman Cometh." *America*, 95 (June 2) 251.
An intellectual challenge. One cannot quite decide what O'Neill is saying, and we do not have to believe him.

MANNES, Marya. "Theatre: A matter of style." *Reporter*, 14 (28 June) 35-36.

O'Neill makes all modern "realists" seem mannered, crude, and sterile. The play moves relentlessly toward Hickey's doom.

MYERS, Henry Alonzo. *Tragedy: A view of life.* Ithaca, NY, Cornell, 1956. V. "Macbeth and the Iceman Cometh: Equivalence and ambivalence in tragedy," pp. 98-109.
For comment see entry under BOOKS.

OPPENHEIMER, George. "Long night's journey." *Newsday*, 25 May.
The stuff of which nightmares are made. Better than *Lower Depths*; a bitter play, reflecting O'Neill's bitter life.

WYATT, Euphemia Van R. "The Iceman Cometh." *Cath. Wld.*, 183 (July) 310.
The fact nobody leaves the play is some kind of proof of O'Neill's "haunted genius."

Further Reviews

*ANDREACH, Robert J. "O'Neill's women in The Iceman Cometh." *Renascence*, 18 (Winter 1966) 89-98.
Feeling that O'Neill's theological frame of reference has been neglected, this critic discusses theological implications relative to the women in his plays who are figures of the Virgin and the attitude of men toward them, especially in *ICEMAN*. The men seek grace through the women, who point up guilt. Names are all related to figure of the Virgin: Cora and Margie mean maiden and pearl, and Pearl herself. Bessie, meaning Elizabeth, kinswoman of Mary; Rosa, for Rose, or Virgin; Mollie, for Mary, etc. While Andreach seems at times to stretch for relationship, the article is thought provoking at least.

*BRASHEAR, William R. "The wisdom of Silenus in O'Neill's Iceman." *Am. Lit.*, 36 (May 1964) 180-188.
Concentrating on tragic, rather than autobiographical aspects, this critic discusses Nietzschean influences: Hickey both victim and agent of antagonistic force; Larry close to tragedy because of his understand-

ing and awareness of the balance between Dionysiac (death longing) and Apollonian (resistance) elements.

*CARPENTER, Frederic I. "Focus on Eugene O'Neill's The Iceman Cometh: The Iceman Hath come." In Madden, David, ed., *American dreams, American nightmares*. Carbondale and Edwardsville, Southern Ill. Press, 1970, pp. 158-164.

The play has continued to grow in stature and significance. It reflects the American dream and its disastrous results: assassination of two Kennedys and Martin Luther King are life copying the melodrama of art: the murder of the ideal dream by Hickey, which is the killing of the freedom dream. The tragic truth is illumination of the American dream and American nightmare—the double nature revealed in affluence and in hate.

CHABROWE, Leonard. "Dionysus in The Iceman Cometh." *Mod. Dr.*, 4 (Feb. 1962) 377-388.

Play is analyzed in detail as a redoing of *LAZARUS* in more modern terms. Close parallels shown between Lazarus and Hickey, choral effects of crowd, etc. Both plays, despair notwithstanding, celebrate life in ritual manner.

DAY, Cyrus. "The Iceman and the bridegroom: Some observations on the death of O'Neill's salesman." *Mod. Dr.*, 1 (May 1958) 3-9. [Reprinted in Raleigh, *Twentieth century interpretations of The Iceman Cometh*, 1968.]

This critic shows O'Neill's pessimism and anti-Christian approach through correlation of Hickey with biblical bridegroom, Mark 25:5-6. Regarding it as nihilistic, Day draws parallels between the play's characters and those surrounding Jesus at time of death.

*FRAZER, Winifred D[usenbury]. "King Lear and Hickey: Bridegroom and Iceman." *Mod. Dr.*, 15 (Dec. 1972) 267-277.

Extended, and often fascinating, development of the concept of the bridegroom of love and the iceman of death as seen in the evolution of the ultimate tragedies of Lear and Hickey. Matters of hopeless hope experienced by both, suggestions of incest, sexual references particularly in Lear, and demonstrated parallels between tragic concepts of both writers make this a highly interesting and provocative article.

*———. *Love as death in The Iceman Cometh.* Gainesville, Univ. of Fla. Monographs, Humanities No. 27., 1967.

A significant 63-page study of the whole concept of love as death as developed in the play. Citing in the introduction the many references in literature about "Cupid's fatal dart," from Edmund Spenser to Leslie Fiedler, the author goes on to develop in three chapters on Setting, Characters, and Action how O'Neill plays upon the theme. Agreeing with Mary McCarthy's views that the play is like no other ever written (see her item "Eugene O'Neill—Dry Ice) the writer concludes : "O'Neill has skillfully imposed the rhythm of life upon the world of action, and in which the theme that love is death is the chief irony, for man nourishes and lives by the illusion that love is life."

KAHN, Sy. "O'Neill's legion of losers in The Iceman Cometh." In French, Warren, ed., *The forties*, Deland, Fla., Everett/Edwards, 1969, pp. 205-213.

Analysis in terms of O'Neill's recollection of a particular time in the past and as reflection of the failed dream experienced individually and by America.

LEE, Robert C. "Evangelism and anarchy in The Iceman Cometh." *Mod. Dr.*, 12 (Sept. 1969) 173-186.

Hugo, Slade, Parritt, Hickey discussed in relation to the symbols of "destructive encroachment" of pipe dreams in evangelical and anarchistic movement, leading to modern tragedy which is not "death-defying" but "self-defying."

PRESLEY, D. E. "O'Neill's Iceman: Another meaning." *Am. Lit.*, 42 (Nov. 1970) 387-388.

Advances the possibility that Hickey is "iceman" in underworld terms: a person whose promises are not to be relied on, or as one who makes ostentatious gifts of worthless and trivial things.

QUINN, James P. "The Iceman Cometh: O'Neill's long day's journey into adolescence." *Jour. of Pop. Cul.*, 6 (Summer 1972) 171-177.
Brief but interesting discussion of the play's portrayal of certain archetypal tragic figures as well as showing the complete inversion of middle-class values and the portrayal of Hope's bar as a kind of womb, benevolent security, providing secure familial love.

QUINTERO, José. "Postscript to a journey." *Th. Arts*, 41 (Apr. 1957) 27-29. [Reprinted in Raleigh, *Twentieth century interpretations of The Iceman Cometh*, 1968.]
Account of discussion with Mrs. O'Neill regarding permission to revive the play, which emerged as "less a permission than a sacred charge."

*ROY, Emil. "The Iceman Cometh as myth and realism." *Jour. Pop. Cul.*, 2 (Fall 1968) 302.
This play applies romantic mythical forms to a realistic content. There are parodies of Christian ritual and social reform and family unity, a "conspiracy of false brotherhood created by arrested hostility" with "final truncation" in a developing pattern of "hopeless desire, mistaken and ambiguous ends."

STAMM, Rudolf. "The Iceman Cometh." In Stamm's *The shaping powers at work: 15 essays on poetic transmutation*. Heidelberg, Carl Winter Universitätverlag, 1967, pp. 254-265.
"Artistically the play is among his few impeccable creations." General review of play, theme, strong dialogue, etc.

WEALES, Gerald. "Eugene O'Neill: The Iceman Cometh." In Cohen, Henning, *Landmarks of American writing*, NY, Basic Books, 1969, pp. 353-367.
"Not only a fine play and an exercise in compassionate nihilism, but an American document as well." Weales takes critics such as Bentley, John Mason Brown, Mary McCarthy to task for failing to recognize its basic style and theme.

WRIGHT, Robert C. "O'Neill's universalizing technique in The Iceman Cometh." *Mod. Dr.*, 8 (May 1965) 1-11.

Examination of O'Neill's development of universal significance with emphasis on methodology and creative processes rather than philosophical implications.

ILE

Reviews of first Greenwich Village production
1918

ALLEN, Kelcey. "Fourth bill presented by Frank Conroy." NY *News Record*, 20 Apr.
   Intensely dramatic, a fine piece of writing.

"Art improves at Greenwich village theatre." NY *Herald*, 21 Apr.
   Displays the start of skill and power in the young writer.

BROUN, Heywood. "Greenwich Village players." NY *Tribune*, 21 Apr.
   Disapproval of making the wife go mad for no adequate reason. It shows lack of inventiveness.

GARDY, Louis. Review of the Greenwich bill. NY *Call*, 22 May.
   Biggest attraction on bill; highly dramatic, if not always artistic.

"Greenwich players in 3 new acts." Brook. *Eagle*, 19 Apr.
   Nothing new here; *ILE* something of a *tour de force*.

"Greenwich Village bill." NY *Telegram*, 19 Apr.
   A grim little play with the writing better than the acting.

"The Greenwich Village theatre." NY *Post*, 19 Apr.
   A certain vigor, but too obvious as a shocker to have much value as realism.

HORNBLOW, Arthur. "Mr. Hornblow goes to the play." *Theatre*, 27 (June) 356.

It's a mercy that the audience does not lose its mind also.

"Ile." NY *Drama Mirror*, 78 (4 May) 620.
Typical of the young writer. Vigorously characterized, tense, cheerless.

MANTLE, Burns. "Greenwich Village players offer 3 short plays." NY *Mail*, 19 Apr. [Reprinted in Miller, *Playwright's progress*, 1965.]
Obviously theatrical, not so good as *IN THE ZONE*, but still this "son of James O'Neill" has gift of realism and characterization.

"New bill at Greenwich." *Billboard*, 30 (27 Apr.) 20.
First mention of Eugene O'Neil [*sic*] in *Billboard*, noted as son of actor James O'Neil.

"New bill at the Greenwich Village." NY *Globe*, 19 Apr.
Much interest in this man O'Neill. This play is the only one on the bill worthy of praise.

"A new bill at the Greenwich Village." NY *Times*, 19 Apr., 13:3.
Not pleasant, but vigorously characterized; another of these sea plays "owed" to O'Neill.

SHERWIN, Louis. "New bill at the Greenwich Village." NY *Globe*, 19 Apr. [Reprinted in Cargill *et al*, *O'Neill and his plays*, 1961.]
Young O'Neill arouses interest, seems to have promise. Wonder what he can do with a three-act.

SMITH, Agnes. Review of Greenwich Village bill. NY *Telegraph*, 19 Apr.
Written with some literary distinction. Effective if you like this sort of thing.

"Village players present best bill." *Jour. Comm.*, 22 Apr.
ILE attracts most attention; morbid, depressing, strongly written.

"Village theatre stirs patriotism." NY *Sun*, 19 Apr.
O'Neill's idealistic sense of drama is perhaps too idealistic

because he pictures the actors carrying his work to the audience with the same refined sense of his own.

IN THE ZONE

*Opening night reviews—New York
Newspapers of 1 Nov. 1917*

BLOCK, Ralph. "The Washington Square players in 4 one-acters." NY *Tribune*.
Not the best play on the bill.

"The Comedy opens season." NY *Sun*.
Tense, but not exciting because of early emphasis on comedy.

DALE, Alan. "Worth while is new bill at Comedy." NY *American*.
The best of the bill; good idea and good thrills.

"Four plays to start season for players." NY *Herald*.
Praise for realism; ingenious dramatic effects.

"In the Zone." NY *Drama Mirror*, 77 (10 Nov.) 5-7.
Appealing and exciting; does not go off into melodrama.

"In the Zone at the Comedy." NY *World*. [Reprinted in Miller, *Playwright's progress*, 1965.]
Creates some real suspense, but dialogue is out of proportion to substance.

MANTLE, Burns. "Washington Square Players present James O'Neill's son as a new playwright." NY *Mail*.
"This boy's first play . . . easily the best thing in the opening bill . . ."

"New play bill from Washington Square." NY *Times*, 13:3.
Tense O'Neill sea play marks top of the evening; sense of tragedy.

"New season of short plays at the Comedy . . ." NY *World*.
Dialogue out of all proportion to substance of play; does have a certain amount of real suspense.

"Play season opens for Washington Square." NY *Sun*.
Much dialogue about the box could have been done away with.

SHERWIN, Louis. "The Washington Square players at the Comedy." NY *Globe*.
A young man capable of writing this has a marvelous gift. This play quite enough reason to go see the bill.

"The Washington Square players." NY *Post*.
A clever thriller of the "sell" variety.

"The Washington Square players at the Comedy." NY *Telegram*.
"A bit of human history which holds the interest and sympathy of the spectator."

WOLF, Rennold. "Players begin Comedy season." NY *Telegraph*.
"Grim little story" most effective because of the unusual setting.

Other reviews and criticism
1917

"In the Zone." NY *Drama Mirror*, 77 (10 Nov.) 5-7.
Appealing and exciting; does not go off into melodrama.

"Washington Square players present four new works." NY *Clipper*, 65 (7 Nov.) 10.
By far the best of the four. Up to date sea tale, with the idea excellently worked up.

Further reviews

BLUEFARB, Sam. "The sea-mirror and maker of character in fiction
and drama." *Eng. Jour.*, 48 (Dec. 1959) 501-510.
   ZONE included in discussion of the sea as an escape theme.

GOLDHURST, William. "A literary source for O'Neill's 'In the
Zone.'" *Am. Lit.*, 35 (Jan. 1964) 530-534.
   Plot outline seems strongly related to Conan Doyle's short story
"That Little Square Box."

LAZARUS LAUGHED

Book

AIKEN, Conrad. "Lazarus Laughed." NY *Post*, 24 Dec. 1927.
   Much that is fine; "pitched a little too high" and comes close
to parody. Lacks humor, too serious and grandiose.

ATKINSON, Brooks. "Man's challenge to death in Lazarus Laughed."
NY *Times*, 27 Nov. 1927, V, 5:1.
   Akin to pre-reformation miracle and mystery plays, recovering
some of the "primordial impulses of drama." Ranks with heroic
poetry in its creative imagination.

———. "O'Neill again on the horizon." NY *Times*, 11 Sept. 1927,
VIII, 1:2.
   If he were not serious, poetic and forceful, this first act would
be dismissed as "incohate, unwieldy figment of madness."

BJORKMAN, Edwin. "A dramatist of moods." NY *Sun*, 26 Nov. 1927.
   The "big idea" is carried out "constructively, dramatically, pic-
turesquely" within O'Neill's limitations. Masks go to verge of absurdity—maybe good on stage but superfluous in reading.

KALONYME, Louis. "Eugene O'Neill's dithyrambic Lazarus Laughed." *Arts & Dec.*, 27 (Sept. 1927) 68-69.
High praise for this "spiritually liberating dithyrambic poem which should convince all that O'Neill is no morbid pessimist."

KRUTCH, Joseph Wood. "Beyond life." *Nation*, 126 (4 Jan. 1928) 19.
Whole idea of death being an illusion and permitting laughter is "so effectively bodied forth that it seems true so long as the play endures." Succeeds because of emotional ardor.

LUSTIG, Norman. "Poetically dramatic." Brook. *Citizen*, 25 Dec. 1927.
Reviews the poetry and legends of this play with Masefield's "Tristan and Isolt." O'Neill seeks truth rather than beauty.

MUMFORD, Lewis. "Lazarus laughs last." NY *Her-Trib.*, 20 Nov. 1927.
This review traces O'Neill's development from earliest plays to present, showing his treatment of human nature up to this arrival at a positive decision in affirmation of death.

Pasadena

The first production of this play was staged on 9 April 1928 by the Pasadena, Calif., Community Playhouse. It followed all of O'Neill's directions concerning multiple settings, characters, and masks. The one review from the San Francisco *Chronicle* is listed because of its publication by Cargill *et al.* The more meaningful critical reviews appeared in the other five references noted below.

HERSEY, F. W. "Lazarus Laughed." *Drama*, 18 (May 1928) 244-246.
Pictures of preparation for production and some actual scenes (pp. 242-243).

KEHOE, M. E. "The amateur stage." *Theatre*, 48 (July 1928) 42-44.
Full page of illustrations of production and general review of the effort put into it.

"Lazarus Laughed." *Rev. of Rev.*, 78 (Oct. 1928) 439-440.
Effectiveness of music discussed. It is possibly a great American opera. Pictures of production.

STECHAN, H. O. "Lazarus Laughed." *Billboard*, 40 (21 Apr. 1928) 11. [Reprinted in Miller, *Playwright's progress*, 1965.]
A not unenthusiastic review which sees much real merit, but the play is not always convincing and the laughter becomes monotonous, at times forced to the point of silliness.

"The tributary theatre." *Th. Arts*, 12 (June 1928) 447-448.
3 pictures and brief review. Reports unanimous critical praise for the effort.

WARREN, George C. "Lazarus Laughed." San Francisco *Chronicle*, 10 Apr. 1928. [Reprinted in Cargill *et al*, *O'Neill and his plays*, 1961.]
Praise for the spectacular production, so well done in scenery, costumes, and control of the immense cast.

Fordham

The second production at Fordham University in April 1948 was the last attempt at staging the play in the style O'Neill demanded. The laughter was not attempted, but was signalled by the ringing of a bell.

ATKINSON, Brooks. "O'Neill's affirmation." NY *Times*, 9 Apr. 1948, 27:4.
Shallow, sophomoric, hortatory, unwieldy, practically unbearable theatre.

FREEDLEY, George. "Fordham ambitiously offers O'Neill Lazarus Laughed." NY *Telegraph*, 10 Apr. 1948
Poor acting, monotonous performance mar the first New York production.

GARLAND, Robert. "University players present O'Neill play." NY *Jour-Am.*, 9 Apr. 1948.

"Over-written, over-wrought, and frequently bombastic." Lazarus talks and talks and talks and the play stands still, or limps in "sophomoric circles."

HARTUNG, Philip H. "Stage and screen." *Commonweal*, 48 (30 Apr. 1948) 674.

The substitution of the musical note for the laughter is approved. But the play is "biggest lemon" in all O'Neill works, worth forgetting immediately.

HAWKINS, William. "Lazarus Laughed—but very gloomily." NY *World-Tel.*, 9 Apr. 1948.

Requires almost superhuman, heroic efforts of even the best players. It is essentially literary.

"Lazarus Laughed." *Variety*, 9 Apr. 1948.

Shows commercial impracticability of the play. As presented it is an ordeal for an evening in the theatre.

WATTS, Richard, Jr. "Fordham players in Lazarus Laughed." NY *Post*, 9 Apr. 1948.

Tedious, verbose, pretentious; written beyond a subject playwright could adequately handle.

WYATT, Euphemia Van R. "The drama." *Cath. Wld.*, 167 (June 1948) 64.

Slumps down into complete ineptitude and bathos.

Further reviews

ALEXANDER, Doris M. "Lazarus Laughed and Buddha." *Mod. Lang. Quar.* 17 (Dec. 1956) 357-365.

An attempt to clarify the character of Lazarus by a list of saviours "upon whom he has been modeled." He is Christian and Greek (Dionysus) as interpreted by Nietzsche, as well as a lot of Zarathustra.

Buddha must be added to make the character completely understandable because of his abstractness in time of family danger and the cool quality of his affections. A well documented article developing the entire thesis in Miss Alexander's typically scholarly fashion.

DAHLSTROM, Carl E. W. L. "Dynamo and Lazarus Laughed: Some limitations." *Mod. Dr.*, 3 (Dec. 1960) 224-230.
For comments see entry under *DYNAMO*.

*DAY, Cyrus. "*Amor fati*: O'Neill's Lazarus as Superman and Savior." *Mod. Dr.*, 3 (Dec. 1960) 297-305. [Reprinted in Gassner, *O'Neill* (Twentieth century views), 1964.]
In plays like *FOUNTAIN* and *BROWN* immortality is shown as "cyclical regeneration of the biological abstraction Man," conversion to which gives "the calm of deep serenity." *LAZARUS* reiterates, basically in Nietzschean ideas, a reinterpretation of Superman doctrine, but O'Neill fails to transmute the ideas into effective drama.

POMMER, Henry F. "The mysticism of Lazarus Laughed." *Crane Rev.*, 8 (Winter 1966) 83-91.
Discussion of O'Neill's mysticism in this adaptation of the biblical legend.

TORNQVIST, Egil. "O'Neill's Lazarus: Dionysus and Christ." *Am. Lit.*, 41 (Jan. 1970) 543-554.
Well-documented advance of thesis that Lazarus is essentially a Dionysian-Zarathrustran figure rather than related to Buddha (see article by Doris Alexander) or a pagan Christ as in Engels' view in *Haunted heroes*.

LONG DAY'S JOURNEY INTO NIGHT

Book—1956

ATKINSON, Brooks. "Tragedy behind a tragic masque." NY *Times*, 19 Feb., VII, p. 1.
Prolix and repetitious, but written "by the mind of a great dramatist." Thoroughly absorbing and characteristic work.

BREIT, Harvey. "In and out of books." NY *Times*, 19 Feb., VII, 8:1.
An explanation of how the book was published by Yale.

CLURMAN, Harold. "The O'Neills." *Nation*, 182 (3 Mar.) 182-183.
A valuable play; better released now than in proposed 25 years.

FAGIN, N. Bryllion. "Remembrance of things past." *New Rep.*, 134 (5 Mar.) 20.
Despite some fog, rises to a poignant clarity.

HEWES, Henry. "O'Neill and Faulkner via the abroad way." *Sat. R.*, 39 (20 Oct.) 58.
Like so many O'Neill plays, a work of desperation; abounds in arguments hashed and rehashed.

KRUTCH, Joseph Wood. "Domestic drama with some difference." *Th. Arts*, 40 (Apr.) 89-91.
More than biography and domestic tragedy; it is modern tragedy of alienation, universal tragedy of search for cause of our fates.

"The last O'Neill tragedy." *Life*, 40 (12 Mar.) 93-99.
A general review of O'Neill's background and the play, with pictures of the Stockholm production and of the O'Neill family.

LEWIS, Theophilus. "Long Day's Journey." *America*, 95 (5 May) 141.
Impressive play, but not inspiring.

PICKREL, Paul. "Unconventional memoirs." *Harpers*, 212 (Mar.) 96-97.
"It is as much an American tragedy as Dreiser's novel, and it has the power of Dreiser at his best."

PRESCOTT, Orville. "Books of the Times." NY *Times*, 20 Feb., 21:4.
O'Neill's tragic pessimism "is one of the most psychologically interesting of American literary problems." Not up to his best.

SELDES, Gilbert. "Long Day's Journey into Night." *Sat. R.*, 39 (25 Feb.) 15-16.
Does not measure up to the tortured genius of O'Neill. Contains his usual weaknesses.

WHICHNER, Stephen. "O'Neill's long journey." *Commonweal*, 63 (16 Mar.) 614-615.
Much of the mood of homelessness and helplessness of the early plays. Completely transcends biography. "If our definitions of tragedy do not fit this work, we should perhaps rethink our definitions."

Opening night reviews—New York
Newspapers of 8 Nov. 1956

ATKINSON, Brooks. "Theatre: Tragic journey." NY *Times*, 47:2.
"The American theatre acquires stature and size" with this play. The tragedy transcends the material facts.

CHAPMAN, John. "Long Day's Journey into Night a drama of sheer magnificence." NY *News*. [Reprinted in Miller, *Playwright's progress*, 1965.]
"Exploded like a dazzling skyrocket over the humdrum of Broadway theatricals." A most beautiful play; one of the great dramas of any time.

COLBY, Ethel. "Entertainment on Broadway." *Jour. Comm.*
A bitter drama. The script's indictment of the father is "incredible."

COLEMAN, Robert. "O'Neill's last drama emotional dynamite." NY *Mirror*.

Needs editing; repetitious, yet fascinating. Sprawling, ruggedly chiseled monument "carved from granite." Never touches the heart, but excites admiration.

DASH, Thomas R. "Long Day's Journey into Night." *W.W. Daily*. [Reprinted in Miller, *Playwright's progress*, 1965.]

Savagely incisive and harrowing, but does not rank with *INTERLUDE* or *ELECTRA*. The very nature of the work prevents catharsis or exaltation. Repeats and meanders exasperatingly.

DONNELLY, Tom. "A long journey but worth taking." NY *Wor-Tel. & Sun*.

Long and tortuous, but the ultimate effect is "tremendously powerful." Requires patience; early scenes come close to parody.

KERR, Walter. "Long Day's Journey into Night." NY *Her-Trib*. [Reprinted in Hewitt, *Theatre USA*, 1959; and in Miller, *Playwright's progress*, 1965.]

Deliberately, masochistically harrowing, but it is an obligation for anyone who cares about the theatre. "It is a stunning theatrical experience."

McCLAIN, John. "Superb cast supplements O'Neill genius." NY *Jour-Am*.

One can never doubt its stature. "O'Neill makes today's playwrights look a little silly."

WATTS, Richard, Jr. "Superb drama by Eugene O'Neill." NY *Post*.

Magnificent and shattering. "Unmistakably" registers O'Neill's giant stature. Play gives the entire season stature.

Other reviews and criticism
1956-1960

APPLEYARD, J. A. "Long journey's end." *America*, 96 (19 Jan. 1957) 452-454.

O'Neill, for all his sensitivity to human problems, is inarticulate and generally beyond his ability in most of his plays.

ATKINSON, Brooks. "One man's truth." NY *Times*, 3 Mar. 1957, II, 1:1.

While the "truth" of O'Neill's family is, of course, hard to determine, even from this play, there is obvious truth in the tensions and loyalties of family life. If it were merely autobiographical the play would not succeed as it has; there are other universal and tragic truths.

————. "O'Neill's journey." NY *Times*, 18 Nov. 1956, II, 1:1.

It is hard to determine if this is O'Neill's greatest, but it ranks with his finest. The end fulfills the tragic definition.

BOLTON, Whitney. "Long Day's Journey O'Neill at his best: Monumental play." NY *Telegraph*, 9 Nov. 1956.

The theatre grows up with this, reaching size and power of which it is capable. One of the most important plays in quarter of a century.

CHAPMAN, John. "A colleague of James O'Neill says 'Journey' is unfair picture." NY *News*, 30 Dec. 1956.

Extensive quotes from David F. Perkins who acted with James O'Neill, proving that although *JOURNEY* is a good play it is not honest in reflection of actor's career as a great star in plays other than *Monte Cristo*.

CLURMAN, Harold. "Theatre." *Nation*, 183 (24 Nov. 1956) 466. [Reprinted in Clurman's *Lies like truth*, 1958; and in Cargill *et al*, *O'Neill and his plays*, 1961.]

A play everybody should see and admire.

COOKE, Richard P. "Formation of a playwright." *Wall St. Jour.*, 9 Nov. 1956.

A strong play, weakened by length. It is difficult for the playgoer to assimilate it all. There is enough for a half-dozen family tragedies.

DRIVER, Tom F. "Long and short of it." *Christ. Cent.*, 74 (20 Feb. 1957) 235.

It takes on artistic stature because it gradually reveals shape of a consistent view of human nature. Here is a picture of Fate which enables us to bear the hell these people are in.

ENGEL, Edwin A. "Eugene O'Neill's Long Day's Journey." *Michigan Alumnus Quarterly Review*, 63 (1957) 348-354.

This major O'Neill critic reviews the play soon after its American premiere, but copy of this periodical could not be secured before publication deadline.

"Eugene O'Neill: A new phase." *Chrysalis*, 9 (1956) No. 5-6, pp. 3-13.

Reviews essence of the play and its place in O'Neill's work. Questions whether or not it is pessimistic or optimistic.

GASSNER, John. "Broadway in review." *Ed. Th. Jour.*, 9 (Mar. 1957) 43-44.

Great vibrancy of life. O'Neill makes most other modern writers seem miniscule.

GIBBS, Wolcott. "Doom." *New Yorker*, 32 (24 Nov. 1956) 120.

Despite need of editing and the fact it is often "barbarously" written, it is impressive. It will not go down as a major contribution to the drama of our time.

HAYES, Richard. "A requiem for mortality." *Commonweal*, 65 (1 Feb. 1957) 467-468.

Spirals inward to the tragic fact; weaves a "seamless pattern of time, suffering, and nobility" typical of tragedy. Final wisdom and love elevates these people.

HEWES, Henry. "O'Neill: 100 proof—not a blend." *Sat. R.*, 39 (24 Nov. 1956) 30-31. [Reprinted in Cargil *et al*, *O'Neill and his plays*, 1961.]

It may be "the most universal piece of stage realism ever turned out by an American playwright."

*KAUFMAN, R. J. "On the supersession of the modern classic style." Mod. Dr., 2 (Feb. 1960) 358-369.
JOURNEY is used as the O'Neill play, together with Camus' Caligula, which heralds the death of "Modern Drama" or "Modern Classic Drama" as we know it. Current plays are becoming as distinct from "modern" as the Restoration was from Elizabethan drama. No longer do we have "purposive" characters in Socratic terms, nor people who, like Antigone, are "relentlessly loyal to the professed higher ideals of culture." O'Neill longs for heroism and in this play acknowledges a world in which there is none.

KRUTCH, Joseph Wood. "The rediscovery of Eugene O'Neill." NY Times, 21 Oct. 1956, VI, pp. 32-34.
A review of O'Neill's artistry in an attempt to determine whether or not he will remain in our literature after this revival of interest. Concludes with a discussion of the tragic view as shown in LONG DAY'S JOURNEY.

LERNER, Max. "To face my dead at last." NY Post, 7 Jan. 1957.
". . . . no one, after seeing it, can be content again with anything less than the unflinching truth about his work, his world, and himself."

"Long Day's Journey into Night." Th. Arts, 41 (Jan. 1957) 25-26.
It is a play as well as frank autobiography and it commands attention. It can lay claim as one of his finest works.

"Long Day's Journey into Night." Vogue, 128 (15 Nov. 1956) 105.
Includes small picture of O'Neill family in New London.

MANNES, Marya. "A dissenting opinion on the O'Neill play." Reporter, 15 (13 Dec. 1956) 38-39.
A rare theatrical experience, but it is not a great play nor a great tragedy. Too embarrassingly personal.

MORRISON, Hobe. "Long Day's Journey." *Variety*, 14 Nov. 1956.
It may stand as O'Neill's finest play. Tremendous and inspiring; an unforgettable theatrical experience.

"New play in Manhattan." *Time*, 68 (19 Nov. 1956) 57.
May constitute his most substantial legacy to the American stage. O'Neill has achieved more here by "stripping himself bare" than he did with masks.

"O'Neill's youth on U.S. stage." *Life*, 41 (19 Nov. 1956) 123-128.
Several fine pictures of the play, and three of interior and exterior of the original home in New London.

OPPENHEIMER, George. "The tragic truth." *LI Newsday*, 16 Nov. 1956.
There has been no family so haunted since Oedipus. But O'Neill never loses his love for his people. It is something to see for all its faults of being prolix, prosy, and monotonous.

QUINTERO, José. "Postscript to a journey." *Th. Arts*, 41 (Apr. 1957) 27-29.
Account by the original director of the progress of the play from the time of first discussion of possibilities with Mrs. O'Neill until opening. Quintero reports Mrs. O'Neill gave him her wedding ring to wear as a good luck charm.

RALEIGH, John Henry. "O'Neill's Long Day's Journey and New England Irish-Catholicism." *Partisan Rev.*, 26 (Fall 1959) 573-592. [Reprinted in Gassner, *O'Neill* (Twentieth century views), 1964; and in Bogard and Travis, *Modern drama: Essays in criticism*, 1965.]
Interesting and detailed study of this play's autobiographical qualities as they reflect the traditions and the mores of American Irish-Catholics.

RUBINSTEIN, Annette. "The dark journey of Eugene O'Neill." *Mainstream*, 10 (Apr. 1957) 29-33.
In reviewing O'Neill's portrayal of his family, this article shows how the playwright has frequently written two plays at once—

philosophic "false conclusion" and the artist's "truthful presentation." This play throws this contradiction into "startling relief."

SHAWCROSS, John T. "The road to ruin: The beginnings of O'Neill's Long Day's Journey." *Mod. Dr.*, 3 (Dec. 1960) 289-296.
    Proof that *AH, WILDERNESS!* is of biographical importance, a "play of old sorrow" more than sentimental interim. Many parallels demonstrated in character and scene. Ghosts are faced in *WILDERNESS*, not quite squarely, but finally and relentlessly in *JOURNEY*.

"Theatre notes." *English*, 12 (Spring 1959) 140.
    Powerfully compelling. Not uplifting; an "orgy of accusation." Stark, excorciating.

"Triumph from the past." *Newsweek*, 48 (19 Nov. 1956) 117.
    Less a play than willful act of autobiographical catharsis. The mark of America's greatest living playwright even in death.

WINTHER, Sophus Keith. "O'Neill's tragic themes: Long Day's Journey." *Ariz. Quar.*, 13 (Winter 1957) 295-307.
    Important play because of the revelation of O'Neill's creative life. Father is symbol of evil, and home as a place of failure and death —items present in the most important of his other plays.

WYATT, Euphemia Van R. "Long Day's Journey into Night." *Cath Wld.*, 184 (Jan. 1957) 306.
    Sartre's Hell is less violent than this.

Reviews of production by
Royal Dramatic Theatre of Stockholm
Newspapers of May 1962

    A touring company of this famous theatre in Stockholm, long a producer of O'Neill's plays, including the premiere of this one in February 1956, presented two performances in New York, in Swedish, on 15 and 17 May 1962. It was reviewed by all the major critics.

BOLTON, Whitney. "Long Day's Journey a Swedish triumph." NY *Telegraph*, 17 May.

Language presents no problem. "A magnificent demonstration of superb theatre," building emphasis on the character of the mother.

CHAPMAN, John. "O'Neill packs punch in 'anything goes' tunes." NY *News*, 16 May.

Enthralling event. Becomes more of a woman's play than when first produced. Inga Tidblad as Mary gives performance of "almost unbearable pathos."

GELB, Arthur. "O'Neill tragedy." NY *Times*, 16 May, p. 35.

O'Neill's poetic weakness enables easy translation, and language here is no barrier. "The violent writhings of O'Neill's self-doomed characters are more native to the Royal Dramatic Theatre ensemble than to O'Neill's countrymen." This shows "what great theatre can be."

KERR, Walter. "Long Day's Journey." NY *Her-Trib.*, 16 May.

Shows the "other play" that O'Neill wrote—the story of the mother instead of the essentially masculine American version. "A curious, fascinating, even most persuasive shift of focus" enabling us to see the play in different fashion.

NADEL, Norman. "Long Day's Journey played by Swedish company at Cort." NY *Wor-Tel & Sun.*, 16 May.

Interesting, but cannot measure up to American production. Most serious misinterpretation is in character of Mary, played here for massive Greek tragedy rather than muted poignancy.

SHEAFFER, Louis. "Swedish specialty: O'Neill's Journey." NY *Her-Trib.*, 13 May, Sec. 4, p. 3.

Review explaining the interest of Sweden in O'Neill from time of Nobel award to the present play.

WATTS, Richard, Jr. "Long Day's Journey in Swedish." NY *Post*, 16 May.

While language barrier provided difficult going, performance of Inga Tidblad as Mary added greatly to play's emotional strength.

Other reviews and criticism
1962-1970

BOWEN, Croswell. " 'Journey' key to understanding O'Neill's life." NY *Wor-Tel* & *Sun*, 13 Oct. 1962.
Upon appearance of film version, this biographer discusses importance of this probable classic in understanding the playwright's life.

*BRYER, Jackson R. "Hell is other people: Long Day's Journey Into Night," in French, ed., *The fifties*, Deland, Fla., Everett/Edwards, 1970, pp. 261-270.
Because the Greek concept of Fate and the gods cannot apply to modern scientific and humanistic society, heredity, environment, and as in this play, love itself and the individual human flaws serve as tragic source. The Tyrones emerge as a group protagonist. "Because no American playwright has depicted more complex and complete characters . . . than Eugene O'Neill in Long Day's Journey, it deserves a place among the great plays written in any age in any language. . . . one of the few American plays which meet most of the measures of modern tragedy."

FINKELSTEIN, Sidney. "O'Neill's Long Day's Journey." *Mainstream*, 16 (June 1963) 47-51.
Re-examination of a "masterpiece" in light of appearance of film version.

LAWRENCE, Kenneth. "Dionysus and O'Neill." *Univ. of Mo. at Kansas City Review* (formerly University of Kansas City), 33 (Autumn 1966) 67-70.
Using terms listed by Gilbert Murray as essential parts of Dionysiac Greek tragedy: agon, pathos, suffering, messenger, lamentation, etc., etc., this shows how *JOURNEY* is closer to tragic structure of the Greeks without use of masks, plot lines, etc.

McDONNELL, Thomas P. "O'Neill's drama of the psyche." *Cath Wld.*, 197 (Apr. 1963) 120-125.
General discussion of certain of O'Neill's family and artistic problems in view of *JOURNEY* specifically.

REDFORD, Grant H. "Dramatic art vs. autobiography: A look at Long Day's Journey Into Night." *Coll. Eng.*, 25 (1964) 527-535.

Opening night reviews—Promenade Theatre revival
New York—Newspapers of April 1971

BARNES, Clive. "Rousing Long Day's Journey." NY *Times*, 22 Apr., p. 36.
Probably greatest of American plays, landmark in 20th century drama. This production "one of the glorious highlights" of the season. A great play.

DAVIS, James. "Eugene O'Neill revival grand night in theater." NY *News*, 22 Apr.
Will set any doubter straight concerning O'Neill as a giant among playwrights. Perfect revival, honest and moving production.

HIPP, Edward Sothern. "O'Neill masterpiece." Newark *Eve. News*, 22 Apr.
Has lost none of its power, still a stunning modern example of catharsis, "probably the most effective in the O'Neill collection." A great stage play.

MISIIKIN, Leo. "O'Neill's Long Day's Journey revived." NY *Telegraph*, 23 Apr.
Stunning revival of what may be the greatest play in the American theatre. Massive power; holds you completely transfixed. Awesome storms and fury shake to the core; theatre in most fierce and penetrating form.

OPPENHEIMER, George. "Going somewhere again." LI *Newsday*, 22 Apr.

Brilliant revival, helps make the theatre the "dwelling place of wonder. . . . One of the major events of the season."

POPKIN, Henry. "O'Neill's 'old sorrow' returns." *Wall St. Jour.*, 23 Apr.
The cast extracts a great deal of wealth; deserves to be seen.

WATTS, Richard. "An O'Neill masterpiece." NY *Post*, 22 Apr.
Towering masterpiece in brilliant revival. Tragedy is "nothing short of heart-breaking . . . wonderfully real to a point rarely to be found in the contemporary theatre."

WOODRUFF, Virginia. "Long Day's Journey." NY *Mirror*, 23 Apr.
Exquisite production; an evening of true theatre.

Other reviews and criticism

BEHRMAN, S. N. "Long Day's Journey into Night." *TV Guide*, 10 Mar. 1973, pp. 37-38.
In advance of the Laurence Olivier television production on this date, this long established playwright tells of his meeting with the O'Neills in 1937 and the thoughts of that meeting upon reading of the suffering and agonies in this play.

CLURMAN, Harold. Comments in Theatre column. *Nation*, 212 (10 May 1971) 605-606.
The great design of the tragic sense seems missing.

GELB, Barbara. "Written in tears and blood . . ." NY *Times*, 4 Mar. 1973, 11:19.
Prior to Mar. 10 production of Olivier's TV version, this biographer of O'Neill reflects upon many of the plays which involve O'Neill and his family, including *CHILLUN*, *DESIRE*, *POET*, *ELECTRA* as well as *JOURNEY*.

KALEM, T. E. "Doom music." *Time*, 97 (3 May 1971) 122.
Greatest drama ever written by an American. O'Neill's closest to neo-Greek tragedy. The dialogue is the "music of doom."

KERR, Walter. "Do the Tyrones live here?" NY *Times*, 2 May 1971, 11:3.

Not until the fourth act with its "last fogbound banshee scream" does the play find its voice. Curious sense that none of the ravaged characters actually live within the setting. Last act is well worth going to see.

KROLL, Jack. "American classic." *Newsweek*, 77 (10 May 1971) 122.

Approaches a "totally tragic purity and directness." O'Neill has achieved what few writers have: "an absolute humanity of vision and utterance."

"Long Day's Journey." *Variety*, 28 Apr. 1971, p. 68

Virtually a powerhouse; overwhelming experience; one of America's finest stage works.

OLIVER, Edith. "Return journey." *New Yorker*, 47 (1 May 1971) 94.

Better than the original. Play now "completely absorbing." Every moment is believable, "which takes some doing with O'Neill."

OPPENHEIMER, George. "On stage." LI *Newsday*, 22 May 1971.

An achievement that towers above work of any other American playwright and most British or European. The most rewarding event of several seasons.

PRIDEAUX, Tom. "When a journey becomes classic." *Life*, 70 (4 June 1971) 17.

An American classic; so broadly human it applies to all of us. Classic because it is a work that "over a period of time and in the deepest sense, we can use."

SIMON, John. "Long Day's Journey." *New York Mag.*, 4 (10 May 1971) 72.

A great play, O'Neill's masterpiece.

THE LONG VOYAGE HOME

The first production of this play was on 2 November 1917, just one year after the first staging of an O'Neill play in New York. next appearance was as a part of the composite production of four one-act sea plays under title *S. S. GLENCAIRN*, which opened seven years later on 3 November 1924. Entries below are reviews of the 1961 production by the Mermaid Theatre. All other items concerning *VOYAGE* will be found under *S.S. GLENCAIRN*.

ALPERT, Arthur. "Mermaid adds play by O'Neill." NY *Wor-Tel* & *Sun*, 5 Dec.
Absorbing but far from fascinating. Fails to reach the emotions.

BOLTON, Whitney. "Long Voyage Home at Mermaid theatre." *Stage Rev.*, 6 Dec.
Not a very good play, but it has historical worth.

GELB, Arthur. "Early O'Neill." NY *Times*, 5 Dec., p. 49.
Though some of the flavor of the revival is perhaps "too genteel," it helps fill out the evening with *DIFF'RENT*.

GOTTFRIED, Morton. "Long Voyage Home flashes O'Neill's genius." *W.W. Daily*, 6 Dec.
"The scrawl of genius is real enough to reach out and bite." Real theatre which rewards the audience.

HERRIDGE, Frances. "O'Neill's 'Voyage' joins 'Diff'rent.' " NY *Post*, 5 Dec.
Effective as a curtain raiser. Through it all comes O'Neill's sense of helplessness and loneliness.

"Long Voyage Home." *Cue*, 16 Dec.
Makes the entire evening more rewarding.

"Long Voyage Home." *Village Voice*, 14 Dec.

"Makes for a fine draught of early O'Neill and a solid evening of theatre."

MORGENSTERN, Joseph. "Long Voyage Home." NY *Her-Trib.*, 5 Dec.
  "Grim fascination" but few in the cast are up to the play which demands it be played "up to its rusty hilt."

LOST PLAYS

The New Fathoms Press edition of *LOST PLAYS* appeared in 1950. It received generally unfavorable reviews of its five very early plays. In 1958 the Citadel Press reissued the plays, and again in 1963 in paperback. No important reviews appeared. In 1964 Random House added five more "lost" plays in *Ten "Lost" Plays of Eugene O'Neill* which contained an introduction by Bennett Cerf, but no editorial comment. The only important review was by biographer Arthur Gelb, included below.

BROWN, John Mason. "Finders keepers, losers weepers; ugly business of publication of Lost Plays of Eugene O'Neill." *Sat. R. Lit.*, 33 (17 June 1950) 28.
  Resounding condemnation of the shoddy, if legal, practice of exploitation of unpublished MMS. No decent excuse for the publication over O'Neill's protest; the copyright laws should be changed.

CLARK, Barrett H. "Lost Plays of Eugene O'Neill." *Th. Arts*, 34 (July 1950) 7.
  Nothing much here; cannot imagine them being produced.

COLIN, Saul. "Without O'Neill's imprimatur." NY *Times*, 18 June 1950, VII, 4:3.

In discussion of other famous works published after death against writers' wishes, Colin finds these plays "extremely stageable."

EATON, Walter Prichard. "Young O'Neill." NY *Her-Trib.*, 25 June 1950.

Publication of these "juvenile ineptitudes" is deplorable; they can cause O'Neill admirers only pain.

FREEDLEY, George. "Lost Plays of Eugene O'Neill." *Library Jour.*, 75 (15 June 1950) 1048.

Crude and bathetic; for library collections only, though there is a spark of genius.

GELB, Arthur. "Onstage he played the novelist." NY *Times Mag.*, 30 Aug. 1964, p. 1.

The many editing flaws are noted, and hope is expressed that no more "lost" plays will be resurrected.

POLLOCK, Arthur. "Guide for the young playwright." NY *Compass*, 7 June 1950.

Plays are condemned as the floundering of an inept writer.

R.H. "Lost plays of Eugene O'Neill." *New Rep.*, 123 (28 Aug. 1950) 21.

Extraordinary workmanship. The plays are tightly organized.

WAGNER, Charles. "Books." NY *Mirror*, 18 June 1950.

This should be welcomed because it fills in a chunk of the O'Neill mosaic never seen before. All of the plays have a "strange fascination."

WATTS, Richard, Jr. "The early sins of Eugene O'Neill." NY *Post*, 23 June 1950.

The publication was a shabby deed, but O'Neill will not suffer.

MARCO MILLIONS

Book

ATKINSON, Brooks. "Marco Polo as an American merchant prince."
NY *Times*, 15 May 1927, III, 6:1.
Common vein of satire, but background and impulses are
O'Neill.

CANFIELD, Mary Cass. "The albatross afoot." *Sat. R. Lit.*, 4 (10
Sept. 1927) 102.
O'Neill's past writing of passion and "blasting sincerity" is
likened to Emersonian "self-moved, self-absorbed" man or to
Baudelaire's albatross afoot.

EATON, Walter Prichard. "A cycle of Cathay." NY *Her-Trib.*, 29
May 1927.
Not a comedy, but the same O'Neill following the Gleam to far
Cathay.

FIRKINS, O. W. "O'Neill and other playwrights." *Yale Rev.*, 17 (Oct.
1927) 173-174.
Real stuff of drama is here, but questions why writers must go
so far in their satire of America. Admiration for O'Neill's "refusal
to be tethered by success."

GARLAND, Robert. "Well, what of it?" NY *Telegram*, 23 May 1927.
"A swell Eugene O'Neill drama to stay away from."

GILDER, Rosamond. "Theatre Arts bookshelf." *Th. Arts*, 11 (Sept.
1927) 724-725.
Gorgeous and far-flung pageant, a challenge to any producer. An
allegory, with moral of definite interest and application.

KRUTCH, Joseph Wood. "Marco the westerner." *Nation*, 124 (18
May 1927) 562-564.
Krutch likes the spiritual depth realized in both the "idealized
Orientals" and the "shallow, bumptious complacency" of Marco.

LEVINSON, André. "A French critic on O'Neill." *New Rep.*, 51 (27 Jul. 1927) 259-260.

Seems to have been influenced by Shaw in the tricks used, with particular charm in its lyricism.

MACGOWAN, Kenneth. "Theatre books—Marco Millions." *Th. Guild Quar.*, April 1927, pp. 22-24.

Though the Babbitry could be laid on with less thoroughness, the play remains a fine satire.

MACY, John. "O'Neill's wise and humorous Marco Millions." NY *World*, 22 May 1927.

Glorious satire, streak of burlesque, does not slide to farce.

"Marco Millions." *Outlook*, 146 (29 June 1927) 292.

Some good poetry. O'Neill still is an "incorrigible mystic" but he can write satire.

"Marco Millions—Theatric travelog." *Dramatist*, 18 (July 1927) 1341-1342.

No plot, no problem, no sequence. It is not a play; O'Neill's style "is not art, it's abortion."

NATHAN, George Jean. "O'Neill's new play." *Am. Merc.*, 8 (Aug. 1926) 499-505.

Long detailed review of plot. O'Neill is a man not unaware of sardonic humor even in most tragic drama, says Nathan, and in this play answers those who say he has no sense of humor.

ROEDDER, Karsten. "The book parade." Brook. *Citizen*, 19 June 1927.

O'Neill's first bid for the library makes perfect transition from stage. In many respects his best play, a "perfectly constructed farce."

SIMMON, Bernard "Some notes on Marco Millions." NY *Her-Trib.*, 22 May 1927.

A superb piece of literature which will depend much on the production for its effect.

Untitled item. *New Yorker*, 28 May 1927.
The satire is superb, with lots of poetry and wisdom.

WATTS, Richard, Jr. "Marco Millions versus Marco Polo." NY *Her-Trib.*, 12 June 1927.
Instead of sympathy, this shows hatred of Polo. Watts wonders why he is made a "bumptious ass" and "clownish dolt."

WHIPPLE, Leon. "Scripts for the summer solstice." *Survey*, 58 (1 July 1927) 390.
"Bravura piece" which shows more sureness instead of the gropings of previous O'Neill. "Intellectual mastery of the material."

*Opening night reviews—New York
Newspapers of 10-11 Jan. 1928*

ALLEN, Kelcey. "Marco Millions is poignant O'Neill satire." *W.W. Daily*, 10 Jan. [Reprinted in Miller, *Playwright's progress*, 1965.]
An eventful night in the theatre. The play is "corruscating satire, biting in irony, suffused with poetry, rich and dramatic."

ANDERSON, John. "Marco Millions gorgeous spectacle." NY *Jour.*, 11 Jan.
Expansive, expensive, opulent, colorful and utterly beautiful. O'Neill in gayest mockery, almost lighthearted. Despite looseness and tiresome verbosity, it has poetic beauty in writing.

ATKINSON, Brooks. "Eugene O'Neill's gorgeous satire." NY *Times*, 10 Jan., 28:2.
It is a tragedy of emotion as well as satire.

COHEN, Julius. "Marco Millions." *Jour. Comm.*, 11 Jan.
Masterpiece of writing. O'Neill was never more poetical or satirical.

COLEMAN, Robert. "Marco Millions fine tragic play by Eugene O'Neill." NY *Mirror*, 11 Jan.
Amusing, heart-breaking, blending humor and grim drama, sym-

pathetic and ironic. Prose soars to meet poetry. A fine play, flawless, without a single dull moment.

DALE, Alan. "Marco Millions by Eugene O'Neill." NY *American*, 10 Jan.
Voluminous, sketchy, occasionally tiresome and "inordinately flimsy"; almost a travelogue with words. Never drab, but a sense of humor might have helped.

GABRIEL, Gilbert. "Marco Millions." NY *Sun*, 10 Jan.
The poetry raises it above being merely dramatic or undramatic. This has much strength and power.

HALL, Leonard. "Theatre Guild presents its first Eugene O'Neill play." NY *Telegram*, 10 Jan.
O'Neill's uppercut to the "quivering jaws" of those who said he had no humor; it is a very comical creation.

HAMMOND, Percy. "Marco Millions." NY *Her-Trib.*, 10 Jan.
Interesting satire; splendid and thoughtful burlesque.

HIGLEY, Philo. "New O'Neill play at Guild." NY *Telegraph*, 10 Jan.
If intended as a spectacle, then it succeeds. If a drama with dominant theme, then perhaps not. But much of it stirs impressively to life in stately, if wearisome, stride.

"Immortal Marco." *Wall St. Jour.*, 11 Jan.
A complete delight; a beautiful play of infinite intent. Not often is such literary achievement so well treated, histrionically and pictorially.

LITTELL, Robert. "Mr. O'Neill pillories a Venetian Babbitt." NY *Post*, 10 Jan.
O'Neill, taking a vacation from his post as our greatest playwright, is way below par, surprisingly "simple minded, obvious, foolish." Delights the eye, distracts the ear.

MANTLE, Burns. "Marco Millions impressive." NY *News*, 10 Jan.

The story is stimulating to the imagination. An unusual and altogether satisfying evening.

OSBORN, E. W. "Marco Millions." NY *World*, 10 Jan.
O'Neill's high mark up to this moment. Almost poetic in handling of Kukachin.

POLLOCK, Arthur. "The Theatre Guild does a play by O'Neill at last." Brook. *Eagle*.
Worth "something less than the time" it takes to present it. Not one of his best. Could be said more easily, briefly, persuasively in simple 3-act play.

WINCHELL, Walter. "O'Neill the clown." NY *Eve. Graphic*.
Pictorially gorgeous. O'Neill never so gay and kidding. For the most part unique and enchanting, an artistic if not prosperous achievement.

WOOLLCOTT, Alexander. "Marco Polo of Zenith." NY *World*.
The Babbitt theme is now a little worn; this is an elaborate way of saying the same thing.

Other reviews and criticism
1928

"After Babbitt what?" *Daily Worker*, 16 Jan.
Excellent satire, fourth rate poetry, excellent fun. But O'Neill really knows nothing about what makes up the modern business man. Despite faults, it should be seen.

ATKINSON, Brooks. "After the battle." NY *Times*, 22 Jan., VIII, 1:1.
Much of value, though it may not come across because O'Neill is not a wit and he cannot express his thoughts clearly.

BENCHLEY, Robert. "The prevalent scoffing." *Life*, 91 (26 Jan.) 19.
Splendid production hurt mainly by satire coming too late.

BRACKETT, Charles. "Tears and spectacles." *New Yorker*, 3 (21 Jan.) 25.
Obvious, repetitious, dull. Others have taken the subject and done it much better.

BROWN, John Mason. "New York goes native." *Th. Arts*, 12 (March) 163-166. [Reprinted in Cargill *et al*, *O'Neill and his plays*, 1961.]
More than a satire, for O'Neill never intended it to be just that. More nearly tragic in the disintegration of Marco.

CARB, David. "Marco Millions." *Vogue*, 71 (1 Mar.) 82-83.
Does nothing, causes nothing to happen, is not even good theatre; it was not worth producing.

CLARK, Barrett H. "Eugene O'Neill and the Guild." *Drama*, 18 (Mar.) 169-171.
Reviews *MARCO* and *INTERLUDE* together, finding the former "minor."

DE CASSERES, Benjamin. "Broadway to date." *Arts & Dec.*, 28 (Mar.) 62.
A "whack in the face" after reading the original. Production is much too heavy with too much caricature.

"Digging for Marco Polo." Brook. *Eagle*, 8 Jan.
Interesting account of some of the historical points which O'Neill observes in the play.

FARQUHAR, E. F. "Marco Millions." *Letters* (Univ. of Kentucky) 1 (Nov.) 33-40.
A provocative comment on the purpose behind writing "poetic" drama. This play, says Farquhar, is not poetry, but he approves of it more than plays like *GREAT GOD BROWN*, which "fuss and fume."

GABRIEL, Gilbert. "The boor of Venice." NY *Sun*, 16 Jan.

The play proves the possibility of singing freely, with tongue in cheek. Admiration for O'Neill power to "read into a curious and devious travelogue such living scorn and modern beauty."

————. "The newer O'Neill." *Van. F.*, 30 (Apr.) 52-53.
MARCO and *INTERLUDE* show that O'Neill is the most influential and contributive playwright America has yet produced.

GOULD, Bruce. "O'Neill takes a crack at Babbitt." *Wall St. News*, 12 Jan.
Thrilling beautiful production, but O'Neill "falls far." Stinging disappointment. Apparently a "slashing thoughtless attempt" to say his angry say about money mad people.

HAMMOND, Percy. "Marco Millions a rich and sardonic extravaganza." NY *Her-Trib.*, 15 Jan.
Further comments upon reflecting back on the play.

HOUGHTON, William M. "East and west." NY *Sun*, 22 Apr.
It is important to behave as we are, rather than to put on appearances of another society; hence Polo's leaving Kukachin behind is approved.

KRUTCH, Joseph Wood. "Marco Millions." *Nation*, 126 (25 Jan.) 104-105.
Great purity of outline with a "delicacy of execution." The other treatments of Babbitt theme now seem "raucous and dull."

LELAND, Gordon M. "Marco Millions." *Billboard*, 40 (21 Jan.) 10.
Can be called "hooey" or "tripe" or whatever; unpoetic, theatrically dull. Shaw does it much better.

MANTLE, Burns. "Mr. O'Neill writes a comedy." NY *News*, 15 Jan.
For once we would like to think of O'Neill as happy, and this play seems written without the burden of the cares of the world on his shoulder.

"Marco Millions." *Variety*, 11 Jan.
    Will add prestige to the Guild.

"Marco Millions O'Neill's latest, done by Guild." NY *Review*, 14 Jan.
    Satire obvious, humor not overly spontaneous or keen.

"Marco Polo masquerading as Babbitt." *Lit. D.*, 96 (4 Feb.) 26-27.
    Three illustrations. Some excerpts from press reviews.

NATHAN, George Jean. "Judging the shows." *Judge*, 94 (4 Feb.) 19.
    "Uncommonly well-wrought play" adding luster to American drama.

"O'Neill and his plays." NY *Times*, 8 Jan., VIII, 2:4.
    Article traces history of development of the play plus a summary of O'Neill's past history with Provincetown and others.

"O'Neill took few liberties with life of Marco Polo." NY *American*, 22 Jan.
    Review of some of the historical facts which O'Neill made use of.

OSBORN, E. W. "The theatres." NY *World*, 14 Jan.
    Osborn reviews some of the facts about Polo which O'Neill did and did not follow in constructing the play.

POLLOCK, Arthur. "Eugene O'Neill and Marco Millions." Brook. *Eagle*, 15 Jan.
    Because O'Neill is "bent on growing" instead of just developing naturally, his plays get longer and less comprehensible. Marco Millions is at times actually banal. Too wide and flat—he should try to make the point, rather than adorn it.

SAYLER, Oliver M. "The play of the week." *Sat. R. Lit.*, 4 (11 Feb.) 590.
    Pales into insignificance beside Nina Leeds; could have been written with his left hand.

SHIPLEY, Joseph. "Babbitt Billions." NY *New Leader*, 14 Jan.
First act weakens it. O'Neill is too indignant about moderns to treat his theme well.

SKINNER, Richard Dana. "Marco Millions." *Commonweal*, 7 (25 Jan.) 986.
Little of dramatic importance, few moments of authentic drama, a "Strange Interlude" in the career of our premiere dramatist.

YOUNG, Stark. "Dilations." *New Rep.*, 53 (25 Jan.) 272-273.
Much promise of an extraordinary drama, but lacks delineation of satire and lyricism. The satire is spread over too wide a field.

MARCO MILLIONS was given a revival of 8 performances beginning 3 March 1930. New York newspapers reviewed the play, finding it very little different from the original.

*Lincoln Center Revival—New York
Newspapers of February 1964*

BOLTON, Whitney. "A good colorful production of O'Neill's Marco Millions." NY *Telegraph*, 22 Feb.
"Almost, but not quite, persuades you that O'Neill was smarter than we thought he was in 1930." Theme is still pertinent. More valid in some ways than it was 34 [*sic*] years ago.

CHAPMAN, John. "Lincoln Center's production of 'Marco Millions' stylized bore." NY *News*, 21 Feb.
"A thudding bore . . . a lead-footed fantasy." Not very good when it first appeared and it is not very important now.

COOKE, Richard P. "The ugly Venetian." *Wall St. Jour.*, 24 Feb.
Not one of O'Neill's good ones. Revival is a "cultural event" rather than a drama to stimulate and arouse. Our ideas toward "inscrutable wisdom" of Orient have changed.

GOTTFRIED, Martin. "Marco Millions" *W. W. Daily*, 21 Feb.
Superficial; too little of O'Neill's genius. Best left alone. "The

play is foolish, . . . relatively uninteresting . . . kind of embarrassing."

KERR, Walter. "Marco Millions." NY *Her-Trib.*, 21 Feb.
Interesting production techniques devised to drive forward a play with little internal momentum. Not one of O'Neill's best; inadequacies still apparent.

McCLAIN, John. "An entrancing O'Neill revival." NY *Jour-Am.*, 21 Feb.
Its message "may be somewhat tired and tarnished" but this production is entrancing and something a repertory company of this type should be doing.

"Marco Millions." *The Villager*, 27 Feb.
Beautiful production directed with imagination.

NADEL, Norman. "O'Neill bares ax in Marco Millions." NY *Wor-Tel & Sun*, 21 Feb.
Imaginative and exotic staging has probably better realized the potential than when first produced. Staging is probably best reason to go see it.

OPPENHEIMER, George. "Repertory group revives O'Neill play." LI *Newsday*, 21 Feb.
Most of the play remains "strikingly fresh." Poetic quality and satiric wit not often found in O'Neill.

SMITH, Michael. "Theatre: Marco Millions." *Village Voice*, 27 Feb.
Deadly bore; bad play badly produced, acting is dreadful. Literary curiosity unsuited for production.

TAUBMAN, Howard. "O'Neill revival." NY *Times*, 21 Feb., p. 33.
The irony has not become outdated; carries meaning even today, despite the heavy-handed satire.

WATTS, Richard, Jr. "O'Neill at war with Marco Polo." NY *Post*, 21 Feb.

Good production does not hide fact that it shows O'Neill in a mood for which he was not equipped. Cardboard Marco is tedious and uninteresting.

Other reviews and criticism
1964

ABEL, Lionel. "Prose and pageantry." *Nation*, 198 (9 Mar.) 249-250.
The pretentious wisdom of the Khan and his wise men give this critic more sympathy toward the American man of affairs than ever felt before.

"Babbitt in Cathay." *Time*, 83 (28 Feb.) 61.
Seemed "ponderous and pontifical" when first produced and has not improved with age. A fault of Broadway producers is that they do not know a bad play when they see one.

FREEDLEY, George. "Marco Millions." NY *Telegraph*, 9 Mar.
Comedy of the original is gone, only "heavy handed satire" remaining. Production more spectacular than original, but O'Neill has gone out the window.

GILMAN, Richard. "Epitaph for Lincoln Center." *Commonweal*, 80 (10 Apr.) 89. [Reprinted in Gilman's *Common and uncommon masks*, 1971.]
"No conceivable case for reviving a work of such radical ineptitude." Banal, dreary, forced; the production is a "Chinese fashion show."

HARDWICK, Elizabeth. "Marco Millions: The soul is a mystery." *Vogue*, 143 (1 Apr.) 40.
Acting commonplace; diction "shocking," though no objection to choice of play.

HEWES, Henry. "Life of a salesman." *Sat. R.*, 47 (7 Mar.) 23.
It is dated. Questions can still be recognized, but production is inadequate and style does not fulfill writer's poetic view.

LEWIS, Theophilus. "Marco Millions." *America*, 110 (9 May) 656.
O'Neill's most thoughtful play. Those who enjoy reading plays
they do not normally hope to see will be grateful for this revival.

MCCARTEN, John. "Good going." *New Yorker*, 40 (29 Feb.) 106-
107.
Highly satisfying spectacle. O'Neill's attitude on materialism is
still pertinent.

"O'Neill magic." *Newsweek*, 63 (2 Mar.) 1956.
"Downright stunning revival." Compare to today's competition,
a "whopper of a play."

TAUBMAN, Howard. "O'Neill revisited." NY *Times*, 1 Mar., 11:1.
[Reprinted in Miller, *Playwright's progress*, 1965.]
Less dated in revival than current *STRANGE INTERLUDE*,
though "undermined by weakness of characterization." What O'Neill
said is still pertinent, despite heavy handedness.

Further reviews

STROUPE, John H. "Marco Millions and O'Neill's 'two part two-play'
form." *Mod. Dr.*, 13 (Feb. 1971) 382-392.
A comparison of various drafts and playscripts of *MARCO* to
show O'Neill's initial experimentation with a two-part two-night play
abandoned for present plan.

———. "O'Neill's Marco Millions: A road to Xanadu." *Mod. Dr.*,
12 (Feb. 1970) 377-382.
O'Neill's narrow reading of Sir Henry Yule's *Book of Ser Marco
Polo*, which saw Polo as a materialistic American business man tourist
of limited vision as translated into the play reveals O'Neill's own
views of corrupting soulless nature of American society. Character
and theme reveal much of O'Neill's own nature.

A MOON FOR THE MISBEGOTTEN

Opening night reviews—Columbus, Ohio, Tryout
Newspapers of 21 Feb. 1947

KISSEL, Bud. "Two much conversation in A Moon for the Misbegotten." Columbus *Citizen*.
 Cast wasted time on an unimportant play. Mostly conversation. Action occurs only when somebody picks up a bottle and drinks. Beautiful story to tell but too much time telling it, a *Tobacco Road* with an all Irish cast.

McGAVRAN, Mary V. "O'Neill lifts curtain on sympathetic drama." Columbus *Ohio State Journal*.
 Represents all the art that is theatre, but it is not arty. Shows O'Neill talent for stripping the comic mask from life and revealing it naked and afraid.

"New play by O'Neill opens in Columbus." NY *Times*, 16:2.
 This "conventional" play is about "straightforward lust to obscure psychological complexes."

WILSON, Samuel T. "A Moon for the Misbegotten has world premiere here." Columbus *Dispatch*.
 Arresting and fine play. Third act has muted beauty, a tremendous emotional impact.

Other reviews and criticism, including published version
1947-1954

ADAMS, Phoebe Lou. "The inner truth." *Atlantic*, 190 (Sept. 1952) 76.
 Thoroughly interesting plot; more readable than most of his works.

BENTLEY, Eric. "Eugene O'Neill's pieta." *New Rep.*, 127 (4 Aug. 1952) 17. [Reprinted in Bentley's *The dramatic event*, 1954.]

Will change nobody's views; not O'Neill's best or worst. Better than some recent plays, so much the worse for recent plays.

CARROLL, Joseph. "A play Broadway could use." *Th. Arts*, 36 (Sept. 1952) 6-7.
Scholars of theatre should take a new look at O'Neill. Other writers may "approach his best or surpass his worst" but none equal his achievements.

CLURMAN, Harold. "Theater." *Nation*, 178 (8 May 1954) 409. [Reprinted in Clurman's *Lies like truth*, 1958.]
Noting the success of *MOON* in Stockholm, Clurman reviews O'Neill's status as an off-Broadway possibility.

DARRACH, Henry B. "Moon in Columbus." *Time*, 49 (3 Mar. 1947) 47.
Brief review of Columbus premiere, with feeling it is much more impressive than *ICEMAN*, but needs much more work.

EATON, Walter Prichard. "A bookshelf premiere for a play by Eugene O'Neill." NY *Her-Trib.*, 3 Aug. 1952.
Increasingly difficult to find a soul in the fumes of Bourbon; not O'Neill's best and only he could or would have written it.

FREEDLEY, George. "A Moon for the Misbegotten." *Library Journal*, 77 (Aug. 1952) 1307.
"Highly recommended."

JONES, Johnny. "A Moon for the Misbegotten." *Billboard*, 1 Mar. 1947.
Usual O'Neill philosphy of frustration. Intricate play that should smooth itself out and do business.

KRUTCH, Joseph Wood. "Genius is better than talent." *Th. Arts*, 39 (Oct. 1954) 22-23.
This general review finds the play to be an *ANNA CHRISTIE* with an unhappy ending. Lacking the facility of talent, O'Neill does have genius, which is probably better anyway.

"Lament for the loveless." *Time*, 60 (4 Aug. 1952) 80.
Scarcely a play to be added to O'Neill's lofty prestige. The lament is gentle and moving, more prolix than profound, but better than most things on current Grey White Way.

McCarthy, Mary. "The farmer's daughter." NY *Times*, 31 Aug. 1952, VII, p. 7. [Reprinted in McCarthy's *Sights and spectacles*, 1956; and in Cargil *et al*, *O'Neill and his plays*, 1961.]
Crude technique. Still exacts "homage" for its "mythic powers."

Opening night reviews—New York
Newspapers of 3 May 1957

Atkinson, Brooks. "Theatre: O'Neill's last." NY *Times*, 21:2.
No stage production can solve the problems of the play which were evident when it first appeared. It is prolix and uneventful, lacking much of O'Neill's elemental power. A tired work.

Chapman, John. "Wendy Hiller is magnificent in A Moon for the Misbegotten." NY *News*.
Without the impact of *JOURNEY*, but still a compelling piece of theatre; another beautiful O'Neill play.

Dash, Thomas R. "A Moon for the Misbegotten." *W. W. Daily*.
It has all of the virtues and many of the vices of O'Neill's plays. A superb study of people tormenting themselves, spasmodic power, trenchantly realistic, but also overwritten. It is not one of his best.

Donnelly, Tom. "A long night's moongazing." NY *Wor-Tel* & *Sun*. [Reprinted in Miller, *Playwright's progress*, 1965.]
The serious playgoer will want to see it, but it will be a labor of love. O'Neill is close to smothering everything in a mass of tedium.

Gilbert, Justin. "O'Neill play grim, uneven work." NY *Mirror*.
Alternately grubby and funny, grim and poetic. O'Neill's incandescence "barely flickers here and there."

KERR, Walter. "Moon for the Misbegotten." NY *Her-Trib*.
First half rattled and blathered, without mercy and without meaning. O'Neill seems to have lost his sense of the theatre, although last act is a superb "dance of death."

McCLAIN, John. "O'Neill opus long but fiercely great." NY *Jour-Am*.
Power and grandeur evident, the same fierce qualities of *JOURNEY*. Brings poetry to this squalid place, never losing control of understanding the characters.

WATTS, Richard, Jr. "Another moving O'Neill tragedy." NY *Post*.
[Reprinted in Miller, *Playwright's progress*, 1965.]
Suffers from typical faults of length and lack of eloquence, but still moving and shattering. Haunting emotional experience, further proving O'Neill was a titan of the theatre.

Other reviews and criticism
1957

ATKINSON, Brooks. "O'Neill's finale." NY *Times*, 12 May, II, 1:1.
A minor work. Only fitfully alive; the tragic drive is missing. O'Neill's grand achievements were over when this was written.

COLBY, Ethel. "Entertainment on Broadway." *Jour. Comm*. 6 May.
The need for condensation is a "glaring fault." Too much reiteration. Rich and vital though it is, it is not up to O'Neill's best.

COOKE, Richard P. "O'Neill's last." *Wall St. Jour*., 6 May.
Minor O'Neill with touches of greatness; lacks tragic inner fires of *JOURNEY*. The recital of drunken deeds is tiresome.

DRIVER, Tom F. "Misbegotten." *Christ. Cent*., 74 (22 May) 657.
O'Neill's loquacity has spun a good one-act play into four. Does not achieve nobility of vision seen in *ICEMAN* or *JOURNEY*. The valid, poignant theme needs lightness.

GIBBS, Wolcott. "A tired Tyrone." *New Yorker*, 33 (11 May) 84.

It is hard to see how this will add much to O'Neill's reputation. His other plays, for all their verbosity, had something to say; this does not.

HATCH, Robert. "Theatre." *Nation*, 184 (18 May) 446.
O'Neill is trying to lay the ghost of his brother. The truth in this play is very evasive; the ending rings false.

HAYES, Richard. "The image and the search." *Commonweal*, 66 (30 Aug.) 541.
"Full of sucking guilt and reddened with whiskey." It does not demand audience response as much as endurance.

HEWES, Henry. "Requiem for a roué." *Sat. R.*, 40 (18 May) 34.
There is too much time spent on trivial things, but it is still a memorable experience.

LEWIS, Theophilus. "A Moon for the Misbegotten." *America*, 97 (25 May) 270.
O'Neill is too long getting started. Many early scenes are written with the frenzy of a man who knew he did not have much longer to live.

"A Moon for the Misbegotten." *Th. Arts*, 41 (July) 12-13.
Comparisons to *JOURNEY* and others are unfortunate, but final impact is worth waiting for. Unhappily the rest of the play does not measure up to the last forty-five minutes.

"More Eugene O'Neill." *Newsweek*, 49 (13 May) 70.
O'Neill can no longer transport his characters to the pinnacle of tragedy. A minor work.

"New play in Manhattan." *Time*, 69 (13 May) 91.
Too much talk. Becomes a ghost of O'Neill's other plays. It is nothing to be remembered.

WELCH, Mary. "Softer tones for Mr. O'Neill's portrait." *Th. Arts*, 41 (May) 67.

Upon the opening of this revival Miss Welch, the originator of Josie in the abortive tryouts on the road, writes of her intimate personal experiences in meeting O'Neill and his wife, in getting the part, and in the rehearsals and performances.

WYATT, Euphemia Van R. "A Moon for the Misbegotten." *Cath. Wld.*, 185 (July) 308-309.

It is still too long, too much talk. There is a limitation to alcoholic values. It is sad to think that O'Neill's play is itself so sad.

Further reviews

FITZGERALD, John J. "Guilt and redemption in O'Neill's last play: A study of A Moon for the Misbegotten." *Texas Quar.*, 9 (Spring 1966) 146-158.

Discussion of play as a purgation of soul of Tyrone through virginal earth-mother Josie. Characters seem almost classic. Hogan is out of Aristophanes, Josie from Aeschlyus, and Tyrone from Euripides.

HEWES, Henry. "Hogan's goad." *Sat. R.*, 51 (29 June 1968) 40.

Good performance which takes emphasis off O'Neills dialogue, which is old-fashioned. Here it is "kind of emotional music symptomatic of characters' inner conflicts."

"A Moon for the Misbegotten." *Time*, 91 (21 June 1968) 67.

An O'Neill play is "somewhat like a confession without hope of absolution." Sense of sin is too deep to be expiated. As usual with O'Neill, language halts short of eloquence, but characters still speak "poignant, subliminal dialogue" making audience hear what does not quite get said.

SIMON, John. "Total theatre: Which way?" *Commonweal*, 88 (26 July 1968) 504-505.

Well-wrought and poignant revival. Much of the beauty of O'Neill's dramaturgy is seen in this play. His tragic vision rears up over and over. "The play is a self-contained monolith dropped on earth from some great, distant cosmic disaster."

WEST, Anthony. "A Moon for the Misbegotten: and yet . . ." *Vogue*, 152 (15 Sept. 1968) 70.
"O'Neill may have wanted to give us another Hamlet, but what we get is a lush Peter Pan." Flaw lies in "humourless innocence." Production tries to look like an American classic, and yet . . .

THE MOON OF THE CARIBBEES

As with nearly all of O'Neill's early one-act plays, critics paid little attention to this one, first produced on 20 December 1918. It appears again as part of the four-act composite known as *S.S. GLENCAIRN*, produced 3 November 1924. The following two reviews are the only ones discovered in a search of the files of major New York newspapers.

1918

BROUN, Heywood. "Susan Glaspell and George Cook have bright one-act play." NY *Tribune*, 23 Dec.
A disappointment in spite of the true dialogue and atmosphere. A pointless tale; Smitty is an uninteresting deep sea snob. The trouble is with the playwright, not the actors.

"Greenwich Village sees new dramas a la Provincetown." NY *Herald*, 21 Dec.
The play is mainly just an interlude; the prelude and afterlude are left to the audience.

Book reviews
1919

The Moon of the Caribbees and Six Other Plays of the Sea was the first volume of O'Neill's plays to be published, other than the abortive *Thirst and Other One Act Plays* of 1914. These are some of the more important notices which it received.

BROUN, Heywood. "The Moon of the Caribbees." NY *Tribune*, 4 May.

O'Neill's very unusual talent is confirmed by these plays, which read well.

CLARK, Barrett H. "The plays of Eugene O'Neill." NY *Sun*, 18 May. [Reprinted in Cargill *et al*, *O'Neill and his plays*, 1961.]

Our most promising young native playwright.

"Eugene O'Neill's plays." NY *World*, 18 May.

Collection is not for weaklings; does not fear ugly truths. Breezy as a sea gale and realistic as a rocky shore.

LEONARD, Baird. "The Moon of the Caribbees." NY *Telegraph*, 17 May.

Pleasant to read, an exception to most published plays.

"Mr. O'Neill's plays." NY *Sun*, 17 May.

These plays show a true theatrical gift.

"The Moon of the Caribbees." *Dial*, 66 (17 May) 524.

Atmosphere of the stage production is still present in the printed version. Action halting; motivation commonplace.

"The Moon of the Caribbees." NY *Globe*, 10 May.

Too many stage directions, but they read better than they act.

"The Moon of the Caribbees." *Rev. of Rev.*, 60 (July) 112.

Should convince us that O'Neill has arrived; he is the Conrad of playwrights.

"The Moon of the Caribbees." *Th. Arts*, 4 (20 Jan.) 80.

"No one has more completely mastered the technique of the one-act play." They read as well as they act.

"Sea plays." NY *Post*, 30 Aug.

Much to gratify the admirers of theatrical thrillers.

"Seven artisans and an artist." *Nation*, 108, (14 June) 948.

O'Neill's best gift is "hard and virile pathos." The introduction of "romantic" women makes the plays lapse almost into melodrama.

Other Reviews and Criticism

SCARBROUGH, Alex. *O'Neill's use of the displaced archetype in The Moon of the Caribbees W. Va. Philological Papers*, 19 (July 1972) 41-44.

Writing of Blessed Isles that are not blessed, of sensuous natives who are not innocent but scheming and mercenary whores, of the displaced Smitty, O'Neill "has not only displaced his archetypes, but allowed the mood of the play to be ironically cast by the displacement."

MORE STATELY MANSIONS

*Premiere Performance—Royal Dramatic Theatre
Stockholm 1962*

COLE, Alan. "Again, a 'new' O'Neill drama." NY *Her-Trib.*, 14 June 1959.

A review of some of the history of O'Neill on the Swedish stage and discussion of the adaptation which Gierow proposes to produce.

EDELL, Frederick. "Swedish Theatre: Unfinished O'Neill play proves disappointment." NY *Times*, 18 Nov. 1962, Sec. 2, p. 3.

Sharp disappointment. A clearly unfinished manuscript.

FLEISHER, Frederic. " 'Mansions' premier in Stockholm continues Sweden's O'Neill romance." *Variety*, 9 Jan. 1963.

Discussion of long history of O'Neill on Swedish stage.

HEWES, Henry. "O'Neill in Sweden." *Sat. R.*, 45 (1 Dec. 1962) 26.

Despite problems of the script, this shows ironically that the later years when O'Neill was neglected by the public are the years when his writing was much better. Should be thankful for this production.

"More Stately Mansions." *Variety*, 28 Nov. 1962.
    Flavor and strength are authentic O'Neill. It may be one of his
great plays, but cannot be compared to *JOURNEY*.

"O'Neill's last play is clobbered by critics." NY *Mirror*, 10 Nov.
1962.
    Summary of the Swedish reviews which, though mixed, were
generally unfavorable.

Book—1964

GELB, Arthur. "Onstage he played the novelist." NY *Times Mag.*,
30 Aug. p. 1.
    Highly dubious that the adaptations by Gierow in Sweden and
Gallup in US have resulted in a play O'Neill himself might have
authorized. Extensive discussion of O'Neill's novelistic style and some
of history of writing this play.

GILMAN, Richard. "Mr. O'Neill's very last curtain call." NY *Her-
Trib.*, 31 May. [Reprinted in Gilman's *Common and uncommon
masks*, 1971.]
    O'Neill's last plays "constitute his strongest claim to permanent
stature." Throughout his plays his "desires outrun his capacities."

OPPENHEIMER, George. "Caught between two furies." *Sat. R.*, 47
(30 May) 46.
    Might have been called "The unmasking of an American."
Simon "ill-defined," being more symbol than man. In reading, one
of O'Neill's less rewarding plays.

Los Angeles performance
1967

BOGARD, Travis. "O'Neill: The message of More Stately Mansions."
Los Angeles *Times Calendar*, 10 Sept.

A review of the *POSSESSORS* cycle, held to be O'Neill's first significant social comment. Discussion of O'Neill's exploring the silent world which terrifies all men and the causes which lead to man's fear, isolation, and pain.

"More Stately Mansions." *Variety*, 20 Sept.

Lavish production given "with such solemnity and reverence as to mitigate its theatrical impact." O'Neill did not provide the characters with the emotional props necessary.

"O'Neill's last long remnant." *Time*, 90 (22 Sept.) 76-77.

"Watching an O'Neill play fail is sometimes as awesome as seeing the Titanic sink." This play however is more like a becalmed Flying Dutchman. Credibility gap between audience and characters. O'Neill shows again "Hell hath no fury quite like a human family."

SMITH, Cecil. "Ahmanson's 'Mansions'—Theatre with a capital T." Los Angeles *Times Calendar*, 24 Sept.

Further discussion in terms of opening night review. Play like this could only be done by non-profit organization instead of commercial producer.

———. " 'Mansions' debuts: Series of theatre firsts in Los Angeles." Los Angeles *Times*, 14 Sept.

"Absorbing, gratingly human and richly textured production." Tragedy is as "massive and miniscule" as man. Verbose and ponderous but has great strength in "immense compassionate insight."

WINDELER, Rob. "Colleen Dewhurst outshines Ingrid Bergman in O'Neill play." NY *Times*, 14 Sept., p. 54.

Comments on production, and mention of two Los Angeles reviews from LA *Times* and *Herald Examiner*, latter of whom found "spiritual writhings and neurotic recriminations" funny to the audience, which later subsided into awe or lethargy.

Opening night reviews—New York
Newspapers of November 1967

BARNES, Clive. "O'Neill's More Stately Mansions opens." NY
Times, 1 Nov., p. 40.
    "In its unfinished, raw and tortured state, it does O'Neill's mem-
ory disservice," but some of his greatest themes are here. One wonders what kind of play it might have been.

BOLTON, Whitney. "Controversial More Stately Mansions." NY
Telegraph, 2 Nov.
    If O'Neill wanted this destroyed he was an excellent judge of
his own work knowing a flawed play when he saw it. Production
sprawls, is unformed, bewilders more than enchants. Should not have
been placed before an audience.

CHAPMAN, John. "Ingrid Bergman is back on stage in Eugene
O'Neill's last play." NY *News*, 1 Nov.
    Solemn and impressive production, but seems a dirty trick on
O'Neill to put the play on in this condition. But as work of our great-
est dramatist, an argument can be made for doing it.

COOKE, Richard P. "Strained O'Neill." *Wall St. Jour.*, 2 Nov.
    Lacks power and poignance of *JOURNEY*. He is better with his
own family; "these scarifying relationships have paled, strained
through the sieve of perhaps too-conscious literary effort."

GOTTFRIED, Martin. "More Stately Mansions." *W.W. Daily*, 1 Nov.
    This is still another example of O'Neill's erratic quality, such
a lesser play as to be positively embarrassing. "Heaviness of dialogue
and absence of humor that was one of his few consistent traits."

WATTS, Richard, Jr. "First view of an O'Neill play." NY *Post*, 1
Nov.
    Tortured and exasperating. Appeal comes from seeing an O'Neill
play never seen before, and from performances of Bergman and
Dewhurst. Far from topgrade O'Neill.

Other reviews and criticism
1967-1970

CHAPMAN, John. "Have we had last O'Neill play?" NY *Sunday News*, 12 Nov. 1967.
Grateful for the production, for *any* O'Neill play is better than no O'Neill "in these days of miniature playwrights." Probably should have been erased as O'Neill wanted it to be.

CLURMAN, Harold. Comments in Theatre column. *Nation*, 205 (20 Nov. 1967) 538-540.
Ham was cursed for telling his brothers of the nakedness of his father. "Sundry Hams commit the sin on the body of Eugene O'Neill, for which they must be chastised. Except that they know not what they do." Truncated body still gives evidence of power. A botch in itself, the production is a paradigm of what is wrong with our theatre.

CROCE, Arlene. "Old Testament man as American." *Nat. R.*, 20 (16 Jan. 1968) 43-44.
Brilliant play. Should not be prone to regard it as inferior unfinished work just because O'Neill said it was not finished. Characters are in control and are of great interest. Chain of dramatic events that keep the audience breathless.

DIESEL, Leota. "More Stately Mansions." *The Villager*, 16 Nov. 1967.
Disappointing as a play, but not as a production. Difficult to believe in Simon, but play is "absorbing to watch."

DOWNER, Alan S., "Old, new borrowed, and (a trifle) blue: Notes on the New York theatre 1967-1968." *Quar. Jour. Sp.*, 54 (Oct. 1968) 199-211.
O'Neill's theatrical history reached its blackest page in this season. The present version is a goulash, a ghost play, a patchwork manuscript.

HARTMAN, Murray. "The skeletons in O'Neill's Mansions." *Dr. Surv.*, 5 (Winter 1966-1967) 276-279.

Brief review of the Cycle plays and place of *MANSIONS*, including its presentation of many of O'Neill themes—war against acquisitive society, Oedipal obsessions, corruption of reality by hallucinations.

HEWES, Henry. "Unreal estate." *Sat. R.*, 50 (18 Nov. 1967) 26.
Plot is so speeded we feel we are watching a synopsis. Seems falsely melodramatic. The talent is misused to turn this difficult attempt into "merchandisable skeleton."

KERR, Walter. "No one will ever live in it . . ." NY *Times*, 12 Nov., Sec. 2, p. 1.
Like a Depression apartment house never finished and then torn down, the play is "born a ruin" which we see before it must be torn down. Great architectural emptiness; no one will ever live there. Failure is not all O'Neill's clumsy style but fact it *is* unfinished. O'Neill's struggle with the play is extraordinarily impressive.

LEWIS, Theophilus. "More Stately Mansions." *America*, 117 (18 Nov. 1967) 622-623.
Authentic O'Neill style and vigor. Ending almost as murky as if it had been written by Pinter.

MORRISON, Hobe. "More Stately Mansions." *Variety*, 8 Nov. 1967.
Numbingly long, sprawling prolix work. At best, second rate O'Neill, lacking firmness and feeling of rhythm.

OLIVER, Edith. "Trick but no treat." *New Yorker*, 43 (11 Nov. 1967) 127.
Opened on Hallowe'en and "if all concerned with the production were haunted by the ghost of Eugene O'Neill that night, it served them right." Creaky melodrama. Very few human or affecting moments. Doing it was a dirty trick, a piece of impudence.

PRIDEAUX, Tom. "A shining return for Ingrid." *Life*, 63 (13 Oct. 1967) 63.
Perhaps O'Neill will be best remembered as an "inspired Ameri-

can primitive." Despite O'Neill's sophistication, there is something ungainly and square about the bulk of his work.

*REAL, Jere. "The brothel in O'Neill's Mansions." *Mod. Dr.*, 12 (Feb. 1970) 383-389.
Discussion of love as a merchandisable object and motif of man's "universal prostitution"—*i.e.*, "the human capacity to bargain away those very qualities that grant individuals that elusive distinction, humanity."

SIMON, John. "Unfinished mansions." *Commonweal*, 87 (8 Dec. 1967) 335-336.
O'Neill probably right in wanting this destroyed. "Stultifying, unmerrygoround of instant reversals of position, lightning arbitrariness, and thunderous absurdity." From the ashes of the manuscript not a phoenix but a turkey.

"These three." *Newsweek*, 70 (13 Nov. 1967) 125.
A ghost, a phantom of a play, a "strange interlude" in the history of our most important playwright. Series of fragments, but has its rewards. A "giant, graceless tension of a statue trying to leap off its pedestal."

WATTS, Richard, Jr. "A question about Eugene O'Neill." NY *Post*, 11 Nov. 1967.
Discussion of whether or not it should have been done. Obviously inferior, but not completely disastrous and it is satisfying to have opportunity to see it.

WEALES, Gerald. "Less stately mansions." *Reporter*, 37 (30 Nov. 1967) 34-35.
Inheritance from O'Neill's father and his father's theatre more obvious and extensive here than in his other plays. Very old-fashioned, century-old devices.

WEST, Anthony. "More Stately Mansions: 'The inevitable.' " *Vogue*, 151 (Jan 1968) 62.

"The house is haunted by a blabber mouthed spook who has written Freud without understanding him."

WETZSTEON, Ross. "Steady as gravity." *Village Voice*, 9 Nov. 1967.
Could be written off as "nothing but a bloated masterpiece" but it is worth seeing. O'Neill could not write down a rough outline without creating a powerful dramatic conflict. Touch of a master dramatist.

MOURNING BECOMES ELECTRA

Opening night reviews—New York
Newspapers of 27 Oct. 1931

ALLEN, Kelcey. "Mourning Becomes Electra seethes with epic tragedy." *W.W. Daily.*
Magnificent tragedy of classic proportions; has quality as pitiless and remorseless as the original Greek.

ANDERSON, John. "O'Neill's trilogy." NY *Journal.*
Unreserved praise for masterpiece with strength, clarity and unflagging intuition, putting flesh of modern psychology on the bare bones of impersonal Greek original. Play of "enduring greatness."

ATKINSON, Brooks. "Strange images of death in Eugene O'Neill's masterpiece." NY *Times*, 22:1. [Reprinted in Miller, *Playwright's progress*, 1965.]
Superb strength, coolness and coherence, much Greek but no slavish imitation. Cause of great rejoicing for O'Neill, Guild, drama.

BROWN, John Mason. "O'Neill's trilogy Mourning Becomes Electra presented at the Guild theatre." NY *Post*. [Reprinted in Brown's *Two on the aisle*, 1938; and in his *Dramatis personae*, 1963; and in Miller, *Playwright's progress*, 1965.]
Proof that the theatre is very much alive; rises above the

"scrubby output of our present day theatre" like the Empire State Building above New York.

COHEN, Julius. "O'Neill's trilogy superbly acted." *Jour. Comm.*
   A difficult job well done. It is not a complicated theme, but the ideas heavily underlying it make a brief review difficult.

COLEMAN, Robert. "Mourning Becomes Electra fascinates brilliant audience." NY *Mirror*.
   It will cause a lot of controversy and be subject of much debate.

GABRIEL, Gilbert. "Mourning Becomes Electra." NY *American*.
   A grand scheme grandly fulfilled. One of the dramatic master-pieces of the world today; O'Neill achieves new stature.

GARLAND, Robert. "Eugene O'Neill turns out a masterpiece." NY *Wor-Tel*.
   Bears out the promise of earlier plays.

HAMMOND, Percy. "Mr. O'Neill blends Athens, New England, and Broadway in an exciting new tragedy." NY *Her-Trib*.
   Easily applauded despite length. O'Neill to be congratulated.

LOCKRIDGE, Richard. "Mourning Becomes Electra." NY *Sun*.
   An implacable and unrelenting tragedy marking O'Neill's emergence as an artist in the theatre.

MANTLE, Burns. "Mourning Becomes Electra." NY *News*.
   If we had to have the old story rewritten it was nice O'Neill did it.

POLLOCK, Arthur. "Broadway sees New Eugene O'Neill play." Brook. *Eagle*.
   May not be his most fascinating, but in many ways his best. O'Neill has grown wiser and calmer.

Other reviews and criticism
1931

ATKINSON, Brooks. "Tragedy becomes O'Neill." NY *Times*, 1 Nov., VIII, 1:1.

O'Neill's only masterpiece, but not a great play because of lack of nobility of character and appropriate language. One of "supreme achievements" of the modern theatre.

BENCHLEY, Robert. "Top." *New Yorker*, 7 (7 Nov.) 28. [Reprinted in Moses and Brown, *The American theatre as seen by its critics*, 1934; and Oppenheimer, Louis, *The passionate playgoer*, 1958.]

Grand, stupendous thriller, with the melodramatic hand of Monte Cristo much in evidence.

BOLTON, Whitney. "By easy stages." NY *Telegraph*, 1 Nov.

Five days after opening it is still possible to feel the impact of great tragedy.

BOWEN, Sterling. "The O'Neill play." *Wall St. Jour.*, 28 Oct.

Hard to place in the catalogue of O'Neill work. The first part is melodrama, the last is dilution. Instead of becoming tragic, the characters are merely exotic.

BROWN, John Mason. "Two on the aisle." NY *Post*, 28 Oct.

A widely quoted article reprinting many of the notes from O'Neill's working diary. Clark also includes excerpts in *European theories of the drama*.

BURR, Eugene. "Mourning Becomes Electra." *Billboard*, 43 (7 Nov.) 17. [Reprinted in Miller, *Playwright's progress*, 1965.]

Written by any other man the play would have been taken as the misguided outpouring of an inferior writer. It is little more than a good three-act "meller."

CANBY, Henry Seidel. "Scarlet becomes crimson." *Sat. R. Lit.*, 8 (7 Nov.) 257-258. [Reprinted in Canby's *Seven years' harvest*, 1936.]

An excellent approach to modern decadence. The Greeks would

not have liked the approach of the abnormal instance. But O'Neill has "consummate skill" as a writer which none can question.

CHATFIELD-TAYLOR, Otis. "The latest plays." *Outlook*, 159 (11 Nov.) 343.
Argument about length and needed editing are unimportant beside the fact it is the most actable play of the year. Some performances that are rare experiences in the contemporary theatre.

CLARK, Barrett H. "Mourning becomes Electra." *Contempo* (Chapel Hill, N.C.), 1 (1 Dec.) 2.
Artful, skillful, magnificent, though it still does not represent the goal O'Neill has set up for himself.

EATON, Walter Prichard. "Powerful but not Greek." NY *Her-Trib.*, 22 Nov.
Not a Greek tragedy, though gripping, because of contemptible and small characters. O'Neill is as near classic as we can ask in modern drama.

EVANS, Harry. "Mourning Becomes Electra." *Life*, 98 (13 Nov.) 19.
Adds stature to the theatre, establishing O'Neill as the "leading dramatist of his time."

FERGUSSON, Francis. "A month of the theatre." *Bookman*, 74 (Dec.) 440-445.
Bad taste shown in attempting to present a case history in classical trappings and confusing psychological approach. The Greek values are not with us today.

GARLAND, Robert. "Second thoughts on prophets, playwrights, the critics of Mourning Becomes Electra." NY *Wor-Tel.*, 29 Oct.
A review of the press comments shows American theatre is not dead.

"Greece in New England." *Time*, 18 (2 Nov.) 34-38.
The significant straightforward treatment of the theme is good. Most of this review discusses O'Neill's background and the play.

JORDAN, Elizabeth. "Mr. O'Neill and others." *America*, 28 Nov.
Drawn as we are to morgues, or around accident victims, we want thrills, and this has them.

KRUTCH, Joseph Wood. "Our Electra." *Nation*, 133 (18 Nov.) 551-552.
A great play, not "meaning" anything in sense of Ibsen or Shaw, but like *Hamlet* it means that human beings are great and terrible when in the grips of passion. One of the "very greatest works of dramatic literature" despite a lack of appropriate language.

LOCKRIDGE, Richard. "Out of the show shop." NY *Sun*, 29 Oct.
The highest point O'Neill has reached; true art. He is now above his early faults, showing the theatre is not trivial.

MANTLE, Burns. "Yankee Electra releases a flood of super-latives—What next?" NY *News*, 1 Nov.
Reviews the critical reaction, wonders if there will not soon be a recession of praise. O'Neill treatment of Electra is a greater writing achievement than the original Greek, but it is probably not as great in character as *INTERLUDE*.

MOTHERWELL, Hiram. "Mourning Becomes Electra." *Th. Guild Mag.*, 9 (31 Dec.) 14-20. [Reprinted in Hewitt, Barnard, *Theatre USA*, 1959.]
This is a modern tragedy of psychology and shows need for shift of emphasis from Orestes to Electra in today's reliance on woman. An interesting counter to criticisms finding the play only a murder melodrama.

"Mourning Becomes Electra." *Variety*, 1 Nov. (?)
Lusty, vigorous drama with more human emotional punch than any gang melodrama ever written. Never lets you out of its grip. Grim, horrifying, intensely absorbing.

NATHAN, George Jean. "The theatre of—" *Judge*, 21 Nov.
One of the most important plays in history of American drama. Monument not only to O'Neill but American Theatre as well.

"O'Neill at top notch." *Lit. D.*, 111 (21 Nov.) 18-19.
Excerpts from other reviews, with two illustrations from original.

"O'Neill's own story of Electra in the making." NY *Her-Trib.*, 8 Nov.
Excerpts from O'Neill's diary, first published by John Mason Brown in NY *Post*, 28 Oct.

POLLOCK, Arthur. "O'Neill does his finest work in Mourning Becomes Electra." Brook. *Eagle*, 29 Oct.
Beautiful play, showing O'Neill improved, no longer a faddist; more self-reliant than ever before.

"Priscilla and Electra." NY *Times*, 31 Oct., 16:4.
Editorial comment; an amusing plea to leave poor old New England alone in its struggle with the Depression instead of accusing it of such horrors as here and in *DESIRE UNDER THE ELMS*.

RUHL, Arthur. "Second nights." NY *Her-Trib.*, 1 Nov.
Brief discussion of the effectiveness of play.

SKINNER, Richard Dana. "The play." *Commonweal*, 15 (11 Nov.) 46-47.
Emotions and artistic ability still not mastered enough to make O'Neill a great playwright, though this is his finest.

———. "What of the new season?" *Commonweal*, 26 (Aug.) 406.
Because O'Neill's future is important to our theatre, Skinner hopes forthcoming *ELECTRA* returns to the "rich intuition" of *BROWN*.

WELLMAN, Rita. "In and out of town." *Town & Country*, 86 (1 Dec.) 46.
No softening element in the tragedy; like a New England boiled dinner the effect does not soon wear off.

WYATT, Euphemia Van R. "Agamemnon turned Puritan." *Cath. Wld.*, 134 (Dec.) 330-331.

Misses Olympus because of complete lack of human nobility and charity, without which human race would have long since perished.

YOUNG, Stark. "Eugene O'Neill's new play." *New Rep.*, 68 (11 Nov.) 352-355. [Reprinted in Zabel, *Literary opinion in America*, 1937, 1951; in Young's *Immortal shadows*, 1948; in Gassner, *O'Neill* (Twentieth century views), 1964, and in Gassner and Allen, *Theatre and drama in the making*, 1964.]

The entire approach of Young's criticism is an objective discussion successfully opposing those who would pick the play apart because of departures from the Greek. He finds modern additions "exhilarating."

1932

The road company, starring Judith Anderson, Walter Abel, and Florence Reed gave 16 performances starting 9 May 1932. New York critics reviewed it briefly, with little change in their original opinions.

ATKINSON, Brooks. "Tempest of the fates." NY *Times*, 22 May, VIII, 1:1.

Revaluation of the play upon return engagement finds it still tremendous, written "with the heat and fume of humanity."

BROWN, John Mason. "Two on the aisle." NY *Post*, 15 Apr.

Extensive quotes from St. John Ervine's criticism of O'Neill in London *Observer*.

CARB, David. "Seen on the stage." *Vogue*, 79 (1 Jan.) 56-57.

Abandoning tricks, O'Neill returns to characters about whom he can write at first hand. Majesty, dignity, tremendous sweep.

CLARK, Barrett H. "Aeschylus and Eugene O'Neill." *Eng. Jour.*, 21 (Nov.) 699-710.

This criticism is good to contrast to Feldman's article. Clark objectively compares the Greek pattern and O'Neill, making clear O'Neill used Aeschylus only where necessary in trying to show a modern idea in psychology in pattern of basic Greek sense of fate. It was ready-made story that did not need explaining.

DE CASSERES, Benjamin. "Broadway to date." *Arts & Dec.*, 36 (Jan.) 52.
Most unique American play ever to be seen on the stage, some of O'Neill's greatest and mightiest characters, the culmination of all his work.

"Electra revisited." *Th. Guild Mag.*, 9 (Mar.) 10.
Second visit shows more visual beauty and expression; a play for both eyes and ears.

FERGUSSON, Francis. "Recalling the highlights." *Bookman*, 75 (June-July) 290-291.
Jones and Nazimova brought brilliance to a "stiff and pretentious monstrosity."

FREDERICK, J. George. "Evening becomes intolerable." *Van. F.*, 37 (Jan.) 46-47.
A T.B.M. (tired business man) taken as guest expresses definite and adverse opinion that things like this do not make drama. A convincing case is made for the theatre of pure entertainment.

HUTCHENS, John. "Greece to Broadway." *Th. Arts*, 16 (Jan.) 13-16. [Reprinted in Gilder, *Theatre Arts anthology*, 1950; and in Cargill *et al*, *O'Neill and his plays*, 1961.]
For the first time O'Neill shows himself the great story teller in this horrific murder melodrama, having none of the uncertainty of former emotional writing.

KIRSTEIN, Lincoln. "Theatre chronicle." *Hound and Horn*, 5 (Jan.-Mar.) 280-282.
A "low high-water mark" of current theatre. Not a great play, not a tragedy, but given so much, one wants so much more.

KNICKERBOCKER, Frances Wentworth. "A New England house of Atreus." *Sewanee Rev.*, 40 (Apr.-June) 249-254.

Close comparison and contrast of Greek and O'Neill. Not great tragedy because Mannons are not great people and there is no "gleam of reconciliation."

KRUTCH, Joseph Wood. "O'Neill again." *Nation*, 134 (17 Feb.) 210-211.
Defending his original enthusiastic response, Krutch finds the criticism against the psychoanalytical approach worthless, because it is merely explaining actions of the characters in a way we today can readily understand.

"Mourning Becomes Electra." *Th. Guild Mag.*, 9 (Jan.) 2.
The one play you cannot walk out on or stop watching; O'Neill doing the thing he can do better than anything else.

NATHAN, George Jean. "Our premier dramatist." *Van. F.*, 37 (Jan.) 24.
Nathan attempts to show why O'Neill, except O'Casey, is the only living writer of English plays of any stature.

———. "Retrospect." *Van F.*, 38 (June) 57.
A less important work than *STRANGE INTERLUDE*.

SKINNER, Richard Dana. "The play." *Commonweal*, 15 (6 Apr.) 636.
Reviewing the season, Skinner discusses the production and what O'Neill tries to do. The next great period of our writing will come when the feelings of O'Neill are harnessed into right direction.

———. "Some thoughts on O'Neill and Sophocles." *Commonweal*, 15 (3 Feb.) 386.
Almost nothing of Greek is in this because of failure to find substitute for fate.

SMITH, Althea E. "Mourning Becomes Electra." *Players Mag.*, 8 (Jan.-Feb.) 11.
Seeing is much different from reading; characters do not move

one to pity on the stage. There is no faith transcending disaster, and we do not identify.

WYATT, Euphemia Van R. "The theater weathers depression." *Cath. Wld.*, 135 (June) 336.

Despite a high price, this production brought the audience in and swept them into a world of imagination, which is art's function.

Further Reviews

ALEXANDER, Doris M. "Capt. Brant and Capt. Brassbound: The origin of an O'Neill character." *Mod. Lang. Notes*, 74 (April 1959) 306-310.

Convincing argument that O'Neill "borrowed" Brant of *ELECTRA* directly from Shaw's Capt. Brassbound.

————. "Psychological fate in Mourning Becomes Electra." *PMLA*, 68 (Dec. 1953) 923-934.

Hamilton and Macgowan's 1929 *What is wrong with marriage* is shown as O'Neill's text in establishing his legitimate elements of psychological fate. The Puritan attitude toward love contributes about half; fate is completed by the Oedipus and Electra complexes handed down through parents to children in a vicious, never-ending circle.

ASSELINEAU, Roger. "Mourning Becomes Electra as a tragedy." *Mod. Dr.*, 1 (Dec. 1958) 143-150.

A carefully detailed analysis of the play, especially Lavinia, to show that O'Neill conceived a tragedy in the genuine classic sense, equal to if not surpassing the Greek, despite his lack of distinctive style.

BARRON, Samuel. "The dying theatre." *Harpers*, 172 (Dec. 1935) 108-117.

The theatre is dying because of narrow traditions unable to handle demands of modern drama. *ELECTRA* fails because of the limits of the stage.

BATTENHOUSE, Roy W. "Mourning Becomes Electra." *Christendom*, 7 (Summer 1942) 332-345.

An interesting and provocative analysis of the characters. O'Neill is writing variations on the one basic human ill, the "original" sin of insubordination to God, which can only end in dismal tragedy.

*DICKINSON, Hugh. "Eugene O'Neill: Anatomy of a trilogy." *Drama Critique*, 10 (Winter 1967) 44-56; and "Eugene O'Neill: Fate as form." *Drama Critique* 10 (Spring 1967) 78-85.

This long item, contained in two consecutive issues (the dates are confusing—Winter 1967 signifies publication after January 1, 1967), is an extensively detailed and annotated scholarly analysis of the play in terms of classic origins and modern realistic adaptation. The artistic success is seen to lie in O'Neill's ability to "control and exploit contrary tendencies at the point of maximum tension" with his vision centered not in Satan but in the human psyche. There is no recourse to supernatural fate. "When O'Neill recasts the ancient myth . . . he abolishes the Olympian gods . . . subconscious becomes mother of demons and intellect becomes the pursuing Furies, and man goes inward to a hell of his own devising."

FELDMAN, Abraham. "The American Aeschylus?" *Poet Lore*, 52 (Summer 1946) 149-155.

A lamentable failure, using theatrical tricks instead of drama to gain an "obscene" interpretation of Freud. Violently opposed to the entire play.

*FRENZ, Horst, and Martin Mueller. "More Shakespeare and less Aeschylus in Eugene O'Neill's Mourning Becomes Electra." *Am. Lit.*, 38 (March 1966) 85-100.

In plot parallels, character emphasis, relationship, and development, this important essay convincingly shows *ELECTRA* to have much closer affinity with *Hamlet* than with the *Oresteia*. Although O'Neill identified the *Oresteia* as his inspiration, the entire pattern of development shows strong, if subconscious, Shakespearean influence.

HANZELL, Victor E. "The progeny of Atreus." *Mod. Dr.*, 3 (May 1960) 75-81.

In a discussion of ancient and modern plays on Electra-Orestes theme, *ELECTRA* is found faithful to spirit of the original, retaining a "delphic atmosphere."

KERR, Walter. "Why revive Mourning Becomes Electra?" NY *Times*, 7 Sept. 1969, Sec. 2, p. 1.

More of a discussion of the philosophy of modern repertory companies such as the Guthrie Theatre in Minneapolis which produced *ELECTRA* during its 1969 season. Kerr questions wisdom of revivals of this sort, finding *ELECTRA* not particularly worthy of the attention it receives.

LECKY, Eleazer. "Ghosts and Mourning Becomes Electra: Two versions of fate." *Ariz. Quar.*, 13 (Winter 1957) 320-338.

Both deal with the power of past over the present, including heredity, environment, and sexual conflict. The structure and effect in both are, of course, different, and they are divergent as regards the future—*Ghosts* essentially optimistic, *ELECTRA* pessimistic.

*O'NEILL, Joseph P., S.J. "The tragic theory of Eugene O'Neill." *Texas Studies in Lit. & Lang.*, 4 (Winter 1963) 481-493.

Discussion of O'Neill's tragic concept finds *ELECTRA* as peak of O'Neill's dramatic development with balance and tension between fate and free will maintained as in all great tragedies. Final redemptive aspect of great tragedy is lacking.

STAFFORD, John. "Mourning becomes America." *Texas Studies in Literature and Language*, 3 (Winter 1962) 549-556.

Detailed analysis of the use of "psychological fate," the "furies of the modern American soul" in this play which represents O'Neill's interpretation of American society with its denial of love and life and spiritual weaknesses of "aristocracy." Mourning becomes not only Electra but America as well.

WEISSMAN, Philip. "Mourning Becomes Electra and The Prodigal: Electra and Orestes." *Mod. Dr.*, 3 (Dec. 1960) 257-259.
Comparison of approaches to the myth by modern writers O'Neill and Richardson.

Stratford, Conn., revival
1971

BARNES, Clive. "Electra gets new twist in Stratford." NY *Times*, 1 July, p. 60.
The characters are among the most complex and arresting that O'Neill ever developed. Questions whether or not the cuts of more than an hour should have been made, as brevity makes no advantage. O'Neill's achievement is considerable.

GAVER, Jack. "Mourning Becomes Electra." NY *Mirror*, 6 July.
A good production which should be seen. It is good to see this play again.

HEWES, Henry. "The theatre." *Sat. R.*, 54 (7 Aug.) 33.
The revival seems to focus more on struggle for family dominance than on Greek tragic aspect. O'Neill may not have liked the emphasis on melodrama, but it is perhaps the only way "this intrinsically artificial" work can now be done.

KERR, Walter. "We see, we hear, but don't believe." NY *Times*, 18 July, Sec. 2, p. 1.
It does not quite come off; O'Neill did not commit himself completely to the Greek nor to contemporary psychology. It straddles two worlds, stands as "two halves of an echo."

NOVICK, Julius. "Mourning becomes electric." *Village Voice*, 8 July.
Preposterously overvalued when it first appeared, but this still has a good deal of very vigorous life left. For the first time in many years grandeur and passion are to be found on the Stratford stage.

OPPENHEIMER, George. "Mourning becomes lackluster." LI *Newsday*, 1 July.

The greatness of the play is measured by its survival in a largely lackluster production. Tragedy is sacrificed to melodrama.

STARK, Larry. "A fresh Mourning." *Boston After Dark*, 6 July.
Powerful, engrossing, and well done. Most successful of the Stratford offerings of the current season.

STASIO, Marilyn. "Mourning Becomes Electra." *Cue*, 10 July, p. 10.
Rewarding production, with possible tendency to overemphasize melodrama.

WATT, Douglas. "O'Neill's Electra joins Stratford (Conn.) Rep." NY *News*, 1 July.
The power is cumulative. Overwhelms in spite of awkward structure and writing. The play remains compelling for all its flaws.

WATTS, Richard. "On crime and punishment." NY *Post*, 12 Aug.
Not a brilliant production. Overwhelming intensity and force, but lacking the sympathy of *ICEMAN* and *JOURNEY*.

Opening Night Reviews—Revival by Circle-in-the-Square
New York Newspapers 16-17 Nov. 1972

BARNES, Clive. "Stage: Mourning Becomes Electra." NY *Times*, 16 Nov. p. 57.
The cuts are regrettable. Thought prosaic and clumsy, a better play to see than read. The more the earlier plays are seen the more O'Neill seems great in plays other than the last three. A distinguished production.

GOTTFRIED, Martin. "Mourning Becomes Electra and a brand new theatre." *W.W. Daily*, 17 Nov.
O'Neill "has to be the worst great playwright in the history of drama." Without other great works of his, plays like this would be historical curiosity and seeing it shows how bad contemporary judgments were. Little literary or theatrical value today. Ludicrous, unwieldly, an unmitigated disaster and never more disastrous than in

this production. Unproduceable, soap opera style, and embarrassing performances.

WATT, Douglas. "Circle in the Square (Uptown) bows with O'Neill trilogy." NY *News*, 16 Nov.
"Passable" production, but awesome logic and strong beauty of the play still hold.

WATTS, Richard. "An O'Neill masterpiece." NY *Post*, 16 Nov.
One of O'Neill's most towering, and one of classics of American stage. A brilliant revival, good to see the play again. The spell of the play is nothing short of tremendous.

Other reviews and criticism
1972

AFRIÇANO, Lillian. "O'Neill." *The Villager*, 30 Nov.
One of the season's "most interesting" productions; four hours well spent.

"The circle moves up." *Newsweek*, 80 (27 Nov.) 78.
On one level a "titanic soap opera" but also one of greatest triumphs of O'Neill's emotional authenticity over his naïveté and clumsiness. Cumulative power, builds tensions and agonies.

CLURMAN, Harold. Theatre column in *Nation*, 215 (4 Dec.) 572-573.
As when first seen, critic regards it "chiefly as Freudian graph on 'classic' themes." High aims of grandeur and grappling with universal human motivations is never achieved. Not the play of heat of lust O'Neill envisioned, blocked by O'Neill's puritanism. The doom is merely "schematic," and really a melodrama.

GILL, Brendan. "Something to celebrate." *New Yorker*, 48 (25 Nov.) 48.
Recommended as a "grave and beautiful embodiment of a grave and beautiful play." Skillfully edited, the suspense mounting "like poison in a vial." Though crushed by O'Neill's approach, we are also

exhilarated, and his personal sufferings "transformed into words . . leave an uncanny residue of joy."

HEWES, Henry. "Frothy Shakespeare; obsessed O'Neill." *Sat. R. (Society)* 55 (Jan. 1973) 72.
A distinguished revival, with style of production forbidding large tragic scope and focusing on inner psychological struggles.

KALEN, T. E. "Day of wild wind." *Time*, 100 (27 Nov.) 73.
Like the Ancient Mariner with "glittering eye" O'Neill harangues with banal tongue but "slings the albatross round our necks" and makes us hear his fearful tale. Like a day of wild wind, the play "reduces everyone and everything to a sodden, nerveless pulp." A+ for enterprise but less for good judgment.

KERR, Walter. "Mourning Becomes Electra doesn't work." NY *Times* 26 Nov., Sec. 11, p. 1.
We keep telling ourselves, says Kerr, that somewhere this will carry the awesome overtones of the Oresteia, but it never does. Audiences do not get emotionally involved; there is no unbidden doom, just the grindstone of a plot.

MORRISON, Hobe. "Mourning Becomes Electra." *Variety*, 22 Nov.
Still monumental, overpowering, a fine opening for the new theatre. Must certainly be O'Neill's finest work, even better than *INTERLUDE* or *LONG DAY'S JOURNEY* with a production worthy of the play.

OPPENHEIMER, George. "Mourning Becomes Electra." LI *Newsday*, 26 Nov.
A generally favorable review, but critic is unable to expunge memory of the original production. A good play that transcends the faults of the production.

THE ROPE

Opening night reviews—Playwright's Theatre
New York—Newspapers of April-May 1918

Broun, Heywood. "Brilliant one-act play called The Rope Provincetown feature." NY *Tribune*, 29 Apr.
Glorious success among other neutral plays; finely imaginative story with surprising ending that comes without trickery.

"Provincetown players give new playlets." NY *Clipper*.
A dramatic gem; the best of the works from this gifted author.

Opening night reviews—Washington Square Players
New York—Newspapers of 14-15 May 1918

"Brace of new plays given at the Comedy." NY *Morn. World*, 14 May.
Ironic and vigorous; better than the companion piece by Susan Glaspell.

Broun, Heywood. "Two new plays at the Comedy." NY *Tribune*, 14 May.
In the best vein of O'Neill.

Dale, Alan. "Two new playlets at Comedy theatre." NY *American*, 14 May.
It may have been meant well, but you make of it what you like or don't like.

Darnton, Charles. "The Rope." NY *Eve. World*, 14 May.
Admiration expressed for O'Neill's ability to draw character.

Gardy, Louis. "The Rope put on at the Comedy." NY *Call*, 15 May.
A tremendous piece of rugged craftsmanship, carrying promise of future greatness. A terrifying spirit throughout.

MANTLE, Burns. "Washington Square players add a dose of tonic to their spring bill." NY *Mail*, 14 May.
Ugly but thrilling little drama; O'Neill's usual "fine, free active imagination."

SHERWIN, Louis. "Two new ones at the Comedy." NY *Globe*, 15 May.
Disappointing, not nearly as effective as others by O'Neill.

"Three comedies and a drama." NY *Sun*, 14 May.
"A very original play."

"Two new playlets instead of Salome." NY *Times*, 14 May, 11:5.
Has O'Neill vigor, lacking "singleness and bigness of motive" of his other better works.

"Two new playlets on bill at Comedy." Brook. *Eagle*, 14 May.
The most striking and best of current bill; strength almost to brutality.

"Two new plays at the Century (*sic*)" NY *Telegram*, 14 May.
Questionable taste at times, but good for those who like their drama straight.

"Two new plays by Washington Square players." NY *Herald*, 14 May.
Review of plot, no comment.

"Two new plays given at Comedy." NY *Sun*, 14 May.
"Lamentably lacking in clearness and motive."

"The Washington Square players." NY *Post*, 14 May.
A happy replacement for *Salome*, though it contributes nothing much of dramatic value.

"Washington Square players win new laurels." NY *Journal*, 14 May.

Frank, direct, even brutal tragedy; its realism fairly makes the audience gasp.

Other reviews and criticism
1918

HORNBLOW, Arthur. "Mr. Hornblow goes to the play." *Theatre*, 27 (June) 358.
O'Neill is a young playwright to be reckoned with, showing much literary value.

"The Provincetown Players." *Vogue*, 15 June.
Much talent for the theatre in this young man.

Untitled note in drama column. *Life*, 23 May.
In spite of repulsiveness, it does get a strong grip on the interest.

"Washington Square players." *Dram. Mir.*, 78 (25 May) 730.
The better of the two plays on the bill.

S.S. GLENCAIRN

The plays of the *Glencairn* cycle—*MOON OF THE CARIBBEES, BOUND EAST FOR CARDIFF, IN THE ZONE*, and *THE LONG VOYAGE HOME*—were each produced separately during O'Neill's early career by both the Provincetown Players and the Washington Square Players. Only the Washington Square productions were generally well covered by the press. The four plays were later combined into the collective *S.S. GLENCAIRN*.

Opening night reviews—New York
Newspapers of 4 Nov. 1924

DALE, Alan. "Cycle of plays offered at Provincetown." NY *American*.
Little significance; too much of the unlovely and squalid.

"Four little O'Neill plays are revived." NY *Times*, 21:4.
This does not seem as good as the originals.

GABRIEL, Gilbert. "The S. S. Glencairn." NY *Telegram & Mail*.
Four stark, beautiful pictures of the sea and its men. They remain among the most affecting and poetical of O'Neill's plays. He has accomplished the music of the sea.

HAMMOND, Percy. "S. S. Glencairn." NY *Her-Trib*.
"Honest relentless bits of humble sea life" told in the best O'Neill way.

"Mr. O'Neill gets three hits and a foul ball." NY *Post*.
If you take your drama seriously here is a program to see. There is less salt, and more hokum than in his later plays, some of it too obvious.

POLLOCK, Arthur. "Young Mr. O'Neill." Brook. *Eagle*.
These plays contain some of O'Neill's best work, but in view of recent plays since they first appeared, they now seem tame. But the force is still here, and they cut deep.

"S. S. Glencairn." NY *World*.
Vivid pulsating drama.

Other reviews and criticism
1924-1925

HORNBLOW, Arthur. "Mr. Hornblow goes to the play." *Théatre*, 41 (Jan. 1925) 22.
A service to English speaking drama in presenting these.

NATHAN, George Jean. "O'Neill steams into port." *Judge*, 87 (29 Nov. 1924) 10-11.
An excellent evening's entertainment.

"S. S. Glencairn." *Drama Calendar*, 10 Nov. 1924.
This should forever cure any young boy who wishes to run away
to sea.

"S. S. Glencairn." *Time*, 4 (17 Nov. 1924) 14.
Best thing on the current Provincetown bill.

SISK. "O'Neill's one acters." *Variety*, 12 Nov. 1924.
Though of little commercial value as plays, production is excellent.

WHYTE, Gordon. "S. S. Glencairn." *Billboard*, 36 (15 Nov. 1924)
36.
"Welded into a fine show."

Opening night reviews—Provincetown Revival
New York—Newspapers of 10 Jan. 1929

"Cast and forecast." NY *World*.
Brief notice of the revival of these "popular plays."

"O'Neill's four plays of the sea revived." NY *Times*, 24:5.
Their vigor and freshness do not abate with the years.

"O'Neill four sea episodes survive second revival." NY *Telegram*.
General praise for the revival.

"O'Neill sea cycle at Provincetown." NY *American*.
Review of the play, no critical comment.

"S. S. Glencairn." NY *Sun*.
Glad to see it back.

"S. S. Glencairn at Provincetown playhouse." NY *Journal*.
Recreates all the rude power and tang of life of the early plays,
which forecast O'Neill's later attainments. This far outweighs most
current plays.

"S. S. Glencairn here on return voyage; drab tale endures." NY *Her-Trib.*
　　Indelible picture of the dregs of human existence.

"S. S. Glencairn revived here." NY *News.*
　　Brief notice of the revival.

WALDORF, Wilella. "S. S. Glencairn." NY *Post.*
　　Decidedly worth the trip to see it.

Other reviews and criticism
1929

ATKINSON, Brooks. "Honor enough for everybody." NY *Times*, 27 Jan., IX, 1:1.
　　Warm praise. O'Neill's later works had roots in nature, sprang from the elemental.

BALLANTINE, C. J. "Smitty of S. S. Glencairn." NY *World*, 6 Jan.
　　Tells of O'Neill's description of an actual young man, model of this character. (Note: Many critics at one time or another have identified O'Neill himself with Smitty.)

CLARK, Barrett H. "The real background of O'Neill in his S. S. Glencairn group." NY *Her-Trib.*, 10 Feb.
　　Discussion of the source material.

"Down to the sea." NY *World*, 3 Mar.
　　Some references to the originals of the stage characters.

"Four O'Neill plays on view." NY *Sun*, 11 Feb.
　　Mostly a review of O'Neill's past. He is in select group of writers with four plays running simultaneously.

LENZ, Elita M. "S. S. Glencairn." *Billboard*, 41 (19 Jan.) 5.
　　"Lusty meat and ale of life"; wonderful evening of drama.

LITTELL, Robert. "Brighter lights: Broadway in review." *Th. Arts*, 13 (Mar.) 172.
Stretches toward something "simple, elemental, fine" but achieves "sentimentality and crudity much too often."

NICHOLS, Dudley. "Testing the play." NY *World*, 10 Feb.
Meets real test of good drama; true sweep of emotion.

"O'Neill drew his gallery of sea characters from life." NY *Post*, 5 Jan.
This review of O'Neill's early life points out the sources.

"O'Neill's one act plays." *Wall St. Jour.*, 16 Jan.
No parallel with these plays so far in the season.

"S. S. Glencairn." *Commonweal*, 9 (23 Jan.) 349.
O'Neill at his best; more so than when he is lost in the subconscious.

"S. S. Glencairn." *Drama Calendar*, 5 Jan.
Grip of the scenes still holds; pulsating, tempestuous.

Opening night reviews—City Center Revival
New York—Newspapers of 21 May 1948

ATKINSON, Brooks. "At the theatre." NY *Times*, 21:2.
The acting makes these still fine sea plays. Honest realism with the perspective of the poet. The modern American theatre has nothing more genuine in its library.

BARNES, Howard. "Smooth sailing." NY *Her-Trib*.
The mood becomes attenuated before the end, but there is evidence of the flowering of great dramatic talent.

CHAPMAN, John. "O'Neill's S. S. Glencairn playlets seem a bit quaint at City Center." NY *News*.
More interesting in history than in performance. The sailor talk once seemed realistic, now seems stilted.

COLEMAN, Robert. "S. S. Glencairn is top-flight O'Neill." NY *Mirror*.
One of the finest contributions by the City Center. These plays form an important page in the chronicles of the drama.

CURRIL, George. "O'Neill's S. S. Glencairn still grips an audience." Brook. *Eagle*.
There are anachronisms and inconsistencies, but the theme still rings true.

DASH, Thomas R. "S. S. Glencairn." *W. W. Daily*.
One can still see the writer in embryo, lacking technical skill and dramatic proficiency.

GARLAND, Robert. "Revival at City Center no credit to O'Neill." NY *Jour-Am*.
Disapproval of the production.

HAWKINS, William. "Four O'Neill plays pale in City Center." NY *Wor-Tel*.
The sense of intimacy is lost. The serious mood cannot be conveyed in this large theatre.

MOREHOUSE, Ward. "Eugene O'Neill's S. S. Glencairn." NY *Sun*.
Curiously flat and unmoving. The theatrical realism of yesterday seems flat and tame here.

WATTS, Richard, Jr. "O'Neill's sea dramas done at City Center." NY *Post*.
These are now accepted as "classics" and much of the excitement and brightness have worn away. Other writers have come forward with more pungent dialogue, but they are worth seeing.

Other reviews and criticism
1948

ATKINSON, Brooks. "The tragic dream." NY *Times*, 30 May, II, 1:1.
A good revival. These plays are an authentic part of our literature

of the stage, truly tragic in theme and beautifully executed in character.

BEYER, William. "The state of the theatre." *School & Society*, 67 (26 June) 478.
"Tepid, contrived, routinely touching."

CLURMAN, Harold. "O'Neill again." *New Rep.*, 118 (7 June) 27-29.
Good to see the classics of our literary heritage brought back, however inferior the production. O'Neill has given a lifetime of service in literature.

COOKE, Richard P. "Early O'Neill." *Wall St. Jour.*, 24 May.
The moods of these early plays at times are poignant and dramatically interesting. At other times, they are lifeless and monotonous.

FRANCIS, Bob. "S. S. Glencairn." *Billboard*, 60 (29 May) 47.
After *Mister Roberts* it is a feeble beep on a steamship whistle.

FREEDLEY, George. "Expert staging of O'Neill Glencairn." NY *Telegraph*, 23 May.
Nobody has done a better job of interpretation of the sea and its men than O'Neill.

GIBBS, Wolcott. "Song and dance." *New Yorker*, 24 (29 May) 43-44.
The plays may have been something new when first produced, but they should now be relegated to the library.

NATHAN, George Jean. "A brief biography of American stage tars." NY *Jour-Am.*, 1 June.
They were amazingly popular because they presented for the first time in the drama the sea very close to reality.

PHELAN, Kappo. "S. S. Glencairn." *Commonweal*, 48 (4 June) 185.
The plays are hardly worth it any more.

"S. S. Glencairn." *Variety*, 26 May.
More fragmentary drama compared to later works.

WILSON, John S. "Four of O'Neill's early one-act plays." *P.M.*

Further reviews

RUST, R. Dilworth. "The unity of O'Neill's S. S. Glencairn." *Am. Lit.*, 37 (Nov. 1965) 280-290.
In theme, character, images, effects, etc., a well-integrated whole.

STRANGE INTERLUDE

*Opening night reviews—New York
Newspapers of 31 Jan. 1928*

ANDERSON, John. "O'Neill's nine-act play opens." NY *Journ.* [Reprinted in Miller, *Playwright's progress*, 1965.]
Profound drama of subconscious. Ordeal by watered dialogue, sprawling, reckless waste—but still "profoundly engrossing." Bursts the seams of theatre in "stretching for deeper meaning and sharper truth." Passages of "soaring poetry," much "unwinking courage."

ATKINSON, Brooks. "Strange Interlude plays five hours." NY *Times*, 28:1.
Atkinson does not offer the high praise that others do, recognizing however that the unoriginal story is not as important as the technique of experiment. The asides are at times "the very stuff" of drama; at other times, used unwisely.

COLEMAN, Robert. "Strange Interlude opens." NY *Mirror*.
Great day for faddists. "Long winded bark at the moon in nine fat acts." Tiresome, jerky, heavy-footed, obvious.

DALE, Alan. "Strange Interlude." NY *American*.
The French would toss it off as a ribald farce. "A sordid mess"; "Pecksniffian outbursts," hysterical analysis of a psychopathic woman. "Six-hour bore."

GABRIEL, Gilbert. "Last night's first night." NY *Sun*.
This "magnificent" venture "cleaves the skyline of tomorrow."
It is a "hewer of ways" in technique, and "enthralling" in theme.

HALL, Leonard. "Eugene O'Neill is off on a huge and ambitious
adventure." NY *Telegram*.
"One of the most astonishing adventures a stage ever held."
". . . great daubs of grays and browns and royal purples on a canvas
the size of the side of a barn." Authentic genius.

HAMMOND, Percy. "The theaters." NY *Her-Trib*.
Contains everything but brevity to make it an exciting evening
in the theatre. Grand interlude for drama lovers who are patient and
above average intelligence.

LITTELL, Robert. "A great play." NY *Post*.
Greatest contribution to our stage, beside which all future plays
in conventional style will seem flat and two dimensional.

MANTLE, Burns. "Strange Interlude nine acts." NY *News*.
Frankly biological. Solid gray in tone, slow-paced, repetitious,
forbidding in length.

"New O'Neill play worthy experiment." *W. W. Daily*.
Momentous and significant experiment in art and technique of
dramaturgy. Wearisome to the layman, but attractive to the "epi-
curean." Less clumsy than masks of *BROWN*.

NICHOLS, Dudley. "Strange Interlude." NY *World*.
Perhaps the most "important event in the present era of the
American theatre." O'Neill catches not only a life but life itself; not
just man and woman, but mankind.

POLLOCK, Arthur. "Eugene O'Neill's nine-act play, Strange Interlude,
proves fascinating." Brook. *Eagle*.
Fascinating as life itself. A novel written for the stage, but not
a stunt. Sharply, beautifully written with a "bitterness and hard truth
that hurts."

VAN DYCKE, Thomas. "Nine-act O'Neill drama opens." NY *Telegraph*.
> The most significant play O'Neill has written. Finest play yet written by an American, perhaps "most remarkable play of our generation." A monument in the history of American dramaturgy.

Other reviews and criticsm
1928 (Two entries dated 1927 also entered)

"Accounting for the popularity of O'Neill's nine-act drama." NY *Post*, 30 June.
> Three factors may explain the play's popularity: desire to see something out of the ordinary, curiosity about what Guild and O'Neill had done to split the critics, and the possibility he wrote a great play.

AIKEN, Conrad. "Strange Interlude." NY *Post*, 21 July. [Reprinted in Aiken's *Reviewer's ABC*, 1958.]
> Book review. "Finest play by an American . . . ever seen on the stage."

ANDERSON, John. "Pieces of eight-thirty." NY *Post*, 3 Dec. 1927.
> This report of the play before production calls it a "jawbreaking endurance contest" which has certain literary, perhaps poetic, qualities. "O'Neill spreads a vast and impressive net to catch a nuance" as he did in *GREAT GOD BROWN*.

ANTHONY, Luther B. "Strange Interlude, disease germs disseminated." *Dramatist*, 19 (Jan.) 1356.
> Brief and strongly prejudiced attack against the play—suggests O'Neill's next step is dissemination of disease germs among audience.

ATKINSON, Brooks. "Laurels for Strange Interlude." NY *Times*, 13 May, IX, 1:1.
> The Pulitzer prize is approved, but the play is not great because of "cramping intrusion of the tenets of science." O'Neill has not ventured far enough into real tragedy to have written great drama here.

———. "Strange Interlude." NY *Times*, 5 Feb., VIII, 1:1.

Listing many faults in technique and philosophy, Atkinson nonetheless admits "when Mr. O'Neill is the black magician" nothing is
boring and it is a very enjoyable evening.

BELLAMY, Francis R. "Lights down." *Outlook*, 148 (22 Feb.) 304-
305.
  Not the last word in a new type drama, but the first, and O'Neill
has given some of the most compelling drama ever witnessed.

BENCHLEY, Robert. "All about Strange Interlude." *Life*, 91 (16 Feb.)
21.
  Only O'Neill could make an audience stick through this kind of
play. Highly important, maybe great, far from perfect.

BRACKETT, Charles. "Not at their best." *New Yorker*, 3 (11 Feb.)
24.
  An interesting stunt, four acts too long. Stream of consciousness
cannot compare to Woolf or Joyce, and has much phony poetry.

BROUN, Heywood. "It seems to me." NY *World*, 1 Feb.
  Broun points up the basic difficulty of getting all thoughts into
words. Try as he might O'Neill can't really get the "lowest part of
the iceberg" in.

BROWN, John Mason. "Intermission—Broadway in review." *Th.
Arts*, 12 (Apr.) 237-240.
  O'Neill taking himself as mystic seer is not so good, crystal ball
in one hand, volume of Freud in another. But play is constantly interesting despite repetitions and asides.

CARB, David. "The prize drama." *Vogue*, 72 (1 July) 62.
  Play is above all else on the boards, but O'Neill's continued use
of trick devices is bad. He is above such fiddle-faddle.

―――. "Strange Interlude." *Vogue*, 71 (1 Apr.) 82-83.
  O'Neill not a thinker or philosopher. His work on contrivance
is both irritating and depressing. If he so continues it will be bad
for him and calamity for American theatre.

COHEN, Julius. "The Strange Interlude." *Jour. Comm.*, 1 Feb.
O'Neill's greatest; also greatest ever written.

DALE, Alan. "Theatre and food cannot mix." NY *American*, 5 Feb.
"The unification of drammer and dinner is no more possible than that of oil and water." A biting attack on the whole matter of demanding that the audience eat during the play.

DE CASSERES, Benjamin. "Broadway to date." *Arts & Dec.*, 28 (Apr.) 65.
Greatest play of the century; with *LAZARUS* it should make him a world figure. Nina is Eternal Woman in all respects.

"The editor goes to the play." *Theatre*, Apr.
A masterpiece—it casts the hard and fast traditions on the scrapheap. O'Neill "shows the mechanism of the human soul under a microscope of verbal power and beauty." High praise for this "magnificent adventure into the guarded secret recesses of the mind."

GABRIEL, Gilbert. "Freud's first play." NY *Sun*, 5 Feb.
. Successful with Freud for first time. Asides and soliloquies vital in probing of past lives, so much more important than what goes on at present.

GILDER, Rosamond. "Plays bound and unbound." *Th. Arts*, 12 (May) 362.
"Surprising dramatic force." Asides bring us one step closer to the "springs of being."

GOULD, Bruce. "Suggestion for cutting O'Neill's Strange Interlude." NY *Post*, 12 Mar.
Reviewing the book, Gould finds the spoken thoughts do not intrude as much as on stage. But even in reading it is too long.

HALL, Leonard. "O'Neill's drama is stirring up the playgoers this week." NY *Telegram*, 3 Feb.
Discussion of the way in which the play is affecting audiences, and the investigation into the matter of life which O'Neill attempts.

HAMMOND, Percy. "Strange Interlude." NY *Her-Trib.*, 5 Feb.
"O'Neill has broken the drama's shackles and escaped from its prison more successfully than other fugitives from its many walls."

HOPE, Edward. "The lantern." NY *Her-Trib.*, 28 Feb.
Devotes full column to the futility of trying to put everything down in the subconscious. Joyce failed, and so does O'Neill. Characters often speak obvious things that don't need speaking, though the play rises above "minor ineptitudes of technique."

"In and out of town." *Town and Country*, 15 Feb.
"Richly wrought, handsome piece of pornography." A slow start, but by the end it is "incredibly fascinating." This critic sees Joyce and Proust as O'Neill's literary antecedents who stimulated him but whom he did not imitate.

JORDAN, Elizabeth. "Mr. O'Neill's dramatic 'stunt.' " *America*, 25 Feb.
The play would be infinitely clearer without the revelation of thought. O'Neill looks at humanity with jaundiced, red-rimmed, astigmatic eyes and sees abnormal people in abnormal situations.

KRUTCH, Joseph Wood. "A modern heroic drama." NY *Her-Trib.*, 11 Mar. [Reprinted in Miller, *Playwright's progress*, 1965.]
Capable of doing on stage what novel could only do before; may start a new form. "Interesting, subtle, great, and also direct."

———. "Strange Interlude." *Nation*, 126 (15 Feb.) 192. [Reprinted in Cargill *et al*, *O'Neill and his plays*, 1961.]
Does O'Neill say anything worth saying in such unusual technique? Krutch believes so, because he has made dramatic those elements of the novel heretofore forbidden to the stage.

LELAND, Gordon M. "Strange Interlude." *Billboard*, 40 (11 Feb.) 10.
Pretty much of a triumph all around, perhaps greatest play written by an American.

LITTELL, Robert. "Two on the aisle." NY *Post*, 4 Feb.

No doubt it is the greatest contribution to our stage. This "brief expedition into the depths" of the play finds any simplified account of it difficult to write.

MANTLE, Burns. "A play that makes history." NY *News*, 5 Feb.

It will be parodied and kidded as a freak for some time, but no doubt will become part of the Guild repertory. Cannot be compared with anything else ever written. Significant milestone in progress of drama. No matter what you think of it, it has significance.

MOELLER, Phillip. "Silences out loud." NY *Times*, 26 Feb., VIII, 4:7. [Reprinted in *Theatre Guild Quarterly*, 5 (Feb.) 9.]

Interesting account of many attempts tried and discarded in the establishment of correct procedure for delivering the asides.

NATHAN, George Jean. "The idea and comedy." *Am. Merc.*, 14 (May) 120.

Asides have gotten rid of infantile stage directions of 19th century which suggest sotto-voice asides, etc. The full and articulate speech is much to O'Neill's credit.

———. "Judging the shows." *Judge*, 94 (18 Feb.) 31.

One of his most important contributions to the American drama, which could have been written in no other way.

———. "O'Neill's finest play." *Am. Merc.*, 11 (Aug. 1927) 499-506.

A long synopsis of play before production with lament that O'Neill has not been properly produced before this time by the Guild. Finds play one of the most distinguished pieces of dramatic writing our stage has known.

OSBORN, E. W. "Strange Interlude." NY *World*, 21 Jan.

An amazing play. Cleverly conceived use of the soliloquy. Characters rounded out and full.

————. "The theatres." NY *World*, 4 Feb.

Comparison of the reading and acting versions. The play definitely becomes an acting play, because of the effect of the spoken asides.

POLLOCK, Arthur. "Eugene O'Neill and Strange Interlude." Brook. *Eagle*, 5 Feb.

His finest drama, in which he is not so much a philosopher as a propagandist against life, which he finds is Hell.

R. S. "Obsessions." *Wall St. Jour.*, 2 Feb.

The story is of questionable material for theatre; more for a mental clinic.

"The rhyming reader." *Bookman*, 67 (Aug.) 692-693.

Amusing eleven-verse rhymed account of play, finding no real human being in entire work.

RUHL, Arthur. "Second nights." NY *Her-Trib.*, 19 Feb.

Deserves the attention it is getting as great news item, but there are many questions as to the value of technique and the fact everybody acts like "so many Freudian rats."

S. M. W. "O'Neill's Strange Interlude is his supreme effort." NY *Review*, 31 Jan.

Clinches O'Neill's right to be called "most individual dramatist in America if not world." His success in defiance of tradition and rules "one of the greatest triumphs of individualism in the history of the theatre."

SAYLER, Oliver M. "The play of the week." *Sat. R. Lit.*, 4 (11 Feb.) 590.

A *tour de force* which may be over-praised too easily, or too easily dismissed. Encouraging to see the work of one who dares the unknown and forbidden.

SELDES, Gilbert. "The theatre." *Dial*, 84 (Apr.) 348-351.

The merits are almost entirely spoiled by "technical infelicities." O'Neill too good a dramatist to have to use the asides.

SELIGMAN, Herbert J. "A diagnostic poet." NY *Sun*, 10 Mar.
This review of the printed version enters into considerable discussion of O'Neill's interest in diagnosing his characters. Regardless of how he does it, O'Neill is plumbing phases of American life with true theatricality, seriousness and profundity.

SHIPLEY, Joseph T. "Strange Interlude." *New Leader*, 11 Feb.
Unique experience not to be missed; a profound study of well-rounded characters. O'Neill's experiments are not within but are without the realms of conventional drama.

SKINNER, Richard Dana. "Strange Interlude." *Commonweal*, 7 (22 Feb.) 1098-1099. [Reprinted in Hewitt, *Theatre USA*, 1959.]
Combination of novel and play makes a very interesting if not necessarily great drama.

SLOAN, J. Vandervoort. "Strange Interlude." *Drama*, 18 (May) 248.
A masterpiece comparable in "elemental quality" to Dostoievsky. The greatest play written by an American.

"Strange Interlude." Brook. *Eagle*, 6 May.
By style and length O'Neill has shown in impressive way facts of our lives and the absence of meaning in much of our desires.

"Strange Interlude." *Christ. Cent.*, 37 (7 June) 737.
Tremendous; has depth. Shows souls turned inside out.

"Strange Interlude." *Independent*, 120 (31 Mar.) 315.
Brief book review. Asides legitimate, if unnecessarily long.

"A Strange Interlude." *Psychology*, Mar., p. 53.
Mainly a review of the play's plot, but raising the question interesting to the psychologist concerning whether or not monagamy is instinctive and what can be done when one cannot live that way.

444   *Strange Interlude—1928*

"Strange Interlude." *Sat. R. Lit.*, 4 (3 Mar.) 641.
Book review. First truly successful drama using "double voice." New power; play becomes more articulate because of it.

"Strange Interlude." *Theatre*, 47 (Apr.) 39-40.
Great days of the drama have returned; O'Neill makes us have reverence for the theatre.

"Strange Interlude." *Time*, 11 (13 Feb.) 36-38.
Reviews the play act by act and gives brief background of O'Neill's life and career.

"Strange Interlude." *Variety*, 1 Feb.
The best thing O'Neill has ever done, throwing much cold water on his disparagers.

"Strangest interlude is one of indigestion." NY *Post*, 31 Jan.
Report on the difficulties of eating the evening meal between acts—and a comparison of the more efficient way the Germans do it when attending Wagner.

STRUNSKY, Simeon. "About books, more or less: Miscellaneous." NY *Times*, 20 May, IV, p. 4.
Reviewing Pulitzer awards, finds interesting contrasts in length of the play and brevity of Wilder's *Bridge of San Luis Rey*. Play has something of the "trick" about it.

"Three dimensional play." *Lit. D.*, 96 (25 Feb.) 26-27.
Realistic drama has recieved a body blow.

VAN DYCKE, Thomas. "The make-up box." NY *Telegram*, 5 Feb.
Looking back on his previous comments about the significance of the play and the writer, this critic still feels O'Neill has made "the most significant contribution to the drama of America."

WENTWORTH, Margaret. "A strange interlude." *Drama Cal.*, 10 (15 Feb.) 2.
At times smacks of the clinic, smells of the dissecting room. If

one cares to think about mysteries of life and death, no play in town is more stimulating.

WINCHELL, Walter. "Another Eugenic O'Neill baby." NY *Eve. Graphic*, 31 Jan.
Gripped, awed, fascinated for six episodes, grew cumbersome last 3. Acutely interesting, powerfully spellbinding, tense and breathless tragedy.

WOOLLCOTT, Alexander. "Giving O'Neill till it hurts." *Van. F.*, 29 (Feb.) 48.
Subtitle: "Unofficial program notes for the most punishing of his plays." The Guild not having given any O'Neill up to now, insists on giving until it hurts.

———. "Mr. Hecht goes to Strange Interlude." NY *World*, 14 May.
Extensive quotes from an unidentified Hecht writing about his amazement at this "cultural shell game" with which Woollcott agrees.

———. "Second thoughts on first nights—Strange Interlude." NY *World*, 5 Feb.
Admiration for the impulse to write this, but finds no living characters after the five hours of "resonant emptiness."

WYATT, Euphemia Van R. "Plays of some importance." *Cath. Wld.*, 127 (Apr.) 77-80.
Despite some unpleasantness, the work of a master dramatist, written with sincere thought; an absorbing play.

YOUNG, Stark. "The new O'Neill play." *New Rep.*, 53 (15 Feb.) 349-350.
Whatever its shortcomings, an overwhelming milestone in American theatre.

1929-1953

*ALEXANDER, Doris M. "Strange Interlude and Schopenhauer." *Am. Lit.*, 25 (May 1953) 213-228.

Extremely convincing development of thesis that Schopenhauer was followed almost completely and that Freudian psychology is not the basis. If accepted, this does explain much of seemingly pointless ending which so many critics disliked.

BATTENHOUSE, Roy. "Strange Interlude restudied." *Religion in Life*, 15 (Spring 1946) 202-213.

Thorough and fresh analysis in terms of failure of individual to find peace by natural conscience or scientific reason when God has been rejected. Critic feels play bears restudying today. Has an interesting set of speculations on possible symbolic meaning of title itself, plus statement that much in the play satirizes the American of its day.

GARLAND, Robert. "O'Neill play's success has critics gasping." NY *Telegram*, 15 June 1929.

After sitting through it again, Garland observes that the "only thing wrong with O'Neill characters is they're crazy." Play is childish, obvious, unnecessarily disagreeable.

KRUTCH, Joseph Wood. "The new American drama." *Nation*, 130 (11 June 1930) 678-679.

Instead of thesis plays which must be explained and contain a "point" the modern American writer as here aims at contemporary American life, making comedy and tragedy acceptable to contemporary audiences.

LITTELL, Robert. "Two on the aisle." NY *Post*, 30 Jan. 1929.

Criticizes O'Neill for his continual identifying characters with himself instead of standing aside. A contrast of this play with other earlier O'Neill shows how far he has come.

McGUIRE, Harry. "Beyond Strange Interlude." *Drama*, 19 (Mar. 1929) 172.

Attempt by this admirer to show O'Neill's faith in life and living despite apparent almost nihilistic disillusion of the play.

MALONE, Kemp. "The diction of Strange Interlude." *Am. Speech*, 6 (Oct. 1930) 19-28.

An attempt to discover if O'Neill realism in language is consistent, reaching obvious conclusion he is as realistic as he wished to be.

NATHAN, George Jean. "Ervine encore." *Am. Merc.*, 16 (Feb. 1929) 246-247. [Reprinted in Downer, *American drama and its critics*, 1965.]
Nathan makes strong defense against Ervine's attack condemning the asides.

PHILIPPS, Alice E. "Strange Interlude and the blah brotherhood." *Drama*, 19 (Mar. 1929) 174.
Based on reading only, takes sharp issue with creation of Nina as a woman, and with critics in general for praise of what to this critic is only an expression of sex.

SHIPP, Horace. "The x-rays up to nature." *Eng. Rev.*, 52 (Mar. 1931) 378-380.
"An amazing, a lovely and provocative play which must be seen by everybody who loves the theatre."

WYNNE, Stella. "The Strange Interlude." *Overland*, 87 (July 1929) 220.
Nina becomes the very ancient and primitive woman desiring to propagate the race.

Actors Studio revival—New York
Newspapers of March 1963

BOLTON, Whitney. "Strange interlude wears well." NY *Telegraph*, 13 Mar.
The excellent impression gained by this critic in seeing the original is retained. The revival shows how in subject and theme O'Neill paved the way for Williams, Inge, and others.

COOKE, Richard F. "Uneven O'Neill." *Wall St. Jour.*, 13 Mar.
Though a stimulating production, values have changed since the

1920s. Not altogether satisfying, but there is no avoiding the power of O'Neill's writing.

GOTTFRIED, Martin. "Strange Interlude revival by Actors Studio brilliant." *W.W. Daily*, 12 Mar.
Magnificent production. Though flawed, the play bears "indelible stamp" of genius. Not a masterpiece and often awkward in style. The woman-God theory becomes adolescent intellectualizing.

NADEL, Norman. "O'Neill is reborn at Hudson." NY *Wor-Tel & Sun*, 22 Apr.
Production has stature and luster lacking in many new plays. Play has held up remarkably well, remaining a kind of masterpiece.

OPPENHEIMER, George. "The electrical display of God." LI *Newsday*, 20 Mar.
Major event of the season; ensemble acting at its best. Critic is not as enthusiastic as in 1928 when it seemed daring, and today it sometimes topples into melodrama and must be viewed in context of the time it was written.

SMITH, Michael. "Theatre uptown." *Village Voice*, 14 Mar.
Sharp disappointment. An impossible play to produce, with nothing new in this production to give it new life. Dated, but the emotions have not lost their power. The entire play moves at a "medium walk."

STERN, Harold. "Interlude revived." NY *Standard*, 13 Mar.
More of a curio than an exalting experience. Not boring, holds attention, but fails to move. What once was the "impact of a pile driver" is now "curiously stilted."

"Strange Interlude." *The Villager*, 21 Mar.
Absorbing, acted with uncommon skill. Despite some of the unbelievable aspects, the emotional power is supreme.

TAUBMAN, Howard. "Actors Studio presents O'Neill revival." NY *Times*, 13 Mar.

Brilliant revival. Now the play seems "shot through with flaws and absurdities" but has plenty of dramatic moments. Asides seem laughable now. Three men scene still one of O'Neill's greatest triumphs.

WATTS, Richard. "O'Neill's Strange Interlude retains its dramatic power." NY *Post*, 12 Mar.

Flaws cannot be denied, but performance shows "an engrossing drama of enormous power and steady fascination."

Other reviews and criticism
1963

BRUSTEIN, Robert. "Revivals: Good, bad, and insufferable." *New Rep.*, 148 (30 Mar.) 28-29.

This critic is "still shaking with rage" four days after. The play is not only the worst play O'Neill ever wrote but it may be the worst *ever* written by a major dramatist. An "ill-born monstrosity" with some of the "most vacant characters ever assembled on a single stage." Audiences that support it now, as those that first supported it, are "hundreds of goofy admirers huddled around an emperor completely naked of intellect or art." Nine acts of "blah-blah-blah."

CLURMAN, Harold. Comment in Theatre column. *Nation*, 196 (30 Mar.) 274-275.

Even as in 1928 it is immature and artistically unconvincing.

GILMAN, Richard. "Between anger and despair." *Commonweal*, 78 (12 Apr.) 72-73. [Reprinted in Gilman's *Common and uncommon masks*, 1971.]

Like an enormous fake elephant, an inflated contrivance. The most atrociously ill-written and ill-conceived play of our time; very likely the worst play ever written by a dramatist with reputation. Quarter-baked Strindberg, tenth-rate Freud.

HEWES, Henry. "Actors Studio's first long pants." *Sat. R.*, 46 (30 Mar.) 36.

Quite a production, reminding us that O'Neill was quite a playwright, which we need to do every now and then. Despite age, seems to be "lingeringly valid criticism" of American life in past, present, and future. Contemporary theatre seems trivial by comparison.

Lewis, Theophilus. "Strange Interlude." *America*, 108 (20 Apr.) 594.
Nina is a "soft shelled" Hedda Gabler. Though Freudian ideas compared to Tennessee Williams are rather primitive, it still is a mirror of life even today.

McCarten, John. "Something old, something new." *New Yorker*, 39 (23 Mar.) 73.
It is probably too long, but does have "galvanic moments." Subtleties of human emotion are never explored as O'Neill apparently wanted. Freud is almost nudged into the wings.

"More curio than classic." *Time*, 81 (22 Mar.) 74.
The brilliant production "merely deepens the shadow of doubt that must now fall heavily on the value of the play." "Indelibly datemarked: Lost Generation, made in the 1920's."

Morrison, Hobe. "Strange Interlude." *Variety*, 13 Mar.
Remains "fascinating tremendous drama." Power and impact remain.

"Overwhelming." *Newsweek*, 61 (25 Mar.) 97.
"Of all O'Neill's galumphing masterworks," this one seemed to have the least chance of revival, but this revival came with "thrilling effect."

Pryce-Jones, Alan. "*Strange Interlude.*" *Th. Arts*, 47 (May) 12-13.
Holds audience with ease; it may tire, but it is never boring.

Brashear, W. R. "O'Neill's Schopenhauer interlude." *Criticism*, 6 (Summer 1964) 256-265.
While most of O'Neill is Nietzschean, this "interlude" fits Schopenhauer. (See Doris Alexander's comment.) Difference between this and other O'Neill plays is that characters do not reach the dignity

nor significance of the tragic individual. They exist under the Schopenhauer idea of the single "will" or "force" which is not that of the characters themselves.

TAUBMAN, Howard. "O'Neill revisited." NY *Times*, 1 Mar. 1964, Sec. 2, p. 1. [Reprinted in Miller, *Playwright's progress*, 1965.]
As a chic play to see in 1928, it has not worn so well. Fatally flawed by the incredibility of central character.

WINCHESTER, Otis W. "History in literature: Eugene O'Neill's Strange Interlude as a transcript of America in the 1920's." In papers prepared on the occasion of and in honor of the inauguration of J. Paschal Twyman as President of the University of Tulsa. Tulsa Univ. Press, 1970.

THE STRAW

Book

FIRKINS, O. W. "Plays for the reader." *Weekly Rev.*, 4 (25 June 1921) 406-407.
O'Neill is not yet the master of the long play. A sense of theatre and honesty should be helpful in the future.

RENIERS, Percival F. "O'Neill's plays." *Lit Rev. of NY Post*, 16 July 1921, p. 3.
Interesting, sincere, realistic; scenes of unquestioned dramatic skill.

"The Straw." *Dial*, 70 (June 1921) 715.
Reviewed with *JONES*. *STRAW* is a less important work.

"The Straw." *Th. Arts*, 5 (Oct. 1921) 334-335.
Strongly and truly written, with good character, but everybody is tied up too much with tuberculosis.

V.S.G.L. "The Straw." *New Rep.*, 26 (25 May 1921) 386.

No half lights, no gray shades, nothing fragile and delicate. Constructed of 2x4's spiked together with O'Neill's reiterated emphasis.

WOOLLCOTT, Alexander. "Second thoughts on first nights." NY
Times, 8 May 1921, VI, 1:2.
Typical O'Neill, recognizable any place. Pure tragedy; a study
of human misery, salted with irony.

Opening night reviews—New York
Newspapers of 11 Nov. 1921

ALLEN, Kelcey. "Eugene O'Neill puts real vigor into The Straw."
W.W. Daily.
Optimism makes it less bitter than *HORIZON* or *CHRISTIE*; well
written dialogue and skillful characterization.

BROUN, Heywood. "It seems to me." NY *World*.
Last act "one of the most thrilling things our native theatre has
ever known."

DALE, Alan. "Tuberculosis dramatized in the latest play by Eugene
O'Neill." NY *American*.
Parody of a play; O'Neill wasting his time on a subject nobody
cares about seeing dramatized.

DARNTON, Charles. "The Straw human and moving." NY *World*.
Does not make this forbidding and gloomy; gives it saving quality
of youth and hope. A memorable play.

DE FOE, Louis D. "O'Neill's triple extract of gloom." NY *World*.
Unbearable and strangely beautiful, superior quality but exceed-
ingly lugubrious and depressing.

"Eugene O'Neill's The Straw is gruesome clinical tale." NY *Sun*.
The sight of a tuberculosis sanitarium in full operation is not a
good tonic. The play is a good example of "morbid Teutonic drama."
The end hardly justifies the tubercular means.

"Eugene O'Neill's The Straw profoundly impressive play." NY *Herald*.

Much could be made shorter, and though moving, it is a painful play.

HAMMOND, Percy. "The Straw." NY *Tribune*.

O'Neill does not make use of any of the TB props for pity, yet manages to bring much new emotion to the viewer.

MACGOWAN, Kenneth. "The Straw." NY *Globe*.

"A drama of character, uneven in emotion until last scene, when it surges into undeniable tragic power."

MANTLE, Burns. "The Straw a hopeful play." NY *Mail*.

More conventional than most O'Neill plays; surprisingly sympathetic.

MARSH, Leo A. "Another O'Neill play presented." NY *Telegraph*.

Striking study on subject of the strength of hope.

"O'Neill scores new triumph in The Straw." NY *Journal*.

Written with great force; the interest of real life is in it.

"The Straw." Brook. *Eagle*.

Not up to *ANNA CHRISTIE*, but still a play that should succeed.

"The Straw by Mr. O'Neill." NY *Telegram*.

Every play assures O'Neill of a strong position, and this play proves him to be the most vital American dramatist.

TOWSE, J. Ranken. "The Straw." NY *Post*.

Not the play admirers of O'Neill might have expected, but it is good realism and absorbingly interesting.

WOOLLCOTT, Alexander. "Another O'Neill play." NY *Times*, 16:2. [In Cargill *et al*, *O'Neill and his plays*, 1961.]

Interesting and moving, with last scene having tragic irony and pathos seldom seen in the theatre.

Other reviews and criticism
1921-1922

ANDREWS, Kenneth. "Broadway, our literary signpost." *Bookman*,
54 (Jan. 1922) 463-464.
A new step in the as yet immature but developing O'Neill. He
is able to weep with characters and feel their passions.

BENCHLEY, Robert. "The great plague." *Life*, 78 (8 Dec. 1921) 18.
Margalo Gilmore should recover because she is such a nice girl.

BOYD, Ernest. "Mr. O'Neill's new play." *Freeman*, 7 Dec. 1921.
Depressing, unpleasant and vulgar.

BROUN, Heywood. "It seems to me." NY *World*, 12 Nov. 1921.
O'Neill's awareness that the greatness in tragedy lies in the
struggle rather than defeat calls for praise.

————. "More moral victories." *Van. F.*, Jan. 1922.
Impossible to place O'Neill in any one category; in this play he
sides with characters against fate.

CRAWFORD, Jack. "Broadway sheds tears." *Drama*, 12 (Feb. 1922)
152.
One of the first of the year's plays worthy of significance.

DE FOE, Louis V. "Our foremost apostle of woe." NY *World*, 20
Nov. 1921.
With continual emphasis on woe and depression, O'Neill's effec-
tiveness and contribution may be limited.

HAMMOND, Percy. "The theatres." NY *Tribune*, 20 Nov. 1931.
The play deals far more in troubles of the heart than the lungs.

HORNBLOW, Arthur. "Mr. Hornblow goes to the play." *Theatre*, 35
(Jan. 1922) 31.
The production is a disappointment.

JAMES, Patterson. "The Straw." *Billboard*, 33 (3 Dec. 1921) 19.
O'Neill is not the hope of the American theatre yet. Reeks with insincerity and theatricalism. Having exhausted all other means of terrorization, O'Neill has gone into the sputum cup for a really good horror. "A creation whose blood is ink and tissue is sawdust."

KAUFMAN, S. Jay. "The Straw." *Dram. Mirror*, 84 (19 Nov. 1921) 737.
O'Neill's power does not ring as strong and ferocious as it could, but it is true, with a tremendous final scene.

MACGOWAN, Kenneth. "The Straw." *Vogue*, Jan. 1922.
Not as well written or well knit as *CHRISTIE*, but tremendously moving at the end.

————. "Year's end." *Th. Arts*, 6 (Jan. 1922) 6.
A disappointment through production and no fault of the writer.

PARKER, Robert A. "An American dramatist developing." *Independent*, 107 (3 Dec. 1921) 236.
Lacks the interest and conviction of *ANNA CHRISTIE*.

POLLOCK, Arthur. "About the theatre." Brook. *Eagle*, 13 Nov. 1921.
No need to fear seeing it for its unpleasant subject, although it does not come off as well as could be hoped.

REAMER, Lawrence. "The Straw shows the effect of the sanitorium drama." NY *Herald*, 20 Nov. 1921.
O'Neill's promise may lead to great popularity uptown as well as down.

"The Straw." *Town Topics*, 17 Nov. 1921.
From the standpoint of logic, integrity and soundness, it is O'Neill's best; ranks as a great American tragedy.

"The Straw and its message." NY *Sun*, 18 Nov. 1921.
Dr. Lyman Fisk, eminent medical authority, sees a message of hope which is always important in medicine.

"The Straw is play of hopefulness, pain, and death." NY *Clipper*,
16 Nov. 1921.

Merely plot review; little critical comment.

"The Straw is repellant study in tuberculosis." NY *Review*, 12 Nov.
1921.
Mostly wasted effort; ugly subject is not embellished with art.

"The Straw . . . remarkably well acted." NY *Call*, 23 Nov. 1921.
Despite the subject matter, play stands on its characterizations,
which are extraordinary.

WHITTAKER, James. "O'Neill's Straw compact history of girl's
heart." NY *News*, 27 Nov. 1921.
Sanitorium used only to telescope an entire life and to indicate
afflictions of a girl's heart.

A TALE OF POSSESSORS SELF-DISPOSSESSED

This is the title of the projected "cycle," discussed fully under
CHRONOLOGY OF COMPOSITION. Most reviews center around *A
TOUCH OF THE POET* and *MORE STATELY MANSIONS*, but the
following items are directly related to the entire subject.

FITZGERALD, John J. "The bitter harvest of O'Neill's projected
cycle." *New Eng. Quar.*, 40 (Sept. 1967) 364-374.
An attempt to reconstruct the content of the cycle based on available chronology supplied by O'Neill and others. The author, despite
references to several other sources, insists on calling the play cycle
"A Tale of Possessors Self-Possessed."

GELB, Barbara. "The 'Child' O'Neill tore up." NY *Times*, 29 Oct.
1967, Sec. 11, p. 1.

Extended review of the history of the cycle and its destruction except for *POET* and *MANSIONS*.

SEARS, William P., Jr. "O'Neill begins another marathon." *Lit. D.*, 119 (27 Apr. 1935) 28.
Brief review of work on the cycle, though it is not named as such.

THIRST

This play first appeared in O'Neill's initial venture into print called *Thirst and Other One Act Plays*, published in 1914 at the insistence of Clayton Hamilton. The entire expense was borne by James O'Neill. The Provincetown Players gave one performance of the play in 1916 at the Wharf Theatre during one of their summer series, but there is no record of any other production. The only printed review of the play was written by Hamilton soon after the book appeared.

HAMILTON, Clayton. "A shelf of printed plays." *Bookman*, 41 (April 1915) 182. [Reprinted in Miller, *Playwright's progress*, 1965.]
Under "Playwright of Promise" Hamilton states that the young writer has a knowledge of the sea, and that the plays have violent emotion.

A TOUCH OF THE POET

Stockholm and Published Version
1957

ATKINSON, Brooks. "O'Neill's Poet." NY *Times*, 22 Sept. II, 1:1.
The book seems a temperate play after *JOURNEY*; it does not probe the "black corners of O'Neill's life." Although Melody somewhat overburdens the plot, it is vigorous and original and the characters come alive.

BELAIR, Felix, Jr. "World premiere for O'Neill." NY *Times*, 7 Apr., II, 3:1.

A review of O'Neill's Stockholm reception and of the play's subject matter, "What is truth?" It is portraying O'Neill's conviction that those who are loneliest are the proudest, and in this play he has found entirely new characters to express what has been called his one obsession.

COLE, Alan. "Touch of the Poet done in Stockholm." NY *Her-Trib.*, 7 Apr.

A "gawking tragedy" which is not true tragedy—instead it is a "romantic historical comedy." Production seems to understand the importance of the play in the American tradition.

FLEISHER, Frederic. "A long day's journey into O'Neill." *New Rep.*, 136 (3 June) 21.

This review of the Stockholm production finds the play reminiscent of *The Wild Duck* in its destroying of the life-lies so typical of O'Neill.

HEWES, Henry. "Self delusion in Stockholm." *Sat. Rev.*, 40 (13 Apr.) 24.

A distinguished and vital example of demon-driven dramaturgy. Even with its shortcomings it shows O'Neill's growth into this final great period.

"The Iceman crumbleth." *Time*, 70 (30 Sept.) 102.

A distressingly flaccid play, but it still makes most Broadway productions seem stillborn, even in its published version.

KRUTCH, Joseph Wood. "Eugene O'Neill's claim to greatness." NY *Times*, 22 Sept., VII, p. 1. [Reprinted in Cargill *et al*, *O'Neill and his plays*, 1961.]

Another *ICEMAN* theme, a nihilistic *Wild Duck*, and it will not add to O'Neill's stature as did *Journey*. Despite strong adverse criticism against him, O'Neill still draws audiences, and seldom is a writer given the second chance he now is. This review of O'Neill's present position offers a convincing case for his permanence in our theatre because, for all his lack of a facile style and his other major and obvious faults, he does communicate to the audiences which have always supported his plays in the past and which are apparently doing so once again.

"O'Neill in Stockholm." *Time*, 69 (8 Apr.) 77.
The play gives an idea of what O'Neill's last words might have been had he not destroyed them. "Great theatre" according to one Stockholm critic.

SELDES, Gilbert. "Small touch of genius." *Sat. Rev.*, 40 (21 Sept.) 21.
This reworking of old themes might just as well be left unproduced. *JOURNEY* had well developed characters, but this is only about a drunkard. O'Neill seems to have lacked conviction in this play.

"This is a gayer O'Neill." *Newsweek*, 49 (8 Apr.) 66.
Brief general review, noting the great applause at the end beyond that given *JOURNEY*.

WEALES, Gerald. "Behind the mask." *Commonweal*, 67 (11 Oct.) 54-55.
Many of the usual O'Neill problems here: awkward exposition, insufficient language. But he has created an unlikeable character in Melody whose final collapse is strangely moving.

Opening night reviews—New York
Newspapers of 3 Oct. 1958

ASTON, Frank. "Touch of Poet at Helen Hayes." NY *Wor-Tel.* & *Sun*.
Without much comment on the play, aside from its being a "garrulous, sardonic, clinical examination of a British major," this review praises the acting and production, particularly the performance of Helen Hayes.

ATKINSON, Brooks. "Theatre: Eugene O'Neill's A Touch of the Poet." NY *Times*, 23:2. [Reprinted in Miller, *Playwright's progress*, 1965.]

A recognizable O'Neill play in its characters and its illusions and
pipe dreams though it is not typical in the lack of death at the end.
Characteristically overwritten, full of O'Neill's bigness, bitterness,
and hatred.

CHAPMAN, John. "Portman, Hayes and Stanley magnificent in Touch
of the Poet." NY *News*.
   O'Neill seems very much alive today; not a great O'Neill play,
but makes much of contemporary theatre look pallid. "Once more
Eugene O'Neill gives stature to the theatre."

COLBY, Ethel. "Entertainment on Broadway." *Jour. Comm.*
   A lesser O'Neill, though nothing he ever wrote can be called
a waste of time. Some brilliant dialogue and effective scene, but the
over-all picture lacks marked effect.

COLEMAN, Robert. "Touch of Poet magnificent." NY *Mirror*.
   One of O'Neill's best. There are touches of O'Casey and Shaw,
but it is genuine O'Neill, including as it does love, compassion and
humor—a heart that is missing in many of his plays. It can be seen
again and again.

DASH, Thomas R. "A Touch of the Poet." *W. W. Daily*.

McCLAIN, John. "O'Neill again proves he's incomparable." NY
Jour-Am. [Reprinted in Miller, *Playwright's progress*, 1965.]
   Even a lesser O'Neill play proves he is "majestically alone" in
American theatre. Intensely created, full-dimensioned characters,
though lack of sympathy weakens them. "Once more Mr. O'Neill
makes everybody else look silly."

WATTS, Richard, Jr. "Eugene O'Neill's Touch of the Poet." NY
Post.
   The season takes on dignity and importance. Not quite what his
others have been, but there is enormous power, compassion, and emotional impact. It is more than the revelation of character; it is a drama
of America's formative years. A powerful, stirring, beautiful play.

WHITTAKER, Herbert. "A Touch of the Poet." NY *Her-Trib.*
It may not rank with O'Neill's greatest, but it is worthy of them.
The power of *JOURNEY* is evident here, and the collapse of Melody
is set forth with force and brutality, hewn out of four compact acts.

Other reviews and criticism
1958 (two entries dated 1959)

ATKINSON, Brooks. "A Touch of the Poet." NY *Times*, 12 Oct.,
II, 1:1.
One of O'Neill's best, which takes skilled acting to bring out
the vigorous internal life of the play. On its many levels of pessimism,
savage quarrels and "boisterous theatricality" it is all O'Neill.

BOLTON, Whitney. "Superb cast makes O'Neill's Touch of the Poet
vivid drama." NY *Telegraph*, 14 Oct.
O'Neill has written scenes of spectacular force and the production
is a "thumping show."

BRUSTEIN, Robert. "Theatre chronicle." *Hudson Rev.*, 12 (Spring
1959) 96-98.
Actually a story of a hero divested of heroism and it has tragic
possibilities. It shows O'Neill was improving as a dramatic draftsman
with an authentic tragic theme.

CHAPMAN, John. "The next-to-last O'Neill." NY *News*, 12 Oct.
Not much comment here on the play; mainly a review of the
cycle and the tragedy of coming to the end of O'Neill's plays.

CLURMAN, Harold. "Mystery, strife, and loneliness." NY *Her-Trib.*,
10 Aug.
General review of the play discusses O'Neill's three main themes:
mystery of life, inability to fathom the object of his own struggles,
and nature of fate.

COOKE, Richard P. "Love and pride." *Wall St. Jour.*, 6 Oct.
Not upper-echelon O'Neill, but has unmistakable mark of

craftsmanship and bears his trademarks of a "great flow of often wonderful words, . . . flashes of dark light."

DENNIS, Patrick. "Rake's progress." *New Rep.*, 139 (20 Oct.) 23.
Power and greatness abundantly evident. "A big evening of real O'Neill fireworks."

DRIVER, Tom F. "Imagination in crisis." *Christ. Cent.*, 75 (26 Feb.) 252-254.
Perhaps our greatest crisis today is that of the imagination—the way man thinks of himself in relation to the world and his dreams. The published version suggests it is an age of meaninglessness because of man's lack of confidence in his ideas. In this play O'Neill is not negative, but merely skeptical.

————. "Kiss of death." *Christ. Cent.*, 75 (3 Dec.) 1401-1402.
The play greets the theatre like a kiss of death. If the theme is "the making of America" it does not fit the script as produced, for the production never focuses but is almost a parody of itself.

GELB, Arthur. "O'Neill's hopeless hope for a giant cycle." NY *Times*, 28 Sept., II, 1:3.
Upon the opening of *POET*, this informative article traces much of O'Neill's plans for the multi-play cycle, of which this play is the only surviving member.

HAYES, Richard. "The music of old manners." *Commonweal*, 69 (7 Nov.) 151-153.
The defect is loss of grandeur, though one must admire the way O'Neill orchestrates and distributes his substance. It is not his best play.

HEWES, Henry. "The playboy goes west." *Sat. R.*, 41 (18 Oct.) 56. [Reprinted in Cargill *et al*, *O'Neill and his plays*.]
It glows "like a beautiful bridge" between the old fashioned theatrical conventions and the new love-filled O'Neill we are now discovering. The last act has some unforgettable moments.

KRUTCH, Joseph Wood. "The O'Neill's on stage once more." *Th. Arts*, 42 (Oct.) 16-17.
It is more than a melodrama with a happy ending, because O'Neill had in mind more than just this play. Krutch assumes the entire *POSSESSORS* cycle was O'Neill's picture of his own family. It is better constructed than many of his plays.

LARDNER, John. "Irish pride and Mexican love." *New Yorker*, 34 (11 Oct.) 87.
Strident, sluggish, overmagnified people and an overly massive point of view. Compensations are found in intensity of purpose and honesty in writing.

LERNER, Max. "The mask and the face." NY *Post*, 22 Oct.
Play reaches to the universal about man's identity. Preferable to *ICEMAN*.

LEWIS, Theophilus. "A Touch of the Poet." *America*, 100 (25 Oct.) 118.
A brief review offering "bravos" for those concerned with the production.

McCARTHY, Mary. "Odd man in." *Partisan Rev.*, 26 (Winter 1959) 100-106.
As in the case of many present-day plays this lacks both hero and villain, seen in *JOURNEY, Epitaph for George Dillon* or *Look Back in Anger*. Main characters alternate between brutality and seeking forgiveness, always needing a woman who "understands."

MANNES, Marya. "A matter of motive." *Reporter*, 19 (13 Nov.) 37-38.
These are real people in real situations, held together in better structure than in *ICEMAN* or *JOURNEY*. O'Neill's purity of intent raises him above everybody else.

MORRISON, Hobe. "A Touch of the Poet." *Variety*, 8 Oct.
Second rate O'Neill. Diffuse, repetitious, somewhat old-

fashioned in technique, but nobody can match its sheer theatricalism. Stunning emotional impact; a tremendous play.

"New play in Manhattan." *Time*, 72 (13 Oct.) 89.
The play has "centripetal force and centrifugal wastefulness, giant strength and giant sprawl." The characters are superior to the action, but it never gets the power of cumulative drama.

"Once again the giant." *Newsweek*, 52 (13 Oct.) 112.
Middling-best O'Neill, but characteristic. It still charges the stage with electricity. "Another belated gift from the greatest."

OPPENHEIMER, George. "The Melodys of O'Neill." LI *Newsday*, 18 Oct.
Sometimes drags, but often breathes drama and life. Not O'Neill at his greatest, but still first rate and constantly absorbing and powerful.

SHIPLEY, Joseph T. "A Touch of the Poet." *New Leader*, 13 Oct.
One of "most tender and poignant" of O'Neill's plays.

TALLMER, Jerry. "O'Neill's last best play." *Village Voice*, 8 Oct.
Objectivity, complexity, levity, and effective symbolism, though none are fully successful, are better achieved here than anything else of recent date. One of O'Neill's best later plays; perhaps the best he wrote.

"A Touch of the Poet." *Th. Arts*, 42 (Dec.) 9-10.
Though a "mellow" O'Neill, it is still strong medicine and has considerable substance. It is not as forceful and convincing as *ICEMAN* or *JOURNEY*.

"A Touch of the Poet." *Vogue*, 132 (15 Nov.) 105.
"Acerbates the nerves" with repetition in the early part, then "excites them" in the last half.

VIDAL, Gore. "Theatre." *Nation*, 187 (25 Oct.) 298-299.
The appeal is strong because of the element of Cornelius Melody

in all of us. It is "human and gently wise," a contrast to the usual O'Neill.

WHITTAKER, Herbert. "O'Neill's :Poet' superbly acted." NY *Her-Trib.*, 12 Oct.
Does not inspire with awe as does *JOURNEY* but it is good O'Neill.

WATTS, Richard, Jr. "Another triumph for Eugene O'Neill." NY *Post*, 12 Oct.
O'Neill can only be compared to his own work, and this is not quite *JOURNEY* or *ICEMAN*. It is not a minor work, either. Enormous force and impact. The American theatre is at its best again.

WYATT, Euphemia Van R. "A Touch of the Poet." *Cath. Wld.*, 188 (Dec.) 243-244.
The play leaves us wondering what came before and what followed in the cycle. Much is needed to understand this vigorous play.

Other reviews and criticism

*MARCUS, Mordecai. "Eugene O'Neill's debt to Thoreau in Touch of the Poet." *Jour. of English and Germanic Philology*, 62 (April 1963) 270-279.
Parallels of more than passing coincidence would suggest strongly that O'Neill made considerable use of *Walden* and the *Journals* in creating Melody (Hugh Quail), Sarah (Ellen Sewall), Simon (Thoreau), and Deborah (Cynthia Thoreau, Henry's mother).

Revival—New York
Newspapers of May 1967

COOKE, Richard P. "O'Neill on illusions." *Wall St. Jour.*, 4 May.
The play needs patience to get through. "Some stretches of dramatic marshland."

KERR, Walter. "Touch of the Poet revived." NY *Times*, 3 May, p. 38.

Worth doing, but doing better. Play seems to have been conceived in an echo chamber.

MISHKIN, Leo. "O'Neill's Touch of the Poet." NY *Telegraph*, 4 May.
Essentially soap opera material. O'Neill said things about dreams and reality better in *ICEMAN* and *JOURNEY*.

NADEL, Norman. "A Touch of O'Neill." NY *World Jour. Trib.*, 3 May.
It is a meatier play than it seems in this production.

OPPENHEIMER, George. "Powerful touch of drama offered by O'Neill's Poet." LI *Newsday*, 3 May.
Production lacks color and excitement, which this play needs. Second-best O'Neill, but remains engrossing and powerful despite tardiness of pace.

"A Touch of the Poet." *Village Voice*, 11 May.
Even at the end O'Neill "had not lost his affinity for inflated guff." Second-rate O'Neill; Melody no tragic hero, though he has his moments.

WATTS, Richard, Jr. "The veteran of Wellington's army." NY *Post*, 3 May.
"Strangely absorbing" play; one of O'Neill's masterpieces.

WARNINGS

This play appeared in the small volume *Thirst and Other One Act Plays*, published in 1914 at the expense of James O'Neill. It has never received any important production.

SHKLOFSKY, Bryna. "Eugene O'Neill and deafness." *Volta Review*, 38 (January 1936) 48.
This publication devoted to the teaching of the deaf relates the

plot of this story of a ship's wireless operator who gradually loses his hearing. To this reviewer the play should be considered a tragedy.

THE WEB

This very early play was first published in Random House's edition of *Ten "Lost" Plays*. It apparently received no production.

*FISH, Charles. "Beginnings: O'Neill's The Web." *Princeton Univ. Library Chronicle*, 27 (Aug. 1965) 3-20.
    Extensive study of the place in O'Neill's plays of this "first play I ever wrote" according to an autograph note appended to the MS in 1944. Facsimile page of MS included.

WELDED

Opening run reviews—Baltimore Tryout
Newspapers of March 1924

CLARK, Norman. "New play by O'Neill at Auditorium." Baltimore *News*, 5 Mar.
    Not in conventional dramatic form and the uncovering of human souls through conversation is not appealing.

"Eugene O'Neill's latest drama here." Baltimore *Sun*, 4 Mar.
    Motionless and wordy, though competent and dignified as is usual with O'Neill, but it probably will not succeed.

GARLAND, Robert. "Welded fails to add to Eugene O'Neill's fame as author." Baltimore *American*, 9 Mar.
    High strung and overly introspective, exasperating; strains our emotions and sense of humor.

————. "Welded is drama of married bondage." Baltimore *American*, 4 Mar.

"Provocative, earnest, not entirely convincing."

"O'Neill play falls short of ideal upon its premiere." Baltimore *Post*, 4 Mar.
It is a disappointment.

"Welded seen as probe of human soul." Baltimore *Sun*, 9 Mar.
An extensive article with dialogue excerpts showing how the play fails mainly because of our own failure to become interested in the characters.

Opening night reviews—New York
Newspapers of 18 March 1924

ALLEN, Kelcey. "Latest O'Neill play Welded is study of marriage." *W.W. Daily*.
Reviews plot only.

CORBIN, John. "Romantic marriage." NY *Times*, 24:1.
Work of an original and distinguished playwright but the play is not up to the writer's ability.

GABRIEL, Gilbert. "Linked bitterness long drawn out in O'Neill's newest play." NY *Sun*.
True and wise and wearisome.

HAMMOND, Percy. "Welded a lugubrious conversazione about life among the artists." NY *Tribune*.
Dull, uneventful, garrulous, about people in whom we have no interest.

MANTLE, Burns. "Welded intense but monotonous." NY *News*.
Uninspiring, repetitious, "written in a single doleful key."

OSBORN, E. W. "Welded." NY *Eve. World*.
Powerful first act, with anticlimactic ending.

SINNOTT, James P. "Welded a drama of married life." NY *Telegraph*.
Not much of a play, little but conversation; O'Neill falls from the heights of realism.

TORRES, H. Z. "Welded displays morbid tendency." NY *Commercial*.
O'Neill capable of better things; repetitious and dull, based on a pathological premise.

TOWSE, J. Ranken. "O'Neill's Welded is disappointing." NY *Post*.
O'Neill befogs whatever he is trying to say and must learn the difference between power and sensationalism.

"Welded." NY *World*.
For 2 acts as bold and true and well written a play as anything on the stage now.

WELSH, Robert G. "Two chatty egotists." NY *Telegram & Mail*.
Characters created with skill and clear dialogue. A masterpiece with so few characters.

WHITTAKER, James. "Eugene O'Neill's play shown at 39th Street." NY *American*. [Reprinted in Miller, *Playwright's progress*, 1965.]
Bilious cupid with poison arrows, a bull in this china shop of high society the same as in the grog shops of O'Neill's other plays.

WOOLLCOTT, Alexander. "O'Neill's new play." NY *Herald*.
Perhaps O'Neill's integrity instead of incompetence is what makes this so prodigiously dull.

Other reviews and criticism
1924

BENCHLEY, Robert. "Three hot ones." *Life*, 83 (3 Apr.) 26.
Moves as if directed for slow-motion movie; very dull.

BJORKMAN, Edwin. "Plays and playmakers." *Outlook*, 137 (11 June) 238.
Brief review together with *CHILLUN*.

CARB, David. "To see or not to see." *Bookman*, 59 (May) 332.
Poor acting and script which is not up to O'Neill standard; distressingly overwritten.

CORBIN, John. "Among the new plays." NY *Times*, 23 Mar., VIII, 1:1.
Characters are human but lack contact with normal experiences; play is uninspiring and dull.

GRUENING, Ernest. "The wings of the children." *Th. Arts*, 8 (July) 497-498.
Harrowing, garish bathos and morbid melodrama; a wild and maudlin night.

HAMMOND, Percy. "Oddiments and remainders." NY *Tribune*, 23 Mar.
Interesting only to those of similar temperament. Romance has never been shown in so miserable a fashion.

HORNBLOW, Arthur. "Mr. Hornblow goes to the play." *Theatre*, 39 (May) 16.
O'Neill is not using his great dramatic gift; talky, morbid, barren.

KRUTCH, Joseph Wood. "Patterns." *Nation*, 118 (25 June) 743-744.
Reviews mainly *ALL GOD'S CHILLUN*.

LEWISOHN, Ludwig. "Pseudo-marriage." *Nation*, 118 (2 Apr.) 376-377. [Reprinted in Cargill *et al*, *O'Neill and his plays*, 1961.]
A "new departure" as O'Neill once more starts his career over again. The play is not thought out; becomes murky.

MACGOWAN, Kenneth. "Crying the hounds of Broadway." *Th. Arts*, 8 (June) 357.
Brief review of season's offerings.

———. "Eugene O'Neill as realist." NY *Times*, 23 Mar., VIII, 2:6.
Being romantic instead of a realist, O'Neill wished to get straight to the emotions and passions which realistic technique could not have done, which is the reason for the style of dialogue in this play.

———. "Seen on the stage." *Vogue*, 63 (15 May) 66-67.
Actually a piece of expressionistic writing instead of realism. More for experiments of Provincetown than Broadway.

METCALFE, J. S. "The need of segregation." *Wall St. Jour.*, 19 Mar.
A sharp attack against O'Neill and those of Greenwich Village who would sell wares like this as dramatic art or literature. Like the brothels of Tokyo, they should be segregated and perform without publicity. Plays of this type incite obscene thoughts and provoke ribald comment. There will be time enough to present O'Nèill when he has written a decent piece.

NATHAN, George Jean. "Welded." *Am. Merc.*, 2 (May) 115-116.
[Reprinted in Downer, *American drama and its critics*, 1965.]
Attempting a Strindberg, O'Neill has missed it completely. Full of "three-alarm dramaturgy" without point.

OSBORN, E. W. "The theatres." NY *Eve. World*, 22 Mar.
Further discussion of the play as a dramatic study of two characters.

POLLOCK, Arthur. "About the theatre." Brook. *Eagle*, 23 Mar.
O'Neill still writes like a young man, refusing to be placed in a rut. The impression of this play is blurred.

"Welded" *Drama Cal.*, 6 (24 Mar.) 1.
Dull entertainment; turgid sex dirge. As unreal and unconvincing as it can be; a singularly ineffective play.

"Welded." *Variety*, 26 Mar.
Mostly a review of story, along with the assertion it will not run long.

"Welded—luminous psychology of neurots." *Dramatist*, 15 (Apr.) 1208-1210.
Only play-going neurots of New York would go to this.

WHYTE, Gordon. "Welded." *Billboard*, 36 (29 Mar.) 34.
"Splendid example of dramatist overreaching himself to get an effect." Caricature of realism. A big theme tackled the wrong way.

WOOLLCOTT, Alexander. "O'Neill's new play Welded a melancholy stage study of quarrel of man and wife." NY *Sun*, 22 Mar.

WHERE THE CROSS IS MADE

These two reviews of the original Provincetown production are the only ones found in the New York Public Library.

BROUN, Heywood. "Provincetown players give fine thrill in sea play." NY *Tribune*, 23 Nov. 1918.
One of the best things O'Neill has done. Sweep of story has exceptional skill.

"Only the captain's daughter stays sane." NY *Telegraph*, 23 Nov. 1918.
A good play to watch to enjoy sensation of going mad.

Graduate Research

O'Neill's name appeared frequently in graduate research in American drama during his lifetime, both on the master's and doctoral levels. Doctoral dissertations devoted exclusively to him, however, were few and far between. With the revival of interest in his plays which began in the late 1950's the total number of dissertations in which O'Neill is the subject either alone or together with other major writers has increased steadily as the playwright's reputation increased and he became eminently respectable as a subject for scholarly research everywhere.

Because of the extremely large number of masters' theses and the obvious impracticality of tracking them all down, plus the fact that they are often of a comparatively superficial nature, the following list has been restricted entirely to doctoral dissertations. The main source of reference has been *Dissertation Abstracts*, volume and page numbers of which are included as available.

ADAMS, William J. "The dramatic structure of the plays of Eugene O'Neill." Stanford Univ., 1957. DA 17:916.

O'Neill is held to be firmly in the tradition of great drama in his structure, but his aim was higher than his accomplishments.

ALEXANDER, Doris M. "Freud and O'Neill: An analysis of *Strange Interlude*." New York Univ., 1952.

Detailed analysis of the play in terms of Freudian psychoanalysis. See Miss Alexander's 1953 article in *American Literature* which holds that the play is influenced essentially by Schopenhauer.

ARBENZ, Mary H. "The plays of Eugene O'Neill as presented by the Theatre Guild." Univ. of Illinois, 1961.

Study of the interrelationship between the plays and their Guild productions, determining matters of textual change and the effect upon O'Neill the artist.

BELL, Wayne E. "Forms of religious awareness in the late plays of Eugene O'Neill." Emory Univ., 1966. DA 28:222A.

The late plays shown to approach a Christian affirmation of the created order, finite freedom of mind, and efficacy of human love.

BELLI, Angela. "The use of Greek mythological themes and characters in twentieth century drama: Four approaches." New York Univ., 1965.

Psychological approach of *ELECTRA* discussed in this study of different treatments of Greek themes.

BELTZER, Lee. "The plays of Eugene O'Neill, Thornton Wilder, Arthur Miller, and Tennessee Williams on the London stage 1945-1960." Univ. of Wisconsin, 1965. DA 26:5590.

ELECTRA, ICEMAN, and *LONG DAY'S JOURNEY* examined to determine the critical reception of these plays as commercial productions.

BERNSTEIN, Samuel J. "Eugene O'Neill: Theatre artist. A description of and commentary upon the craftsmanship of four plays by Eugene O'Neill." Brandeis Univ., 1964. DA 25:4683.

WHERE THE CROSS IS MADE, DESIRE, HAIRY APE, and *ICEMAN* discussed as particularly good theatre pieces whose nonverbal dramatic effects show how O'Neill reads so badly and performs so well.

BLACKBURN, Ruth M. "Representation of New England rustic dialects in the plays of Eugene O'Neill." New York Univ., 1967. DA 28:4616A.

O'Neill's use of dialect as in *DESIRE* is found to be substantially accurate, but not as good or "linguistically versatile" as his Irish dialect.

BROUSSARD, Louis. "The modern allegorical plays in America." New York Univ., 1963. DA 26:2203.

O'Neill and Elmer Rice regarded as the first writers of allegorial drama influenced by expressionism.

BURIAN, Jarka Marsano. "A study of twentieth century adaptations of the Greek Atreidae dramas." Cornell Univ., 1955. DA 15:2524.

ELECTRA included in this study which feels the positive values of Greek tragedies are best conveyed to modern audiences by effective and imaginative translations and productions rather than merely adaptations.

BURNS, Sister M. Vincentia. "The Wagnerian theory of art and its influence on the drama of Eugene O'Neill." Univ. of Pennsylvania, 1943.

Indirect influence of Wagner's theory through Nietzsche, Strindberg, French symbolists, and new theatre techniques of the period.

CALVERY, Catharine A. "Illusion in modern American drama: A study of selected plays by Arthur Miller, Tennessee Williams, and Eugene O'Neill." Tulane Univ., 1964. DA 25:6111.

POET and *ICEMAN* discussed in this investigation into the nature of illusion or phantasy.

COHEN, Sandra H. "The Electra figure in twentieth century American and European drama." Univ. of Indiana, 1968. DA 29:4000.

ELECTRA considered together with plays by von Hoffmansthal, Giroudoux and others in terms of psychological matters and religious skepticism.

COOK, Thomas E. "Eugene O'Neill's use of dramatic imagery 1920-1930: A study of six plays." Tulane Univ., 1962. DA 23:4353.

JONES, APE, BROWN, MARCO, DYNAMO, DESIRE discussed in terms of dramatic imagery as a visual symbol of a dramatic idea or motive.

CORRIGAN, Robert W. "The Electra theme in the history of drama." Univ. of Minnesota, 1955. DA 15:1612.

Inquiry into what happens to a mythological legend used by different writers, with *ELECTRA* included to demonstrate aspect of inheritance of guilt.

CRONIN, H. C. "The plays of Eugene O'Neill in the cultural context of Irish-American Catholicism." Univ. of Minnesota, 1968. DA 29:2384A.

"If one views the plays of O'Neill in the cultural context of Irish-American Catholicism, this can provide an extremely rich critical facility and a deeper understanding of the plays."

CUNNINGHAM, Frank R. "Eugene O'Neill's romantic phase, 1921-1925." Lehigh Univ., 1971. DA 31:5394A.

Some of O'Neill's least successful plays—*GOLD, STRAW, FIRST MAN, WELDED, FOUNTAIN* are contained in the "romantic" period together with outstanding successes such as *ANNA CHRISTIE, APE,* and *DESIRE.*

DALVEN, Rae. "The concepts of Greek tragedy in the major plays of Eugene O'Neill." New York Univ., 1961. DA 22:4343.

Thirteen plays from *HORIZON* to *POET* held to be closest to the Greek tragic writers discussed, with conclusion that in his earnest quest for truth O'Neill was related to all the Greek dramatists.

DAWSON, William M. "The female characters of Augustus Strindberg, Eugene O'Neill, and Tennessee Williams." Univ. of Wisconsin, 1964. DA 25:2663.

Eight plays by each writer show how attitudes toward women were influenced by childhood and adolescence, with each writer confusing love and lust in demonstrating how women are motivated by the will to power.

DECKER, Philip H. "The use of classic myth in twentieth century English and American drama 1900-1960: A study of selected plays." Northwestern Univ., 1966. DA 27:3536.

Modern adaptations of Atreidae, Hippolytus-Phaedra, and Alcestis-Admetus myths indicate writers have not fashioned first class dramatic literature.

DEW, Deborah S. "Expressionism in the American theater, 1922-1936." Yale Univ., 1968. DA 29:595A.

APE examined in depth in a study of expressionism in America as an independent movement sharing many of the qualities of European counterparts.

DUBLER, Walter. "Eugene O'Neill, Wilder, and Albee: The uses of fantasy in modern American drama." Harvard Univ., 1964.

DUSENBURY, Winifred L. "The theme of loneliness in modern American drama." Univ. of Florida, 1956. DA 16:2160.

O'Neill among others found the theme of loneliness meaningful, and it is held to be the most important theme in serious American drama between 1920 and 1950. (Published as a book, Univ. Fla. Press, 1960, *q.v.*)

ELROD, James F. "The structure of O'Neill's serious drama." Univ. of Indiana, 1959. DA 20:1898.

Thirteen plays from *ILE* through *JOURNEY* demonstrate O'Neill's idea that man must suffer with little hope of reconciliation with God and life.

ENGEL, Edwin A. "Recurrent themes in the drama of Eugene O'Neill." Univ. of Michigan, 1953. DA 13:1193.

Analysis of the plays in chronological order including naturalistic, mystical, and religious aspects, finding that although many of the plays do not bear up well, O'Neill's achievement is greater than the sum of the parts.

FALK, Doris V. "Eugene O'Neil and the tragic tension." Cornell Univ., 1952.

Study of O'Neill's works, later expanded into a major book (*q.v.*), showing the "tragic tension" of the pull of opposites of good-evil, joy-suffering, etc.

FICCA, John. "Eugene O'Neill's critical reputation in America." Univ. of Iowa, 1962. DA 23:1827.

Newspaper, magazine, and scholarly attitudes toward O'Neill, showing general and specific reactions to the plays and the playwright.

FIRESTONE, Paul A. "The educational value and power of the Pulitzer prize plays." Columbia Univ., 1968.

O'Neill's plays included in study of the prize plays 1918-1965 with regard to their "educational value" as originally specified by Pulitzer.

FISKIN, Abram M. "Eugene O'Neill: The study of a developing creed through the medium of drama." Univ. of Minnesota, 1964. DA 25:4697.

Traces development of a philosophic system through *DAYS WITHOUT END*, mainly the Godhunt and interpreting life as Being and Becoming.

FITCH, Polly M. "The language of the last three major plays of Eugene O'Neill." Stanford Univ., 1966. DA 27:273A.

MISBEGOTTEN, JOURNEY, POET examined to show certain incompetence in language use. O'Neill found to lack an awareness of the mechanics of the sound of language.

FLOYD, Virginia I. "Eugene O'Neill's 'New England' cycle: The Yankee Puritan and New England Irish Catholic elements in five autobiographical plays of Eugene O'Neill." Fordham, 1971. DA 32:963A.

FOX, Josef W. "Probability in the plays of Eugene O'Neill." Univ. of Chicago, 1953.

O'Neill establishes probability by excellence of structure design rather than by any "adventitious devices" incorporated into the plays for that purpose.

GADDIS, A. G. "Eugene O'Neill's Desire Under the Elms: The fortuitous blend." Oklahoma State Univ., 1967. DA 28:4932A.

ELECTRA and *ICEMAN* included to show that *DESIRE* is a "fortuitous blend of ancient and modern concepts of tragedy . . . a nearly perfect tragedy" except for language.

GOBRECHT, Eleanor A. "A descriptive study of the value commitments of the principal characters in four recent American plays, Picnic, Cat on a Hot Tin Roof, Long Day's Journey Into Night, and Look Homeward, Angel." Univ. of Southern California, 1963.

Exploration of the hypothesis that plays indigenous to a culture and which receive praise of their contemporaries provide, through their characters, the source for the study of the values articulated by the people of that culture.

GOULD, Arthur. "The idea of tragedy in modern American drama." Univ. of Michigan, 1948. DA 8:105.

Among modern playwrights O'Neill comes nearest to resolving the conflict between humanistic and naturalistic values in tragedy.

HAHN, Vera T. "The plays of Eugene O'Neill: A psychological analysis." Louisiana State Univ., 1939.

O'Neill's "unerring analysis and interpretation of the man of today" and familiarity with Freud, Adler, and Jung, make his fame and recognition deserved.

HALLINE, Allan Gates. "Main currents of thought in American drama." Univ. of Wisconsin, 1936.

Royall Tyler to O'Neill, this study devotes ten pages to plot summaries of major O'Neill plays and ten additional pages focusing mainly on *APE*.

HARTMAN, Murray. "Stringberg and O'Neill: A study in influence." New York Univ., 1960.

Parallels in lives and dispositions shown to demonstrate influence upon O'Neill's themes and techniques.

HERNDON, Genevra. "American criticism of Eugene O'Neill, 1917-1948." Northwestern Univ., 1948.

Extensive coverage of O'Neill criticism from all domestic sources.

HIGHSMITH, James M. "Eugene O'Neill: Apprenticeship with dramatic presentationalism." Univ. of North Carolina, 1967. DA 28:3671A.

Through dramatic presentationalism O'Neill provides full theatrical experience, combining Dionysiac, or ritualistic, with Apollonian, or aesthetic, elements.

HILL, Philip G. "Irony as a structural device in selected plays of Eugene O'Neill." Tulane Univ., 1964. DA 25:4302.

Study of eight plays from *HORIZON* to *JOURNEY* shows O'Neill's "masterful grasp" of the technique, the height of his theatrical effectiveness.

HORNER, Harry N. "Love, agony, ambivalence: Background and selected studies in the artistic failures of Eugene O'Neill." Kent State Univ., 1972.

FIRST MAN and *DYNAMO* form the focus of this study of O'Neill's difficulty with the theme of love, particularly influenced by the "almost cyclic motifs of betrayal, hate, revenge, guilt, forgetfulness and death" resulting from relationships with his own mother.

ITKIN, Bella. "The pattern of verbal imagery as found in the ten major works of O'Neill." Western Reserve, 1955.

JASPE, Arthur. "Critical theory and playwriting practice of contemporary American playwrights: A study of the relationship of critical theory to playwriting practice as evidenced in the prize-winning plays of contemporary American playwrights during the years 1920-1940." New York University, 1958. DA 20:290.

Eight O'Neill plays included in discussion of eighty-one plays by eleven prize-winning playwrights (Pulitzer, Critics, Burns Mantle listing, etc.) which attempts to ascertain a consensus or lack of it with regard to the major prizes in terms of fundamental structure of the craft of contemporary playwriting.

KAUCHER, Dorothy J. "Modern dramatic structure." Univ. of Missouri, 1928.

One of the very earliest dissertations to include major discussion of O'Neill. *GOLD* is given extended treatment to demonstrate O'Neill's structural technique.

KETELS, Arthur O. "The American drama of the twenties: A critical revaluation." Northwestern Univ., 1960. DA 21:3192.

O'Neill included in this study which finds the "renaissance" of American drama in retrospect to be highly derivative which achieves importance only in light of what went before. .

KILKER, Dorothy K. "Eugene O'Neill's methods of characterizing the secret self." Univ. of So. Calif., 1971. DA 32:3311A.

KOPLIK, Irwin J. "Jung's psychology in the plays of O'Neill." New York Univ., 1966. DA 27:3872A.

Discussion of Jungian philosophy in O'Neill, rather than Jung's influence, concluding that O'Neill's "preoccupation with the inevitable tension between conscious and unconscious forces underlies the entire corpus of his work."

LANGLEY, Stephen G. "Three puritanical stage figures in the American drama." Univ. of Illinois, 1966. DA 27:2215.

O'Neill included in a broad study of important relationship between Puritanism and the American drama, delineating the reformer, the aristocrat, and the sinner.

LEE, Robert C. "Eugene O'Neill: A grapple with a Ghost." Univ. of Michigan, 1965. DA 26:2754.

O'Neill held to have failed to attain creative maturity because of the conflict between the artist's needs and the need for self-examination.

LEVY, Valerie B. "Violence as drama: A study of the development of the use of violence on the American stage." Claremont Grad. School (Calif.), 1971. DA: 31:6618A-19A.

Especial emphasis on O'Neill, Williams, Albee.

LONG, Chester C. "A study of the role of nemisis in the structure of selected plays by Eugene O'Neill." Northwestern Univ., 1962. DA 23:4784.

Nemisis is developed as the idea of justice in action—social, tragic, and "ultimate" nemisis—with characters having the power to choose and therefore help to shape the nemisis that overtakes them.

MANFULL, Helen A. "The new realism: A study of American dramatic realism 1918-1929." Univ. of Minnesota, 1961. DA 22:2912.

HORIZON and DIFF'RENT included in discussion showing development of interest in common man's life, providing more mature and skilled realism than heretofore.

MILLER, Jordan Y. "A critical bibliography of Eugene O'Neill." Columbia Univ., 1957. DA 17:1556.

The original version of this present volume.

OLSON, Esther J. "An analysis of the Nietzschean elements in the plays of Eugene O'Neill." Univ. of Minnesota, 1956. DA 17:695.

The whole body of O'Neill's plays could be considered a discussion of the "sickness of today," with the playwright succumbing to Nietzschean idea of God is dead.

POAG, Thomas E. "The Negro in drama and the theatre." Cornell Univ., 1943.

JONES and CHILLUN discussed in chapter devoted to the Negro themes of white dramatists after 1920.

PORTER, Thomas E., S.J. "Mythic elements in modern American drama." Univ. of North Carolina, 1965. DA 26:3961.

Myths and ritualistic aspects of modern drama are investigated, despite assertion of an essentially "mythless" society. ELECTRA included.

RAGHAVACHARYULU, Dhupaty V. "The achievement of Eugene O'Neill: A study of the dramatist as seeker." Univ. of Pennsylvania, 1959. DA 20:2300.

O'Neill seen as a "significant link" between American drama and fiction by applied "Christian allegorical tradition" in his search for meaning and identity.

RAY, Helen H. "The relation between man and man in the plays of Eugene O'Neill." Univ. of Kansas, 1965. DA 26:7324.

A demonstration that O'Neill continually denies the validity of his stated interest in relation between man and God; except for *LAZARUS*, protagonists are depicted in relåtionship to other characters.

SALEM, James M. "Revolution in manners and morals: The treatment of adultery in American drama between the wars." Louisiana State Univ., 1965. DA 26:4674.

O'Neill shown as maintaining a consistently "morally conservative position," showing in such plays as *WELDED, ELECTRA, INTERLUDE*, and *DAYS WITHOUT END* that adultery is never acceptable and leads to decay and destruction.

SARHAN, Mohamed Samir G. "Ibsen and O'Neill: An analysis of structural parallels." Univ. of Indiana, 1968. DA 29:1519.

By parallels drawn between early and late periods of both writers, both shown as romantics who passed through period of experimentation. O'Neill's later plays held in true tradition of Ibsenesque realism.

SCANLAN, Thomas M. "The American family and family dilemmas in American drama." Univ. of Minn., 1971. DA 32:1529A.

Especial emphasis on O'Neill, Williams, Miller.

SCARBROUGH, Alex. "Eugene O'Neill's sense of place: A study of his locative archetypes." Tulsa Univ., 1970. DA 31:2938A.

An examination of evolution of O'Neill's usage of locative archetypes from earliest to latest plays. By the twenties he demonstrates assurance with "locative archetypes" and prevalent avatars of Gothic house, sea, tavern, etc., have arranged themselves. Final plays demonstrate final development of an archetypal evolution.

STEENE, Kerstin B. "The American drama and the Swedish theatre: 1920-1958." University of Washington, 1960. DA 21:268.

Discussion of acceptance of American plays by Swedish theatre, mainly the experimental works of Wilder, Williams, Miller, and most respected of all, O'Neill.

STEIN, Daniel Alan. "O'Neill and the philosophers: A study of the Nietzschean and other philosophical influences on Eugene O'Neill." Yale Univ., D.F.A. thesis, 1967.

Emerson, Strindberg, Freud, Jung, Schopenhauer also included, with conclusion O'Neill rejected messianism in his search for artistic truth.

STROUPE, John H. "O'Neill's Marco Millions: A road to Xanadu." Univ. of Rochester, 1962.

Evolutionary study of various drafts of MARCO in the Yale collection determines that O'Neill meant the play as a two-part two-night production.

TEMPLETON, Joan. "Expressionism in British and American drama." Univ. of Oregon, 1966. DA 27:2548.

O'Neill's techniques and themes explored in a separate chapter of this study devoted to determining the part expressionism played in the attempt to form a non-realistic theatre in England.

THURMAN, William R. "Anxiety in modern American drama." Univ. of Georgia, 1964. DA 25:5945.

ICEMAN included with Death of a Salesman for intensive study in this analysis of concept of anxiety in mid-twentieth century American drama.

TINSLEY, Mary A. "Two biographical plays by Eugene O'Neill: The drafts and the final versions." Cornell, 1969. DA 31:1297A.

JOURNEY and MISBEGOTTEN explored to show ways O'Neill manipulated biographical material, and how he changed his approaches during composition of the plays.

TURNER, Clarence Steven. "Man's spiritual quest in the plays of Eugene O'Neill." Univ. of Texas, 1962. DA 23:1709.

O'Neill's search for God reveals such varying religious attitudes as Christian pantheism and agnostic existentialism from *HORIZON* to *JOURNEY*.

VALGEMAE, Mardi. "Expressionism in American Drama." Univ. of California at Los Angeles, 1964. DA 26:377.

JONES, APE, ANCIENT MARINER, ALL GOD'S CHILLUN, BROWN included in study demonstrating pattern in American drama of German rather than Strindbergian expressionism. (Basis of *Accelerated grimace*, 1972, *q.v.*)

VIRSIS, Rasma A. "Eugene O'Neill's aesthetic expression of time." New York Univ., 1968. DA 29:4025A.

Investigation of O'Neill's shortcomings and success in relation to his theme of conflict between past and present.

VUNOVICH, Nancy W. "The women in the plays of Eugene O'Neill." Univ. of Kansas, 1966. DA 28:1089A.

A study of the women in six categories: prostitute, nags and meddlers, the disturbed, innocents, driven, and mothers.

WHITE, Jackson E. "Existential themes in selected plays of Eugene O'Neill." Arizona State Univ., 1967. DA 27:4270A.

Though accused of incoherence and philosophical anarchy, O'Neill seems to have explored all important themes of recent existential literature.

WILLOUGHBY, Pearl V. "Modern dramaturgy, British and American." Univ. of Virginia, 1928.

This limited (16-page) discussion of O'Neill is significant in that it is one of the earliest graduate dissertations in which O'Neill is seriously treated.

WINCHESTER, Otis W. "A rhetorical analysis of Eugene O'Neill's *Strange Interlude*." Univ. of Oklahoma, 1961.

Exploration of the relationship between the arts of rhetoric and drama approached from social and cultural values of the 1928 audience.

Index

The change in format of this Second Edition has necessitated some significant alterations in the organization of the Index. The elimination of the consecutive numbering of entries as found in the First Edition has avoided the confusing duplication of numbers printed in both italic and Roman typeface. All Index entries now refer to page numbers only.

A bibliography of this type is only as good as its index, which has been made as comprehensive as possible. Every pertinent item, even if noted in passing reference within an. annotation, has been included. Every subject and every proper name or title which appears within the text has an entry somewhere within this Index.

Entries are organized as follows:

NAMES. This category includes authors, editors, actors, producers, producing companies, publishers, publishing houses, theatres, organizations, colleges, universities and so on. All material following each entry is designed to convey as accurately as possible information concerning the content of the reference. The following entries will serve as good examples:

> Atkinson, Brooks, vii, 159-162; repr. Atkinson on
> Nobel prize 106; AHW 222, 228; ANNA 246;
> BB 250; DAYS 262-263; DES 275; etc.

Under Atkinson, therefore, will be found an initial reference in the introductory pages, general references on four consecutive pages within the bibliography, a reprint of his own article on the Nobel award, and reviews of individual plays on indicated pages.

> Random House, pub. *NINE plays* 32, 34; *Plays* 34, 36;
> *10 "lost" plays* 39, 183, 381, 467; *Selected plays* 40;
> AHW 31; ANNA 35; DAYS 31; etc.

Information concerning this publisher's volumes of play collections and individual editions will be found on the various pages as indicated.

TITLES. *Books, monographs, pamphlets, etc.* All items of this type appear in italics with initial word only capitalized, together with the name of author, editor, or, if anonymous, the source, followed by the pages on which they are found. The great majority appear but once. However, on occasion a title may appear more than once. In such cases, the *main entry* is marked with an asterisk as follows:

> *Eugene O'Neill, the man and his plays* (Clark), 3, 15, 41, 90-93 *passim,* 113*, 147, 163, 169, 175, 178; O'N letters 90-91.

This book by Clark will be found under references of a general or passing nature as indicated, except that page 113 contains the book's *main entry,* with full bibliographic information and annotation.

Periodicals. Magazines, quarterlies, scholarly publications of regular or irregular nature, and newspapers all appear in italics with full capitalization to distinguish them from books, followed by an indication of contents and pages. Example:

> *Theatre Arts (Magazine, Monthly)*, pub. DK 21; EJ 22; *General:* Anderson 160; Clark 169; Downer 174; Gassner 183; etc., *Reviews:* AHW 226, 228, 230; ALL 234; AM 237; ANNA 245, 248; etc.

Under this entry, in one of the magazine's three titles, will be found information concerning the publication of two plays, general articles by authors named, and individual criticisms and reviews of specific plays as noted.

The same general procedure is followed for newspapers. All New York newspapers are grouped together in one section of the Index.

Articles. Only articles of general interest are listed. Specific reviews of individual plays, particularly newspaper reviews, are *not* indexed. The reasons are many and obvious: the repetition of play title as the only title for newspaper reviews, or the repetition of column titles are the most immediately apparent reasons. Sheer volume of the number of reviews is another. No problem is really involved in finding specific articles about individual plays, because all may be found by consulting the play titles within the Index, or simply by leafing through the bibliography itself under the section on Individual Plays.

All articles listed in the Index, wherever published, appear in quotation marks, first word only capitalized, with the name of the author or the source in parentheses, followed by the page numbers. Almost without exception articles have but a single reference. Because all articles entered in the bibliography proper contain full information concerning sources of reprints, the Index lists *only* the main entry.

SUBJECTS. *O'Neill himself.* While the "subject" of this entire volume is indeed Eugene O'Neill, the Index includes listings under his name in order that particular references of a specific nature concerning various aspects of O'Neill's life and artistry may be located. Virtually all "subjects" within the bibliography are thus listed under O'Neill's name, with the exception of the plays themselves.

O'Neill's plays. All are spelled out in CAPITAL LETTERS, followed by page references as follows:

> DYNAMO, 110, 117, 141, 149, 170, 475, 480; copyr. 28; pub. 29, 32-34; prod. 65; Simonson set 148; *Reviews.* NY opening: 292-294; Other 1929: 294-299; Further 300.

Under this play are various general and passing references, information concerning copyright, publication, and production, and the various reviews and further references to date.

A list of abbreviations used within the Index follows. Abbreviations of O'Neill's plays have been devised to follow as closely as possible the alphabetical position of the full titles.

Abbreviations and Short Titles

AHW—AH, WILDERNESS!
ALL—ALL GOD'S CHILLUN GOT WINGS
Am.—American
AM—THE ANCIENT MARINER
ANNA—ANNA CHRISTIE
BB—BEFORE BREAKFAST
BH—BEYOND THE HORIZON
biog.—biography, biographical, etc.
bk.—book
BOUND—BOUND EAST FOR CARDIFF
chor.—choreography
copyr.—copyright
cost.—costume(s)
DAYS—DAYS WITHOUT END
DES—DESIRE UNDER THE ELMS
DIFF—DIFF'RENT
dir.—direction, directed (by)
DK—THE DREAMY KID
DYN—DYNAMO
EJ—THE EMPEROR JONES
EO'N—Eugene O'Neill
expl.—explains, explanation (of, by, etc.)
FM—THE FIRST MAN
FOUN—THE FOUNTAIN
gen.—general
GRGB—THE GREAT GOD BROWN
HA—THE HAIRY APE
ICE—THE ICEMAN COMETH
IZ—IN THE ZONE
LAZ—LAZARUS LAUGHED
LDJ—LONG DAY'S JOURNEY INTO NIGHT
lit.—literature
LOST—*Lost Plays of Eugene O'Neill*
LVH—THE LONG VOYAGE HOME

MM—MARCO MILLIONS
mag.—magazine
MMIS—A MOON FOR THE MISBEGOTTEN
mod.—modern
MOON C—THE MOON OF THE CARIBBEES
MORE SM—MORE STATELY MANSIONS
MOURN—MOURNING BECOMES ELECTRA
MOVIE—THE MOVIE MAN
O'N—O'Neill
PE—THE PERSONAL EQUATION
pref.—preface
prod.—production, produced (by), etc.
pub.—publisher, published (by), publication, etc.
RECK—RECKLESSNESS
rev.—review, reviewed (by)
ROPE—THE ROPE
SSG—S S GLENCAIRN
SNIPER—THE SNIPER
SI—STRANGE INTERLUDE
STRAW—THE STRAW
TALE—A TALE OF POSSESSORS SELF-DISPOSSESSED
th.—theatre, theatrical
TP—A TOUCH OF THE POET
WARN—WARNINGS
WEB—THE WEB
WCM—WHERE THE CROSS IS MADE
WIFE—A WIFE FOR A LIFE
(Single word titles—GOLD, ILE, etc., are of course indicated in full)